D0897649

Dependence and Interdependence

Essays in Development Economics

Dependence and Interdependence

Jagdish N. Bhagwati

ESSAYS IN DEVELOPMENT ECONOMICS
VOLUME 2

edited by Gene Grossman

Basil Blackwell · Oxford

© Jagdish N. Bhagwati 1985

First published 1985

Basil Blackwell Ltd
108 Cowley Road, Oxford OX4 1JF, UK

British Library Cataloguing in Publication Data

Bhagwati, Jagdish N.
  Dependence and interdependence. – (Essays
  in development economics; v.2)
  1. Developing countries – Economic conditions
  I. Title
  330.9172′4   HC59.7

  ISBN 0-631-14222-3

Phototypeset by
Dobbie Typesetting Service, Plymouth, Devon
Printed in Great Britain by
Bell & Bain Ltd, Glasgow

For
ANNE KRUEGER
friend and collaborator
over the years

Contents

Editor's Preface

In these two volumes I have collected many of Professor Bhagwati's writings in the broad area of development economics. This set of papers complements nicely the collection assembled by Robert Feenstra on the theory of international trade (*Essays in International Economic Theory*, MIT Press, 1983). Whereas the earlier volumes concentrated on Bhagwati's contributions to the academic theoretical literature, the current selection is more diverse, and is intended to highlight the close relationship and mutual reinforcement in Bhagwati's research and professional activities between economic theory, empirical validation, and policy debate.

The two volumes are organized with domestic or internal development problems discussed in volume 1 (e.g. theory and regularities in growth and development, poverty and income distribution, employment and technology issues), and international or external problems comprising volume 2 (e.g. North–South issues, import substitution versus export promotion, foreign assistance and international migration). Most of the papers have been included in their original published forms, although in several places some minimal editing has been performed to avoid significant duplication of material or to make the current volumes self-contained when the meaning of the original was obscure out of context. Groups of papers on the same topic are preceded by brief introductions in which the author discusses his current views of the nature of the contributions and the relationships between them. In several cases unpublished papers have been included (e.g. volume 1, chapter 16) or postscripts have been added (volume 1, chapters 7 and 10), where these add substantially to the coherence of the presentation of a topic.

As one who is a student and admirer of Professor Bhagwati's work in the field of international trade theory, it has been a pleasure for me to assemble and read through these papers on policy problems arising in a development context. While these works tend to be less technical in style than the ones with which I am more familiar, they are no less logically rigorous in their argumentation. In them, it is possible to see the wellsprings of many of the well-known theoretical investigations and to observe the development of this scholar's coherent world-view. Professor Bhagwati's writings, theoretical or otherwise, have always been deeply rooted in real-world policy problems, and motivated by a keen concern for the plight of the world's poor. One cannot help but admire the breadth and scope of their contribution, as well as an expositional style that is at once entertaining, insightful, and provocative.

Gene Grossman

Author's Preface

First and foremost, I must thank Gene Grossman, now at Princeton University, for editing these two volumes with great care, assisting with the selection and organization of the papers and with much else that needs to be done to prepare such selections for the printers. He is one of the most gifted young theorists whom I had the good fortune to have among my students at MIT. It has been a privilege to have him edit these two volumes.

Both he and I have been at pains to eliminate overlaps in the essays. Affinities in ideas, as between papers, cannot, however, be removed altogether. Unlike in the natural sciences, economics lends itself more readily to expression of similar ideas in different contexts, with new nuances lending an important new shade of colouring to one's ideas. This is why natural scientists race for the Nobel, losing out if their rivals get ahead by epsilon time, while economists are typically happy to lend an applauding hand to those who 'rediscover' ideas even years apart, as in the case of Harrod and Domar who arrived at the same 'exponential' growth model but developed it in very different ways. And then again, I draw comfort, not just from Keynes' example, but also from Alexander Herzen's wise remark, citing Proudhon:

> I have said this a dozen times, but it is impossible to avoid repetitions. Persons of experience know this. I once spoke to Proudhon of the fact that there often appeared in his journal articles which were almost identical, with only slight variations.
>
> 'And do you imagine,' Proudhon answered, 'that once a thing has been said, it is enough? That a new idea will be accepted straight off? You are mistaken. It has to be dinned into people, it has to be repeated, repeated over and over again, in order that the mind may no longer be surprised by it, that it may be not merely understood, but assimilated, and obtain real rights of citizenship in the brain.'[1]

I must also thank Panayotis Varangis, my student at Columbia, for reading all the essays, checking out the references, and even making excellent editorial suggestions beyond the line of duty. Brian Lancaster, Marta Cabrera, Mary Conroy and Deborah Breslof, my secretaries, have

---

1. Alexander Herzen, *My Past and Present Thoughts* , (Berkeley: University of California Press, 1982, abridged edition by Dwight MacDonald), p. 666.

also weighed in with typing, cutting and pasting, all with good cheer; they too deserve my gratitude. Sunil Gulati has helped enormously with the proofs and prepared the index with great care.

A word is in order on the title of the volume: *Dependence and Interdependence*. Idiomatically, these two words have acquired different, and contrapuntal, ideological meanings. Radicals often talk about the former as characterizing North–South relationships, though the dependence (of the South) is frequently distinguished from 'dependencia', the latter being thought of as a particular model (though, anyone familiar with the Latin American intellectual literature on the subject will be unable to deny that numerous variants obtain here none the less). While therefore dependence suggests some kind of vulnerability and hence an inequality of power relationship, interdependence is at best a neutral word, and has often been used by bourgeois or liberal writers to suggest simply interaction among the different actors or its possible consequence in the form of sensitivity of an actor's situation, on some parametric dimension, to what happens in the other's economy. Often, however, interdependence has been used in contexts where mutuality of interests and benefits has been stressed, so that in *popular* conception, interdependence has acquired in effect a benign connotation.

Dependence therefore suggests a negative perception of the world economy's impact on the developing countries and interdependence a happier one. Since, as the reader will discover, my views on the constraints and opportunities implied by the world economy for the developing countries, in areas of North–South interaction, on dimensions such as capital and labour flows, trade and technology, are complex and textured enough not to be readily categorized as belonging to either the dependence or the interdependence ideological school, the elevation of both to the title seemed a logical step!

In conclusion, I am grateful to my distinguished co-authors, Professors Richard Brecher, Anne Krueger, Paul Krugman and T. N. Srinivasan, for permission to reprint my joint work with them.

Jagdish Bhagwati

New York
November 1984

Acknowledgements

Thanks are due to the following for permission to reprint articles: MIT Press for chapters 1–3; American Economic Association for chapter 4; Cambridge University Press for chapter 5; Johns Hopkins University Press for chapter 6; National Bureau of Economic Research for chapter 7; Japan Economic Research Center for chapter 8; Oxford University Press for chapter 9; *Economic and Political Weekly* for chapter 10; Overseas Development Council for chapter 11; United Nations for chapter 12; National Bureau of Economic Research for chapter 14; Oxford University Press for chapter 16; United Nations for chapter 17; American Enterprise Institute for Public Research for chapter 18; North-Holland Publishing Co. for chapter 19; Macmillan Publishing Co. for chapter 20.

Introduction

These two volumes contain a selection of writings on developmental economics over the last 25 years. They range over a great number of problems and issues, and they extend to both the internal and external aspects of the developmental process and designs for its acceleration.

While the selection is mainly confined to published essays, scattered in several sources, I have also taken the opportunity to take a few brief excerpts from book-length writings of my own (volume 1, chapter15; volume 2, chapters 7, 14 and 15) where they add to the coherence and value of the other selections under these topics. On the other hand, I have omitted several theoretical essays, which have a direct and immediate relevance to the analysis of developmental issues, simply because they are equally relevant to the theory of international trade and have already been reprinted in a two-volume selection of 70 essays of mine, entitled *Essays in International Economic Theory*. This was edited by Robert Feenstra and published by MIT Press (Fall 1983) and is referred to in the present volumes simply as *EIET*. To ensure ease of reference, and to provide a more complete view of my developmental writings, editorial cross-referencing to *EIET* has been provided here, in several places.

The present Introduction offers a broad-ranging review of my thinking on developmental problems, based on the contents of both volumes, and is therefore carried in each of them. The introductory section at the beginning of most parts, on the other hand, provides more specific discussion of that particular group of papers.

So much for organizational questions. In regard to the intellectual and scholarly contents, the essays speak for themselves. However, several broad themes in my thinking and evolution as a developmental scholar may be spelled out, since they parallel the growth of the discipline in the postwar period.

As regards the *objective* of development, I should emphasize, as I always have, that growth was seen by me (and indeed others such as the Indian planner, Pitambar Pant, with whom I was privileged to work), from the early 1960s, as simply an 'instrumental variable', as a means to an end, and the end was clearly the elimination of poverty. As I note in volume 1, chapter 1, my Distinguished Speakers Program Lecture at the Asian Development Bank in Manila, and as I have remarked at length in an interview with me by the distinguished editor of *The Third World Quarterly*, the very first piece of research I undertook in the Indian Planning Commission in 1962 was to examine the available statistical evidence on functional and personal income distribution for as many countries, with as many diverse economic and political systems, as we could find. The idea was to see whether we could detect significant variations in income distribution, and whether we could then relate better incomes for the poor with specific policy options. Rapid growth rates, sustained by internal savings mobilization supplemented by foreign aid flows, were then *deduced* as providing perhaps the most promising method for a sustained attack on Indian poverty, coupled with land reforms. The basic theme, i.e. growth with a view to eliminating poverty, may have been too optimistic; indeed, I think it was. But it will not stand scrutiny to say that growth was conceived as an end in itself! The emphasis on poverty and income distribution, especially the former, as the targets of developmental planning, recurs explicitly in chapter 1 of my 1966 volume on *The Economics of Underdeveloped Countries*, a work that developed the 'planning approach' to development, as contrasted with the *laissez faire* approach underlying the work of Professors Peter Bauer and Basil Yamey who wrote a similar, mass-appeal tract on the problem at about this time. The theme was again explicitly set forth, in the context of the design of world order, with contrast being drawn between the targets of providing 'minimum income' to all and the objective of raising per capita or total income *per se*, in my 1972 introductory essay to the volume I edited on *Economics and World Order*, an essay which is not being reprinted here.

2

With regard to the *techniques* or methods of development, so as to achieve the desired objectives, the approach advocated by me has from the beginning been a blend of planning for 'key decisions', land reforms where required, and a generous and judicious use of the market mechanism. In his *Times Literary Supplement* review of my 1966 volume on the underdeveloped countries, Peter Bauer mistook my message wholly, entitling his review fetchingly 'Planning without prices'. I, of course, envisage a far more substantial role for the government than he does: I cannot be a determinist who thinks that governments are destined to be malign, whether intentionally or inadvertently! But excluding prices from a major role in developmental strategy is a wholly different matter, and certainly not part of my game plan for the developing countries!

If there were any doubt in this regard, it should have been dispelled by the later volume that I and Professor Padma Desai wrote for the OECD on India's trade and industrial policies, *India: Planning for Industrialization*. In that book, as also in subsequent writings (e.g. the Shastri Lectures reprinted as volume 1, chapter 2, and also the joint piece with Padma Desai from *World Development*, which is volume 1, chapter 3), I have castigated the intellectual flabbiness that confuses and equates mindless controls with genuine socialism and, in the process, also hampers the very accumulation and growth process that could impact on poverty. In advocating the dismantling of much of this control apparatus from India's modern trade-and-industrial sector, I have long been the principal intellectual advocate of 'liberalization' in the modern-industrial and trade sectors in Indian policymaking. This major theme has been further analysed and advocated in the later Bhagwati–Krueger-directed NBER-Project sequel with Professor T. N. Srinivasan, *Foreign Exchange Controls and Economic Development: India*, written in 1975. Here, we examine systematically the dynamic, as against the static, consequences of India's control and allocational policies.

3

Again, in the classic and indeed a central issue of developmental economics, i.e. the relative merits of import-substituting (IS) and export-promoting (EP) developmental strategies, my sympathies have generally been with the latter, though I have expressed scholarly *caveats* to guard against treating the EP strategy as being virtuous on all counts and indeed myself raised several pertinent questions about why precisely the EP strategy seems to be more efficacious in general (as particularly in volume 2, chapter 5, where I am playing the devil's advocate in full and hostile view of several EP-strategy proponents at an After-Conference performance, and rather more carefully, and after much further reflection when the NBER Project's full results had come in, in volume 2, chapter 7).

My scientific work on the theory of trade and welfare (especially my 1963 *Journal of Political Economy* paper with V. K. Ramaswami), reprinted in *EIET*, had argued in the early 1960s that trade protection was generally an economically inappropriate first-best policy instrument, whether conferred through tariffs or quotas or exchange controls under overvalued exchange rate regimes, except in the case of what I christened as a *foreign* distortion, i.e. monopoly power in trade. Where the distortions were domestic, the appropriate policy to be used was *domestic*, e.g. production subsidy or subsidy to training workers in infant industries characterized by learning-by-doing. This fundamental insight was utilized and developed at great length, in an explicit policy context, in my 1967

Frank Graham Lecture at Princeton University on *The Theory of Commercial Policy*, reprinted as chapter 1 in my *EIET*, vol. 1. I noted, in particular, that import-substituting policies, as in India, could involve both an excessive *degree*, and a chaotic *pattern*, of import substitution, that an overvalued exchange rate regime typically led to the latter, given the precise manner in which exchange quotas were allocated: a theme which I took up later more fully in the NBER Synthesis volume; *The Anatomy and Consequences of Exchange Control Regimes*, 1978. Indeed the critical relationship between the QR (quantitative-restriction) regime implied by overvaluation and the resulting impact on the degree, and more so on the pattern, of import substitution is the hallmark of this work as distinct from the other overlapping and indeed important work of major trade-and-developmental economists such as Professors Bela Balassa, Ian Little, Maurice Scott and Tibor Scitovsky. The Graham Lecture also developed the notion of Phase sequencing of exchange control regimes, which was refined and developed to advantage by Professor Anne Krueger and myself in the NBER-Project studies of 10 developing countries.

I should add that the key role played by exchange control regimes and the overvaluation of the exchange rate in my thinking on the problems of the IS outcomes was a result of several years of prior reflection in the context of Indian policy debates, as exemplified in my earlier advocacy of exchange auctions to replace import allocations in 1962 (volume 2, chapter 9) and the later urging of devaluation in the early 1960s in India (volume 2, chapter 10). There I argued, in response to critics who pointed to the orthodoxy that devaluation would be inflationary, that it could be deflationary instead: a contention now made by several distinguished economists including Professors Richard Cooper, Lance Taylor and Paul Krugman. A contribution towards my thinking on the problems with IS strategy and the desirability of outward-orientation was also made by my early clarification of the widespread confusion over the different concepts of 'foreign exchange bottlenecks' and 'balance of payments deficits', where I sharply differentiated between the two notions (volume 2, chapter 8), thereby helping to dampen the dominant view that the payments difficulties of many developing countries implied that there were foreign exchange bottlenecks and therefore IS strategy was *ipso facto* sensible.

My general advocacy of non-distorting, 'neutral' EP policies, and criticisms of the IS policies as actually observed in the OECD and NBER Projects for example, I should like to emphasize again, must be read in the context of the caveats and questions that I have simultaneously raised. In particular, we need to know more about the relationship between the EP strategy and R&D, economies of scale, and X-efficiency, for instance. But, as Dennis Robertson once said of a distinguished theorist, it is easy to be 'silly–clever'. I think that we know enough by now to conclude that the EP strategy – *not* to be confused with 'export maximization' – is indeed a more promising policy to adopt.

4

But, if I have come out in favour of greater outward integration in trade policies in the shape of the EP strategy, while theoretically and empirically noting several *caveats*, I should add that this is not quite the case with the other areas in which the developing countries interact with the developed countries and with one another.

Thus, in relation to international migration, my theoretical researches on skilled migration, the so-called brain drain or reverse transfer of technology, have focused on highlighting and formally modelling the manifold linkages between such migration and national welfare, and indeed clarifying the important question of how national welfare ought to be defined in the presence of international personal mobility. After the important work of Professors Harry Johnson, Herbert Grubel and Anthony Scott, in particular, the dominant orthodoxy was in favour of a relatively benign view of the phenomenon of skilled migration from the underdeveloped countries. My theoretical work in the 1970s (reprinted extensively in volume 2 of *EIET*) was designed to show why and when such orthodoxy was often inappropriate. In regard to *policy* implications, however, I have shifted the debate pointedly away from its early preoccupation with measures to 'stop the brain drain' or its opposite tendency to 'let things be'. Rather, I have proposed that such migration indeed be left free, as a humane value in itself, but that skilled-migration-*related* tax policies be adopted. A variety of such ideas, and principally the idea that the income tax jurisdiction of the underdeveloped countries be extended to bring the nationals abroad into the tax net (as indeed has been the US practice), and their economic and moral–philosophical rationales, have been developed at length in many writings (especially the two volumes in 1976 on *The Brain Drain and Taxation* and a Symposium in the *Journal of Public Economics*, 1982), including a recent review (volume 2, chapter 18). The relationship of these tax ideas to one another and, in turn to the altogether different question of extending international resource flow accounting to embrace international skilled migration has been extensively analysed as well (volume 2, chapter 17). All have been elevated to international policy discussions within the UNCTAD and other UN agencies.

In regard to private foreign investment, or equivalently and more colourfully the question of multinationals or transnationals, my views have been equally sceptical of those who claim virtue in laissez-faire. Rather, my theoretical research has aimed to develop arguments for welfare-improving intervention. Among the more notable of such arguments is the demonstration (in chapter 6 in volume 1 of *EIET*) that the inflow of foreign investment in a tariff-distorted small economy may be immiserizing, and the further stronger proposition that it would be necessarily so under additional restrictions such as that the import-competing activity in a 2×2 model is capital-intensive, as demonstrated by Professors Hirofumi Uzawa, Koichi Hamada, Richard Brecher and Carlos Diaz-Alejandro independently of one another. This argument has been recapitulated, and applied to the analysis of the relative merits of EP and IS strategies in volume 2, chapter 7, in turn. Yet more recently, Professor Brecher and I have argued (volume 2, chapter 20) that the *theoretical* case for extending GATT to include foreign investment, as urged by the United States presently, needs to be recognized as not being symmetric with the classical gains-from-trade argument of Professor Paul Samuelson that every agent benefits (at least none loses, strictly speaking); with free trade initially, a transition to free capital mobility across countries may be shown to result in immiseration for one agent and improvement for another. Again, in the V. K. Ramaswami Lecture (reprinted as chapter 42 in volume 2 of *EIET*), I have reviewed, synthesized and extended several arguments that point to the conclusion that foreign investment may legitimately be examined by the host country governments to eliminate cases where it is counterproductive of the welfare of its citizens.

As for foreign aid, whose merits and demerits have preoccupied many distinguished developmental economists, my views are considerably more sanguine. The case for aid is, in the end, moral. It is also not compromised, in my view based on empirical reflections, by gross inefficiency to a degree that is radically greater than the inefficiency that characterizes all enterprises and programmes, public or private. As I have often argued, even the capitalist private sector is supposed to secure social good, not by getting everything right at once (which is impossible) but by eliminating the wrong things, once they have come to pass, fairly expeditiously. To expect total *ex post* efficiency and success from all aid expenditures is to make the impossible the enemy of the possible good. Elsewhere (in two essays that I wrote with Professor Earl Grinols reprinted as chapters 65 and 66 in volume 2 of *EIET*) I have formalized the notion that aid can nonetheless create serious political-cum-economic situations, as in Allende's Chile, where an aid cutoff to the recipient because of ideological shifts unpalatable to the donor can generate a significant 'resource crunch' that may destabilize even without active covert intervention. Doubtless, individual countries and regimes, both recipient and donor, occasionally present disturbing examples of waste and worse. But, on balance, I remain convinced that aid has done 'net good' and must continue to remain an important component of the international economic order, whether old or new.

5

My intellectual position on the manner in which developing countries ought to integrate into the world economy, and manage what Raul Prebisch has christened centre–periphery relations, is thus not readily classifiable as either 'liberal' or 'radical'. This is equally true of the positions I have taken over the years, as the North–South dialogue has unfolded during the 1960s and 1970s, on the question of how such a dialogue ought to be managed and how the developing countries (the South) should proceed. My analysis of these issues is in the tradition of political economy as well as theoretical economics. I have analysed both the possibilities of negotiations and their scope in terms of the power configurations that have obtained over the postwar period between the North and the South (volume 2, chapters 1–3) and also probed in depth the appropriateness of several of the demands of the South for reform in the international economic regime from the standpoint of rigorous economics. Both these aspects, i.e. the desire to place the negotiating possibilities into a realistic perspective so as to ensure progress in the desired direction *and* the insistence on examining the merits of each specific proposal embraced by the Southern leadership, have imparted a certain degree of critical stance in the writings reprinted here. Thus they fit into no group's political and economic positions, while seeking to influence the process and the scholarly views of economists, political scientists and international-relations specialists on these questions.

6

The final theme that I should like to touch on is the theme of political economy. While, along with such major figures as Professors Assar Lindbeck, Ronald Findlay, Stanislaw Wellisz, and Anne Krueger, I have increasingly turned to the issues raised by the question of integrating politics seriously into economic theorizing (see my work on the theory of DUP activities, especially chapters 17–27 in volume 1 of *EIET*), developmental economics has been among the principal areas where I have found this type of cross-fertilization (or what Hirschman calls 'trespassing') extremely useful from the outset. My 1973 paper on income distribution and education (volume 1, chapter 11) is a telling example of this type of work. There, I discuss questions such as the interaction between class structure and income distribution, on the one hand, and the choice of educational expenditure levels and composition as among different types of education, on the other hand. Included here is also an extended analysis of the question now increasingly raised: namely, the nutritional bias, aside from educational bias, against female infants and women respectively in household allocational decisions.

I think that, in these broad themes that have characterized my thinking on developmental processes and problems, I have been fortunate to have been present at the creation. Orthodoxy has gradually but firmly changed in the direction of these themes. Objectives have increasingly been defined by developmental economists, fairly explicitly, in terms of poverty-eradication (witness, e.g., the talk of 'basic needs'). Few now equate controls with egalitarianism; and an increased role for the market mechanism, appropriately exploited to pursue one's objectives, is increasingly appreciated. Not merely have the principal command-oriented underdeveloped countries experienced generally lukewarm economic performance, but the major centrally planned economies including the Soviet Union and China have acknowledged strains on their economies attributable in large part to their overly-quantitative and rigid command systems. There has also been increasing convergence to the view that the EP strategy is more effective, with strenuous objections being increasingly confined to ideologues or armchair economists who have made no contact with the reality of the postwar experience on these questions. And questions of political economy (e.g. why is the transition to the EP strategy held up in countries such as India while it has progressed swiftly in the 'Gang of Four' countries of the Far East?) have become all the more interesting for economists to ponder and address seriously: trespass has yielded to legitimacy.

In its concern with the fundamental issue of poverty and wealth of peoples and nations, developmental economics cannot but continue being animated and lively. It rose as a discipline in the postwar period under the guiding hand of many great economists (volume 1, chapters 19–22 should convey a glimpse of the ideas of several of them); the proclamation of its decline is certainly premature.

REFERENCES

Bhagwati, J. N. (1966): *The Economics of Underdeveloped Countries*, World University Library Series (London: Weidenfeld & Nicolson; New York: McGraw-Hill).

———— (1968): *The Theory and Practice of Commercial Policy: Departures from Unified Exchange Rates*, Frank Graham Memorial Lecture (1967), Special Papers in International Economics, No. 8 (Princeton: Princeton University Press); reprinted in *EIET*, vol. 1, ch. 1.

———— (ed.) (1972): *Economics and World Order: from the 1970s to the 1990s* (London and New York: Macmillan).

———— (ed.) (1976): *The Brain Drain and Taxation: Theory and Empirical Analysis*, (Amsterdam: North-Holland).

—— (1979): 'International factor movements and national advantage', V. K. Ramaswami Memorial Lecture, *Indian Economic Review* 14(2), pp. 73–100; reprinted in *EIET*, vol. 2, ch. 42.

—— (1980): 'North–South dialogue: an interview' (by Altaf Gauhar), *The Third World Quarterly* (April).

—— (1982): 'Structural adjustment and international factor mobility: some issues'. Paper presented at the IEA Conference at Yxtaholm, Sweden, August 1982; forthcoming in a volume of the Proceedings edited by Karl Jungenfelt.

—— (1983) *Essays in International Economic Theory EIET*, vol. 1: *The Theory of Commercial Policy*, vol. 2: *International Factor Mobility*, edited by Robert C. Feenstra (Cambridge, Mass. and London: MIT Press).

—— and Desai, Padma (1970): *India: Planning for Industrialization* (London: Oxford University Press; Paris: OECD).

—— and Grinols, Earl (1975): 'Foreign capital, dependence, destabilisation and feasibility of transition to socialism', *Journal of Development Economics*, pp. 85–98; reprinted in *EIET*, vol. 2, ch. 65.

—— and Partington, Martin (eds) (1976): *Taxing the Brain Drain: a Proposal*, vol. I (Amsterdam: North-Holland).

—— and Ramaswami, V. K. (1963): 'Domestic distortions, tariffs and the theory of optimum subsidy', *Journal of Political Economy*, 71 February, pp. 44–50; reprinted in *EIET*, vol. 1, ch. 14.

—— and Srinivasan, T. N. (1975): *India* (New York: Ballinger for NBER).

Grinols, E., and Bhagwati, J. N., (1976): 'Foreign capital, savings and dependence', *Review of Economics and Statistics* 58 (4), pp. 416–24; reprinted in *EIET*, vol. 2, ch. 66.

Hirschman, A. O. (1982): *The Economics of Trespassing* (Cambridge: Cambridge University Press).

The Times Literary Supplement, review of *The Economics of Underdeveloped Countries*, 8 December, 1966.

This list excludes essays published in the present collection.

PART I
North–South Issues

The first three essays in this volume analyse the international economic framework, or what is now increasingly described as the question of the 'governance of the world economy', as it touches on the interests of the developing countries. More precisely, these essays use historical, political and economic analysis to understand and then seek to shape the evolution of international economic relations between the developing and the developed countries, between the North and the South.

1

The New International Economic Order*

North–South economic relations, three decades after the decline of colonial empires and the emergence of new developing countries on the international scene, have come to the forefront of international economics and politics. The concerted demands of the South for a new international economic order (NIEO), and the problems they raise for the North in setting the stage for negotiations on concrete proposals related to the NIEO, now define the agenda, as well as the political climate, of the numerous conferences and intergovernmental negotiating groups on international economic matters.[1]

In assessing North–South relations and their prospects and in suggesting the optimal reforms NIEO demands should and can sensibly (in terms of political feasibility) be directed to, a historical perspective is essential. It is necessary to trace the evolution of the economic and political philosophy of the developing countries that currently animates and conditions their views of the current international economic order and prompts their demands for changes therein.

1   DEVELOPING COUNTRIES: SHIFTING POSTURES

In fact, the present postures of the developing countries can be traced to three factors.

(1) A substantial shift has occurred in the developing countries' perception of the gains to be had from economic relations with the developed countries under the existing rules of the game; the shift has been toward the gloomier side.

(2) At the same time, the developing countries now perceive their own economic and hence political power vis-à-vis the developed countries to be sufficiently substantial to warrant a strategy of effective 'trade

---

1. Among the major, recent conferences, UNCTAD IV at Nairobi in May 1976 and the Paris Conference on International Economic Cooperation (CIEC) are the principal ones. The 1976 ILO World Employment Conferences and the earlier, 1975 UNIDO Lima Conference should also be mentioned.

---

*Introduction to J. Bhagwati (ed.), *The New International Economic Order: The North–South Debate* (Cambridge, Mass.: MIT Press, 1977), pp. 1–24. References to that volume are abbreviated as *NIEO*.

unionism' to change the rules of the game and thereby to wrest a greater share of the world's wealth and income.

(3) Finally, a straightforward political desire to participate more effectively in decision making on international economic matters is now evident: this is the 'populist' aspect of the current situation.[2] Participation is thus demanded, not merely to ensure that the developing countries' interests are safeguarded but equally as an assertion of their rights as members of an international community and as a desired feature of a just international order.

A correct appreciation of each of these striking new aspects of the Southern postures is critical for a proper evaluation of the prospects for improved North–South collaboration on international economic issues.

Shifts in perception of existing international economic order[3]

The developing countries are linked to the developed countries through trade, aid, investment, and migration. The central issue for them is whether these links work to their detriment or advantage. Several ideologies compete for attention on this question; the influential policymakers in a number of developing countries have moved from more cheerful to gloomier ideologies as they have progressively made more forceful demands for changes in the world economic order.

The ideology that has traditionally been dominant is aptly characterized as that of 'benign neglect'–links with the rich nations create benefits for the poor nations. This view of the world economy parallels the utilitarian economists' view that the invisible hand works to promote universal well-being. In this model, the laissez-faire view that private greed will produce public good translates on the international scene into the notion that, while the different actors in the world economy pursue their own interests, the result will nonetheless be to benefit the developing countries. Thus, while multinational corporations invest in these countries to make profits, they will increase these countries' incomes, diffuse technology, and harness their domestic savings.[4] The exchange of commodities and services in trade will reflect the principle of division of labour and hence bring gains from trade to these countries.[5] The migration of skilled labour, instead of constituting a troublesome brain drain, will help to remove impediments

2. The characterization as 'populist' comes from Kindleberger (1975).

3. The alternative ideologies noted in this subsection were distinguished earlier in Bhagwati (1976a).

4. For a lucid statement of this viewpoint, see Vernon (1972).

5. This is, of course, the central conclusion of the conventional theory of international trade and welfare.

to progress such as inadequate remuneration of the educated elite.[6]

In direct contrast to this classical economic viewpoint, there is the doctrine of 'malign neglect' which views the impact of these links between the rich and the poor nations as primarily detrimental to the latter group. In the apt description of Osvaldo Sunkel, integration of the developing countries in the international economy leads to their domestic disintegration. This doctrine also supports the economic notion, used extensively by the Swedish economists Knut Wicksell and Gunnar Myrdal, of growing disequilibrium and exploding sequences, rather than the classical notions of equilibrium. Thus, multinational corporations disrupt domestic salary structures by introducing islands of high-income jobs that cause exorbitant wage demands by others seeking to keep up with the Joneses in the multinationals. International trade leads to the perpetuation of the role of developing countries as producers of primary, unsophisticated products that relegate them to a secondary and inferior position in the international division of labour. Furthermore, in the classic Prebisch thesis, the terms of trade of the primary-product-exporting developing countries have declined and will continue to do so, conferring gains on the developed and inflicting losses on the developing countries.[7] The brain drain to the developed countries deprives the developing countries of scarce skills and the talents that make economic progress possible.[8] The attractions of Western standards of living make domestic setting of priorities and raising of savings difficult if not impossible.

These 'malign neglect' views are merely the logical extension of the disenchantment with the 'benign neglect' model. This disenchantment initially took the form of complaints that, instead of diffusing

6. Harry Johnson, among others, has noted several positive effects of the brain drain on developing countries. For a review, see Bhagwati and Partington (1976, ch. 1, appendix).

7. This view appears to be factually erroneous, though one could construct theoretical models to explain it. Ian Little has argued:

UNCTAD was founded on the mistaken view, which it has enshrined by constant repetition into the myth, that there is a trend in the terms of trade against developing countries as a result of an adverse trend in the terms of trade between manufactures and commodities. The mistake was originated by a League of Nations publication in 1945, and repeated by an early U.N. publication. Some more recent work suggests an *improvement* in the manufactures/commodities terms of trade for nearly a century before 1952–5, when there was a highly favourable and unsustainable peak in developing countries' terms of trade associated with the Korean War boom. Thereafter for at least seven years they worsened, but then improved for a decade, even excluding oil. Any reasonably objective observer would have been saying for many years now that the evidence cannot possibly be held to give grounds for maintaining that there is a trend in the terms of trade against developing countries. Theories have been invented to explain this non-existent trend: they are treated with respect even though they explain what does not exist. (1975a, p. 227)

8. For several models of such adverse impact, see J. Bhagwati (1976b); note the contributions of Koichi Hamada and J. Bhagwati.

development, the links with the international economy were of no consequence to the developing countries. Thus, the early revisionist critics of foreign investment argued that these investments led to enclaves and had little genuine impact on the developing countries: the latter remained in consequence at the periphery of the world economy.[9] As Naipaul remarks wryly in his *Guerrillas* (1975, p. 5), 'Tax holidays had been offered to foreign investors; many had come for the holidays and had then moved on elsewhere.' The 'malign neglect' school takes this revisionism to its logical extreme and turns the argument on its head by claiming that the trouble with foreign investment is not that it makes no impact on the national economies of the developing countries because of its enclave nature but rather that it does and that this impact is adverse.

Also contrasting with these models are the two major ideological positions that focus not on the impact of the links but rather their intended objectives. Thus, the 'benign intent' school of thought, to which the 'white man's burden' philosophy belongs, considers the international links and institutions to be designed so as to transmit benefits to the poor nations. Private investment is regarded as motivated by the desire to spread the fruits of modern technology and enterprise to the developing countries. In particular, the foreign aid programmes are conceived as humanitarian in origin, reflecting the Western ideals of liberalism and the enlightened objective of sharing the world's resources with the poor countries.

The polar opposite of this model is the 'malign intent' view of the world, typically favoured by the Marxist and New Left writings on the international economy. Foreign aid is seen as a natural extension of the imperialist designs on the poor nations aimed at creating dependence.[10] Private investments, following the flag in past models, are seen now as precursors of the flag, with brazen colonialism replaced by devious neocolonialism (Nkrumah, 1965).

Clearly, none of these models in their pure form capture the full complexity of the effects that the links with the outside world have on the developing countries' prospects for economic progress. However, it is clear that policy makers in several developing countries have moved over the three postwar decades from a world-view based primarily on the benign neglect and intent models to one characterized more by varying shades of the malign neglect and intent models.

Thus, the early posturing of these countries was based on the view that the existing mechanisms governing trade and investment flows were primarily beneficial. Furthermore, aside from utilizing and expanding trade opportunities and attracting foreign investment funds, the developing countries could appeal to the developed countries on a purely moral plane

9. The writings of Hans Singer developed this theme; see, for example, Singer (1975).
10. An excellent statement of this type of viewpoint can be found in Weisskopf (1972).

for the provision of technical assistance and foreign aid for developmental programmes. These premises were the basis for the first UNCTAD conference in Geneva in 1964, which led to a permanent creation of the UNCTAD secretariat and its eventual emergence as the principal forum for airing the problems of the developing countries.

UNCTAD I at Geneva and UNCTAD II at New Delhi thus concentrated primarily on defining and underlining aid targets for the developed countries, while laying principal stress on two aspects of trade policy: preferential access by developing countries into the markets of the developed countries, and the principle of non-reciprocity.

The trade efforts were to bear fruit, yielding to the developing countries the satisfaction of having utilized collective action at UNCTAD to some advantage. This advantage, however, was rather small; in retrospect, it is evident that the grant of preferential entry by the EEC and by other developed countries, including the United States in 1975, has been of limited value because of numerous exceptions and because of the importance of nontariff barriers to which it did not extend (see Malmgren [in *NIEO*]). As for the principle of non-reciprocity, it is now increasingly obvious that the developing countries probably threw away the main instrument that governments have at their command to lower their own trade barriers–the ability to tell their protected industries that the protection must be reduced as part of the reciprocal bargaining process. Recent studies on the foreign trade regimes of the developing countries have shown[11] that the degree and dispersion of the protection enjoyed by the industries of these countries have been disturbing; a continuation of reciprocity would have been most useful if effectively used by willing governments in the developing countries.[12]

The principal disappointments were to be in the field of international aid flows. The developing countries were faced with the incongruous contrast between the UNCTAD targets on foreign aid and the declining overall flows from the leading aid donors, particularly the United States, once the leader of the enlightened donors. Not merely were nominal aid flows decelerating, but their real worth was falling with inflation. It was increasingly clear that their worth was seriously reduced by practices such as aid-tying, which compelled the aid recipients to buy from the donor countries at artificially high prices. Their worth was further reduced because few of the aid funds were anything but loans to be repaid and

---

11. For a review of the principal findings on this and other related issues in research by Little-Scitovsky-Scott for the OECD, Bhagwati-Krueger for the NBER, and Balassa for the IBRD, see Bhagwati (1976c).

12. One must concede, however, that for the 1950s and most of the 1960s, many of these governments were of the view that their protectionist policies were desirable.

hence were substantially less by way of genuine aid transfers than the publicized figures implied.[13]

Aside from the failure to meet the obligations which the developed countries appeared to have endorsed, however reluctantly, at international forums such as the UNCTAD, there was also an emerging sense that the declining efforts at international assistance were a reflection of the steady thaw in superpower relations. Thus, it became increasingly difficult to maintain that humanitarian motives, rather than the political necessities of the Cold War, were the major motivating factors behind the aid programmes of the 1950s. These cynical perceptions of the aid efforts of the developed world were only to be reinforced by the misguided attempts at enforcing performance criteria in aid distribution. Typically, the aid donors, following economically wise but politically foolish precepts, insisted on examining and endorsing the entire set of economic policies of the recipient nations to ensure that their meagre aid assistance was being utilized to advantage,[14] thereby generating resentments and charges of calculated attempts at imposing ideological solutions in the guise of 'scientific' economic prescriptions.[15]

The confirmation of covert political interventions in the developing countries, euphemistically described as destabilization operations, engineered by developed countries from which one expected better behaviour, often prompted and encouraged by multinational corporations (such as the ITT in Chile), must have helped in strengthening the radical theses regarding the Northern designs and impact on the South.

The growing sense that the benign intent and impact of the developed countries on the well-being of the developing countries could not be taken as the natural order of things under the existing international arrangements was finally to be accentuated and reinforced from yet another direction. The focus during the 1950s on the 'gap' in the incomes, living standards, and wealth of the developing and the developed countries and on the gearing of international targets to narrowing and eventually eliminating such differences, was probably helpful in lending animation to the development decades and the attendant programmes for developing

13. See Bhagwati, (1970, Chs I and II). Several different estimates are reviewed here and it is reported that the net worth of foreign aid to recipients was reduced to less than half of the alleged amounts and, in some cases, to little more than a third.

14. That aid may be misused unless the whole economic programme of the receipient country is examined is a lesson that was learned by economists during the Marshall Plan. Needless to say, politically it seems outrageous to sovereign nations receiving such assistance to have their entire economic process be subjected to scrutiny and control by donors who contribute, in general, no more than 1–2 per cent of the overall resources in the recipient countries.

15. Such resentments are inevitable as economic policies inevitably reflect ideological preferences and value judgments. An articulate expression of these resentments from a frustrated aid-recipient negotiator can be found in I. G. Patel's contribution in Ward (1971).

countries. But it was also to lead inevitably to frustration–such gaps cannot possibly be narrowed in any significant manner in the foreseeable future despite any optimism as to the prospects of the developing countries' growth rates.[16] Thus, despite the fact that the developing countries, as a group, grew at the historically remarkable rate of 5.5 per cent per annum during the first development decade of the 1960s, the awareness grew that these rates of growth could neither help measurably in 'catching up' with the developed countries nor could they adequately diffuse the fruits of growth to the poor in the developing countries.[17] Poverty, both absolute at home and relative vis-à-vis the developed countries, thus seemed to be inescapable under the existing economic regimes. As a result, as far as domestic policies are concerned the intellectuals have turned increasingly to distributive implications of their developmental pro- grammes: the faith of many in the 'trickle-down' process has been shaken. At the international level the implication is again for distribution: it is felt now that the growth rates of the poor countries, no matter how rapid, have to be supplemented by increasing transfers of resources on a simple, progressive argument. It is a question of a *moral* imperative that the world's limited wealth and incomes be shared more equitably. This is only the international counterpart of the sociological fact that as access to affluence diminishes, the resentment of success increases and the stress on redistribution is keener. For example, the greater American mobility surely explains the lack of success of socialist doctrines there whereas the social and economic rigidity of the British society explains the stresses on the social contract that are quite evident in their macroeconomic failures. The erosion of faith since the 1950s in the ability of developing countries to catch up with the developed countries has surely contributed to their present 'trade unionist' demands for greater shares in world income through the creation of a new international economic order.[18]

Post-OPEC emphasis on collective action: the rise of 'trade unionism'

It was against the backdrop of this slow but certain shift in several developing countries' world-view that the dramatic event of the successful

16. The consequent need to redefine the goals of international efforts at development in the developing countries has been stressed by several writers. See, for example, the contributions by Pitambar Pant, Göran Ohlin, and J. Bhagwati in Bhagwati (1972).

17. One can only agree with Little, however, in the judgment that the so-called statistics on income distribution for developing countries, which suggest *absolute* impoverishment of millions during the 1960s, are totally unreliable. See his critique in Little (1976) and also my rejection of these claims in volume 1, chapter 1.

18. An alternative view is that the demands for the NIEO have resulted from the 'revolution of rising expectations' following the high rates of growth in the developing countries.

cartelization of oil producers, nearly all members of the Third World, was to materialize. The OPEC had existed for a number of years prior to its dramatic success since 1973, but practically no serious analyst had considered its success probable. Indeed, my colleague Morris Adelman had the singular misfortune of writing a superb analysis of the oil industry (1972), predicated entirely on the assumption that OPEC would not succeed, and having it published just as this basic assumption was being falsified!

The Third World's reaction to the nearly sevenfold rise in oil prices and the accentuation of the resource and foreign exchange difficulties of many of the poorer nations among the Third World, was to baffle the rich nations that sought to mobilize the poor against the OPEC. The developing countries refused to condemn, and indeed seemed to take great delight in, the oil price increases. This reaction can only be understood in light of the shifts in their views about the rich nations. Clearly there was a need for prudence *vis-à-vis* the *nouveaux riches* to whom the developing countries would have to turn for aid. But, far more than that, the developing countries seemed to feel that finally there was one dramatic instance of a set of primary producers in the Third World who were able to get a 'fair share' of the world incomes by their own actions rather than by the unproductive route of morally persuading the rich nations for fairer shares. Even while many of them suffered from the fallout of the oil price increases, many developing countries therefore felt a sense of solidarity, a *corps d'esprit* with the OPEC countries and the exhilarating sense that they could finally take their economic destiny in their own hands. Thus, the stage was to be set psychologically and politically for the present phase of 'trade unionist' militancy. The nascent sense that collective action, as crystallized in the developing countries' Group of 77 and the activities at UNCTAD, could yield some results (such as the schemes for preferential entry), was now to be transformed into an act of faith: solidarity in international bargaining, alternatively termed 'collective self-reliance', on a variety of fronts would yield much more than had ever been thought possible.

The OPEC success crystallized the concepts of strength through collective action and 'solidarity rather than charity'. The developing countries also seemed to infer from the OPEC experience that their commodity exports, which had traditionally been viewed as a sign of weakness, could be turned instead into weapons of collective action. Thus, the notion of 'commodity power' emerged and has shaped not merely the politics but also the economics of the demands for the NIEO (as typified by the Corea plan for commodities at the UNCTAD).

Populism

The OPEC example was also to hold the further attraction that, contrary to aid flows (whether bilateral or multilateral), the earning of the new resources through improved terms of trade implied that the OPEC countries retained their national sovereignty in deciding how to spend these resources and also began to qualify as nations that commanded some voice in the management of international monetary affairs and therefore in other deliberations on the world economic regime as well.

Many developing countries, seeking both the assertion of fuller national sovereignty over their economic programmes and increased participation in international deliberations on trade, aid, and monetary rules, thus saw the OPEC as an ideal case which they would hope to emulate.

The foregoing analysis underlines the complex nature of the current attitudes and demands of the developing countries while defining the limits within which the amicable evolution of a new international economic order will have to be defined. Several major points must be stressed.

(1) Our analysis shows that the developing countries' objectives are economic and political. The economic objective is principally to increase their share of the world's income and wealth. The political objectives are that they should have better control over the use of these and their own resources and that they should also be allowed to participate actively in devising the new rules for managing world trade, aid, and monetary and other matters of global concern. Needless to say all of these objectives may not be in harmony; it may be possible to get more resources transferred if their use is not entirely within the prerogative of the recipient country–a conflict that is quite important in practice. However, these objectives do exist manifestly; the twin political objectives are the new elements on the scene, as compared with the 1950s and 1960s.

(2) The developing countries' assessment of their capacity to achieve these objectives is grounded in their assessment of their capacity for collective action. There is some evidence that the early optimism about the use of commodity power has receded: except for bauxite, the results of collective cartelization seem to have borne little fruit. This should, in fact, have been expected from a realistic assessment of commodity markets since oil is a very special case with exceedingly low elasticities, considerable macro effects, and no real parallel for other commodities. The 'commodity power' that exists, outside of oil, is therefore only a short-run, disruptive power; it may be currently exercised to some advantage[19] but is certainly self-destroying through high elasticities of substitution and through the use of augmented inventory policies by the developed countries (such as those proposed recently in the United States for certain raw materials).

19. For example, Japan as well as Western Europe (as noted by Bergsten in his paper [in *NIEO*]) have raw material 'dependence'–ratios that are of concern to their governments: the short-run disruption to their economies from interruptions of supplies could be quite substantial.

Interestingly therefore the emphasis has shifted from the proposed use of weak and essentially short-run 'commodity power' to improve prices to pressuring the consuming developed countries to collaborate in the raising of the prices of these commodities to 'fair' levels; this 'indexing' idea parallels the domestic US parity programme for agriculture.[20] As Kindleberger has remarked, this is tantamount to asking the chicken to help in plucking its own feathers! And yet, the idea is not quite absurd; the developing countries now see their power not as accruing from commodities *per se* but rather from their capacity to create confrontations and impede agreements on a variety of global concerns such as the Law of the Sea. Thus, commodities today have become a chief vehicle through which the developing countries want resources transferred via increased prices, this increase being forced by the use of political power rather than the use of admittedly small commodity power.

(3) It should finally be noted that the new affluence of the OPEC countries has already split the Third World into the Third and Fourth Worlds, the former being almost wholly the OPEC developing countries and the latter the rest. The two worlds have managed to collaborate effectively. Thus, the OPEC nations have extended credits and aid on a massive scale to the developing countries while also championing their cause politically.[21] As Fred Bergsten has noted, the OPEC countries managed to get developmental NIEO-type issues included on the agenda by withdrawing from the first ministerial session of the 'energy dialogue' in Paris in April 1975. They also successfully pushed for further liberalization of IMF credits at Kingston in January 1976 by linking the usability of their currencies directly to liberalization of the credit tranches and by prompting the liberalization of the compensatory finance facility through their negotiating strategy in Paris (see Bergsten, panel discussion [in *NIEO*]). Thus, far from compromising the collective action potential of the developing countries, the emergence of the more powerful OPEC countries has only served to increase the political potential for collective action by the developing countries.

(4) In fact, the specific demands of the developing countries for institutional reform in the international economic order clearly reflect both the new objectives and the new political and economic realities that

20. For example, the 1972 Algiers demands and the resolutions of the special 1975 United Nations Conference on Raw Materials seem far more optimistic in regard to unilateral initiatives on commodities than does the February 1976 Manila Charter of the Group of 77 which sought to define the concerted position of these countries at the May 1976 Nairobi Conference of the UNCTAD. The Manila Charter demands the indexing of prices of exports of primary commodities by the developing countries to the prices of manufactured goods imported from the developed countries; this indexing is clearly to be achieved by cooperation toward that goal by both producing and consuming nations.

21. See Table 2.2 in the Edelman-Chenery paper [in *NIEO*] for the statistics on this.

the oil price increases have imposed on the poor countries. Few of the current demands for specific reforms are entirely novel, but the choice of those that have been highlighted at UNCTAD IV and propagated at other forums is revealing. Two principal proposals have been the *Integrated Programme for Commodities*, christened the Corea Plan after the UNCTAD Secretary-General, and the demand for general *debt relief*.

The debt relief proposal would eliminate the accumulated debt burden, which many of the poorer developing countries find particularly onerous after the terms of trade losses from the increased oil prices. The elimination of this burden would provide for a transfer of resources (measurable as the present discounted value of the repayments cancelled) in a form that is free of strings and high on the sovereignty scale. Generalized debt relief would also be politically and psychologically reinforcing to the developing countries because bilateral debt reliefs have usually been accompanied by extensive scrutiny and provisions by the creditor nations. Similarly the Integrated Programme for Commodities would also appear to do extremely well in light of the three objectives that were distinguished. Indexing of commodity prices (implied by the phrase 'establishment and maintenance of commodity prices at levels which, in real terms, are . . . remunerative to producers')[22] would yield transfer of resources by suitably raising them and maintaining them there. Indexing would mean that the developing countries had earned these increased incomes and therefore their national sovereignty over them would have been guaranteed. By participating in the arrangements designed to run these schemes, the developing countries would have earned the right to deliberate in international policy making in this sphere of international economic management.

2 DEVELOPED COUNTRIES: FACTORS AFFECTING RESPONSE

While these two proposals do not constitute the totality of the demands made by the developing countries nor have they been pushed with continuing vigour by the developing countries since UNCTAD IV—in fact, the demand for a generalized debt relief or moratorium has, if anything, lost ground within the Group of 77 itself and the Group of 24 at the Fund/Bank Manila meetings in the fall of 1976 avoided or even repudiated the subject altogether—they do illustrate the problems that the present aspirations and postures of the developing countries pose for the developed

22. Secretary-General of UNCTAD, 1975, *An Integrated Programme for Commodities: Specific Proposals for Decision and Action by Governments*, Report TD/B/C.1/193, 28 October 1975. For further details on the Integrated Programme, see the paper by Harry Johnson [in *NIEO*].

countries as the latter contemplate the nature of their response to the demands for the NIEO.

In particular, there are two dimensions to these proposals that are guaranteed to make the response to them lukewarm, if not hostile, in the United States: the developed country whose consent is critical to orderly adoption of such proposals, as it clearly constitutes a *force majeure* on the international economic scene. These dimensions relate to sovereignty and efficiency, both of which can add up to an ideological confrontation that will have to be cooled, if not circumvented, to usher in reforms in the international economic system.

Sovereignty

While the developing countries have come to stress the sovereignty over the use of their (and the transferred) resources, the rise of intellectual neoconservatism in the United States has tended to move the aid philosophy precisely in the opposite direction. To the exaggerated complaints about the misuse and inefficiency of aid programmes, one must now add the moral concern that the developing countries suppress civil liberties and oppress their populations and that therefore aid cannot be justified any longer on 'humanitarian' or progressive principles; the latter should apply to transfers between individuals, not governments.

Indeed, in the year of Adam Smith's bicentennial, it must be sadly admitted that the invisible hand has yielded to the iron fist in a number of developing countries. However the neoconservative inference that therefore resources should not be provided to developing countries' governments on progressive principles is a nonsequitur.

The nation state, as an entity that transposes itself between individuals in the developing and the developed countries, cannot be wished away; world order therefore must surely be defined in terms of morality as between nations. Moreover, the freewheeling description of developing countries as dictatorships and tyrannies is an exaggeration and self-righteously ignores the moral lapses of the developed countries themselves.[23] In defining the new international economic order, it would therefore seem perfectly legitimate to apply the progressive tax principles to nation states, none of which is characterized by moral perfection and few of which can ever share a common perception of morality in all its dimensions.

However, the neoconservative arguments do have a superficial appeal, especially in the United States where Vietnam and Watergate have crystallized a psychological need for assertion of moral values in policy

23. Indeed, it is arguable that some of these lapses (for example, the Vietnam war) were a greater affront to one's moral sense than the lapses that the developing countries are accused of.

making. Thus the argument that 'we cannot allow ourselves to be pushed around and lectured into giving aid to an undeserving, corrupt Third World' has several adherents in fashionable intellectual circles in the United States.[24] This attitude of hostility to the developing countries has been reinforced by the subtle but propagandistic caricaturing of the positions of developing countries in regard to the New International Economic Order by conservatives and neoconservatives alike in the United States. *Ignoratio elenchi* is a favourite fallacy of intellectuals who are writing extensively in this area; it works very well in its intended purpose, but it must be exposed. In particular, it has been argued that the developing countries wish to establish 'Western guilt' for their own underdevelopment; thus developing countries seek transfers of resources as reparations for past and present damage to their economic success. On the other hand, no such guilt can be established since internal institutional changes are critical for development and account for the growth of countries; hence the demands for the NIEO are ill-founded and must be rejected. This argument would be laughable were it not so superficially plausible, effective, and pernicious.[25] The argument for progressive redistribution of income and wealth does not rest on whether the rich have hurt the poor in the past or are currently doing so. Nor are the majority of the intellectuals in the developing countries so naive as to assume that the colonial rule was necessarily harmful economically; what many do challenge is the opposite thesis of the imperialist historical school that the colonial rule was necessarily beneficial. Moreover, the critical nature of internal reform for rapid economic advance is logically compatible with the importance of external factors in shaping both the nature and the momentum of domestic development. Moreover, the many developing countries that launched five-year plans designed to direct principally domestic efforts at development and many of their left wing intellectuals (who ridiculed Western economists' naivete about the ease with which foreign aid programmes would take the developing countries to 'self-sustained' growth without radical internal reforms) would both (for different reasons) find the present lecturing by these Western intellectuals on the role of domestic reforms to be astonishing, and the inference that the external environment needs no fundamental changes to be a self-serving nonsequitur.

Turning from the conservative and neoconservative arguments, we must note next that the few remaining liberals who favour resource transfers

24. Among the magazines that have encouraged an unduly critical approach to Third World issues is *Commentary*.

25. Variations on this basic theme have appeared in articles by Daniel Moynihan, Peter Bauer, and others, in American magazines such as *Commentary*. Even the *New York Times Sunday Magazine* (7 November 1976) carried an article on the theme of Western guilt and its untenability written by two staffers of the Hudson Institute.

to the developing countries on an increased scale do not adequately consider two compelling lessons from aid experience. First, economics rarely gives unique solutions *ex ante*–when you had six economists including Keynes, a witticism went, you had seven opinions–so that imposing donor-country economic solutions on recipient countries must often require an act of missionary zeal and faith. And second, local constraints on political action, much like in the donor countries, will often require the adoption of *n*th-best policies, contrary to the desires of the unconstrained policy advisers. They continue to see the application of strict, overall, economy-wide performance criteria as essential to a foreign aid policy. Experience points to the infeasibility of having such criteria scientifically and to the general inability to find such criteria. Assuming that consensus could be reached on what was the optimal policy to adopt in the first place, it would be impossible to apply such criteria meaningfully in light of local constraints. Thus, witness the following argument by Richard Cooper (panel discussion [in *NIEO*]), an influential international economist of liberal persuasion and enormous sophistication:

> If we are to justify resource transfers on ethical grounds, then, it must be on the basis of knowledge that via one mechanism or another the transferred resources will benefit those residents of the recipient countries that are clearly worse off than the worst-off 'taxed' (including taxes levied implicitly through commodity prices) residents of the donor countries. That is, general transfers must be based on some kind of performance criterion satisfied by the recipient country, or else transfers should be made only in a form that benefits directly those who the ethical arguments suggest should be benefited. But this proposition has profound implications, . . . for it implies that no completely general transfer of resources from country to country can be supported on ethical grounds. This restriction would encompass the organic SDR link, general debt relief, actions to improve (not merely stabilize) the terms of trade of developing countries, and a brain drain tax that automatically remit the revenues to developing countries. Ethically based transfers should discriminate among recipient countries on the basis of performance in improving, directly or indirectly, the well-being of their general population, and/or they should discriminate among uses of the transfers to maximize the flow of benefits to those who are the intended beneficiaries, which generally means concentration on general nutrition, health care, and education in the recipient countries.

While this quote speaks for itself, one might note particularly that emphasis on nutrition, education, and health care leaves open important issues of the type that have traditionally created friction between recipients and donors on the utilization of aid and hence problems regarding national sovereignty. What should be the balance between these three areas? How much in total, by way of current and investment expenditures, should be allocated to the three sectors together? What should be the time profile of benefits provided in these sectors, given the limited volume of resources? Within education, what should be the allocation to education at different levels and in different geographical areas? All of these questions raise both economic and political issues and involve issues of intertemporal allocations of costs and benefits; in none of these cases does an analyst have any ability to proceed without making several value judgments and not simply economic behavioural assumptions. No wonder that the overly sensitive developing countries have occasionally felt that the zeal of the donor-country economist and his value-unfree (in Nobel laureate Gunnar Myrdal's sense) recommendations, which are to be imposed by arm twisting at the aid-consortia meetings, reflect not just economic naivete but also ideological intentions.

Whether one takes the neoconservative or the liberal position, the fact remains that the developing countries' growing insistence on sovereignty in the use of resources conflicts increasingly with the preferred stress of the intellectuals in the United States on evaluation of economic performance, on monitoring, and on the morality of their internal and even international conduct. The dilemma therefore is that, while the developing countries by and large have centralized political regimes and are able to formulate and coordinate their demands for resource transfers, the developed countries generally have democratic, decentralized regimes where resource transfers must be justified to the electorates. These transfers cannot be defended when the neoconservative position assiduously tries to undercut the moral case for such actions and the liberal case is undermined by the insistence on performance criteria that are now sought to be rejected by the developing countries seeking sovereignty. If only the developing countries had the democratic political regimes and the developed countries the centralized ones, the dilemma would disappear!

This dilemma obtains chiefly in the United States, and far less so in the European countries and in Japan. In fact, Erik Lundberg has observed that in Sweden, uneasiness over the political conditions in several developing countries has not, as in the United States, been taken to rationalize a neoconservative position of opting out of aid; rather the Swedish political parties have unanimously agreed that the aid transfers are a moral obligation and the debate between the parties has only been about which developing countries ought to get what share of the total Swedish aid. This is of small consolation, however, since the United States still remains the force majeure in this area.

Efficiency

Both the generalized debt relief scheme and the Corea Plan for commodities offend the tenets of efficiency as far as the transference of resources is concerned, thus raising serious doubts as to the advisability of these schemes as the principal props of current efforts at negotiating a new international economic order.

(1) Generalized debt relief has already been seen as such and has already been dropped from the active shopping list of the developing countries. The main problems with the scheme were that many developing countries (among the medium and higher *per capita* income groups) had come to borrow increasingly from the private capital markets and presumably must continue doing so for the foreseeable future. A generalized default or moratorium could not but adversely affect the creditworthiness of the developing countries; it would also make it extremely difficult to regulate future borrowings since such largesse would affect expectations as to possible gains from similar largesse later–as Paul Streeten observes (in his comment on Kenen's paper [in *NIEO*]), in economics bygones are rarely bygones.

Recent statistical analyses suggest that the major beneficiaries would be the poor developing countries only when the debt relief was biased toward them.[26] Since these are the countries that have been hit badly by the rise in oil prices and their ability to borrow petrodollars has been inversely affected (whereas the not-so-poor developing countries are better off and have been able to borrow more successfully to tide over their current foreign exchange *and* real resource difficulties), the simpler and least-cost solution[27] to debt relief seems to be to deal with the debt problems of the poor countries on a case-by-case basis; this was, in fact, suggested by the United States at UNCTAD IV (and has been carried out for many years for several countries).

(2) The commodity schemes have not met quite the same fate. This is because that part of their objectives that deals with price stabilization allows for accommodation among both developed and developing countries, whereas the part that deals with indexing, to secure explicit resource transfer to the primary producers in developing countries, raises no enthusiasm and generates much hostility.

The stabilization part, despite the ambiguities of the UNCTAD documentation (which unhappily does not record the analytical work that

26. See Kenen's paper for the magnitudes involved [in *NIEO*].
27. This would be equally true for the not-so-poor developing countries (such as Brazil and Mexico) which fear being tainted by a generalized debt write-off or moratorium.

underlies the declaration of the proposed objectives and hence unnecessarily creates the impression of being economically untutored)[28] appeals to many policy makers in the developed countries. The extremely wide and rapid shifts in commodity prices during 1972–5 appear to have baffled and upset both producers and consumers, suggesting that international buffer stocks are not entirely unacceptable. Besides, except to a Chicago economist, the fact that Keynes had also proposed a third international institution, the *Commod Control*, to supplement the bank and the fund precisely for commodity price stabilization after the war appears to have endowed the idea with some legitimacy![29]

Unfortunately, the developing countries have set the scheme back by muddling it up, deliberately no doubt, with the indexing idea. As most sensible economists will agree, indexing is crude, simplistic, inefficient, inequitable (among developing countries, exactly like oil price increases), and virtually impracticable (administratively perhaps, and certainly politically to developed countries).

It is apparent that the developing countries have chosen to focus on particularly ill-designed measures to translate their objectives into reality. We have also identified the problem that the developing countries' demand for sovereignty in use of resources is likely to raise in the developed countries, a problem that must somehow be circumvented if the resources are to be transferred on anything like a significant scale via one feasible scheme or another. On the other hand, there are also favourable signs that the conflicts may turn into constructive cooperation. The generalized debt relief scheme has been dropped thus pleasing those who believe that the failure to perceive failure is the chief impediment to progress. And the North–South dialogue continues at UNCTAD, in Paris, and elsewhere, with developing countries participating as they wished, and on more harmonious terms than the early 'Algerian-style' rhetoric and the 'Moynihan-style' ripostes (both of which were petty but popular in their own spheres of influence), thus pleasing those who believe instead that the failure to perceive progress is the chief impediment to progress.

28. It is worth noting that Mr Corea, the Secretary-General of UNCTAD, obtained a First in the Economics Tripos at Cambridge University, and that the UNCTAD draws in many consultants with considerable professional expertise and of much distinction. Unfortunately, it has become customary in certain professional circles (in this connection, read Harry Johnson [in *NIEO*] and elsewhere) to equate the UNCTAD Secretariat with economic illiteracy–a charge that cannot be sustained, certainly relative to other international secretariats (such as the GATT) that also operate under governmental control rather than as autonomous university departments of economics!

29. Keynes' memorandum on the subject was discovered by Dr Lal Jayawardene, then on the Committee of Twenty; I hastened to publish it in the *Journal of International Economics*, 4 (3) (1974).

3 DESIRABLE AND FEASIBLE DIMENSIONS OF THE NEW INTERNATIONAL ECONOMIC ORDER

In a sense there is already a transitional international economic order. The developing countries are already active participants in negotiations where they were previously either ignored or regarded peripherally. Recall that the Committee of 20 grew out of the Committee of 10 in negotiations on international monetary reform which, until that recent shift, were regarded as of immediate concern only to the developed countries. 'Populism' therefore is here to stay. However, the developing countries have learned the virtues of avoiding unwieldiness and, within the Group of 77, of biasing participation toward those who are most affected by the decisions being deliberated. It is in fact arguable that such participatory democracy in international economic negotiations has served to cool the inflammatory rhetoric and to reduce the confrontational content of North–South relations: Lord Acton has observed that absolute power corrupts absolutely, but lack of power corrupts equally.[30]

The interesting issues from an economist's viewpoint concern the desirable dimensions, in the form of concrete reform proposals, that the ongoing North-South negotiations should impart to the new international economic order. The record of the developing countries in finding and backing imaginative proposals, as is evident in the foregoing analysis, is not exactly exciting; nor have the developed countries put sufficient energy and initiative into developing a coherent and imaginative response to the specific demands of the developing countries.[31] In short, an overall categorization of desirable targets for the architects of the new international economic order is still to be evolved.

In my view, such a delineation must rest on a judicious combination of two major principles of reform: (1) the developing countries

---

30. One might add with regard to the subset of dictators, that lack of absolute power corrupts absolutely as well!

31. Thus, the *Tinbergen Report on Reshaping the International Order* (New York: E. P. Dutton & Co., 1976), concludes:

It became apparent at the Seventh Special Session that, with few exceptions, the *Western European* Market economy countries and *Japan* although they have potentially more to lose than the US from a failure to forge new international structures, were not only reluctant to take the initiative in redirecting the process of change, but were quite prepared to take refuge behind the United States' position when discussions became serious. That they are unwilling or unable to take serious initiatives is witnessed by the results of the first meeting of EEC Ministers for Development Cooperation held after the Seventh Special Session (3). It ended in complete failure; no agreement was reached on any important agenda point. *Despite a considerable effort, the 'nine' also failed to formulate a common position for UNCTAD IV.* (p. 54; italics added for emphasis)

must receive an increased share of resources under the NIEO; and (2) bargains must be struck which are mutually profitable and which therefore appeal also to the developed countries' interests in areas of trade policy, regulation of multinationals, transfer of technology, migration, and food policy. By focusing on the transfer-of-resources proposals that can raise substantial resources *while circumventing the objections in the developed countries to the autonomous use of such resources by the developing countries* (as can be done), and by appealing to the interests of all concerned parties through the mutual gain proposals (that can indeed be developed) in several different areas of international economic policy, the NIEO can be made a reality that accommodates the major political preferences and economic objectives of the developing and the developed countries. These two principles may now be developed briefly by spelling out the major reform proposals that might be entertained under them.

Resource transfers

There are two proposals that can qualify as raising fairly substantial revenues for developing countries that are least likely to be perfect substitutes for normal aid flows because of the nature of the rationales on which they are justified and also because of the incidence of the revenues within the developed countries. These proposals are also least likely to raise the moral questions that are attached to uncontrolled transfers of resources from the developed to the developing countries.

The first and major proposal relates to the grant of a share in the profits of seabed mining to the developing countries and extending the arrangement further to oceans generally thereby bringing into the net the possible revenues from regulation of 'overfishing' as well. Politically, such proposals are less likely to give rise to objections and therefore be more acceptable to developed countries because rights over these resources are still the subject of international negotiation; thus it is difficult to conceive of the allocation of some of the profits or revenues from seabed mining and licensing of overfished fisheries to the developing countries as a simple grant *from* the developed *to* the developing countries. Furthermore, since the regulation of overfishing is an efficiency-improving business (whereas the taxing of seabed mining would be tantamount to taxing rents unless the returns to innovation and risk were also taxed away), the gut reaction of neoclassical economists is to welcome such methods of yielding resources to the developing countries; in such a case one has that rare example of transfers that may even improve welfare (for fishing) and, at worst, not hurt it (for seabed mining).

The Law of the Sea Conference, which has just terminated its fifth session without reaching any agreement, is the forum for transacting such a resource transfer to the developing countries. The developing countries have, to date, held out for far more substantial control of the ocean resources while resisting lucrative offers of revenues as proposed here.[32] In the end, since the major developed countries are poised to mine the seabeds and will probably effectively threaten to continue unilaterally to do so, it is certain that a bargain will be struck and a substantial source of revenues for the developing countries will emerge. Richard Cooper has put together estimates of the sums that could be raised from the oceans and, while they are necessarily rough and ready, they do indicate the orders of magnitude that one is dealing with: by 1985 a full capture of rents on fish at 1974 levels of output could yield $2.2 billion, a 50 per cent profits tax on offshore oil coming from waters more than 200 metres deep would yield $2.2 billion, and a 50 per cent profits tax on manganese nodules would yield $0.1 billion. This is a total of $4.5 billion in revenues from the oceans (Cooper [in *NIEO*]). Thus, even if half of this revenue was allocated to the developing countries in an international oceans bargain, the developing countries would receive over $2 billion worth of revenues as of 1985. These would be characterized by autonomy in use; because they would be untied grants, they would be worth at least twice as much in grant-equivalent terms as an equal aid flow under the average terms would generally imply.

Yet another example of a proposal that would raise resources/revenues for the developing countries is the suggestion of a brain drain tax. The proposal is to levy a supplementary tax on the incomes earned in the developed countries by skilled migrants from the developing countries. The tax would be levied by the developing countries (for legal-constitutional reasons), collected by the developed countries (for administrative reasons), and the revenues would be transferred *en bloc* to the developing countries via the United Nations (the UNDP) for developmental spending.[33] Given the entry restrictions of the developed countries, the tax may be seen as essentially a tax on the rents generated by such quantitative interferences with the international mobility of labour; it would again be consistent with human rights for the identical reason that the countries that create such interferences on human mobility are the developed countries with their immigration quotas. A moral rationale for taxing the immigrants exists, quite aside from the case for taxing rents, and has been spelled out by me elsewhere:[34]

---

32. It appears that the desire for full control stems again from residual notions of commodity power: it is feared that the access to seabeds would enable developed countries to reduce the potency of the developing countries' major weapon. Note that manganese is among the commodities that are included in the developing countries' list of commodities for exercise of commodity power!

33. For details, see Bhagwati and Partington (1976).

34. Bhagwati and Partington (1976), p. 22. Also quoted in Koichi Hamada [in *NIEO*].

The rationale behind the tax implementation would consist of two arguments; in order of their importance: (1) Firstly, one would assert the moral principle that, in a world of imperfect mobility, those few who manage to get from LDCs to DCs to practise their professions at substantially-improved incomes ought to be asked to contribute a fraction of their gains for the improved welfare of those left behind in the LDCs; this would effectively be extending the usual principle of progressive taxation across national borders. (2) Moreover, since there is a widely-held presumption, based on several sound arguments and embodied in numerous international resolutions, that the brain drain creates difficulties for the LDCs, it would also constitute a simple and rough-and-ready way for the emigrating professionals to compensate the LDCs for these losses. In fact, the moral obligation to share one's gains with those who are unable to share in these gains would be reinforced if these others were also hurt by one's emigration.

The revenues from imposing the brain drain tax have been estimated with some thoroughness and are to be found in Koichi Hamada's contribution [to *NIEO*]. They add up to half a billion US dollars for 1976. Allowing for inflation at 5 per cent to arrive at a figure comparable to Cooper's 1985 oceans-revenue estimate of over $2 billion (at half of the $4.5 billion overall revenue figure, as that allotted to the developing countries), the brain drain tax revenues would exceed a significant sum of $1 billion.

The brain drain tax proposal is based on well-defined moral principles and ought also to appeal to the developed country populations which often feel that the skilled immigrants from the developing countries also ought to make their contribution to their part of the world;[35] the human-rights objections to it are easily dismissed once the proposal is examined in any depth. In addition, the developed country policy makers should realize that the contributions will come from the skilled immigrants as a supplementary tax; hence the revenue is hardly a matter of significant concern for the overall fiscal policy of the developed countries any more than voluntary contributions to foreign countries under the existing US laws for example. Given the great concern expressed over the brain drain in many developing countries, and Mr Kissinger's declaration of willingness to do something in the area at UNCTAD IV[36] ('Finally, the

35. See the sociological evidence on this point in Partington's contribution in Bhagwati and Partington (1976).
36. Note the speech delivered on 5 May, 1976, in Nairobi; text available from Department of State, Press Release No. 224, p. 14.

United States proposes that appropriate incentives and measures be devised to curb the emigration of highly trained manpower from developing countries'), it seems logical to place a measure such as the brain drain tax on the agenda for the new international economic order.[37]

Mutual-gain bargains

While these two examples of significant resource-flow proposals are appealing because they benefit developing countries in a manner that does not hurt the economic interests of the developed countries or offend their political sensibilities on the issue of the sovereignty of the developing countries in the use of these resources, there are several possibilities of mutual-gain bargains in other areas of international economic reform. These possibilities should prove to be more readily negotiable and are discussed in the concluding remarks of this paper.

In the field of trade policy it is clear that mutual gains can be had in two major spheres of policymaking. First, The Corea Plan needs to be explicitly modified to remove any traces of indexing: it should be clearly focused on stabilization. Further, the latter should explicitly distinguish among commodities that have supply problems and those that suffer from demand fluctuations if there is to be any clarity in the kinds of objectives such a stabilization is going to address itself meaningfully to; this also implies that the catch phrase 'Integrated Programme' may be fetching but is certainly poor economics. Second, the developing countries have a clear interest in market access for the *sale* of manufactured exports that have run into nontariff barriers and often interrupted entry on the pretext of market disruption. At the same time, the developed countries (since the flourishing of commodity power by the OPEC countries) have become concerned with assuring market access for their *purchases* of raw materials. Here again therefore there is a prospect for a mutual-gain joint deal whereby the developed countries agree to new rules for regulating the use of trade barriers to handle market disruption problems in exchange

---

37. While these two proposals do generate substantial magnitudes of resource flows to the developing countries in a manner that is consistent with the new political objectives and constraints spelled out earlier, they are to be regarded as supplements to the traditional aid programmes. Indeed, aid flows need to be raised to more substantial levels; this is particularly the case for the poorest countries, many of which have been most seriously affected by the oil price increases. This group of 'most affected countries' in the Fourth World is badly in need of substantially augmented resource transfers to maintain pre-OPEC performance, as is evident in the Edelman-Chenery paper [in *NIEO*]. Furthermore, Edelman and Chenery underline the need to focus on these countries in deciding on the allocation of any given aid funds: the distribution of aid could be improved by giving more weight to poverty and need criteria than to bilateral, strategic and political criteria. Whether the overall aid flows and their distribution could be substantially moved in the directions that are so required is a matter about which one might be sceptical.

for an agreement from developing countries (as well as the developed ones) to a new set of rules for regulating their use of export restrictions. Detailed proposals for such new rules, aimed at reforming the GATT on both counts, have been proposed recently and await policy makers' attention.[38] There is a clear case here for a joint bargain as against the piecemeal, issue-by-issue negotiating strategy that the developing countries seem to be following to little advantage, with little overall vision, in their current efforts at GATT and elsewhere.[39]

In the area of food policy the situation again seems to call for mutual-gain deals. The events of 1972–4, leading up to the crisis-ridden Rome Conference of November 1974, are probably too unique to be repeated. The combined failures of the Soviet, Chinese, and Indian harvests, the depletion of the food surpluses in the United States, the unwillingness of the food exporting countries to part with grain because of inflation fed by the dramatic oil price increases, the foreign exchange difficulties that combined with high prices of fertilizers (related to the high oil price increases) to produce shortages of fertilizer availability in the developing countries where the Green Revolution had been important and could not be sustained without the fertilizers, the additional factor of the tragic drought in Sahel and Saharan Africa–all of these were to produce unprecedented panic in the grain-importing developing countries and confuse thinking on three separate issues that the world food problem raises for solution on a long-term basis.[40] These issues include (1) the need to have buffer stocks, exactly as with other commodities in the Corea Plan, to stabilize wild swings in prices such as happened most dramatically in 1972–4; (2) the need to insulate the drought-affected developing countries from fearsome consequences by providing them with the assistance, not necessarily but most conveniently, in the form of food; and (3) the need to have an aid programme for transferring food to the needy developing countries whose developmental programmes cannot be sustained without such aid inflows and attendant food imports (which serve as the wage-goods, in the classical sense, supporting the needed investments for growth).

There is clearly nothing to be gained by the developed countries from having unplanned calls upon their food stocks for emergency relief in situations of drought; nor is it possible for them, on a long-term basis, to deny food aid to needy countries–after all, food has that special quality

---

38. Proposals related to market disruption (addressed to developed countries but now awaiting the initiative of the developing countries) have been delineated in my paper [in *NIEO*]. On the other hand, Bergsten's paper develops, at equal length, the proposals for GATT reform to regulate the use of export controls.

39. On the latter point, see Gardner Patterson's observations [in *NIEO*].

40. These issues have been distinguished, and their consequences for policy neatly analysed, in the paper by Sarris and Taylor [in *NIEO*].

where conscience does hurt! For both these objectives, therefore, systematic planning ahead will be necessary. As for buffer stocks to handle stabilization, there are now sensible plans afloat that show both the relatively low levels of stocks that such an international operation will have to carry, as well as the feasibility of building up such stocks. The developing countries (such as India) are currently holding very substantial stocks of grain, largely because of successive good harvests but in part because of the immediacy of the lessons learned from the crisis of 1972–4. Thus, the need for international stockholding seems to be correspondingly reduced; and this is also partly because the possibility of entering the grain market seems much more feasible now that the oil-price-hike-induced inflation has decelerated and harvests in the West, especially the United States, have been good.[41] Clearly, therefore, the time has come for an initiative on a world buffer-stock-for-food programme, or a substitute that also sounds like an excellent scheme: the grain insurance scheme of Gale Johnson who has proposed that the United States (and any other interested developed countries) join in a scheme under which they would assure, and build stocks to deliver on such an assurance, the developing countries that join such an insurance scheme that any shortfalls in their trend production larger than a prespecified percentage would be made up by the scheme (see Johnson [in *NIEO*]).

Finally, there is now clearly scope for a code on multinationals (MNCs) and their activities in the developing countries. Until now the developing countries that worried about the MNCs were considered to be somewhat bizarre, if not depraved and corrupted by socialist doctrines. Nothing works to cure one of illusions faster than to be proved naive by unpleasant revelations. The evidence of destabilization efforts directed against foreign regimes, the conviction that the oil companies collaborated in enforcing the Arab oil boycott, the exposé about the corporate bribing of foreign officials that has already ruined a prince and a prime minister,[42] are developments that have come just as the developing countries realized that they do need the technology and management expertise that MNCs can bring. Thus the awareness seems to have grown in influential circles in both the developing and the developed countries that MNCs are a good thing but need to have their international conduct regulated by explicit codes and legal sanctions, including the extension of trust-busting legislation to external operations in the social interest.

In trade, food, MNCs, brain drain, oceans, and a host of other smaller

41. Calculations of buffer stock requirements on alternative assumptions have been made recently by Lance Taylor, Alexander Sarris and Philip Abbot at MIT; others no doubt are in progress.
42. Here, as elsewhere, one should distinguish between demand-determined and supply-determined bribes, however.

impact areas of international policy making, there seems to be scope for acceptable resource transfers and for mutual-gain bargains. Whether these initiatives will be taken constructively and the current momentum for creating a new international economic order will be directed toward these constructive channels will depend critically on the imaginativeness, empathy, and tolerance that the developed nations show toward the sentiments of the developing nations. For, it is only then that it will be possible to shift the developing countries toward the preferred reforms, as opposed to the ill-conceived proposals now current, and to collaborate with them in constructing a desirable and desired international economic order.

In conclusion, I might address my fellow economists who worry, quite naturally, about efficiency in international economic arrangements, and note explicitly that the only feasible way of guaranteeing such an outcome to the present debate on the new international economic order is to have the world system respond, in some significant manner, to the demands for distributive justice; the alternative politically is disorder from disenchanted developing countries, and that can hardly be expected to lead to conditions for international efficiency. Moreover, the programme of reforms set out here fully meets these requirements, while ensuring a sense of fair play and justice to the developing countries and while moving substantially in the direction of assuring them of their sovereignty-newly discovered and therefore much valued. Thus, the brain drain tax, preferably matched by equal contribution from general taxation, would provide some sense of recompense to the developing countries for their present sense of loss of skills thereby making it easier for them to maintain freer flow of such skilled people. The evolution of new rules at the GATT to regulate the use of trade barriers and export controls for so-called market disruption and the holding back of supplies would guarantee freer trade. Commodity price stabilization, aimed at eliminating wild fluctuations in prices of the type that Keynes noted and that were acutely observed in 1972–5, would supplement, not supplant, the market and would make it more efficient. And, by assuring that resources were transferred through the taxation of disexternalities (such as overfishing) and of rents (such as those from seabed mining and others from skilled migration from developing countries into highly-restricted developed countries), the developing countries would be assured of substantial, automatic, and continuing claims on revenues.

Such a programme for the new international economic order can be judiciously embedded in an overall programme of aid flows, restored to the higher (aid to GNP) levels enjoyed during the late 1950s and early 1960s, refocused on the poorer Fourth World, and disbursed with judicious surveillance, performance criteria, and scrutiny that would make these more substantial flows acceptable to the public opinion and parliamentary institutions of the donor countries.

The full agenda for the new international economic order, as developed and proposed here, is surely fully deserving of economists' support – support that is critical for its adoption by the developed countries.

REFERENCES

Adelman, M. A. (1972): *The World Petroleum Market* (Baltimore: Johns Hopkins University Press).
Bhagwati, J. N. (1970): *Amount and Sharing of Aid* (Washington, DC: Overseas Development Council).
——— (1976a): 'The developing countries', in *The Great Ideas Today* (Chicago: Encyclopedia Britannica Inc.).
——— (1976b): *The Brain Drain and Taxation: Theory and Empirical Analysis*, vol. II (Amsterdam: North-Holland).
——— (1976c): 'Protection, industrialization, export performance and economic development'. Paper prepared for the UNCTAD IV conference in Nairobi, May; this formed the basis of the essay reprinted in this volume, ch. 6.
——— (ed.) (1977): *The New International Economic Order: The North–South Debate* (Cambridge, Mass.: MIT Press).
——— (1972): *Economics and World Order: from the 1970s to the 1990s* (London and New York: Macmillan).
——— and Partington, M. (eds) (1976): *Taxing the Brain Drain: a Proposal*, vol. I (Amsterdam: North-Holland).
Kindleberger, C. P. (1975): 'World populism', *Atlantic Economic Journal*, 3 (2).
Little, I. (1975a): 'Economic relations with the Third World–old myths and new prospects', *Scottish Journal of Political Economy* (November).
——— (1976): 'Review', *Journal of Development Economics*, 3(1), pp. 99–105.
Naipaul, V. S. (1975): *Guerrillas* (New York: Alfred S. Knopf).
Nkrumah, K. (1965): *Neocolonialism: The Last Stage of Imperialism* (New York: International Publishers).
Singer, H. (1975): *The Strategy of International Development* (New York: International Arts and Sciences Press).
Vernon, R. (1972): *Sovereignty at Bay* (New York: Basic Books).
Ward, B. (ed.) (1971): *The Widening Gap: Development in the 1970s* (New York: Columbia University Press).
Weisskopf, T. (1972): 'Capitalism, underdevelopment and the future of the poor countries', in J. Bhagwati (ed.) (1972).

2

Rethinking Global Negotiations

The Global Negotiations at the United Nations have been stalemated ever since the UN General Assembly resolved at the 34th Session in 1979 to launch them in 1980 at a special session. The continued frustration of the South over this stalled situation and the bitterness generated by the sense that the North has been intransigent inject a sorry note into the ongoing North–South dialogue that traces back at least to the 1964 UNCTAD Conference. As attempts are currently being made to seek yet again a successful launching of the Global Negotiations during 1983, it is important to assess the underlying objectives that the South aspires to, and indeed to ask whether the Global Negotiations are the ideal, or possibly even a feasible, way to achieve these objectives.

1   A HISTORICAL OVERVIEW: OIL AND ALL THAT

The story of North–South relations, and the dialogue concerning them, could be written in oil. In fact, the present state of Global Negotiations and the constraints and prospects that it presents in the evolving North–South situation cannot be meaningfully understood unless the key role played by oil is appreciated. Before oil entered the picture, North–South issues were already on the international scene, but they were to be transformed with the triumph of OPEC. A backward glance at that transformation is most illuminating.

Phase I: LIEO, Pax Americana, and the pre-OPEC era

The postwar period was indeed the era of the Liberal International Economic Order (LIEO) par excellence. Under US leadership, which was tantamount to *Pax Americana*, the international institutions founded at the end of the war (IMF, IBRD, and GATT) provided the institutional umbrella under which trade, investments, and growth prospered. Unprecedented growth rates characterized the 1950s and 1960s, a Golden Age that has sadly vanished. But already the seeds of Southern unhappiness were sprouting during this period. Two, in particular, need to be noted.

From J. N. Bhagwati and J. G. Ruggie (eds), *Power, Passions and Purpose: Retrospect and Prospect in North–South Negotiations* (Cambridge, Mass.: MIT Press, 1984), pp. 21–31.

First, the process of decolonization created many of the new nations of the South. In consequence, they played no role in shaping the specialized international agencies that defined the LIEO: Many of these nations simply did not exist at the time of this creation! This meant that they had little weight in the voting patterns; they were sceptical that their interests would be properly accounted for in the deliberations of these agencies; and even if they stood to gain from the workings of these agencies, perhaps the division of the gains was skewed against them. Politically, therefore, this translated into the familiar position which divides the South from the North: a preference for the one-nation one-vote approach, which in turn implies a preference for negotiations at the United Nations rather than at the international agencies with their traditionally weighted voting procedures.

Second, the dominant ideological position embodied in the LIEO was not fully shared by the new countries. And it could not be, especially in matters dealing with the classical choice between protection and freer trade. Historically, few countries have embraced free trade when they were behind. Moreover, export pessimism was fairly rampant in various guises during the 1950s, when several developing countries opted for import-substituting (IS) industrialization. But if views diverged on this fundamental issue, they were to grow apart on several others too. The LIEO reflects the traditional, mutual-gain approach under which benign neglect, with the right Benthamite framework, leads to the improvement of all. But as developing countries struggled with their problems and the early optimism about aid-assisted takeoffs gave way, and aid programmes withered with the decline of the Cold War, rival philosophies appeared, accentuating the differences in perceptions, prejudices, and principles. In particular, the benign neglect school had now to compete with the malign neglect school–recall the famous aphorism: 'Integration into the world economy leads to disintegration of the national economy'–and, in certain influential radical critiques, with the malign intent school as typified by the view that aid was an extension of the imperialist arm that sought to suffocate the new countries in a neocolonial embrace.[1] *Rashomon* is rooted in reality; and only an ideologue would deny these harsh possibilities altogether. So the ideological picture became increasingly blurred, with the South often not quite in harmony with the dominant ideological position of the North on the LIEO.

The period up to 1973 was therefore characterized by a growing, but still manageable, ideological and political disharmony between the politically influential countries of the South and the North. The postwar institutional structure, and its basic underlying rationale, were not yet

1. These diverse schools of thought were delineated and discussed at some length in my introductory essay in Bhagwati (1977) [this volume, ch. 1].

subject to any radical onslaught. In fact, the developed countries had already made some accommodating responses by modifying the specialized agencies to reflect the Southern desires and concerns–introducing Part IV in GATT in 1964 and clearing the grant of GSP through waiver of Article 1 of GATT for ten years in the area of trade; instituting new low-conditionality facilities at the IMF to benefit Southern nations, the Compensatory Financing Facility in 1963 and the Buffer Stock Facility in 1969;[2] and creating at the IBRD the International Finance Corporation in 1956 and the International Development Association in 1960. Even the creation of UNCTAD in 1964 to oversee the manifold development problems of the developing countries, although a result of their aspirations and efforts at the UN, can also be viewed in this light, despite UNCTAD's later identification with Southern positions and the resulting tensions with specialized agencies such as GATT, and hence the disfavour it has subsequently incurred in the North.

Phase II: the rise of OPEC and NIEO

The mildly accommodationist status quo of the postwar international regime was sharply interrupted by the success of OPEC, beginning in 1971 (see Figure 2.1). Four aspects of the resulting shift in the tone and content of the North–South dialogue must be emphasized.

First, the example of OPEC suggested to the developing countries that other commodities could be cartelized to extract resources unilaterally from the North. Hence reliance on commodity exports, which had always been thought of as a sign of dependence and the necessity for industrialization, was now considered a source of strength! The economic concept of 'commodity power' was born. The use of the 1973 oil embargo also suggested the political concept of commodity power: the North might be dependent on the South for commodities if the South could take unified positions and threaten interrupted supplies of commodities.

Hence, the early 1970s witnessed a definite shift of gears. The South entered, with a perception of new strength, the negotiations phase, for negotiations cannot occur meaningfully between grossly unequal partners.

Second, and this is a critical point, the South's perception of new power was largely shared by the North at the time. OPEC's demonstrated strength made commodity power seem credible; and it was also directly pitted alongside the South in mutually supportive legitimation roles. Western Europe, feeling particularly vulnerable to OPEC and by and large also intellectually less antipathetic to Southern positions than the United States, played a major role in the conciliatory Northern response, which also led to the Conference on International Economic Cooperation (CIEC) at Paris during 1975–7.

2. For an illuminating discussion of several of these changes, see Ruggie (1983).

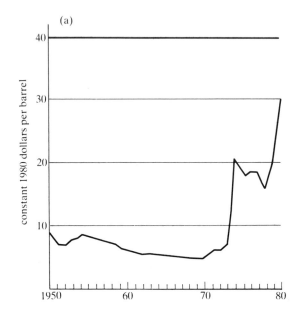

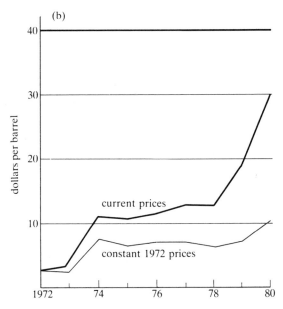

FIGURE 2.1   Petroleum prices, 1950–80 and 1972–80 (annual averages). (From *World Development Report*, 1982. IBRD, Washington DC.)

Third, the key role of OPEC and commodity power in this equation made emphasis on commodities in the new situation inevitable. Just as GSP had become the symbol of the New Delhi UNCTAD II in 1968, commodity schemes were the symbol of the early 1970s and indeed at the Nairobi UNCTAD IV in 1976 where the negotiations on the Integrated Program for Commodities were agreed upon.

Fourth, this key focus on commodities went hand in hand with the stance that the entire range of international economic issues–trade, money, aid, energy, raw materials, etc.–be negotiated together. This was partly a negotiating ploy, to prevent energy being negotiated in isolation to the North's advantage. But it also reflected the view, embodied in the New International Economic Order proclaimed at the 1973 Algiers Non-Aligned Conference and embraced at the UN General Assembly's 1974 Sixth Special Session, that the postwar LIEO institutional structure had to be reorganized to reflect the South's aspirations and interests. This approach was followed also at the CIEC in Paris.

Phase III: déjà vu *and regress*

The euphoria that attended OPEC's success, however, soon vanished. The 1976–9 period was therefore characterized by a sense of *déjà vu* and frustration for the South.

First, OPEC itself gradually dimmed as a threat once the first oil shock (especially the quadrupling of oil prices during 1973) was absorbed, oil prices stabilized in subsequent years and conservation programmes got hesitantly under way. Second, commodity power was soon realized to be illusory; oil was seen to have been a special case. The desired commodity schemes were therefore de facto transformed from unilateral OPEC-type producer cartels into joint arrangements between producers and consumers, thus destroying their original *raison d'être* for superstellar status in North–South negotiations. Therefore, the Northern sense of vulnerability diminished during this period, and the urgency of reaching an accommodation with the South in a global negotiation, either at CIEC or elsewhere in the UN, vanished quickly from the scene.

Third, from the South itself, this tendency was reinforced in a paradoxical fashion. The successful recycling of petrodollars to several of the more developed of the developing countries meant that these were now being integrated into the current international regime. Their capacity to adopt militant, radical-reformist positions with respect to the North was thus increasingly undermined, making Southern solidarity somewhat less of a reality.

The result was regress in the North-South negotiations, with the South unable to exert effective pressure for its demands but still wedded to them. The North basically played along, conversing but making no real concessions. While the Northern lack of response was generally premised on the belated perception of lack of Southern power, it was also reinforced, in my view, by the paradoxical fact that OPEC's success, while whetting the South's demands politically, had also weakened significantly the Northern leaders' macroeconomic situation and hence their political and financial capacity to respond constructively, especially in regard to redistributive measures such as foreign aid flows. Thus, even the Carter Administration, despite its early professions of commitment to Third World causes, failed to deliver. A *Guardian* cartoon at the time captured this latter point rather well by showing Carter, Schmidt, *et al.* on the beach, busy reading a book on how to swim, while the Third World is drowning in the ocean. The caption read: 'Hang in there; we will come out and get you as soon as we have learnt how to swim.'

Phase IV: return to strong posture: the global negotiations

During 1978–80, the 6 per cent cut in world supply triggered by the Iranian Revolution led to the second set of sharp increases in the real price of oil: this time by 80 per cent. This turn of events was the catalyst for a new lease of life for the notion of negotiating from strength.

At the Manila UNCTAD Conference in 1979, several developing countries had raised afresh the question of a special energy deal for the South. This was taken up at other Southern meetings throughout the succeeding months. The dramatic rise in oil prices that preceded the 1979 Havana Conference of the Non-Aligned Nations seems to have prompted Algeria to resurrect in Havana the NIEO approach it had launched in 1973 and to move these nations into resolving that comprehensive, global negotiations should be launched on North–South issues. This approach again found favour both with OPEC, which sought to defuse the Southern demands by linking energy to non-energy issues, and with the North that again was reacting to the energy situation with renewed concern. As with Algiers, the Havana consensus was followed up at the UN General Assembly in its 34th Session where it was resolved that, at its 1980 special session, a round of global negotiations on international economic cooperation for development would be launched. These Global Negotiations, as a legacy from the unsuccessful CIEC attempt during 1975–7, would simultaneously embrace a whole range of issues: trade, finance, aid, energy, raw materials, etc. And the venue would be the UN, with the Committee of the Whole of the General Assembly acting as the preparatory body for these negotiations.

Phase V: the world recession and its aftermath

But the consensus for launching Global Negotiations has been followed by inaction. Why?

The most compelling reason is that the oil card is currently played out. The success of conservation played a minor role. But ultimately the world recession, following on the tight-money policies of the Federal Reserve combined with the expansionary budget deficits and the resulting phenomenal rise in US interest rates, delivered the coup de grâce. In a sagging world oil market, as OPEC is increasingly in public view as a cartel in distress, the Global Negotiations have lost their political rationale once again. OPEC has nothing to offer, nothing to threaten: no quid pro quo therefore can be demanded from the North. Negotiations from strength, therefore, are simply unrealistic once again. And, hanging over the entire issue is the ideological orientation of the Reagan administration which has shifted the United States from the traditional, sympathetic, and accommodating role to a rather unabashed 'rejectionist' one, as evidenced most dramatically in the refusal to sign the Law of the Sea treaty in Jamaica.[3] We are therefore back to regress on the Global Negotiations. Where should we then turn?

2   WHAT SHOULD WE DO?

If the current capacity of the South to negotiate from strength, to extract concessions from the North, is virtually negligible, it is imperative that the Global Negotiations be re-examined realistically.

A principal lesson seems to be the futility of persisting with the Global Negotiations at this juncture, if at all. The most attractive option from the viewpoint of the South seems therefore to be an adjournment–at least until further notice. Or, if this sounds too drastic, a time limit for formally returning to efforts at launching them could be negotiated: a period of one year might be best, since it would broadly coincide with the beginning of a new presidential term in the United States and also with the anticipated recovery of the world economy. Given the South's political investment in the Global Negotiations, this step, in either of the two forms suggested, would naturally be preferable to abandonment of the talks altogether.

But this step, while disappointing to those wedded to the Global Negotiations, can be combined with simultaneous positive initiatives that seem presently to be negotiable and also consonant with some of the key objectives of the South. In particular, the fears over the international debt situation, in the midst of a profoundly disturbing world slump, have opened up a genuine area of mutual concern that draws into its ambit a number of influential countries of the North and the South.[4] The

3. The increasing influence of Secretary of State Shultz, however, may blunt the cutting edge of this reversal of the US role.
4. In this context, it is relevant to note that where genuine mutual interests obtain,

resulting recent exploratory thoughts by Mr Regan, and in response by several Europeans, suggesting that an international monetary conference might be organized outside the IMF framework, and evidently with wider participation, represent an opportunity for the South to enter the scene actively. The South's spokesmen ought to move in on the ground floor of this idea, ensure that they participate constructively in its agenda, and thereby promote both their interests and their desire for more effective participation in the design of the resulting changes in the international monetary regime. Such an initiative would require both political action (e.g. active mobilization of the political leadership of the South, to get the US administration to support the conference proposal) and economic preparation (which would mean that the South provides the expertise to itself and assurance to the North that its participation at the conference would be mutually rewarding).[5]

I must emphasize the need for a thorough and careful preparation for entering and performing at such a conference. It is important that the Southern interests be realistically defined, and interests that do not concern us directly be dealt with at arm's length. In my view, the South ought to urge steps by the North for a quick recovery of the world economy. However, it should leave the matter of macroeconomic co-ordination and management, including the disharmony on exchange rate stability, as a debate between the Europeans and the United States. Nor should the South get involved in OPEC concerns (which were yesterday's Northern concerns) about stabilizing oil prices. The Southern interests lie, of course, in world recovery but the methods ultimately settled upon to institute it are for the most part not ones where we have special expertise or immediate interests.

I stress this last point particularly since the South, especially India and Colombia, attracted unnecessary irritation from the United States at the November 1982 GATT ministerial meeting in Geneva by opposing the proposal to extend the GATT to services. This matter was of special concern to the United States, which sees its comparative advantage shifting to services, and since the threat was greater to the Europeans and Japanese,

---

North–South cooperation seems to emerge without our urging. The problem with the Brandt Commission's eloquent plea for more aid for the South, among other things, was simply that it appealed to mutuality of economic interests that simply were implausible except to those who wished to assist the South anyway. In this, the Commission was of course playing the same game, and with even less success, as the early aid advocates who proposed enlightened self-interest as an argument in favour of aid, but who invoked it in a political form (i.e. that aid would make the world safer for democracy).

5. The serious handicap under which the South operates in international negotiations owing to inadequate technical preparation has been documented by several observers. A particularly frank appraisal is to be found in Commonwealth Secretariat (1982).

who were nevertheless willing to go along with the studies of this proposal, the appropriate response of the developing countries should have been simply to say: 'If you wish to open up this can of worms, fine; but we assert our right to protect our infant service sectors and therefore any extension of GATT to services will have to exempt the developing-country members through suitable clarification of Part IV *et al.*'[6] I might also add that the South missed a fine opportunity at the GATT ministerial meeting in Geneva of putting UNCTAD into the services picture by reminding the developed countries that UNCTAD already had been studying the services for many years and that the proposed studies could be organized jointly under UNCTAD and GATT auspices.

Furthermore, the South should not attempt to resurrect the grandiose notions that have no bearing on the present crisis: a world central bank or the SDR-link are proposals that, no matter how attractive in certain circles and meritorious perhaps in the classroom, have simply no place in the South's current repertoire if it is planning to play a constructive, self-helping role at such a conference.

In my view, the South ought to concentrate instead on two interrelated items. First, the question of appropriate institutional structure and governing principles for debt management for the lucky few 'middle-income' developing countries who borrowed heavily during the 1970s and who now have the Northern banks in their embrace: and second, the question of how to assist the unlucky low-income developing countries, many in Africa, but also including Bangladesh, which need official assistance, official debt relief and the like, especially in view of the collapse of their primary earnings.[7]

While the monetary conference, if it transpires, can provide an instructive departure from the specialized agencies in favour of a wider participation, it would also bring into play a possible role model for a compromise between the South's and the North's positions on the specialized agencies versus the UN as forums for negotiating on North–South issues. The monetary conference would discuss the substance of what ought to be done, trying to reach a consensus. But it does not rule out, in its present conception, the possibility that the ultimate negotiations would be conducted at the IMF itself (unless of course new institutions outside the IMF were to emerge from these deliberations, as seems

6. I should add that the United States also erred in trying to open up GATT to services while simultaneously trying to raise the graduation issue, thus arousing the fears of the SOUTHNICs that they would be under pressure to sign a service protocol without necessary exemptions being granted eventually.

7. There is enough mutuality of interests in the case of the middle-income countries, between Northern banks and Southern borrowers, for such a dialogue to be rewarding. The question of the low-income countries has, rather, to be put on the moral plane, much like famine relief.

unlikely). A way of breaking the impasse at the Global Negotiations would be precisely to explore this possibility: that the UN Global Negotiations become, in effect, a discussion forum where the different issues are addressed within a comprehensive view of the problems facing the world economy and the North–South relations therein; whereas the actual negotiations are conducted at the specialized agencies. A possible enlargement of the UN role could then also be to bring the negotiated agreements at the specialized agencies back to the UN for a wider ratification. Attention would then have to be paid also to strengthening the specialized agencies in the direction of a greater Southern voice and Southern interests, a phenomenon that has certainly occurred, albeit slowly, in the preceding two decades. But this overall shift in focus and conception of what Global Negotiations ought to aim at and accomplish is something that we need to discuss seriously at this conference.

REFERENCES

Bhagwati, J. N. (ed.) (1977): *The New International Economic Order* (Cambridge, Mass.: MIT Press).

Commonwealth Secretariat (1982): *The North–South Dialogue: Making It Work* (London: Commonwealth Secretariat).

Ruggie, J. (1983): 'Political structure and change in the international economic order: the North–South dimension', paper presented to the conference on Rethinking Global Negotiations, International Economics Research Center, Columbia University and Indian Council for Research in International Relations, New Delhi, January.

3

Retrospect and Prospect
in North–South Negotiations

Sudden changes in style and substance have afflicted the North–South dialogue since the 1960s. The tortuous twists are traceable to the fact that the North-South debate and negotiations have reflected shifting realities and perceptions (which are not necessarily rooted in realities) of the configuration of power within and between these two political entities. In the postwar period, there have been sharp and discontinuous shifts as a result of dramatic changes (such as the rise of OPEC) and gradual ones in response to underlying trends (such as the increasing integration of the Southern nations into the world economy).

The style of the dialogue has therefore shifted from a civilized, bourgeois conversation during periods of undoubted Northern power and tentative Southern probing in the early postwar years, to the passionate Southern voice of solidarity and confrontation in the immediate aftermath of OPEC, and then to a frustrated Southern monologue ever since as the early post-OPEC Northern perception of Southern strength yielded to reality.

The substance, in turn, has shifted equally from 'minimalist' ameliorative demands for changes in the international economic management structure devised at Bretton Woods, to 'maximalist' demands for a major 'restructuring' of this edifice, and then back to seeking 'immediate measures' to confront (in the Brandt Commission's words) the common crisis.

The changing substance has reflected underlying philosophical differences in the way North–South interactions (and hence the optimal global institutional design and objectives) are conceived. It has also embraced what appear superficially to be matters of mere form but are matters of certain import: the question as to whether the North–South negotiations must be comprehensive or global in format rather than sectoral and addressed only to segmented issues at a time.

The volatility of the perceptions of power configurations and the complexity of the interaction among these perceptions and negotiating

---

Introduction to J. N. Bhagwati and J. G. Ruggie (eds), *Power, Passions and Purpose: Prospects for North–South Negotiations* (Cambridge, Mass.: MIT Press, 1984), pp. 1–18. References to that volume are abbreviated to *PPP*.

positions and processes have contributed to the malaise that afflicts the current state of the North–South dialogue. As is argued here in *PPP* (in the chapters by Bhagwati and Bressand, in particular), a substantial disjunction arose in the late 1970s, and even more in the early 1980s, between the ambitious negotiating style and stances adopted by the Southern leadership and the objectively weak negotiating power of the South (which was further recognized as such by the North). The Global Negotiations on North–South issues, which the South had sought at the United Nations since 1979, presupposed a power configuration that obtained fleetingly in the first flush of OPEC's success; they were incongruent with the power configuration that soon followed. The power had vanished; the passions had not subsided; the grand purposes still endured.

My objective at the New Delhi conference in January 1983 that led to the *PPP* volume was to illuminate this disjunction between power and purpose and to explore its consequences. In particular, this question had to be asked: Should the South persist in trying to launch these negotiations, or is a different approach to North–South negotiations called for? The answer would have to confront realistically the prevailing power configuration and judgments as to its stability. It would also have to address both the forum for and the substance of the negotiations that would be advocated.

These issues are variously addressed by the authors in the *PPP* volume. However, their thoughts need to be synthesized with one another and put into a coherent historical and analytical perspective. This chapter seeks to do that by exploring alternative views (each of which is historically relevant to some segment of the ` postwar period) of the power configuration characterizing the North and the South and the consequences of these views for the issues at hand.

1   POWER CONFIGURATIONS AND CONSEQUENCES
FOR NORTH–SOUTH NEGOTIATIONS

If for the present we set aside the issues raised by intra-South and intra-North power distribution and concentrate on the North–South power configuration,[1] we can distinguish four different sets of such configurations. Each of them has led to divergent views about what kinds of North–South dialogue and relations can be expected to materialize and evolve.[2] Because reform proposals (except when proposed as utopias)

---

1. Strictly speaking, this is not always a valid procedure. If Algeria was dominant within the South and the South was strong *vis-à-vis* the North, the North–South power configuration would be very different from what it would be if Algeria was replaced by Taiwan or Brazil.

2. Each has had relevance to some part of the postwar period, and my description and analysis of each therefore will be intertwined with that historical experience.

must reflect implicit assumptions of feasibility, these in turn have varied according to the implicit views concerning the North–South power configuration.

Virtual dominance of the North

At one end of the spectrum, the South has no bargaining power at all. This was possibly true of the 1950s, when countries were still emerging into independent nationhood or struggling with the manifold problems attendant thereon.

In this situation the South can be expected to go along with the international economic management structure devised by the North–in this instance, Bretton Woods–reflecting the North's economic, philosophical, and ideological conception of what the world order should be like. With the United States dominant at the end of World War II, the economic ideology was naturally what I earlier described (Bhagwati, 1977) as one of 'benign neglect' within a Benthamite framework, extending to the international arena the viewpoint held equally at the national level. Alternatively, this order has been described as the Liberal International Economic Order (LIEO) and as *Pax Americana* in view of US dominance (or hegemony, in the Gramscian sense as adapted by the political scientist Cox and discussed immediately below).[3]

Evidently, no real negotiations between North and South can be expected if this view is held, and indeed none were expected in the postwar period through much of the 1950s. The South was simply supposed to fit into the LIEO and (in views made more explicit by the Reagan administration ideologues recently) to gain like everyone else from the LIEO framework. The World Bank extended a small hand to the private sector in the Southern nations. Aid programmes were beginning, but they were largely altruistic, not the result of demands from a strong South that had to be accommodated.

Northern hegemony and the voice
of the Southern nonhegemons

The Gramsci-Cox version of the postwar period of 'benign neglect' or the LIEO, however, goes one step further toward endowing the South with some voice. In this view, the North's dominating position implied a hegemonic role. A hegemon is a stability-seeking power that recognizes that its dominant ideology and the attendant institutional structure cannot endure for long unless the nonhegemonic members of that structure accept

3. Evidently I mean 'liberal' in the Manchester School sense rather than the US sense, where 'liberals' have been more akin to European social democrats.

C

its legitimacy. This legitimacy is secured through incrementalist, gradualist, marginalist accommodation of non-hegemonic discontent. The voice of the non-hegemons therefore does matter, for it can be stilled only at a price. The South is therefore not entirely powerless.[4] Probed deeper, this thesis is perhaps only a variant of the 'enlightened self-interest' doctrine that keeps re-emerging, especially in the service of social democrats. Moreover, although *ex ante* the hegemonic distribution of accommodationist largesse in search of legitimacy seems sensible, *ex post* realities may be wholly unexpected; for example, such accommodation may destabilize rather than co-opt.

There may be something in the hegemonic view, however, if we think of North-South relations through the late 1950s and the 1960s. As I note in my *PPP* chapter, and as Ruggie also observes in his,[5] several of the changes in the Bretton Woods international economic management structure, such as the enactment of part IV at the General Agreement on Tariffs and Trade (GATT) and the start of the Compensatory Finance Facility at the International Monetary Fund (IMF), responded to Southern, non-hegemonic discontent without compromising the central thrust of the LIEO as devised by a hegemonic United States and its willing quasi-hegemonic allies in Western Europe.

That Southern dissent and discontent were growing through this period is beyond doubt. Several non-hegemons certainly did not subscribe wholeheartedly to the 'benign neglect' philosophy underlying the LIEO, and the hegemonic consensus over the LIEO was beginning to fray at the periphery since what I have termed elsewhere (Bhagwati, 1977) as the 'malign neglect' and 'malign intent' views of how the LIEO operates with respect to the South came into vogue and competed for attention. Moreover, these were the years when a growing number of Southern nations came to be politically conscious of the fact that they did not have much say in the creation of the Bretton Woods institutions, nor (owing to weighted voting) were they influential in their operation. Accommodation in some respects was therefore prudent. In some respects it was not even expensive, as in the granting of exemptions from most-favoured-nation (MFN) obligations and reciprocity requirements at the GATT, which, given the low interdependency in trade at the time, could be safely conceded without serious damage to the North's own interests.[6]

---

4. Evidently the USSR and the Soviet bloc do not fit this mould; here legitimacy is hard to get and power must come from the end of the barrel.

5. See Bhagwati (1977) and Ruggie (1982) for earlier, extended analyses of this period.

6. It is arguable, however, that it may have damaged the South's interests to have conceded the South's demands for such exemptions, as suggested by Wolf in his chapter in the *PPP* volume.

Consistent with the presumed lack of strength on the part of the non-hegemonic South, these accommodations were made on a single-issue basis at the specialized international agencies: the International Monetary Fund (IMF), the International Bank for Reconstruction and Development (IBRD), and the GATT.[7] The United Nations Conference on Trade and Development (UNCTAD) was indeed created in 1964, over initial US hesitation. However, while it did evolve into an institution that increasingly adopted positions reflecting Southern aspirations and demands, it did not play an executive, negotiating, and implementing role in regard to any of the substantive matters falling traditionally within the jurisdiction of the Bretton Woods agencies. The action was still at those agencies, where hegemonic dominance was ensured.

North–South interdependence and mutual gains

If the hegemonic paradigm argues that the South has an element of strength simply because the hegemon seeks legitimacy, the 'interdependence' school endows the South with a somewhat greater and more effective voice by suggesting that the world economy offers, in view of the multifarious interactions among the nations of the North and the South, several opportunities for creative 'partnership'.[8] Seizing these opportunities provides the rationale for international cooperation; failure to do so implies an opportunity cost in terms of benefits forgone. Indeed, failure to cooperate in certain areas, such as the human environment, may imply a positive harm to all.

This is indeed a 'super-functionalist' view of North-South relations, and it stands, in my judgment, in contrast to the Cox-eyed hegemonic conception, which implies that the North ideologically opts for the LIEO and then modifies its institutional structure marginally to accommodate the South simply to secure legitimacy. On the other hand, the super-functionalist view implies that the LIEO, while constructed to everyone's advantage, has to be modified and supplemented through institutional changes that benefit all.[9] The contrast between the two viewpoints is

7. The specialized international agencies referred to here are not what the phrase stands for in UN bureaucratic jargon, where they refer rather to FAO, WHO, and similar agencies. Also, while I and many authors include the GATT as part of the liberal Bretton Woods superstructure, it was not created at the Bretton Woods Conference.

8. This was the key concept in the Report of the Pearson Commission, the body that preceded the recent Brandt Commission.

9. I call this a 'super-functionalist' rather than simply a functionalist view because, while the 'structure and function' approach introduced into social anthropology by Radcliffe-Brown was general in its scope, some political scientists have used the word *functionalism* in a much narrower sense. See, for example, Jacobson (1979).

evident if one considers foreign aid and institutions dispensing it. The hegemonic thesis would view such aid as a pacification device, a bribe to buy stability. The super-functionalists, if they do not wish to regard it as an altruistic phenomenon, as they well might (in contrast to the Coxian conception), will be inclined to look for a broader range of non-ideological arguments that show the North to have an indirect self-interest in parting with funds such that mutual gain follows. A classic example is provided by the Brandt Commission's first report, issued in 1979, which proposed that aid would generate demand for Northern goods and hence redound to Northern advantage. This was, of course, the economists' counterpart of the political argument advanced during the 1950s and later by several aid proponents that aid, in addition to being altruistic and a moral obligation, would promote democracy and social harmony in the South by accelerating development and would thereby serve the political interests of the democratic Western nations.

However, while the advocates of redistributive programmes, with their essential zero-sum-game thrust, have often tried to pull them out of the altruistic arena, the 'interdependence' thesis is in its most natural habitat when rather more direct and plausible 'mutual gain', or non-zero-sum-game, opportunities are detected and institutions plus programmes suggested for seizing them. Since economists have been trained to recognize mutual-gain situations ever since the invisible hand was seen by Adam Smith, it may be inevitable that they have been in the forefront of the proponents of this approach. These proponents include Richard Cooper (1977) and me (1977), and they also have influential converts, such as the Brandt commissioners.

Super-functionalists are not necessarily gradualists or incrementalists, whether in relation to the LIEO philosophy or in regard to the magnitude and nature of institutional reform. Thus, they have occasionally argued that the North and the South can find mutual advantage in instituting commodity schemes; if so, this leads to the Common Fund and certainly a departure from the vulgar, purist version of the LIEO philosophy. Again, I have argued that there are now both moral and mutual-gain arguments for filling the institutional vacuum in regard to international migration, via a code of conduct and possibly through the creation of an agency (similar to the UNCTAD) to oversee and review developments comprehensively in this field.[10]

Yet another fallacy that needs to be laid to rest is that super-functionalist mutual-gain proposals promise assured progress in North–South negotiations. What is valid, and what has really been the assertion of

10. Cf. my letter to *New York Times*, 13 February 1983, and an Associated Press interview, *New Haven Register*, 1 March 1983.

the super-functionalists, is rather that mutual-gain schemes are more likely to be accepted than zero-sum-gain redistributive proposals–unless the South is strong (as was fleetingly thought during the mid-1970s). I believe that this assertion is unimpeachable. The progress in acceptance of most mutual-gain schemes is, however, likely to be slow, simply because such mutual gains have to be perceived as such by the parties, and they have to be seen as substantial enough relative to alternative arrangements over which they have greater control for governments to undertake the process of institutional change or innovation. The problem is further compounded by the unending dissensions among economists themselves on the consequences (and hence the merits) of alternate proposals such as commodity schemes, and by the fact that different countries within the broad groups such as the South and the North are often differently affected by specific changes of policies and institutions so that coalition can become an arduous and often an insuperable process. Telling evidence of the former difficulty is the deep division among eminent economists on the merits of commodity schemes aimed at price or revenue stabilization and the volatility of opinion on the subject by the same economists.[11] A distressing example of the latter difficulty is the question of debt relief in the mid-1970s. Proposals for granting generalized debt relief to the developing countries, as against treating them case by case, eventually divided the poorest developing countries from the newly industrialized countries (NICs), which had massively entered the post-OPEC financial market and did not wish to see their access to these sources of funds jeopardized by talk of generalized debt relief.

In fact, the mutual-gain approach, while capable of being pursued on a single-issue negotiating track, has provided some momentum instead to a many-issue, comprehensive-bargaining approach for precisely this coalition-forming reason, and not simply because, from a theoretical viewpoint, simultaneous bargains on many fronts can lead to greater payoffs than segmented bargains on single issues.[12]

At the same time, however, the all-embracing bargaining approach has been pursued largely in the context of a militant posture of Southern

11. Thus, for example, Johnson (in Bhagwati, 1977) was far more critical of these schemes than in his earlier writing (1967) on the subject for the Brookings Institution.

12. If each party in a two-agent, two-issue game loses on one issue but gains on another, there could well be no bargain struck although there is net gain from striking a bargain on each issue, whereas a simultaneous bargain on both issues could leave each party better off and hence make a deal feasible. The Law of the Sea negotiations are perhaps a telling example of how a many-issue negotiation, balancing commercial and military interests, made a treaty possible that otherwise would have been non-negotiable. The eventual objections by the new Reagan administration were almost wholly ideological.

strength that stressed maximalist, zero-sum-game-type demands or restructuring. It is difficult, therefore, to judge whether the approach has yielded few results because of maximalist demands or because of the difficulties inherent in such an ambitious bargaining approach (for reasons such as those explored by Zartman and Sewell [in *PPP*] from the theoretical perspectives of negotiating theory and the practical perspectives of several recent multilateral negotiations). These difficulties are, primarily, that the negotiations would become excessively cumbersome; that coalition forming among the 117 members of the Group of 77 (G-77), which speaks for the South, is too impractical in scope; and that the pluralistic, democratic countries of the North have bureaucratic structures and single-issue political lobbies that make it difficult to contemplate the governments' sacrificing on one issue to gain on another in an overall, grand North–South bargain. Partial derivatives are, unfortunately, difficult to take in the analysis of such phenomena.

Southern strength: commodity power, NIEO, and Global Negotiations

Without doubt, a contributory factor in the stalemate on North–South negotiations to date has been that the immediate post-OPEC-success years, especially 1973 and 1974, witnessed the emergence of the perception that the South, in conjunction with the 'newly emancipated' OPEC countries, had significant political strength in relation to the North. OPEC signified a role model for several other commodities exported by the South; unilateral cartelization would lay the importing North open to unavoidable redistribution of income. Besides, such redistribution would be accompanied by sovereign capacity to use the redistributed resources, whereas aid entails restrictions and performance criteria.

The notion of 'commodity power' plus OPEC's political support of the developing countries (evidently with a view to legitimating their cartel to minimize the risks inherent in the exercise of such dramatic economic power in conjunction with total military impotence with respect to the North) combined with the North's immediate perception of economic vulnerability to produce a fleeting but significant period when the South's negotiating ability was remarkably enhanced.[13]

The result was that the sound level of the North–South dialogue, which hitherto had variously reflected elements of the three paradigms I have just outlined, went up several decibels. The militancy of style was matched by a shift in the negotiating substance toward increased emphasis on redistributive programmes such as producers' cartels, the Special Drawing

---

13. A detailed exploration of this theme is provided elsewhere by me [this volume, ch. 1]. The argument is updated in my paper [in *PPP*, also this volume, ch. 2].

Rights (SDR)-link proposal, increased aid flows, and a managed shift of industries from the North to the South to conform to definite targets. A New International Economic Order (NIEO), no less, was the objective.

It may have been inevitable that such objectives would require negotiating everything together. If the South were to set ambitious targets, it had to stick together in solidarity; the bargains to be struck therefore would have to be to everyone's advantage, and hence the issues could not be taken up in isolation. Moreover, restructuring the LIEO into an NIEO also meant taking a comprehensive view. It was also, perhaps, inevitable that eventually the South would consider the United Nations the ideal place to strike the grand bargain; that is where the South had the voting strength, not in the specialized agencies.[14] Part of the grand bargain would then also be the simultaneous, ongoing shift of the foci of control and operation of international economic management away from the specialized agencies to the United Nations.

2 A REQUIEM AND A NEW BEGINNING?

None of this, however, made political sense once commodity power was seen to be ephemeral. And, as I note in my chapter [in *PPP*; also this volume, ch. 2] once OPEC itself began its slide as the world slumped, the negotiating strength of the South waned. The ambitious substance and the all-embracing nature of the Global Negotiations sought by the South therefore lost their *raison d'être*. The failure to get the North to launch the negotiations since 1980 was easily understood once one saw clearly the sharp disjunction between Southern demands and Southern strength.

If the Global Negotiations are not in conformity with the North–South power configuration that obtains and is likely to endure, then a quiet requiem is appropriate. This is what many–including Bressand, Gwin, and me–suggest [in *PPP*]. Temporarily suspending the Global Negotiations, or bypassing them, is the agreeable version of this prescription; it may also be the wise one in view of the potential for disrupting the South's political solidarity that an excessive influx of reality might pose.[15] Ruggie reinforces this viewpoint by underlining that

14. Yet another contributing factor in the desired shift to the United Nations appears to have been the fear of the weaker Southern countries that their interests would be inadequately served if only a few of their Group of 77 members were participating in any negotiations. Global participation, as at the United Nations, would give them direct voice.

15. While politics puts a premium on compromise and therefore suspension rather than abandonment of Global Negotiations appears to offer an advantageous option, it is equally true that forceful leadership may be able to go further. My own assessment, which is consonant with later events, is that the ideological diversity within the non-aligned movement is so great that compromise is the only diplomatic option.

restructuring cannot take place without power. It is remarkable that, although this position aroused controversy at the time of the conference [leading to *PPP*] in January 1983, it had won wide acceptance by the time of the non-aligned nations' meeting in March 1983, at which the Global Negotiations were put on the back burner for a year.

If the Global Negotiations are to be effectively suspended, what prescriptions follow at the constructive level? One long-term remedy from the power-configuration analysis is that the South ought to build up its bargaining strength. Economic relations with the Centrally Planned Economies (CPEs) and within the South have often been considered in this light. *PPP* explores these possibilities.

Desai's chapter offers little comfort to those who would look to the South–CPE arena toward this end. The Soviet Union rejects multilateral obligations of the kind envisaged under the North–South negotiating umbrella, preferring to stick wholly to what Desai christens as the philosophy of *quid pro quo* bilateralism. The South therefore gets little in the way of formal commitments to its advantage. At the same time, the Soviet Union and the other centrally planned economies have become competitors with the South for credits in the world's financial markets. Their technology, principally in the heavy sector, is also no longer appropriate; the NICs have moved on to sophisticated know-how from the North, whereas the newly developing countries at the bottom of the scale embrace developmental programmes that require agricultural, educational, and other technologies where the Soviet comparative and absolute advantages are minuscule. A faltering economic partnership with the Soviet bloc is in prospect.

South–South economic prospects are more promising, and Sanjaya Lall's chapter [in *PPP*] helps to put them into perspective. While he touches lightly on technology flows within the South, it is evident that these are emerging between the NICs and other developing countries, as would be expected from the fact that the NICs have achieved a degree of industrialization and attendant technological sophistication that puts them ahead of the lesser developing countries. However limited they are to date, these flows constitute an improvement in the Southern capacity for better bargains in some cases in a highly imperfect technology market. An interesting example is provided, in fact, by Desai in the Soviet context: The Nigerians used Indian design engineering capacity, partly assisted originally by Soviet training programmes for Soviet-aided steel plants at Bhilai and Bokaro, to evaluate Soviet plans for a steel mill in Nigeria. Southern technology also has diversified somewhat the range of technological choice open to other developing countries. Trade in goods has also witnessed a surge, reflecting again a nascent and growing NIC comparative advantage with respect to the less industrialized developing countries in skill-intensive goods. Perhaps this momentum will sustain itself. I imagine that the outcome will depend ultimately on whether more developing countries will learn to operate relatively open trading systems. The lesson of the postwar period has been that remarkable growth in world trade is feasible as long as access to markets is preserved under the 'rule of law' as was more or less managed under GATT. By contrast, planning trade by quantities, under managed systems, tends to undercut trade expansion, since bureaucrats simply cannot perceive and seize trade opportunities that a multitude of profit-seeking entrepreneurs can under ensured market access. As long as developing countries fail to ease restrictions on access to their markets, it is not likely that significant South–South trade expansion can be sustained in the long run.[16]

Therefore, although in specific instances and areas the South–CPE and South–South economic interactions are certain to be useful in themselves and may even at times contribute to better bargaining ability vis-à-vis the North, they are not an alternative to North–South relations. Nor can they be expected to serve as a method of securing general concessions from the North.

Can we nonetheless derive greater optimism concerning Southern bargaining ability via the interdependence and mutual-gain route? The super-functionalists can point to two phenomena that have intensified North–South linkages. On the trade side, 40 per cent of US exports are now to developing countries. More compelling is the world debt situation, which links Southern financial solvency, and hence Southern economic prosperity, directly with Northern bankers' health and hence with Northern economic prosperity.

However, the former linkage via trade does not quite translate into effective power for several reasons. That this linkage implies that the North would benefit from Southern prosperity does not mean that the South has power, any more than such linkage means that the North has power; the vulgar fallacy of dependency should apply symmetrically if at all. Moreover, as Ruggie notes, the enhanced linkage is only with a very small group of developing countries, the NICs. As it happens, many of these NICs, such as Brazil, Taiwan, and Singapore, are not even members of the non-aligned movement and often are unsympathetic to G–77 opinions on North–South issues.

The latter linkage, via the explosive debt situation, is far more of a useful linkage than trade provides, for it does pull into the game more of the influential Northern pressure groups (in the shape of banks) than

16. This pessimism is equally applicable to the prospects for CPE trade. While CPEs are indeed capable of dramatic deals, their capacity to build up exports is severely limited by their inability to free up their system to perceive and exploit trading opportunities. Their denial of market access rights to developing countries, as indeed to all others, in turn dampens seriously the prospects for South–CPE trade, as Desai concludes in her chapter.

trade ever does (since, for reasons that economists interested in political economy have begun to explore systematically, the exporting pressure groups are far less effective than import-competing lobbies).[17] But again the efficacy of this linkage in improving the Southern bargaining capacity is limited by several facts. For one thing, the Southern countries deeply affected by the debts are the NICs. Their general inclination is likely to be cautious, precisely because they would like to continue borrowing, for the political survivability of their governments is a function of their continued borrowing. Moreover, as discussed above, many of the NICs are not exactly enthusiastic supporters of Southern positions in North–South issues; not only are these prosperous developing countries under both internal and external psychological and political pressure to be co-opted into Northern postures, but a combination of political circumstances has made it costly for them to take more militant positions against the North, especially the United States. Nonetheless, the debt position does imply a certain bargaining advantage. The possible nature of this advantage is discussed by Diaz-Alejandro in his chapter [in *PPP*]:

> How much pressure can LDCs exercise in international financial bargaining? Can Southern debts be aggregated into one powerful bargaining chip? One is skeptical: Mexico is unlikely to want its debt lumped with that of Bolivia or even Brazil for bargaining purposes. One may recall that during the December 1933 Pan American conference held in Montevideo, the Mexican delegation proposed a general moratorium on external debts, an initiative promptly shot down by the distinguished Argentine Foreign Minister, Dr. Saavedra Lamas . . . Yet demonstration effects among debtors could occur during a severe international crisis, leading them to sequentially suspend normal debt service, as during the early 1930s. This may be enough to give at least some LDCs a bit of influence to press for reexamination of international monetary and financial arrangements, perhaps in the context of a 'new Bretton Woods'.

Recognizing this possible bargaining advantage, I propose in my chapter [in *PPP*; also this volume, ch. 2] that the Southern leadership ought to seek a movement in the stalled North–South relations by asking for an international monetary conference, stressing for diplomatic reasons that the original idea was put forth by US Secretary of the Treasury Donald

17. For a useful survey of this literature, see the essay by Robert Baldwin in Bhagwati (1982).

Regan. Such a conference would not merely provide a forum for dealing with the debt situation by examination and possible negotiation of one of the many schemes currently canvassed by prominent proponents;[18] it also would provide a means to underline the critical relationship between holding protectionism in the North at bay and ensuring the solvency of the debtors who must sell to repay and borrow. Such market access can be provided by negotiating for a protectionist 'standstill' – for example, while the world works its way out of the Reagonomics-caused world slump.

Since the NICs are the ones who are most affected by potential protectionism, the linkage of the debt-management solution to the ensuring of market access is of interest, and hence of negotiating value, to the same Southern countries that are endowed with the bargaining 'strength' by the debt situation. It can therefore be confidently expected that such Southern concerns in trade matters would find their way on to the agenda of such a proposed conference. At the same time, the NICs can fully expect the North to raise the issue of 'graduation', such that the NICs wind up 'losing' their non-reciprocity and preferential-entry privileges under the GATT (as amended to permit the developing countries to be granted such privileges). This is a difficult issue for the NICs, but it must be confronted some time. As both Wolf and Behrman emphasize in their chapters [in *PPP*] the advantages of an open trading system have by now been sufficiently demonstrated, not just theoretically by the theorists of international trade[19] but also by the contrasting postwar experience of the developing countries that adhered too long to the import-substitution strategy and those that moved rapidly on to an export-promoting and outward-oriented posture.[20]

If such advantages do occur, and if the advantages from preferential-

18. These are the 'structural' reforms schemes such as the one proposed by Kenen, for example, which require going beyond the simple augmentation of the IMF quotas and SDR allocations, and the provision of funds under the General Agreement to Borrow (GAB). However, the willingness of the US administration to consider such schemes is not currently noteworthy; in fact, the conversion of this administration to the view that GAB is not GRAB by the debtors was a relatively slow business. But the situation is volatile, and one cannot rule out further conversion of the administration to an acceptable structural reform plan at a monetary conference.

19. See, in particular, the arguments in the theoretical works of Bhagwati, Johnson and Meade, and other theorists cited by Martin Wolf [in *PPP*].

20. For a survey of this literature, see my 1979 review with T. N. Srinivasan,'Trade policy and development'. Several eminent economists at the start of the postwar period had raised the question of the appropriate strategies in this regard, among them Ragnar Nurkse, Gottfried Haberler, Jacob Viner, and Raul Prebisch. The younger generation of economists who have illuminated this area includes Bela Balassa (who has conducted several studies for the World Bank), Ian Little, Tibor Scitovsky and Maurice Scott (who conducted major studies for the OECD), and Anne Krueger (who codirected an ambitious project with me for the NBER). For a recent assessment by a group of political scientists, see Ruggie (1983).

entry schemes have been both small and negligible compared to those derived from non-discriminatory access to the markets of the North, as Wolf also stresses, then the case is indeed rather strong for dispensing with the protectionist structure that many developing countries (especially the NICs) still embrace. It is not clear that the willingness to graduate can be translated into firmer market access at the bargaining table where the NICs would face the North, but it is certainly a card that will need to be played soon. Besides, as Wolf notes, the NICs' ability to argue plausibly for a protectionist standstill and for continued, ensured access to Northern markets cannot be expected to carry weight as long as the NICs refuse to accept some form of market-access obligations themselves, despite their new status in the world markets.

Where does all this leave the developing countries that have neither substantial debt-related bargaining power nor market-access interests that can be linked to it? For such Southern countries (and there are many) there is really no effective bargaining power except that which emerges from bilateral, political considerations (for example, the strategic importance of the Central American countries gives them some bargaining power with the United States), as indeed does occur in some instances for the NICs as well (as in the case of Brazil, Argentina, and Mexico with respect to the United States). There is really no such consideration that yields effective bargaining power to the bulk of the developing countries, however. Yet these are among the majority of the Southern countries. What are their concerns? Can they be fitted into the NICs' concerns somehow at an international conference of the type proposed in my paper [in *PPP*; also this volume, ch. 2].

The most compelling questions for these developing countries relate to their export earnings, which are heavily dependent on primary exports, and to their need for official assistance. Both problems have been extremely serious during the recent world depression. The cyclical aspect of the former problem has led to a renewed demand for commodity schemes aimed at price or revenue stabilization, including at the Belgrade UNCTAD meeting in June 1983. Unfortunately, such schemes typically tend to come apart, even when successfully launched, since the producers tend to lose interest when prices are rising and the consumers when they are falling. But there is also a theoretical reason to prefer a different, two-policy-instrument approach. Revenue destabilization over the cycle may be alleged to create two different problems. One is in the foreign exchange market, where liquidity problems can arise from such exchange earning fluctuations; the other is an internal problem of shifting incentives for producers and instability for consumers. If these are indeed problems, then the Tinbergen theory that the number of necessary instruments should generally equal the number of targets implies that it would be necessary, and more efficient, to use two instruments in the present problem rather than one. Commodity schemes to use international buffer stocks to stabilize earnings represent the use of one instrument to solve both problems. On the other hand, the use of two instruments–say, the Compensatory Financing Facility (CFF), suitably augmented, to address the international liquidity problem, and national buffer stocks to address the domestic producer and consumer effects .if they are considered detrimental–would seem to be a more efficient solution. The answer to the problem of the cyclical instability of the developing countries' primary exports earnings therefore lies, in terms of international implications, in the area of the CFF and its reform and augmentation. The details of this are discussed by Diaz-Alejandro [in *PPP*] in the context of the overall cyclical instability of the world economy and its effects on the downside of the business cycle in the present age of heavy financial integration and indebtedness in the world economy.[21]

Since, then, the primary export earnings problem of the developing countries itself embraces reform and expansion in international monetary facilities such as the CFF, it is evident that the proposed international monetary conference can readily be extended to address the chief concerns of not merely the NICs but also the rest of the developing countries.

An international monetary conference, therefore, provides both an appropriate format and the possibility of a realistic and useful agenda for seeking negotiable changes in the international regime in the present power configuration. By contrast, the pursuit of Global Negotiations at this stage could prove to be a distraction–indeed a wasteful and counterproductive diversion–with no rationale in the current power configuration. These conclusions are stark and must sound like a betrayal to the faithful, but Southern interests and aspirations are ill served by politically irrelevant rhetoric that is aimed at the unnegotiable; they are advanced, rather, by realistic analysis and prescription.

It is interesting, therefore, that the New Delhi summit of the non-aligned countries decided to put the Global Negotiations on the back burner for at least one year and embraced the objective of an international monetary conference. Both of these proposals had been advanced during the deliberations by the contributors to this book [*PPP*] two months earlier in New Delhi.

These initiatives, which will need Southern leadership to be translated into effective action, need to be supplemented by a further set of actions concerning what Diaz-Alejandro and I (in a statement issued before the

---

21. Admittedly this solution does not extend to the desire to have commodity schemes that aim not just at revenue stabilization but also at increasing the trend price in favour of the developing countries. Quite aside from whether such schemes can be effectively implemented, there is the problem that these schemes are not what one can put on a North–South agenda any more than the OPEC oil price hikes were a matter of negotiation rather than unilateral acts that had to face the test of economic and political survivability.

non-aligned summit and annexed [to *PPP*] have called 'medium-term reform': first, further changes within the specialized agencies such as the IMF and the World Bank to give greater voice to the South without compromising (and indeed often improving) the efficiency of their operation, as extensively argued by Gwin in her chapter [in *PPP*]; second, a serious examination of the working of the United Nations to restructure it such that it can play a role where a comprehensive view of the world economy and its functioning and implications for institutional action can be provided,[22] with the negotiations for institutional changes being undertaken at the specialized agencies; third, the filling of institutional lacunae to deal with new international economic problems such as international migration. There is indeed much here to keep the North–South diplomats and negotiators productively occupied. The radicals in the South will fear that this means abandoning the grand design and purpose of yesteryear, but did not Mao Tse-Tung say that even a long journey starts with a small step?

REFERENCES

Bhagwati, J. N. (ed.) (1977): *The New International Economic Order: The North–South Debate.* (Cambridge, Mass.: MIT Press).
—— (ed.) (1982): *Import Competition and Response* (Chicago: University of Chicago Press for NBER).
—— and Srinivasan, T. N. (1979): 'Trade policy and development', in R. Dornbusch and J. Frenkel (eds) *International Economic Policy: Theory and Evidence.* (Baltimore: Johns Hopkins University Press); reprinted in this volume, ch. 6.
Cooper, R. (1977): 'A New International Economic Order for mutual gain', *Foreign Policy* (Spring).
Cox, R. (1980): 'The crisis of world order and the problem of international organization in the 1980s', *International Journal*, 35.
Jacobson, H. K. (1979): *Networks of Interdependence: International Organizations and the Global Political System* (New York: Knopf).
Johnson, Harry G. (1967): *Economic Policies toward Less Developed Countries* (New York: Praeger).
Ruggie, J. G. (1982): 'International regimes, transactions, and change', *International Organization*, 36.
—— (ed.) (1983): *The Antinomies of Interdependence* (New York: Columbia University Press).

22. The *London Economist*, 11 June 1983, p. 14, suggested such a role on North–South issues for UNCTAD. The respective roles of the UN Secretariat in New York and the UNCTAD in Geneva in these matters would also need to be clarified as part of the examination I propose. The Office of the Director General for Development and International Economic Cooperation in New York was originally conceived to play a role that could have provided the comprehensive-view function I suggest.

PART II
Developmental Strategy: Import Substitution versus Export Promotion

The export pessimism that characterized much developmental thinking in the early postwar period created a classic and central confrontation between those who unfortunately continued to theorize, and recommend policies, on the assumption that the world was characterized by rigidities and unresponsive world markets and those who quickly surmounted the early gloom and proceeded to advocate successful outward orientation in trade strategy.

Associated with the former position was, of course, the unwillingness to adjust exchange rates: the familiar Marshall–Lerner conditions for a successful devaluation were not likely to be met if countries were being managed as if they were closed economies. The resulting regime of 'reluctant exchange rate adjustments' implied continuing overvaluation, consequent bias against exports and promotion of chaotic import substitution and corresponding economic costs.

That, therefore, the trade and payments regimes had to be analysed in unison was a critical feature of my writings, principally in the 1967 Frank Graham Lecture at Princeton, but developed at greater length in the National Bureau of Economic Research project which Professor Anne Krueger and I co-directed during the early 1970s. The critical role played by exchange controls in analysing the costs of import substitution, and the successive Phases (reproduced at the end of chapter 14) through which countries tended to go in handling the trade-and-payments regime, were therefore both the central and the distinguishing features of our thinking and this is reflected in chapters 4, 6 and 7. These themes and concepts have also found an echo in the work of Professor Michael Bruno (1981) and in the perceptive review article which Professor Ronald McKinnon (1979) wrote on the findings of the NBER project.

The export pessimism therefore promoted deleterious inward-looking trade strategies not merely directly but also indirectly by leading to overvalued exchange rates. But its effect was pernicious also in encouraging the widespread notion that developing countries suffered from 'foreign exchange bottlenecks' and hence reinforcing the reluctance to use realistic exchange rate policies. Chapter 8 is among the earliest attempts in the literature to define the *ex ante* bottlenecks or 'gap' concept and to distinguish it sharply from the concept of an open or suppressed balance of payments deficit. These two notions were at the time hopelessly confused to the point where, in an earlier contribution (1965) in the shape of a comment on Professor Arthur Lewis's paper at the 1964 Vienna Congress of the International Economic Association, I had been startled enough by this confusion to note sharply that the payments difficulties of the developing countries were by no means a sure-fire proof that they faced either inelastic foreign trade elasticities or that they were in a foreign-exchange-gap situation. I have returned to this theme in greater depth in Desai and Bhagwati (1979); and it has been dealt with also in elegant contributions by Professors Ronald Findlay (1971) in a value-theoretic framework, Ronald McKinnon (1964) in variations on the Harrod–Domar model, and Hollis Chenery and Michael Bruno (1962) in the context of a computable model for the Israeli economy.

The question of transiting from the overvalued-exchange-rate Phase II of a country's trade-and-payments regime to increasing reliance on exchange rate adjustment and less resort therefore to exchange controls *via* Phase III 'liberalization episodes' had long engaged my interest, in view of my involvement in Indian policy debates during the 1960s. In the specific Indian context, this meant meeting head-on several conventional objections to rationalization of the payments regime. While chapter 9 examines an 'intermediate' proposal to adopt exchange auctions in preference over controlled allocations, chapter 10 analyses the objection that a full-scale adjustment of the exchange rate would be inflationary. The latter is of particular significance since, written in 1962, it must be among the earliest analyses to note that, if one devalued from a position of a supposed deficit with an overvalued exchange rate, a devaluation was unlikely to be (price-)inflationary as it would cut into the import premia to begin with and hence also, as Professor Krueger and I were to emphasize later and is now a cliché, one had to distinguish between net and gross devaluations. This paper also notes explicitly that a devaluation, in the context of a current-account deficit reflecting foreign assistance for example, would in itself be (demand-)deflationary, i.e. contractionary: a startling idea that has become subsequently more readily accepted with the more substantial critiques of Professors Richard Cooper (1973) and Paul Krugman and Lance Taylor (1978) on precisely the issue that a devaluation could be contractionary.

These insights and questions were to be more systematically developed in the Bhagwati–Krueger NBER project, and especially in Professor Krueger's and (less so) my synthesis volumes on the findings of this project.

The problem of the optimal sequencing of steps in going through Phase III to the liberalized trade regime in Phase IV without overvaluation is now the subject of an important follow-up project, under the guiding hand of Professor Michael Michaely, at the World Bank; its seeds were sown in the NBER project.

REFERENCES

Bhagwati, J. N. (1965): Comment on W. A. Lewis, 'Economic development and world trade', in E. A. G. Robinson (ed.), *Problems in Economic Development* (London: Macmillan).

—— (1968): *The theory and practice of commercial policy: departures from unified exchange rates*, Frank Graham Memorial Lecture (1967), 'Special Papers in International Economics', No. 8 (Princeton: Princeton University Press); reprinted in *EIET*, vol. 1, ch. 1.

Bruno, M. (1981): 'Short-term policy trade-offs under different phases of economic development', in S. Grassman and E. Lundberg (eds), *World Economic Order: Past and Prospects* (New York: St Martins Press).

Chenery, H. and Bruno, M. (1962): 'Development alternatives for an open economy: the case of Israel', *Economic Journal*, 72.

Cooper, R. N. (1973): 'An analysis of currency devaluation in developing countries', in M. B. Connolly and A. K. Swoboda (eds), *International Trade and Money* (Toronto: University of Toronto Press).

Desai, P. and Bhagwati, J. (1979): 'Three alternative concepts of foreign exchange difficulties in centrally planned economies' *Oxford Economic Papers* (November); reprinted in *EIET*, vol. 2, ch. 70.

Findlay, R. (1971): 'The foreign exchange gap and growth in developing economies', in J. Bhagwati *et al.* (eds), *Trade, Balance of Payments and Growth* (Amsterdam: North-Holland).

Krugman, P. and Taylor, L. (1978): 'Contractionary effects of devaluation', *Journal of International Economics*, 8.

McKinnon, R. (1964): 'Foreign exchange constraints in economic development and efficient aid allocation, *Economic Journal*, 74; reprinted in J. Bhagwati (ed.) (1981): *International Trade: Selected Readings* (Cambridge, Mass.: MIT Press), ch. 26.

McKinnon, R. (1979): 'Foreign trade regimes and economic development: a review article', *Journal of International Economics* 9(3).

4

Exchange Control, Liberalization and Economic Development

For the past three years, the National Bureau of Economic Research (NBER) has been sponsoring a research project on exchange control, liberalization, and economic development. In this project, a number of country studies have been undertaken, focusing upon the quantification and analysis of individual developing countries' experiences with exchange control regimes and attempts at liberalizing those regimes, focusing equally on the interaction between the country's trade and payments regime and its economic development.

The countries studied have included Brazil (A. Fishlow), Chile (J. Behrman), Colombia (C. Diaz-Alejandro), Egypt (B. Hansen), Ghana (C. Leith), India (J. Bhagwati and T. N. Srinivasan), Israel (M. Michaely), South Korea (C. Frank, Jr.), the Philippines (R. Baldwin), and Turkey (A. Krueger). Each study has been undertaken within an analytical framework devised by us and agreed upon in advance by all participants. These studies are now completed or nearly so, and they are to be published by the National Bureau of Economic Research through 1973 and 1974.[1] They should be of interest to students of the individual countries as well as to those concerned with trade and development issues more generally. When all the studies are final, we shall have a great deal of material for analysis on a comparable basis of different countries' experiences.

The final stage of the NBER project consists of our attempt to synthesize the results of the individual studies in an overall volume. This paper represents a preliminary report on some of these results.[2] We therefore present an overview of some of the major topics in Section 1. In Section 2 some of the more detailed results pertaining to the effects of exchange control regimes are presented.

---

1. These studies were subsequently published in nine volumes by Columbia University Press, New York. [The NBER-Project country studies and synthesis volumes are listed in the references at the end of chapter 6 in this volume. GG]

2. The two synthesis volumes, one by Bhagwati and the other by Krueger, were published by Ballinger Press, Cambridge, Mass.

Written with Anne Krueger, from *American Economic Review*, 53(2), 1973, pp. 419–27.

1 AN OVERVIEW

For each country covered by the Bureau project, individual researchers were asked to trace their country's experience with a view to identifying: (1) when and why exchange control was adopted, and how the control regime was intended to relate to the country's domestic economic goals; (2) the evolution of quantitative restrictions after their initial imposition; (3) efforts, if any, to ameliorate the undesired results of the payments regime; (4) experiences with attempts at liberalization and the timing of the economy's response to those attempts; and (5) the resource-allocational, income-distributional, and growth effects of the country's experience. Within that framework, each country's author singled out for in-depth analysis a particular point in time during which the detailed working of the exchange-control regime was analysed, and selected one liberalization effort for intensive analysis.

On the basis of the results from individual studies to date, we have been surprised at the degree of similarity among seemingly diverse countries. On each topic, certain broad conclusions have emerged.

Motivation for quantitative restrictions (QR)-regimes

Initial adoption of exchange controls was generally an *ad hoc* response to external events. Rapidly, however, quantitative restrictions were perceived as a means of furthering domestic industrialization policies. Whether it was the rapid shift in international market conditions during the 1952–4 period or memories of the Great Depression, most policymakers were pessimistic – probably to an objectively unwarranted degree – about prospects for growth through industrialization based upon export growth and diversification. The optimal resource allocation dictum – that the marginal cost of earning foreign exchange should be equated with the marginal cost of saving foreign exchange – was generally abandoned in favour of saving foreign exchange at all costs.

In the process of using exchange control to foster the growth of domestic industry, however, the internal working of the QR systems generally frustrated, at least partially, the very domestic goals they were designed to achieve. Bureaucratic allocational procedures, political pressures surrounding the administration of controls, and the private sector response to the unintended incentives created by the regimes led to frustration of the goals the QR regimes were designed to serve. We shall return to more detailed examination of the logic of QR systems in section 2.

Export promotion versus import substitution

Among the more interesting results that appear to emerge from our preliminary analysis of individual countries' experience is that countries which have had export-oriented development strategies appear, by and large, to have intervened virtually as much and as 'chaotically' on the side of promoting new exports as other countries have on the side of import substitution. Yet, the economic cost of incentives distorted toward export promotion appears to have been less than the cost of those distorted towards import substitution, and the growth performance of the countries oriented toward export promotion appears to have been more satisfactory than that of the import-substitution oriented countries. If that conclusion is valid, the lesson is that policy should err on the side of allowing a higher marginal cost for earning than for saving foreign exchange.

There are several theoretical reasons which would explain such an asymmetery in outcomes, and the empirical evidence does point in their direction. In theory, there are four reasons why export promotion may be the superior strategy.

(1) Generally speaking, the costs of excess export promotion are more visible to policymakers than are those of import substitution. If there are departures from unified exchange rates, export-promoting growth can be sustained only by subsidies or other incentives costly to the government budget. Thus, there are built-in forces within the government against excessive export subsidization and promotion. The equivalent costs of import substitution are borne by firms and consumers and, hence, no obvious intragovernmental pressure group emerges as rapidly when incentives are biased toward import substitution.

(2) An export-oriented development strategy generally entails relatively greater use of indirect, rather than direct, interventions. There is considerable evidence from the individual country studies that direct intervention may be considerably more costly than is generally recognized (see section 2 below). When policymakers are concerned with export promotion, direct controls cannot be as pervasive as they can be under import substitution. Price controls, distribution controls, and a host of other detailed interventions make little sense, even to bureaucrats, when firms' outputs are intended largely for overseas markets, but appear attractive when production is oriented toward the home market under import substitution. The fact that, under import substitution, government officials have power to remove or enhance domestic monopoly positions of import-competing firms implies that those firms can be induced to accept otherwise intolerable (and socially unprofitable) interventions with their decisions. By contrast, officials simply do not have the same degree of power over firms engaged primarily in the export market.

(3) Exporting firms, however much they may be sheltered on the domestic market, must face price and quality competition in international markets. Import-substituting producers, with no competition for domestic markets, are a pervasive fact of life in the developing countries where

import substitution has been stressed. While there is little hard evidence on the subject, there is considerable reason to believe that sheltered monopoly positions may be important explanations of low productivity growth in the newly established manufacturing industries in developing countries. Insofar as the adverse side effects of inadequate competition are less severe under the export-oriented strategy, it may be that export promotion is superior simply because it reduces the incidence of the problem.

(4) If there are significant indivisibilities or economies of scale, an export-oriented strategy will enable firms of adequate size to realize them. When import-substituting incentives dominate the domestic market, import-substituting firms generally are confronted with powerful incentives for expansion through diversification; each new product line provides one more domestic monopoly position. If indivisibilities and/or economies to scale are important, an export-oriented strategy will provide better incentives for expansion of capacity in existing lines. As such, an export-oriented growth strategy is better suited to achieving whatever economies of scale are present than is an import-substitution strategy where firms are generally limited in their horizons by the size of the domestic market.

These and other arguments supporting the case for an asymmetrical behaviour of the export-promoting versus import-substituting economies appear to be borne out by the contrast in the success of South Korea and the relative failure of India, for example, in the countries studied in the project. Since approximately 1960, the economic policies of South Korea have been heavily oriented toward growth through exporting. The rate of growth of exports has been almost double that of real GNP. Close inspection of South Korean policies indicates that the kinds of detailed and chaotic interventions which we have found in other countries are abundantly present in Korea's case as well: numerous QRs, high tariffs, and physical targeting of exports and imports. The striking difference, however, is in the remarkable degree to which the government has been willing to use exchange-rate changes and to lean in favour of export promotion via preferential allocation of import licences, etc. Thus, aside from other special factors, such as the high inflow of foreign resources (official and private), the one striking aspect of Korean success has clearly been the significantly less discrimination against exports than in other developing countries, and *not* (it would appear) the presence of a neoclassically efficient allocation mechanism *in toto* in the system.

Whether this asymmetry between export promotion and import substitution is important or not awaits further exploration as the final results of the country studies emerge. What is clear is that, of the countries which have stressed export promotion, none have been free from interventions of the type that economists generally identify with QR regimes and import-substitution strategies, and that the export-promotion strategies generally appear to have higher payoffs.

Nominal versus effective devaluation

Export rebates, tariffs, surcharges, import entitlement schemes, and a host of other devices are generally employed under QR regimes, and they lead to a wide dispersion in effective exchange rates (the amount of domestic currency paid when a good is landed per dollar of c.i.f. value) by commodity categories. Moreover, the increasing resort to changes in surcharges and export subsidies and to alterations in effective exchange rates means that, even without a formal devaluation, there are many degrees of partial devaluation in QR regimes.

Usually, formal devaluation is accompanied by the partial or total removal of export incentives and surcharges upon imports. The result is that changes in the parity, as reported by the International Monetary Fund, do not necessarily provide a good indication of the economically relevant magnitude of the devaluation. Thus, in Egypt, Bent Hansen's study shows that the 1962 devaluation was little more than a tidying up operation: complicated export bonuses and import charges were replaced by across-the-board measures, so that the average local currency payments and receipts per dollar of international transactions increased by only one-fourth the amount of nominal devaluation. For Chile, Jere Behrman's study shows effective devaluations to be about two-thirds the nominal ones in 1959 and 1963. By contrast, when Chile adopted frequent exchange-rate adjustments in the late 1960s, the effective devaluations slightly exceeded the nominal, although real devaluation was much smaller.

Determinants of success of liberalization

Because of the significant differences in practice between nominal and effective devaluation, we believe that it is important, under QR-regimes, to distinguish between devaluation and liberalization.

Liberalization may be said to occur when the official price of foreign exchange assumes an increased role in the allocation of resources, whereas devaluation occurs whenever nominal exchange rates are altered. Thus, as illustrated by Egypt's 1962 episode, it is possible to have a devaluation in which the altered nominal price of foreign exchange has little or no effect on resource allocation, and quantitative restrictions and other direct interventions maintain their importance as allocative instruments. In other cases, such as the Turkish devaluation of 1958 and the Indian devaluation of 1966, the devaluations more than offset the reductions and removals of surcharges, taxes, and export premia. In those circumstances, the official price of foreign exchange increased in importance as an allocator of scarce foreign exchange, at least in the short run.

The difference between nominal and effective devaluations has the important effect that, as happened with the 1966 Indian devaluation, the criteria by which the devaluation is judged are typically confused; and the 'rationalization' implicit in shifting from a *de facto* to a *de jure* devaluation (resulting in no effective devaluation) is ignored and the nominal devaluation is assessed as though it was also the effective devaluation.

The studies also point up a number of interesting conclusions regarding the likelihood of effective devaluations leading to *continued* increases in the allocative function of the price of foreign exchange. A few vignettes are worth pointing out here. (1) Starting from the long exposure to automatic protection under the QR-regime, few industries will accept the consequence of effective devaluation and reduced reliance on QRs; namely, the need to compete or contract. As Michaely's study of Israel and the Bhagwati–Srinivasan analysis of the 1966 Indian episode show clearly, liberalization works only insofar as imports of non-competitive goods are involved, and the degree of protection to import-using industries may even increase as imported intermediates get liberalized. (2) The effect of liberalization is often to induce a recessionary tendency rather than the traditionally feared inflationary impact. The recessionary impact follows from governments typically trying to contract monetary and fiscal policy, while ignoring the fact that the devaluation itself sets up endogenous recessionary tendencies. These come from several sources: (a) the excess of imports over exports, thanks to influx of aid and private capital, itself implies deflation with devaluation; (b) the increased imports of materials can lead to increased output and lowered profit margins and may adversely affect investment in the import-competing activities whereas the exporters may not push up investment in time because they expect the increased export incentives to be neutralized *or* the system remains so loaded against exports that exporters find it difficult to increase their investments sufficiently; and (c) as in Turkey, the initial effect of an effective devaluation seems at times to be to reduce construction activity, with adverse effects (at least in the short run) on employment and income.

Payments regimes and economic growth

The determinants of a developing country's overall growth rate are numerous, and the payments regime is only one such factor. The interaction between the payments regime and economic growth is complex and depends upon a host of other factors in individual countries.

That the effects of the payments regime on growth cannot be analysed without regard to other aspects of the domestic economy cannot be stressed enough. Clark Leith's findings on Ghana provide a good illustration. Its major export, cocoa, is almost unaffected by the payments regime directly. The price paid to producers is determined by the Cocoa Board and is independent of the exchange rate. On the import side, government control over credit allocation under credit rationing, combined with severe capital market imperfections, means that the demand for imports is more a function of government policies in the credit market than it is of the price of foreign exchange. All new investment projects must be approved by the government, which has power to grant or withhold subsidies and other privileges large enough to make the difference between profit and loss on virtually all investment projects. Under such circumstances, it would be folly to analyse the payments regime as if entrepreneurs were responding in perfect markets to price signals alone. This is not to say that the payments regime does not have its own effects upon resource allocation and growth, but rather that analysis of those effects is considerably more complex than is generally assumed. The individual country studies and our forthcoming synthesis explore these interactions in some detail.

2   THE ANATOMY OF QUANTITATIVE RESTRICTIONS

Tariffs versus quotas

It is always true that every quota has a non-negative tariff equivalent at each point in time for every recipient of an import licence. However, it is not always the case that there is a single tariff-equivalent for a quota for a given homogeneous import commodity, and it is generally false that the resource-allocational effects of a quota are the same as those of the tariff-equivalent even when there is a single tariff-equivalent.

The reason why there may not be a single tariff-equivalent for the import of a homogeneous commodity is that resale of imports is often illegal. In that case, there is no reason to expect a common implicit domestic price in the absence of a perfect and costless black market. Thus, the criteria for allocation and the actual detailed bureaucratic decisions as to who should receive an import licence, and how much each should receive, will in general affect resource allocation.

Even when there is a single domestic price for the imported good, the method of licence allocation makes an important difference to resource allocation and income distribution. It is useful to think of the differences between the c.i.f. price of the good (at the nominal exchange rate) and the domestic price as consisting of two parts: (1) the duties, surcharges, and other costs of landing paid by the actual importer, including his normal costs of forgone interest, handling, and so on; and (2) the premium accruing to the recipient of the import licence. The local currency cost of the c.i.f. import plus the first item equals landed cost. Landed cost in local currency divided by the c.i.f. price in foreign currency equals the effective exchange rate. Landed cost is then the price that would prevail in the domestic market if there were no QRs upon the import. The premium, therefore, is the windfall gain accruing to the recipient of an import licence.

The precise allocation of import licences makes for important differences because it determines *who* will receive the premium; we note two here. (1) If licences for intermediate goods imports are allocated directly to producers, these producers are implicitly being subsidized in their production process. A devaluation would increase the costs of the manufacturers using the intermediate good. If, however, licences are allocated to importers who then resell to the manufacturers, the premium accrues to the importers. If devaluation is then carried out, there will be no effect on manufacturers' costs unless the size of the devaluation exceeds the size of the premium. (2) The calculation of effective protection again must allow for the fact that some imports would be obtained directly by producers at premium-exclusive prices and others at premium-inclusive prices. The resulting estimates of protection can be significantly different than if no adjustment was made for the indirect allocation of imports of intermediates to producers, as illustrated for example by the Bhagwati–Srinivasan study of India.

That the distinction between premium and landed cost is important can be seen by inspection of Turkish data for 1968 presented in Krueger's study. At an official exchange rate of TL9 = $1, it appeared that the average landed cost of $1 of imports was TL23.8 and the premium was TL23.1.

Logic of QRs

Once a QR regime is established, it seems to have an internal, self-contradictory logic all its own. The tariff equivalent of existing quotas tends to fluctuate widely and the unintended side effects of QRs tend to force other changes. Decision makers do not receive visible feedbacks as to the effects of their actions. Thus, one finds quota categories where the quotas are redundant and there is a zero premium side by side with quota applications exceeding the amount of the quota by exorbitant multiples. Yet these multiples provide little information to those allocating quotas, because the amount of applications is itself influenced by expectations as to the probable disparity between the amount applied for and the amount received.

But that is only a small part of the story. For, once a QR regime is established, quotas inevitably become a tool seized upon by governments to accomplish a host of purposes other than the initial one of restraining *ex ante* payments imbalances. Thus, 'priorities' are established and preferential treatment is given to applicants willing to further an officially desired goal. For example, efforts are generally made to encourage capital goods imports at the expense of consumer goods imports, in the hope of accelerating the rate of investment. In turn, the newly established manufacturing capacity often has intermediate goods import 'requirements' which can be met only at the cost of reducing capital goods imports, thus defeating the initial purpose of the priority. Moreover, in increasing capital goods imports, consumer goods imports are the first to go, and the production structure of the domestic economy becomes increasingly oriented toward consumer goods.

Once that happens, growth in investment becomes increasingly dependent upon expansion of imports, itself a function of export growth. Yet the protection afforded to producers in domestic markets by QRs is so great that profitability lies in expanding domestic sales and disincentives to export increase. By this point, governments are trapped: if they devalue the currency (which could have been done in the first place as an alternative to QRs), they fear that the rate of capital formation will decline as capital goods become more expensive. If they do not devalue the currency, they must resort to *ad hoc* measures such as export rebates, import entitlement schemes for exporters, and the like in order to stimulate export growth. As these 'incentives' grow over time, the regime becomes increasingly piecemeal. In virtually all the countries studied in the project which have had QR systems, governments themselves have reacted against these undesired effects and proliferation of special regulations that seem to result from QR systems.

The tendency toward increasingly detailed, often internally inconsistent, controls and the resulting frustration of initial intentions shows up in numerous ways. In India, a major goal was the reduction of concentration in economic power, which presumably meant reducing the share of the large industrial concerns in industrial output. Yet the regulations and procedures surrounding licensing applications (for investment and for imports) became so complex that the large firms had a strong competitive advantage in satisfying licence requirements: their share actually increased. In Turkey, import licences were granted to establish assembly industries in the expectation that those (import-substitution) industries would save foreign exchange and provide incentives for domestic production of parts and components. Instead, people invested in the assembly industries in order to earn import licences, and the value of licences for assembly industry requirements of intermediate goods increased, rather than decreased, during the 1960s, while domestic content requirements had to be employed to induce investments in parts-and-components producing activities.

Wide variations in economic costs

When producers know that they will benefit from complete protection from imports once domestic productive capacity is established, there are powerful profitability incentives to establish capacity regardless of the social opportunity costs of so doing. The drive to industrialize has been such an important goal that few of the countries covered in the Project have been able to resist using QRs to provide those incentives. In India and Turkey, goods have simply become ineligible for importation once domestic productive capacity was established. In Egypt and Ghana, the same thing happened *de facto*. In Brazil, the Law of Similars, combined with domestic content requirements, and a provision that tariff rates be doubled once domestic production started, achieved the same result.

It is easily predictable that under such systems the variation in domestic resource cost among and within industries will be great. One of the purposes of the country studies was to quantify the extent of this variation, and the results show remarkably wide differences. We do *not* find that all import-substitution firms are inefficient. On the contrary, some appear to have very low costs while others require a large multiple of all resources in order to save an equal amount of foreign exchange.

In view of this, a major defect of the QR system seems to be its inevitably indiscriminate nature. If, within such a system, low-cost activities could be differentially encouraged, the excess costs of the system should be significantly lower. Yet, the workings of the system seem invariably to result in an inability to reflect differentials in social profitability to individual decision makers.

Actual user licensing

We have already shown that the allocation of import licences to firms using imported goods in their production process has different resource-allocational implications from those that arise when premia on licences accrue to individuals who then resell to actual users. One feature of most QR systems is that they have tended to become increasingly actual-user oriented, and the fraction of import licences allocated directly to user firms has increased over time.

The motive for this method of allocation seems reasonable enough: it is designed to avoid allowing large windfall gains to accrue to persons who apparently do nothing but apply for import licences and, in addition, it rewards those individuals who have contributed toward the industrialization goal, as well as providing an implicit subsidy for recipient firms.

Difficulty, however, arises from the fact that criteria for allocation of licences among actual users are needed in the presence of excess demand. Without such criteria, the allocating officials are naturally accused of favouritism. The most frequently adopted criterion has been to allocate licences to recipients in proportion to different firms' capacities, although almost all countries have made provisions whereby new entrants would be entitled to an initial allocation.

This allocational criterion has had two closely interrelated and deleterious side effects: (1) it has, predictably enough, encouraged the development of excess capacity, and (2) it has resulted in roughly proportionate expansion of all firms in a given industry with little competition between them.

Turning to excess capacity first, in many newly established industries, firms' output levels are determined, within fairly narrow limits, by the volume of imports they obtain. Hence, summing over firms within an industry, the industry's output is closely tied to the imports of intermediate goods allocated to it. The fact that there are excess profits to most firms at that level of output is reflected by the premium on import licences: any individual firm could increase its total profit if it obtained more imports.

The only way to get more imports, however, is to expand capacity, since one's import rights are a function of his share in total capacity of the industry. Thus, even with existing excess capacity, it may pay to build more, since the return on the investment is the premium to be earned per unit of imports times the expected increment in import licences.

When policy makers perceive this result, a natural response is to attempt to control the expansion of capacity. Then, investment licensing follows import licensing. Again, criteria are needed and the circle has one more twist: profitability cannot be used as a criterion, since it emanates from import-licensing procedures, and also is regarded with suspicion (the bureaucrats are rewarding the already rich large firms). Thus, the natural temptation is to allow expansion proportionately over all applicants or over all firms. Decisions about the relative rates at which different industries shall be expanded must then be made and private profitability departs further and further from social profitability.

This brings us to the effect of import, and investment, licensing upon competition. For those industries where a firm's imports determine its output, the firm-specific allocation of imports determines market shares. With output fixed in the short run, there is little competition among firms. If there were no investment licensing, it might be that more profitable firms would expand more, with higher equilibrium levels of excess capacity in the long run. In general, however, investment licensing rules out even that form of competition, perhaps diminishing excess capacity, but insuring the growth of efficient and inefficient firms alike. We spoke earlier of the symmetries of export promotion and import substitution. It may well be that, in dynamic terms, the inability of QR systems to foster relatively more rapid growth of more efficient firms is one of the gravest drawbacks of the QR-import-substitution development pattern.

3 CONCLUDING REMARKS

We have only been able to scratch the surface of the results of the NBER project. Many of the statements we have made require, and indeed have, careful documentation and elaboration. Moreover, there are numerous topics on which we have been unable to touch due to space limitations –evidence on export responses to altered real exchange rates, macro-economic considerations in exchange-rate policy, many of the factors (such as effect on R&D) involved in the trade-regime-growth interaction, and the limits to QR regimes resulting from illicit transactions.

5

What We Need to Know

I shall be brief, not merely because I have a stern Chairman who insists on the ten-minute ration for the panelists, but because to be asked to tell this distinguished audience what we should all be doing in the coming years is to be asked to cast pearls before prima donnas.

I would like to address myself principally to the issues raised in the first session, on trade policy and development in particular. That is the area where I have comparative advantage when I put on my empirical hat. Also, at MIT where I now teach, one learns that Paul Samuelson has absolute advantage in everything, so that everyone has to teach according to comparative advantage (and Paul does not have to teach at all).

The interaction of trade policy (in its widest sense, including exchange-rate policy) with economic variables such as income, growth rates, income distribution, and employment is an intricate problem. It is by no means settled, in my view, and is still open to much more research–despite the excellence of the Little–Scitovsky–Scott (LSS) analysis and contrary to the main burden of the intervention at the earlier session by some of the participants commenting on Diaz-Alejandro's paper.

The current state of research in this area was indeed well surveyed by Diaz-Alejandro, who captured very well the 'temperament', as he calls it, that I would like to see more people bring to this field. Commenting on the role of economic history and of economic theory in comprehending reality, a wit has observed that one says precisely nothing and the other says nothing precisely. Diaz-Alejandro takes correctly the more prosaic and realistic view that both disciplines offer useful insights *but that* our missionary spirit to change things over to 'free trade' or 'export promotion' or the like needs to be moderated by a healthy scepticism and desire for yet more research.

I applaud this position, and not merely because, like the Hindu in E. M. Forster's *A Passage to India*, I have an infuriatingly eclectic approach to the important things of life such as Economics, an approach that corresponds to Diaz-Alejandro's equally noncommittal and sceptical

From Peter B. Kenen (ed.), *International Trade and Finance* (Cambridge and New York: Cambridge University Press, 1975), pp. 506–16. The original text has been edited. The references to Carlos Diaz-Alejandro and others are to contributions in Kenen (1975), or to oral remarks made at the conference whose proceedings are printed there.

Hispanic stance. It is also because my occasional involvement in empirical research in this field has made me somewhat sceptical of the *unqualified* claims concerning the cost of protection, the misallocation of resources, the wastefulness of import substitution, etc. Let me speculate why these views are held with such strong conviction.

(1) Partly, I think that the reaction against the LDC import-substitution strategies of the 1950s and 1960s has been a result of the swing of the pendulum that so often occurs in the philosophy of economic policy (as on fixed versus flexible rates).

(2) Partly, it is also a result of the fact that the LDCs have pursued their import-substitution policies at a time when world trade has grown rapidly – a growth that has been significantly affected by Japan's phenomenal expansion, which is not sufficiently allowed for in reaching judgments on this issue. (Even if Japan were not accumulating surpluses, a balanced-trade growth by Japan at its remarkable postwar rate, combined with Japan's high propensity to import and consequent need to export, would imply, for a faster-growing world economy, continuing shock waves requiring continuous adjustments. Part of the US problem in recent years has been that Japan's rapid export expansion has affected the United States more drastically than Japan's import intake.)

At the same time, some LDCs have clearly managed remarkably better export performance than others, leading to the view that exports could be increased by *all* LDCs – although (a) some LDCs have prospered at the expense of other LDCs (e.g. Pakistan and India on jute exports), (b) the ability to exploit some markets may have depended on political and cultural ties (e.g., the Korean access to the US market?, (c) it is improbable that all LDCs could have expanded exports at high rates without running into DC protectionism, and (d) higher rates of export expansion could not plausibly have been high enough in some cases to alter significantly the import-substitution strategy.

(3) I think that, among the important psychological reasons for the disillusionment of many economists with the import-substitution strategy has been the shock of finding that LDC governments (as much as DC governments in other areas of economic policy) have import-substituted in an economically chaotic way! In our theory classes, we spend a lot of time discussing why the Invisible Hand may not work or, as Joan Robinson once put it graphically, why it may work by strangulation. When, however, we go and see the actual nature of the intervention, and the maze of controls, quantitative restrictions, and automatic protection in many LDCs, we find the intervention chaotic and comprehensive. As a friend of mine in Ghana lamented, 'The Invisible Hand is nowhere to be seen!' It is easy then to lose one's balance and reach an extreme conclusion like the one quoted earlier by Hufbauer from Johnson in respect of multinational corporations:

It is evident that with sufficient analysis one can construct cases in which there is a second-best argument for restriction of inward foreign direct investment. The fundamental problem is that, as with all second-best arguments, determination of the conditions under which a second-best policy actually leads to an improvement of social welfare requires detailed theoretical and empirical investigation by a first-best economist. *Unfortunately, policy is generally formulated by fourth-best economists and administered by third-best economists;* it is therefore very unlikely that a second-best welfare optimum will result from policies based on second-best arguments.

Needless to say, such prescriptions ignore the evidence of useful interventions in a number of areas of policy as well as the evident failures of the market system when left completely to itself. But such prescriptions and attitudes do tend to be the result of exposure to the reality of LDC policy.

(4) And, finally, once one is so shocked, it is easy to fall into the two major pitfalls of economic research and inference: (a) the production of simple regressions, with the right R^2's, which support these views; and (b) the rough-and-ready calculation of numbers, accepted by us with relative ease because they seem to validate the disillusionment with what has been observed to be a chaotic policy.

The distinction between Economics and Econometrics may cynically be said to be that Economics is based on casual empiricism and Econometrics on selective empiricism. It is not uncommon for the best of us to regress (implicitly or explicitly) growth of income on protection levels or to argue that labour productivity has grown less in countries with reliance on import substitution. We then convince most people that this proves import substitution to be bad even when we know that labour productivity is *not* a proper index or that, if this hypothesis is indeed to be tested, it may be more useful to take a cross-section among industries in the same country and see if the export-oriented industries do better on technical change than import-substituting industries (something which Srinivasan and I have tried to do, with no clear results, in our study of India for the Bhagwati–Krueger NBER project). And we have all succumbed in varying degrees to the fallacy of *post hoc ergo propter hoc*, as Diaz-Alejandro reminded us in an earlier session in the context of arguments attributing more rapid growth rates to preceding liberalizations – an example which is matched in my country by the reverse assertion that the difficulties in India's economy after the liberalization attempt of 1966 were 'obviously' the result of the liberalization.

In the area of trade policy and development, where the phenomena involved are fairly complex, one is in danger of being seduced subconsciously into accepting as confirmation of one's ideas the limited aspect of reality that is consistent with one's thesis, and even into thinking that this reality is somewhat more consistent with one's notions than it really might be. A good example is provided by the contrast between Taiwan and India in the OECD series of country studies. In their excellent overall volume, LSS are fairly cautious and guarded in many of their sound recommendations, and they are always scholarly. But I cannot help detecting, as in their argument that Taiwan (which performed very well) 'give[s] an impression of more moderate [protection] rates than in other countries, except Mexico (another fine performer)' (p. 185), a tendency, as in the work of nearly all of us, to underplay the limitations of such 'impressions'. One should really highlight forcefully the tenuous character of all these estimates of protection, the non-comparability of these estimates across countries owing to differences in data quality, the nature of protection (e.g. quantitative restrictions versus *ad valorem* tariffs versus specific tariffs), and the sensitivity of these estimates to the classifications used and the aggregation implied. I cannot help feeling that we are all tempted to conclude that Taiwan must be following more closely the prescriptions of LSS (who, I am often chided by those who see nothing wrong with the trade policies of the import-substituting LDCs, relied heavily on Bhagwati–Ramaswami for their theory and Bhagwati–Desai for their policy lessons) because Taiwan has done better economically! In fact, the secret of Taiwan's success may lie elsewhere. Indeed, looking at the chaotic nature of Taiwan's governmental intervention in investment allocation, which the OECD study of Taiwan itself suggests very strongly, I would be inclined to consider other factors myself, much as I have a vested interest in showing that the Bhagwati–Ramaswami–Johnson prescriptions on how to run trade policy are very important in practice! I cannot help mentioning Mexico also in this context. Was Mexico's relative success the result of her better trade policy? The interventions were again rather extensive, and by no means suited to our prescriptions in any manifest fashion. But, arriving at an explanation that would suit the strategy which we would consider (with them) eminently sensible, LSS found that internal competition and 'smuggling' from the United States must have helped to reduce the protection to which Mexico otherwise would have been condemned! In short, Mexico's policies were not too good, but her proximity to the United States saved her for the LSS strategy and for economic prosperity. My good friends, Little, Scitovsky, and Scott, will forgive me, I hope, if I say with levity and obvious exaggeration that they are almost turning on its head the famous remark of Porfirio Diaz: 'Poor Mexico! How far from God and how near to the United States!'

I must confess also that I am a little sceptical about the meaning of the statistical description of tariff structure, whether nominal or effective,

D

which Corden cited in his review of the trade policy of LDCs. These tariff numbers need to be placed in their policy and economic context. Thus a 400 per cent tariff, calculated implicitly from a high import premium, may be the result of restrictive industrial licensing and not merely an import quota: it does *not* then signify a successful and massive pull of resources. A system of automatic protection may signify a different qualitative insight into the process of industrialization than the resulting tariff structure calculated on any one point in time; it would imply a tariff structure *adjusting* to changing competitiveness and therefore have allocational effects quite different from those of an unchanging tariff structure. One must go way beyond these descriptions toward understanding *functionally* the economic system of the LDC in question (as the NBER project explicitly tries to do). The trouble is that this does hamper cross-section regression analysis and it also calls for more intensive analytical 'country studies'. Fortunately, this is no longer difficult. Fraser, the great evolutionary anthropologist, in the pre-Malinowski–Radcliffe–Brown era, was asked if he had ever visited the exotic areas he wrote about. He is reported to have said:'I only write about savages, I don't mix with them.' Thanks to the Foundations, USAID, the World Bank, and the eager jetsetting propensity of the modern economist, we need no longer fear that our search for knowledge, if not pleasure, will be handicapped by Fraserian attitudes.

In conclusion, while there are many serious questions about the trade policies of LDCs in the last two decades, and indeed the excellent analytical work of the OECD authors and the detailed statistical descriptions of tariffs turned up by the IBRD projects under the able guidance of Bela Balassa have helped to raise them, we are *not* very close to saying: 'Definitive knowledge gained, let us now turn to other things.' This conclusion also bears on the issue that came up in an earlier session: Corden and Johnson, among others, asked for work on why politicians refuse to accept our wisdom (and related work on what political forces constrain them to act as they do). Are we to disregard the fact that this wisdom of ours changes and is fickle on both a cross-section among economists and a time series for any given economist? It would be very entertaining, if not instructive, to study the policy advice of economists on this panel (including myself) over the last ten years: You would probably find that the conviction with which any one of us considers governments to be senselessly recalcitrant in taking economic advice varies positively with the number of times one has changed one's mind on important policy issues! But let us suppress such self-destructive thoughts. We are *still* left with two alternative explanations.

One, produced by Johnson with eloquence in an earlier session, is that politicians *use* economists to justify selectively what they wish to do anyway: Economics becomes the handmaiden of political perfidy. This is an egocentric, econocentric view. My experience does not really coincide with it. Political leaders have rarely sought to justify industrialization in a strictly economic sense; images of modernization, reaching technological maturity, national military power, etc., have played a much more important role in the ideology of industrialization and import substitution. Few politicians have bothered to convince our profession that they were right.

The alternative explanation, to which I am partly inclined, is that policymakers have *something* on their side. Recall that deficit spending as an instrument to create aggregate employment preceded the *General Theory*. Economists should be a little more cautious in assuming that policy wisdom is necessarily on *their* side.

So we need to know more, to do more research. Let me throw out a few things that worry me, as the results of the NBER Bhagwati–Krueger project come in, where more research seems to me to be needed.

(1) Instead of the chaotic selectivity of the incentive policies for 'import substitution', which seems to be the main focus of our trade-theoretic analysis, a more *important* inhibition on growth may in practice be the speed with which 'import substituting' industrialization is geared toward 'export promotion'. Here, again, as the Korean study in the Bhagwati–Krueger project seems to underline, the key to success is not the absence of detailed, selective, and target-oriented export promotion; Korea shows as much variation in domestic resource costs as you could now expect to find among the import-substituting industries in 'inward-looking' countries. And, as Bent Hansen's study of Egypt for the same project also shows, you can have low variance among domestic resource costs even when trade and other incentive policies seem to be chaotically set!

The distinguishing feature of superior economic performance seems to be the pursuit, not of neutral and uniform, but rather of *energetic* policies to promote exports from industries which have been nurtured under protection in the first place.

If this is true, however, we may not find in our Bhagwati–Ramaswami–Johnson models the mainsprings of superior performance. We have to look elsewhere. (This seems to have been the case with Japan since 1898 as well–as suggested by a detailed, original study, by Ippei Yamazawa, of Japan's extensive resort to protection during this period, sponsored under the Bhagwati–Krueger project.) Krueger and I expect to develop this theme at greater length in the overall volumes which will cap the NBER country studies, much as the LSS volume grew out of the OECD country studies, but some preliminary thoughts on this issue were spelled out in our paper at the AEA meetings in Toronto in December 1972. This is clearly an area that needs to be explored much more intensively than we will–with both theoretical and empirical work of the highest quality.

(2) Among the issues related to the possible advantage of rapid export promotion is the question of the impact of import-substituting LDC strategies on technical change and X-efficiency. I must admit to thinking, as did most economists who pondered these issues in the last decade, that sheltered markets generated by quantitative restrictions destroyed incentives for research and development. We should have known better. There is evidence of growing R&D in India, little evidence that it is stronger in export-oriented firms, much evidence that it springs out of the desire generated by the trade regime to promote the use of locally available materials–a variant of the Kennedy-type thesis on technical change–and ample evidence that large firms matter in this game. Is such R&D desirable? What does it do to growth and hence to our overall evaluation of the import-substituting growth strategy from which it springs? There is clearly need for more research here. One has only to recall Japan's transition from shoddy manufacture under bad imitation to decent manufacture under good imitation to excellent manufacture under outstanding imitation to innovative manufacture, and the growing evidence that India is beginning to transit to decent manufacture, to at least pause and ask if there is much more to our choice of strategies than meets our trade-theoretic and cost-benefit-analysis-oriented eye. Historical, current-LDC-oriented *and* theoretical research in this difficult area is urgent.

(3) Let me next join with Johnson in suggesting that we reintroduce political and sociological factors into our analysis of trade policy and development. This is necessary if we are really going to understand complex phenomena such as the impact of policies on growth. As we all know by now, first-best policies applied in second-best contexts can be counterproductive. The Bhagwati–Krueger project again helps to illustrate this very nicely. Unlike the OECD project, ours extends the analysis to specific attempts at liberalizing trade regimes, putting this analysis into its specific political context. Thus, the Israeli and Indian liberalization attempts of the 1960s demonstrate clearly that import liberalization is unsuccessful when it results in greater domestic competition but is eminently successful when it involves only greater access to non-competitive imports: the influence of pressure groups created by the earlier 'automatic protection' type of strategy is evident. Similarly, the analysis of the 1966 Indian devaluation brings out the specific interaction between the success and repeatability of a liberalization package and the political framework (espcially the pressure from the Aid Consortium) within which the package was implemented. I am convinced that a full analysis of the feasibility and success of liberalization would have to take into account these and similar political factors, and that a 'scientific' economic analysis cannot ignore them altogether; the distinction sometimes drawn between 'political economy' and 'scientific economics' is really a false one.

I am sure that we should now also be addressing ourselves to much more developed country research of a similar type. The original Marshall–Taussig concern with the criteria by which tariff protection was actually granted (at the LDC level, one such detailed analysis is Padma Desai's volume on the Indian Tariff Commission) needs to be revived and supplemented by examination of such questions as the characteristics of the industries which managed to get exemptions in the Kennedy Round (a task in which John Cheh at MIT is now engaged).[1] If we knew more about why tariff exemptions are granted, we could construct interesting and relevant theories of tariff retaliation which would add to the existing analytic literature to which theorists such as Johnson and Gorman have contributed in the past.

(4) Finally, let me emphasize the need for more research on the impact of multinational corporations on LDCs. In this area, we have had diverse theories: (a) the 'dualism' notions of the Dutch sociological school, leading to the *enclave* models and approach, where the MNCs bypassed the hinterland, having no effect, either malign or benign; (b) the *benign neglect* model, which has emphasized the beneficial side-effects of MNCs in the guise of diffused technology, increased competitiveness for domestic entrepreneurs, and the like; (c) the *malign intent* model, which finds its validation in the experience of the Union Minière du Haut Katanga, the United Fruit Company, and the ITT of recent vintage; and (d) the *malign neglect* model, which focuses on how the presence of MNCs exercises adverse influence on LDCs via a Hirschman-type inhibition of domestic entrepreneurship or a Sunkel-type accentuation of taste formation, which distorts the pattern of development away from a preferable, more equitable mould or affects the income distribution (as when the granting of salaries comparable to the MNC salary levels to local nationals creates an upward pull on the salary levels of the elite groups in the host LDCs, at the expense of egalitarian ideas). We know far too little about these issues at an empirical level, even about the relatively more tractable issues such as the diffusion of technology; our theories are correspondingly inadequate to the important task of relating the MNCs to the past and future performance of the LDCs.

[1. The references are to: Padma Desai, *Tariff Protection in India, 1947–1965* (New Delhi: Hindustan Publishing Corporation, 1971); and John Cheh, 'United States concessions in the Kennedy round and short-run labor adjustment costs', *Journal of International Economics*, 4(4), 1974, 323–40. GG]

6

Trade Policy and Development

The interaction between international trade and development is a subject of such complexity and importance that it has rarely ceased to attract the attention of economic theorists, analysts of the world economy, and designers of the international economic system. Inevitably, therefore, it has drawn into its fold and its many controversies some of the best minds of each generation of economists: dating from Adam Smith, David Ricardo, and John Stuart Mill, down to Alfred Marshall and, in our own times, to Dennis Robertson, Ragnar Nurkse, Jacob Viner, Gottfried Haberler, and Arthur Lewis.[1]

There are far too many questions that the topic raises: witness, for example, the elegant recent review by Carlos Diaz-Alejandro (1975). We propose rather to concentrate on two sets of analyses that have currently been the focal point of theoretical, empirical, and policy discussions.

In section 1 we review the evidence that is currently available on the question that Nurkse had raised in the early 1950s regarding the optimal trade and developmental strategy for a postwar LDC (less developed country) planning to accelerate its economic growth. Arguing that the nineteenth-century mechanism of trade as 'an engine of growth' (in Dennis Robertson's catching phrase) was not available to present-day LDCs for a number of reasons, he noted that a policy of 'balanced growth', reflecting essentially domestic demands, was inevitable. Remarkably, he did contrast this, what we would today describe as an IS (import substitution) strategy, with the policy alternative of promoting new, manufactured exports, *à la* what we would now call the EP (export promoting) strategy: but felt that the latter offered little promise, as it was likely to run into DC market disruption-related trade restraints, as with textiles. As it happens, the postwar period did witness both sets of policies, starting in the early 1960s, and we have the evidence of two major projects on these issues so that we can, with hindsight, see which strategy was the more successful *ex post*. Our analysis will not merely review these

1. Cf., in particular, Jacob Viner (1953), Ragnar Nurkse (1959), Gottfried Haberler (1959), and W. Arthur Lewis (1969).

Written with T. N. Srinivasan, from R. Dornbusch and J. A. Frenkel (eds), *International Economic Policy: Theory and Evidence* (Baltimore: Johns Hopkins University Press, 1979), pp. 1–35.

empirical results, it will also indicate the unsettled questions on which only future research can generate persuasive evidence.

Therefore, while section 1 focuses principally on the trade policies of LDCs in regard to the optimal methods of utilizing the available trade opportunities, we turn in section 2 to the complementary subject of how those trade opportunities ought to be defined. In particular, we will consider two subjects of recent policy interest, namely, (i) the theoretical and policy issues raised by the problem of market disruption-related threats of trade restrictions on imports of manufactures by DCs; and (ii) the recent demands by LDCs, as part of the New International Economic Order (NIEO), for commodity agreements.

The reader should be forewarned that this chapter is therefore a selective review of the major trade-and-developmental policy issues; it is certainly not intended to be an exhaustive guide to the voluminous literature on the subject.[2].

1 PROTECTION, INDUSTRIALIZATION, EXPORT PERFORMANCE, AND ECONOMIC DEVELOPMENT

We turn now to the 'foreign trade strategy' issues that were admirably, and with much prescience, raised by Ragnar Nurkse.[3] Cairncross, in an insightful review of Nurkse and Haberler, having reviewed the general argumentation couched in terms of trends in world trade and whether these justified elasticity pessimism or optimism and whether these in turn required balanced growth or not, summed up as follows:

> At the end of it all, the reader may still feel that neither Nurkse nor Haberler has settled the primary issue: how far a shortage of foreign exchange (contrasted with capital, skilled labour, land, etc.) is a limiting factor in economic development. The majority of the under-developed countries are monocultures, dependent for their earnings of foreign exchange on a single commodity (or at most two or three). These earnings are highly inelastic except when exports of the principal commodity form a small fraction of the world's consumption. At the same time, nearly all the plant and machinery that they require has to be imported, so that the scale of industrial investment is limited by the foreign exchange available to pay for it. In those circumstances, what should be the policy of a country seeking

---

2. The many distinguished researchers whose contributions are not noted explicitly should equally take note of this fact!
3. This section draws heavily on Bhagwati (1976).

to accelerate its development? We know what most countries have done; it would be interesting if we could be told, by an economist of the standing of Nurkse or Haberler, what the results have been and what they should have done. (Cairncross, 1962, p. 208)

Modesty should prevent us from laying claim to the 'standing of Nurkse or Haberler'. However, we are certainly now in a position to respond to Cairncross's query, thanks principally (though not exclusively) to two major projects on foreign trade regimes and their effects on economic development: the OECD project, directed by Ian Little, Tibor Scitovsky, and Maurice Scott, whose results have been known since the early 1970s; and the NBER project, directed by Jagdish Bhagwati and Anne Krueger, whose results have now become generally available.[4]

In particular, we now have statistical evidence and economic argumentation on the following, related issues: (i) The degree and structure of protection that have been practised in the developing countries; (ii) The analytical rationale for relating this to the pattern of industrialization and export performance of these developing countries via the effect on the relative incentives for import substitution and export promotion; (iii) The statistical evidence for the argument that such incentives affect the pattern of industrialization and export performance in the developing countries; and (iv) The question whether, and if so why, better export performance is related to better economic performance.

The degree and structure of protection: concepts

In analysing protection, one needs to distinguish among three sets of concepts: (i) Trade policy protection versus domestic policy protection: an activity may be protected through tariffs and quotas (QRs), on the one hand, or through domestic subsidies, etc., on the other hand;[5] (ii) Tariffs versus quota protection, or alternatively, explicit versus implicit protection: within trade policy, we can distinguish between protection furnished by tariffs or by QRs; in turn, QR may be specifically designed

4. The Organization for Economic Cooperation and Development (OECD) project (organized by the OECD Development Center) covered Brazil, India, Mexico, Pakistan, the Philippines, and Taiwan; whereas the NBER project covered ten countries: Brazil, Chile, Colombia, Egypt, Ghana, India, Israel, the Philippines, South Korea, and Turkey. The NBER project (National Bureau of Economic Research [1975, 1976]) essentially takes off from the OECD project, in extending the analysis to much more systematic attention to the exchange-control aspects of the foreign trade regimes in the developing countries; it also considers dynamic aspects of the trade regimes and the problems of trade liberalization. The OECD studies (Organization for Economic Cooperation and Development [1970]) have been published in five country volumes and one overall volume:

for protecting the activity in question or they may be a result of an overvalued exchange rate that results in the use of QRs as a technique for balancing international accounts; and (iii) nominal versus effective protection: the protection may be measured in the conventional way as on goods and services (i.e., as nominal rates) or on value added (i.e. as effective rates).

It is clear from these conceptual distinctions that, in examining protection, the international economist aims at comparing the total structure of incentives (to import-competing and other activities) as contrasted with those that would be provided under a regime of laissez faire, or what has been more aptly described as a regime of unified exchange rates.[6] Thus, the incentives for domestic import substitutes that would follow from overvalued exchange rates, and the attendant implicit tariffs implied by QRs, must be allowed for; and so must the use of domestic subsidies, in several forms, to domestic production. The early studies of protection in the LDCs allowed for neither the use of QRs nor the presence of domestic taxes and subsidies.[7] However, the well known IBRD (International Bank for Reconstruction and Development) studies (Balassa and associates, 1971), as also the NBER studies, typically attempt to allow for implicit tariffs (i.e., QRs) and, occasionally and partially, for indirect taxes insofar as they affect domestic prices of inputs or differently affect import substitutes and imports.

The use of implicit tariffs involves, typically, the conversion of import premium data or, alternatively, data on differentials between domestic and c.i.f. prices of comparable items into equivalent tariffs. This procedure is subject to both empirical and conceptual difficulties, a few of which may be mentioned here:[8] (i) quality differences exist between imports and import substitutes, which imply that some of the differential in prices,

---

(1) Little, Scitovsky, and Scott (1970), overall; (2) Bergsman (1970), Brazil; (3) Bhagwati and Desai (1970), India; (4) Lewis (1970), Pakistan; (5) Hsing, Power, and Sicat (1970), Taiwan and the Philippines; and (6) King (1970), Mexico. The NBER studies are being published in ten-country volumes and two synthesis volumes; the following are already published: (1) Krueger (1975), Turkey; (2) Michaely (1975), Israel; (3) Baldwin (1975), the Philippines; (4) Leith (1975), Ghana; (5) Frank, Westphal, and Kim (1975), South Korea; (6) Bhagwati and Srinivasan (1975), India; (7) Hansen and Nashashibi (1975), Egypt; (8) Diaz-Alejandro (1976), Colombia; and (9) Behrman (1976), Chile. Bhagwati (1978) and Krueger (1978) have written two separate synthesis volumes, focusing on different parts of the project results. Note: The Brazil study was not completed.

5. The choice between these alternative instruments of protection has, of course, been the subject matter of contributions by Meade, Bhagwati, Ramaswami, Srinivasan, Corden, Johnson, and other theorists of trade policy. We do not discuss these issues here.

6. This phrasing was used in Bhagwati (1968).

7. This was true of the early estimates for Pakistan, for example, by Soligo and Stern (1965).

8. Cf. the treatment in Balassa (1971, ch. 3); also consult Bhagwati (1978, ch. 5) for a more detailed discussion.

when used for estimation, is attributable to this factor; (ii) frequently the QR regime may be so restrictive that imports are prohibited and there is, in consequence, often no easy and reliable way to get comparable c.i.f. prices; (iii) if perfect competition in quota allocation and use, and in foreign and domestic supply and demand, cannot be assumed, the import premium cannot be meaningfully converted in general into an equivalent implicit tariff; (iv) where domestic licensing contributes to the generation of monopoly profits, the import premium will reflect this factor as well and hence is not interpretable as protection from the viewpoint of inferring resource allocational shifts; (v) in the nature of the case, QRs will be, and are, associated with fluctuating premiums, so that it is extremely difficult to arrive at one set of premiums to convert into implicit tariffs, and totally misleading to use one such set to indicate the tariff structure (which is to be taken, in turn, to indicate the structure of price incentives to domestic protection).

Given these, and other, serious shortcomings, it is best to treat the resulting estimates of the implicit tariff structure as descriptions, in varying degrees of loose approximation, of the pattern of incentives that may be appearing in the developing countries in question, thanks to QRs.[9]

Similarly, the description of the tariff structure in effective tariff, as distinct from nominal tariff, terms raises both conceptual and empirical questions.[10] In particular, it is not possible to utilize the computed effective tariff rates to indicate in an unambiguous fashion the direction of change in resource allocation that is resulting from the set of nominal tariffs that we use to compute the effective tariffs.[11]

In light of these problems, it is best perhaps to regard the effective tariff structures that have been estimated in the OECD, NBER, and IBRD studies, among many others, as also essentially descriptions that, in a very loose way, indicate the differential nature of incentives that the combination of tariffs, QRs and (in some instances) domestic subsidies and taxes seem to throw up in the economy being studied.

9. In some of the studies, the protection granted is broken down into that resulting from explicit tariffs and the additional element due to QRs, when the implicit tariffs exceed the explicit tariffs. Cf. the Bhagwati–Desai–Panchamukhi estimates in the OECD India volume (1970), and the Leith estimates in the NBER Ghana volume (1975).

10. For a detailed consideration of the empirical questions, see Balassa (1971, chs 3 and 4); for conceptual problems, see in particular the contributions by Bruno (1973) and Bhagwati and Srinivasan (1973), to the *Journal of International Economics Symposium on the Theory of Effective Protection in General Equilibrium* (1973).

11. This point has been established, and sufficient conditions under which the direction of change in resource allocation may nonetheless be inferred, investigated, by international trade theorists recently. A good starting point for reading this literature is in the *Journal of International Economics Symposium on the Theory of Effective Protection in General Equilibrium* (1973). The statistical evidence on this question, discussed in the text above, also corroborates this theoretical scepticism, while indicating a few of the reasons for it. For fuller discussion, see Bhagwati (1978, ch. 5).

While the tariff structures are defined and estimated in the manner indicated above, and must be interpreted with great caution, the concept of the degree of protection reflects essentially a weighted average of such tariffs.[12] In addition to such averages, some economists have also attempted to adjust the average degree of protection downward by arguing that the removal of the tariffs would generally generate a balance-of-payments deficit that would have to be eliminated by devaluing the exchange rate. The devaluation, in turn, would imply that the domestic price of the imported commodities would fall by less than the tariff removal would imply.[13] While this is a theoretically correct thing to do, if one is interested in what happens (net) to the nominal domestic price of importables as a result of the tariff imposition,[14] the practical estimation of this adjustment factor, as attempted in several of the IBRD studies, relies on procedures that can be defended only by making highly restrictive assumptions.[15]

Finally, in anticipation of the analysis on pages 101–104 of the interaction between protection and export performance, it may be noted that the degree of protection is often taken as a reasonable explanatory variable for export performance. Additionally, three other concepts are used frequently as explanatory variables in analysing export performance, two relating in some fashion to protection in the broad sense defined above. First, the ratio of the effective exchange rate on exports (EER_x) to that on imports (EER_m) is taken as an index of how far the average exports are profitable relative to average import-competing production.[16]

12. The nominal tariffs may be weighted by shares in imports or in domestic production; effective tariffs may be weighted by shares in nominal value added of the activities in question.

13. Thus a removal of an average tariff of 50 per cent, resulting in a devaluation of 20 per cent, would imply a net, adjusted average tariff of 30 per cent; the domestic, nominal price of the imported items would fall only by 30 per cent when the tariffs were removed and the balance-of-payments position left unchanged.

14. Note that it would require, even in theory, special restrictions to infer from such a (net) effect on the average domestic (nominal) price of importables that, for example, the share of trade in national income is reduced by such a tariff.

15. Cf. Balassa (1971, app. 3) for the specification of the procedures used, and an excellent theoretical survey of them in Dornbusch (1974). Aside from the theoretical objections, spelled out by Dornbusch, one might note also the general inconsistency between using less than infinitely elastic foreign elasticities of demand for exports to compute exchange rate change and constant international prices for computing effective protection (as required by the fact that the general equilibrium analyses of effective protection in the available literature universally make the assumption of constant international prices).

16. The effective exchange rate on exports (EER_x) is defined as the units of domestic currency that can be obtained for a dollar's worth of exports, taking into account export duties, subsidies and surcharges, special exchange rates, input subsidies related to exports, etc. The effective exchange rate on imports (EER_m) is then defined as the units of domestic currency that would be paid for a dollar's worth of imports, taking into account

Second, for any one activity, the effective tariff rate as applicable to production for domestic sales may be compared with the effective tariff rate as applicable to exports and the ratio thereof, when exceeding unity, would be described as the 'export bias' characterizing that activity.[17] But, if the EER_x and EER_m are defined (as they were traditionally in the 1960s in India) as including the incentives and disincentives on outputs as also those related to inputs,[18] then the definition of export bias as the ratio of effective tariffs in export and domestic markets is identical with the better-known and earlier definition of export bias in terms of the ratio EER_x/EER_m.[19] Third, we may note the concept of real effective exchange rates, or what the NBER project calls the price-level deflated effective exchange rates ($PLDEER$s). In contrast to the EER_x/EER_m ratio, the $PLDEER_x$ would show the relative price of the exportables to home goods (as distinct from importables) and hence capture a different element of the total picture regarding incentives to produce for exports. Furthermore, the NBER project utilized, in some studies, the concept of purchasing-power parity effective exchange rates, $PPPEER$s, which adjust also for changes in the foreign price level.

We shall return to these concepts when we examine the relationship of protection with export performance. For the present, it is important

tariffs, surcharges, interest on advance deposits, etc. In principle, the EER_m should include premia on import licences; however, in the NBER studies, the EER_m was defined exclusive of them, for the simple reason that for many countries no reliable data on import premia could be obtained either directly or via suitable surveys of c.i.f. and retail prices. As stated later, the ratio EER_x/EER_m as an index of export bias dates back to before even the OECD project studies and was used, without detailed quantification, in Bhagwati (1968).

17. This concept was used in the International Bank for Reconstruction and Development (IBRD) studies and is used in the South Korean study of the NBER project; it was not used in the OECD project at all. However, as noted below, it reduces in effect to the (properly defined) ratio of EER_x/EER_m in any case.

18. Thus, for example, exporters in India typically receive imported materials at international prices, so that EER_x is defined as inclusive of the implied subsidy from this scheme. See Bhagwati and Srinivasan (1975), for example.

19. This is seen readily by stating that, for the usual notation, export bias under the former concept amounts to:

$$\frac{t_j^x - \Sigma_{a_{ij}} t_i^x}{t_j^d - \Sigma_{a_{ij}} t_i^d} < 1$$

where the superscripts x and d relate to export and domestic markets respectively, and the latter amounts to:

$$1 + (t_j^x - t_j^d) + \Sigma_{aij}(t_i^d - t_i^x) < 1.$$

to distinguish broadly between two basic implications of any observed tariff structure: (i) the import-competing activities are being, broadly speaking, encouraged relative to what the absence of protection would imply: this is what might be called the 'degree of import substitution' aspect of the protective structure; and (ii) there are (usually) differential tariffs on, and therefore differential incentives to, different activities within the import-competing sectors: this is what could be called the 'pattern of import substitution' aspect of the protective structure.[20] In an approximate fashion, we can then argue that the degree-of-protection concept corresponds to the degree of import-substitution aspect, and the structure-of-protection concept corresponds to the pattern of import-substitution aspect, of the process of economic expansion and, in effect, of industrialization in the LDCs.

In the rest of this section we will essentially deal with both these aspects: on pages 95–101 we shall consider the pattern of import substitution; the subsection after that, in considering export performance, will simultaneously imply consideration of the question of the degree of import substitution. Prior to these analyses, however, a brief review of the empirical studies on the degree and structure of protection is presented.

The degree and structure of protection: evidence

Although both the OECD and NBER projects contain, within their more ambitious and wide-ranging framework, estimates of the protective structure, the best-known and standardized estimates for a set of developing countries are to be found in the six IBRD studies for Brazil, Chile, Malaya, Mexico, Pakistan, and the Philippines.[21]

Essentially, these estimates relate to specific dates, typically deploy the effective tariff concept, and utilize implicit tariff estimates (based largely on estimated differentials between foreign and domestic prices of imports).

20. The terminology of degree and pattern of import substitution was introduced in Bhagwati (1972).

21. The OECD and NBER studies offered much more comprehensive and detailed analyses of the countries being studied than the IBRD study. In particular, most of the NBER volumes examined export performance in depth, systematically analysed the evolution of the exchange-control regime over time, examined fully the conditions determining the outcomes of liberalization attempts (including political factors plus the role of foreign aid, etc.) and attempted (in some cases) more systematic examination of dynamic arguments relating to investment, innovation, savings formation, etc. and their interaction with the foreign trade regime. In all these respects, the NBER studies were, for the most part, more comprehensive and ambitious than other efforts, such as, for example, the IBRD project, though the latter did touch marginally on some of the issues (e.g., Balassa's brief treatment of 'dynamic' effects in his introductory essays, relating however mainly to static, scale economies and competition aspects). The relationship between the NBER and the OECD projects, which were both ambitious, has been spelled out above.

Net protection estimates (adjusting for exchange rate change) are also included. The studies also proceed to present effective protection by export and domestic markets, so that export bias, so defined, is also typically estimated by the authors.

The IBRD studies indicated that the manufacturing sector was protected relative to the primary sector in nearly all the countries in question and, in the case of Chile and the Philippines, the average tariff rate for manufacturing was fairly sizeable.

The OECD synthesis volume by Little, Scitovsky, and Scott also contained estimates of average tariff levels for manufactures that indicated again that the degree of protection used for manufactures by developing countries was extremely high: protection being defined as nominal, explicit tariffs alone. By contrast, they argued that most of the present DCs had used substantially lower tariffs in the course of their development.[22] This contrast was sustained by examination of the effective tariffs as well.

While the OECD project did note the 'variability of protection' to different manufacturing activities, the main focus of the NBER studies has been precisely on this aspect of the overall foreign trade regime. Thus, while stressing the many difficulties in interpreting the structure of protection, the estimates were used to underline the differential-incentives-generating nature of the regime, while stressing equally the administrative-cum-allocational procedures that led to automaticity of protection, fluctuating incentives through varying import premia reflecting changing allocations and rules, and numerous other facets without whose adequate understanding the analyst of the effects of tariff structures would be making, at best, misleading inferences.[23] While using the estimated tariffs on several manufacturing activities (and, in the case of Egypt, for agricultural crops as well)[24] to show the wide dispersion in the implied incentives, the NBER project also utilized concepts and measures such as domestic resource costs (DRCs) to indicate rather the varying social rates of return to production in alternative manufacturing activities.[25]

The major conclusion of the NBER studies is that the protective structure, when inclusive of the implicit tariffs (implied by QRs) under exchange controls, is characterized by considerable dispersion and unpredictability, and that the effects are to create resource misallocation

22. Cf. Little, Scitovsky, and Scott (1970, ch. 5). It should be added, however, that an unpublished NBER project-commissioned examination of Japanese tariff protection during the period of early industrialization, by Ippei Yamazawa, suggests a substantially greater role of tariffs, and other forms of protection, than the Little-Scitovsky-Scott figure indicates for Japan.

23. For details, see Bhagwati (1978, ch. 5).

24. Cf. Hansen and Nashashibi (1975) on Egypt.

25. Of course, if shadow prices for domestic factors, and marginal revenues for commodities facing declining prices as exports increase, are not used to calculate DRCs, they can be reduced by a simple transformation to effective rates of protection.

whose incidence is indicated by the DRC-dispersion observed in the empirical studies.[26]

Protection and pattern of industrialization

The effect of the structure of protection on the pattern of industrialization may first be noted, before proceeding to consider the effect of the degree and pattern of such protection on export performance.

While it is true in reality that protection of the manufacturing sector, *in toto*, is supportive of industrialization in the LDCs, it should be noted that it does not follow that the pattern of manufacturing production, or import substitution, also is explainable by the pattern of protection that is being measured for the LDCs. Thus, it is tempting to argue that industries when arrayed in ascending order by their (effective or nominal) protective rates should also be ranked in ascending order by their growth rates, or their import-substitution ratios. But there is neither analytical, nor clear empirical, support for such a hypothesis; and, in fact, it is encouraging that where theory suggests there should be no such correlation, there is mixed evidence to be found in practice as well.

Among the favourable results for the hypothesis stated is that for Colombia. Thus, in the NBER study of Colombia, Carlos Diaz-Alejandro cites the earlier work of Hutcheson on Colombian protection that regresses growth rates successfully on effective protective rates.[27]

Similarly, Frank *et al.*, in the NBER study on South Korea (1975, ch. 10) report on rank correlation coefficients between various measures of effective protection, and of effective incentives (defined so as to include the effects of tax rebates, credit preferences, and such incentives) and resource-allocational indices such as import-substitution ratios (or export shares for export industries) and growth contribution. Their results, however, are generally poor on the import side: the correlation between import ratios and effective incentives is significant and positive, suggesting that import substitution had progressed the least [rather than the most] in those sectors that had a high level of effective incentives on domestic sales, and the correlations between effective incentives to domestic sales

26. The stress on dispersion of incentives is to be found particularly in Leith's NBER Ghana volume (1975) and in Bhagwati and Srinivasan's NBER India volume (1975), and is spelled out overall in Bhagwati's NBER synthesis volume (1978, ch. 5). Balassa (1971) also stresses the variability of incentives in the tariff structure but does not pay the same degree of attention to interpreting it in light of the unpredictability, built-in automaticity of future protection, and other integral aspects of QR regimes that define the context, and hence the true meaning, of these tariff estimates. More is said on this in the next subsection.

27. The Hutcheson estimates of effective protection use the early Balassa method for treating non-traded goods as enjoying zero protection rather than as value added *à la* Corden. Note, however, that in the case of Chile, at least, the distinction between the two measures is not empirically important. Cf. Behrman (1976) on Chile.

and growth contributions are not significant, though they are negative (Frank *et al.*, 1975, p. 56).

Additional cross-sectional analysis of this variety was also conducted by Jere Behrman in his NBER study of Chile, to determine whether the price structures created by the international economic regimes were associated with growth across sectors. (See Behrman (1976, ch. 12) on Chile, for full details of this analysis.) He found a positive relation between growth in value-added and in horsepower capacity between 1961 and 1967 and the implicit tariff rates (ITRs) for 1967 and also for the incremental ITRs between 1961 and 1967. But this relationship has little plausibility, as Behrman notes, and may be rationalized only by argument, such as that the ITRs 'perhaps . . . served as signals, however, of the government's intentions to favour particular sub-sectors' (1976, ch. 12). Interestingly, Behrman found no evidence for a link between effective rates of protection and growth: in fact, the only significant non-zero correlation coefficient, using alternative estimates, was a negative one between effective rates and growth in production from 1953 to 1961.[28]

Going beyond the NBER studies, furthermore, we may note two successful sets of regressions: for Pakistan by Guisinger (1971) and for Nigeria by Oyejide (1971). The Pakistani analysis was unsuccessful for import-substitution ratios, but successful for growth rates for a 23-industry study. The Nigerian analysis, for 42 industries, resulted in successful regressions of import-substitution ratios on effective rates of protection and changes therein.

While, therefore, the results for the different countries are fairly mixed, we also need to note that the construction of a theoretical rationale for a successful regression of import-substitution ratios or growth rates in cross-section analysis is difficult, and one may reasonably expect to find no relationships of the kinds postulated. It should be useful to spell out why this is so, taking the import-substitution ratio as the dependent variable and effective tariffs as the independent variable.

(i) To begin with, effective tariffs being the independent variable, a basic difficulty arises. The effect on the import-substitution (production-to-total-supply) ratio is not uniquely determined by the effective tariff: for the same effective tariff is compatible with different combinations of nominal tariffs on output and inputs and hence with different effects on production and consumption of the output. Therefore, even if the partial-equilibrium, supply-and-demand curves were identical across the industries, the relationship postulated would not follow unless the input-output structure and the structure of nominal tariffs on each industry's outputs and inputs were identical.

28. Nor, for that matter, did Behrman manage to find any significant association between DRCs and growth indicates.

(ii) Once we go beyond partial into general-equilibrium analysis, furthermore, the hypothesis refuses to hold up for the added reason that the theory of general equilibrium tells us unhappily that, in an n-output ($n > 2$) economy, if more than one price changes, the direction of individual output changes cannot be predicted from this fact alone: one really has to work out the full general-equilibrium solution.[29] This nihilistic conclusion carries over, of course, to a general equilibrium model with imported inputs as well.[30]

(iii) Finally, while the analytical points made above relate to the effects of the tariffs vis-à-vis the free trade situation, with given resources, the exercises testing the postulated hypothesis relate often to a situation of growing resources. But, in this event, there is even less presumption theoretically in support of the hypothesis.[31]

Thus, even within the confines of conventional economic theory, one would have serious difficulties with the hypothesis that higher effective tariffs lead to higher import-substitution ratios on a cross-sectional basis. In the context of actual developing countries, these difficulties are accentuated indeed. For example, the growth of industries is likely to reflect industrial licensing and targeting; and, as noted below in the context of QRs, anticipation of tariff protection, as distinct from initial protection, once the industry has built up to size leading to an effective political pressure group,[32] may be quite important in determining growth incentives.

29. One may further be tempted to infer (as we did in the Conference paper upon which the present paper is based) that, if there are n (> 2) different tariffs, resulting in n prices changing, there is no theoretical presumption at all for asserting that the changes in the n activities' outputs will be *correlated* with the n tariffs. However, as noted by Alan Deardorff this would be an invalid inference.

30. In fact, for predicting output changes (as one must do, if one's interest is in the import–substitution ratio), as distinct from 'value-added' changes, in models with imported inputs, the effective protection measures run into trouble even if we confine ourselves to *two* goods. This problem was first raised by V. K. Ramaswami and T. N. Srinivasan (1971) and is extensively analysed in the contributions of Bruno (1973) and Bhagwati and Srinivasan (1973) to the 'Journal of International Economics Symposium' (1973).

31. Thus, take a simple two-sector example, using the standard two-by-two model of trade theory. We know from Rybczynski's theorem that the supply curves of the two commodities will shift differentially rather than identically, so that even if the supply curves were identical in the initial situation across activities, they would cease to be so with economic expansion (unless all factors expanded uniformly). And hence any effect of the tariff structure on the import-substitution ratio would be 'muddied' by this additional growth effect. This is clearly a pertinent point when one is relating the import ratios for 1967, for example, to effective protection in 1962 (as in the Nigerian exercise reported above): a period over which the capital stock may have increased by nearly 30 per cent (assuming a capital–output ratio of 3:1 and an average savings rate of 15 per cent of GNP), and hence certainly in excess of the labour force.

32. Thus, the causal relationship may well run from the growth and size of an industry to the magnitude of its tariff protection. In fact, it is only recently that economists have begun to concern themselves with the question of why tariff structures are what they are, as distinct from what they should be. At an institutional-analytical level, the work of Padma

In fact, we must recognize many additional difficulties, specific to exchange control regimes, (where QRs typically may dominate tariffs), with the notion that observed protective structures will tell the analyst anything terribly conclusive about growth incentives. In particular, an important fact is that many developing countries have operated with rules of 'automaticity' in protection: QRs were used to grant protection as soon as domestic production was started. Once this 'institutional' feature of the system is taken into account, it is easy to see that any observed (implicit) tariff structure fails to incorporate the incentive effects of guaranteed, 'potential' tariff protection, which is clearly a significant factor on the scene. More precisely, we should not expect the resource-allocational effects of n prespecified tariffs to be identical with the effects of a process of tariff-imposition that is characterized by automatic protection to any potential activity, the degree of protection, in turn, being expected by potential investors with uncertainty regarding its precise extent (this, in turn, being dependent largely on the restrictiveness of the foreign exchange situation), and which process winds up with the n observed tariffs in place.

It is for this set of reasons that the notion of relating tariffs, effective or nominal, to the pattern of industrial expansion – no matter how measured – seems to be lacking in sufficient rationale, especially for countries with restrictive exchange-control regimes: as, indeed, several developing countries have been for the bulk of the postwar period. This may well account for the mixed nature of the statistical results reported in this section.

On balance, therefore, we should be content to take the view, admittedly less ambitious, that the differential tariff structure among different activities merely indicates, very broadly indeed, the differential nature of the incentives that exchange-control regimes in developing countries tend to generate: a conclusion that, in itself, is sufficiently interesting and important.

Next, we may note, in this context, that the differential nature of the incentives, as indicated by the differential rates of protection to different manufacturing activities, can be shown rather to result simultaneously in differential social returns from the allocation of resources in producing these alternative items. This can be done qualitatively by showing that the actual allocational criteria used for making production and investment decisions, whether through the use of QRs or through the use of domestic licensing or via both sets of instruments (as in India and Pakistan), can hardly be expected to yield anything like an economically rational

Desai on the criteria used by the Indian Tariff Commission in granting tariff protection represents one approach of interest and importance (cf. Desai, 1970). At a statistical-econometric level, the work of Basevi (1966) on examining the factor intensity of protected industries in the United States represents a different, and equally useful, approach; for an interesting analysis of the relationship between the labour force characteristics of an industry and the degree of exemption secured by it from the across-the-board 50 per cent tariff cut in the Kennedy Round, see Cheh (1974).

allocation of resources.[33] Quantitatively, it can be done by doing sophisticated cost-benefit analysis on a number of different activities, thereby showing the differential social returns resulting from different activities encouraged (or enabled to exist) by the entire framework of protection. It can also be done by using somewhat rough-and-ready calculations, such as those implied by DRC estimates, of the kind deployed in the NBER studies, which essentially use 'illustrative' shadow prices and arrive at notions of differential returns produced by different activities by estimating the foreign exchange that the same value of domestic, primary factors is producing in alternative activities. Primarily using the DRC method therefore as a rough device for estimating social returns, the NBER project does show the wide variations that obtain in the restrictive foreign trade regimes that have been deployed in the LDCs studied under the project.[34]

Finally, note that the NBER studies explicitly extend the analysis of the economic consequences of protection, as generated by restrictive foreign trade regimes, to issues such as underutilization of capacity, excessive inventory holdings, etc., with findings generally adverse to the case of those who favour the use of restrictive trade regimes. They also investigate the dynamic aspects of foreign trade regimes quite explicitly, examining the effects on domestic savings formation, foreign capital inflows and efficiency thereof, quality of entrepreneurship, technical change and innovation, etc. The general conclusion from such analyses is that there is little empirical support for those who would argue that restrictive regimes generate dynamic gains that offset the static inefficiencies that are documented in the NBER studies and that, in fact, were spelled out also in the earlier OECD studies at some length.[35]

Protection and export performance

We turn now to the issue of the degree of import substitution that corresponds, as noted earlier, to the question of the degree of protection. Two points need to be noted at the outset. First, recalling that protection is defined here, as in the NBER studies, as inclusive of the effects of the

33. This, in fact, was done in the India study of the OECD Project (Bhagwati and Desai, 1970) and was also the reason for the analytical focus on methods of exchange control in the NBER studies.

34. For detailed analytical and empirical discussion, see Bhagwati (1978, ch. 5).

35. Many of these dynamic questions were dealt with explicitly for India in Bhagwati–Srinivasan (1975), in particular; they have been considered more generally, with an eye on the entire set of countries in the NBER project, in Bhagwati (1978, chs 6–8). Note equally that, contrary to the enthusiasm of many proponents of liberalized regimes, there is no systematic evidence on their side either of dynamic efficiencies. The facts, and for that matter, the theoretical arguments, in these dynamic areas go in both directions and no general conclusions seem warranted. Cf. Bhagwati (1978).

exchange control regime via import premia etc., the analysis in this subsection will extend to the issue of whether restrictive foreign trade regimes, associated with high import premia, lead to deteriorating or inferior export performance, whereas liberalized foreign trade regimes tend to have improved export performance. Second, we should also note that the common distinction drawn between import-substituting strategy and export-promoting strategy may be made, in sharper analytical terms, by observing that the former group essentially works with a degree of protection that implies that the ratio of *EERs* for exports is less than unity, whereas the latter group of countries essentially has this ratio close to unity (as export subsidies of various types bring the *EER* for exports much closer to that for imports).[36]

There are several different types of evidence available in the NBER studies, to suggest that restrictive foreign trade regimes, with high explicit or implicit tariffs and lower-than-unity EER_x/EER_m ratios, are associated with lower export performance and that changing the overall foreign trade regime successfully in the direction of reduced reliance on exchange control and increased liberalization pays handsome dividends in terms of higher exports.

First, there is the usual type of evidence that, after successful liberalization (normally accompanied by devaluation), exports first decline and then tend to show responsiveness. This phenomenon, known in the literature on devaluation as the *J*-curve behaviour (with initial decline and later rise), has been documented for several (though by no means all) of the liberalization episodes that the NBER countries experienced and that have been studied in depth. Thus, for example, the June 1966 Indian devaluation and liberalization policy package, once adjustment was made for the exogenous decline in exports brought about by two serious agricultural droughts, showed this type of pattern of export behaviour.[37] Occasionally, attention has been focused on the short-run export response, so that the medium and long-run response, which was more favourable, has been missed by earlier analysts.[38]

Second, there is a considerable amount of statistical analysis, in the NBER studies, of the responsiveness of minor exports in particular and manufactured exports in general, which (on the basis of regression analysis using mainly time series estimates) suggests strongly that the exports of

36. In practice, the export-promoting countries do not seem to make the export *EER* identical to that for imports; but they do make it substantially closer. In theory, one should want to define export-promoting strategy as making the EER_x/EER_m ratio exceed unity, so that there is a net incentive to export rather than serve the domestic market! These issues are discussed in Bhagwati (1978, ch. 8).

37. For a full discussion of the cross-country evidence, see Krueger (1978).

38. For a notable exception, see Cooper (1971).

these developing countries are, in general, responsive to price changes. This evidence is at the microlevel for specific commodities (including sometimes even primary products) and also for broad aggregates by sectors.[39] It should be noted that the studies do deploy different indices for their price variable; and there is, indeed, here some of the tendency among econometricians to keep shifting among alternative price variables until something works. But, with this customary *caveat* in mind, we should note that the evidence broadly supports those who contend that prices do matter.

Third, Krueger's cross-sectional analysis of the ten NBER countries in her synthesis volume also seems to underline the significance of prices in improving or inhibiting the growth of exports. In her regressions, she uses dummies to represent Phases I, II, IV, and V: these refer to different degrees of restrictiveness of the trade regime (as spelled out in the NBER studies), where Phase I primarily initiates in a simple way the QR regime, Phase II represents proliferation of QRs and increased restrictiveness, Phase III is attempted liberalization, Phase IV represents successful movement toward liberalization, and Phase V is a full shift to a liberal-payments regime.[40] The Krueger regressions indicate that *PLDEER*s on exports seem to affect both traditional and non-traditional (otherwise described as minor in many of the studies) export values, and that Phases IV and V do seem to affect export performance favourably.[41]

In this regard, note furthermore that there seems to be a general case, underlined by the detailed analysis in the NBER studies, for arguing that it is really a shift to successful liberalization and therefore continuing liberalization that is critical to improved export performance on a sustained basis: i.e., a shift to Phase IV from Phase II will show such an improved performance, but not really occasional jabs at liberalization, each resulting in eventual relapse into Phase II (from Phase III liberalization attempts). Thus, it is the sustained transition during the 1960s and later from Phase II to Phase IV by South Korea, Taiwan, and Brazil that has been attended by high rates of export growth.[42]

39. This evidence would suggest that while the 2×2 trade-theoretic model, where both goods are traded, is unrealistic, the augmentation of this model with a preassigned non-traded good is also incapable of capturing reality adequately. What one needs is a model where, depending on the policy equilibrium, a good may be traded or may cease to be traded. Such a model, on Ricardian lines, was considered by Samuelson (1964) many years ago and has been recently explored by him in a joint study: Dornbusch *et al.* (1977).

40. For more systematic and careful definitions of the Phases, see any of the NBER volumes; for convenience, they are stated fully in the Appendix.

41. Cf. Krueger (1978). *PLDEER* stands for price-level deflated *EER*s.

42. The role of expectations ensuring that export incentives are seen to have been made favourable over continued periods is obviously critical to this result, for that is when entrepreneurs will wish to make investments in export markets.

Additionally, it is also worth noting that it is not just the price aspects of the restictive Phase II regimes that inhibit export performance. As has been documented in the Indian case, for example, and by contrast in the South Korean case, in the NBER studies, the whole framework of exchange controls in a Phase II situation militates against export performance. Thus, for example, the ability to expand production to fill export orders requires access to import licences for raw materials and capacity expansion requires import (and industrial) licences: in each case, red tape and uncertainty cloud the scene.[43]

Fourth, statistical analysis of the usual decomposition variety, where the export performance of several LDCs is decomposed into that attributable to overall growth of demand, regional composition, commodity composition, and a residual 'competitive' factor effect, contrasting the 1950s when most LDCs were in Phase II and the 1960s when some had successfully shifted to Phase IV, shows that the latter group of Phase IV countries had dramatically improved export performance and that a sizable share of it could be assigned to the residual, 'competitive' factor.[44] Such analysis of the 'competitive' factor is not generally considered to be as persuasive as the time-series analysis deployed in many of the NBER studies. However, it has considerable suggestive value and is corroborative of the conclusions arrived at through use of other analytical approaches.

Protection and economic performance

We may finally address the central question of whether LDCs with superior export performance also have superior economic performance and, if so, why?

There is little doubt that, in the NBER studies for example, the countries that have managed to shift to improved export performance by reducing export bias have also managed to register acceleration in their growth rates, whereas countries that have not done so (and have remained in Phase II regimes) have had poorer growth rates. The contrast between the success of South Korea and the failure of India, in this regard, is cross-sectionally the most telling.

A recent statistical analysis of Irving Kravis also supports this conclusion (1970, pp. 868–9 in particular). Using decomposition analysis to differentiate LDCs with high export performance based on domestic policies, and taking a 39-country sample, Kravis has noted a 0.51

43. Again, this is the kind of effect on exports that only Phase-change analysis can pick up statistically, if at all.

44. Cf. Askari and Corbo (1975). This statistical study also distinguishes between 'minor' and other exports, defining the 'minor' as all those exports that were below 10 per cent of the total value in the initial year.

Spearman coefficient between ranks with respect to the index of such export performance and ranks regarding the growth rate of real national product.

That the superior-export-performance countries do better compared to both their own earlier growth performance under restrictive trade regimes and other countries with inferior export performance seems therefore to be, generally speaking, a valid assertion. The interesting question is: why? Here, we have a few answers and many questions.

(1) First, it would appear that the pattern of incentives, and hence of export promotion, is less skewed in practice than the chaotic pattern of import-substituting incentives under the restrictive trade regimes. The statistical quantifications of *EER*s for several activities in South Korea, for the mid-1960s, for example, suggest that the variability (including the extremes) of incentives is significantly lower than the EER_ms for several activities in the restrictive Phase II-type regimes in other countries, such as India.[45]

Similarly, the average ratio EER_x/EER_m also seems much closer to unity (at times even exceeding unity, but remaining closer to it) under the liberalized Phase IV- or V-type regimes than under the restrictive Phase II-type regimes.[46]

Thus, it would appear that, on both the degree and the pattern questions, distinguished earlier, the export-promoting countries with liberalized regimes seem to do better. For both types of allocative reasons, therefore, one could argue that the resulting reduction in allocative inefficiency must provide some of the explanation of the improved export performance that is observed for the liberalized-regime countries. But, in turn, one must ask the question as to why these incentives are less chaotic and more 'neutral', by and large, under the liberalized trade regimes.

The reasons would seem to consist in the fact that the successful shift to export-promoting strategy (or Phase IV) generally takes place within the overall context of continuing exchange controls, and that the QR-caused bias against exports is offset by giving the import premia to exporters through schemes such as supply of imported materials at international prices, etc.,[47] and by using exchange rate adjustment more freely and thereby directly reducing import premia and hence the bias against exports. The result is generally (not always) to eliminate or reduce the bias against exports rather than to create excessive bias for exports.

45. For a more detailed analysis, including statistical and analytical reasons for possible scepticism regarding this observation, consult Bhagwati (1978, ch. 8).

46. In fact, Bhagwati (1978) therefore defines the export-promoting strategy as one where EER_x/EER_m is brought fairly close to unity.

47. There is much documentation of these schemes of export promotion in the NBER studies. Cf. in particular, Bhagwati-Srinivasan (1975) on India and Frank *et al.* (1975) on South Korea.

Because of budgetary considerations, cash subsidies that could conceivably create massive bias for exports are usually not substantial (though not unknown). On the other hand, the import-substituting strategy, especially via the mechanisms of import premia from QRs, can and has typically caused EER_m to get way out of line with EER_x (which was then determined almost exclusively by the exchange rate): and the costs of such a substantial rise in EER_m/EER_x above unity are generally not understood and, in any case, do not fall directly on the budget.

(2) Next, the sheer improvement in export performance, following from the elimination of the bias against exports, must surely play the major role in the full explanation. The links here are possibly diverse.

(i) The NBER studies suggest that there is little evidence that the export-promoting countries are technically more progressive or that they have higher savings rates because of a larger export sector.[48] The asymmetry in the export-promoting and import-substituting countries' economic performance cannot thus be traced, at least on current evidence, to superiority of the one strategy over the other on these dynamic grounds, even though the proponents of each strategy often indulge in assertions to that effect.

(ii) Part of the answer rather appears to be in the fact that a more comfortable balance-of-payments position, resulting from improved export incentives and earnings, generally eases up the excesses of the import-substituting strategy. This should be obvious from the well-known demonstration that, under a foreign exchange bottleneck (in the sense of Chenery), additional foreign exchange is more productive than under a savings bottleneck. But it is also apparent from the fact that it eases excess capacity (generated largely by the QR regime in the first place[49]), may reduce the need to hold excess inventories, and leads often to elimination of critical bottlenecks, etc. It is perhaps remarkable that these kinds of problems, attendant on economies in the restrictive Phase II, are rarely to be found in the liberalized Phase IV and V economies that have successfully transited to export-promoting strategy on a continuing basis.

(iii) In regard to the general easing of the balance of payments (and hence of the losses that attend restrictive payments policies) under the export-promoting strategy, it is also worth noting that this effect is reinforced by the substantial inflow of foreign capital that can attend such a strategy. While political factors help to explain the substantial inflows of foreign private investment in South Korea, these are undoubtedly to be supplemented by economic factors. And here one

48. These questions have been examined in detail, analytically and empirically, in Bhagwati (1978, chs 6 and 7).
49. On this point, see the arguments in Bhagwati and Srinivasan (1975, ch. 13).

probably ought to attribute to the export-promoting strategy itself the sizable magnitude of the inflow of non-aid foreign funds and its efficacy in promoting economic growth. By contrast, under import-substituting strategy, both the magnitude of the inflow and its social returns are likely to be lower. This contrast may be explained as follows.

Regarding magnitude, an export-promoting strategy, with its lack of discrimination against foreign markets, is likely to attract foreign firms essentially on the nineteenth-century pattern of factor-endowment advantages. Whereas in the nineteenth-century, this meant natural resources, today it means exploiting Heckscher–Ohlin style low wages. On the other hand, by creating artificial inducement to invest via tariffs and/or QRs, so that one gets 'tariff-jumping' investments oriented to the domestic market alone, the import-substituting strategy provides an artificially limited incentive to invest in the LDC. Furthermore, even the substantial official borrowings by South Korea and Brazil in the international capital markets surely must have been facilitated by the demonstration of a superior export performance (for, that would assuage fears of excessive borrowing and inability to repay).

Then again, in regard to efficiency, it is easy to show that 'tariff-jumping' investments, induced under the import-substituting strategy, are more likely to imply social losses or (at minimum) reduced gains than investments attracted by Heckscher–Ohlinesque factors. That foreign capital inflow can be not merely less productive when inspired by QRs and/or tariffs, but actually immiserizing, has been shown elegantly by Brecher and Diaz-Alejandro in a recent paper.[50] For the traditional 2×2 model of trade theory, they show that social utility for the small country, having declined with the tariff, will decline further with the initial inflow of foreign capital when the importable good is capital-intensive. It will continue to decline with additional inflows of foreign capital until autarky is reached, then rise gradually to the level under free trade (a situation discussed by Mundell, 1957), remain at that level for further inflows and, finally, start rising after complete specialization in production is reached (a situation discussed by MacDougall, 1958).

While the factors noted in the preceding paragraphs would seem to be critical in defining the asymmetrical outcomes under the import-substituting and the export-promoting strategies, some additional factors may be cited that might contribute to the asymmetry, but for which no systematic evidence is yet available.

(iv) Thus, one could argue that the export-promoting strategy may lead to a generally reduced reliance on direct or physical, as distinct from price,

---

50. Brecher and Diaz-Alejandro (1977). This possibility was noted, in the context of the same model, but less fully, in Uzawa (1969); Hamada (1974); Minabe (1974); and Bhagwati (1973).

measures.[51] Direct controls have been argued with plausibility, in both the OECD and NBER studies, to be very costly in practice. It is possible that the general incidence of such direct controls may be significantly less under export promotion, because price, distribution, and other controls may make little sense to bureaucrats when firms' outputs are mainly addressed to overseas, rather than domestic, markets. A different, and perhaps more perceptive, formulation of this kind of contrast was well put by an economist familiar with both the Indian (Phase II) and the South Korean (Phase IV) trade regimes: the Indian regime consists mainly of 'don'ts' whereas the Korean regime consists mainly of 'do's'. Whether these contrasts are, in a basic political sense, endemic to the two strategies being contrasted is not clear; but the NBER studies do suggest that they exist currently.

(v) In the still more grey area, one may further argue that the export-promoting strategy must produce, through international competition, greater efficiency than the import-substituting strategy, with its sheltered markets. While this argument is plausible *a priori*, there is as yet no real evidence at all on the subject. The issue is also complex, as the domestic competition may be sufficient to provide the incentive to efficiency under import-substitution, whereas exports may be to imperfectly competitive foreign markets or may simply be subsidized to the point necessary to offset any possible inefficiency-raised cost disadvantage.

(vi) Finally, there is the factor of economies of scale, long recognized in international trade theory and policy discussions relating to customs unions, free trade areas, and similar areas where the size of the market is critical to the analysis of economic efficiency. In relation to export promoting strategy, it seems plausible to argue that the creation of incentives (or rather, the elimination of the disincentives) to enter the foreign markets augments the size of the market and hence should enable greater exploitation of economies of scale. Again, however, the issue is more complex insofar as the growth of firm size may be constrained by other policies and objectives (as in India), so that export promotion may take place from firms with constrained sizes by diversion from domestic production and/or by growth of new, licensed firms of small size. Again, therefore, the statistical evidence and analysis of this possible cause of asymmetrical advantage of the export-promoting strategy is not yet available in anything like a degree that would be reasonably compelling; but it does remain a plausible hypothesis.

It is finally important to note that once industrialization is on its way the basic difference between the two trade strategies is not in the degree of

51. The points in this paragraph and the next two were made, with slight differences in emphasis, in Bhagwati and Krueger (1973).

industrialization opted for; rather it is in the efficiency of the industrialization process. In fact, the export-promoting strategy merely implies a more rapid transition from import substitution to a substantial reduction of the bias against manufactured exports and, insofar as it is successful, may yield both more rapid and more substantial industrialization than the continued reliance on import-substituting strategy would. The familiar view in some developing countries and of their policy-makers that the export-promoting strategy may result in reduced industrialization is therefore not based on an accurate understanding of the strategy and its precise contrast to the import-substituting strategy.

2   THE INTERNATIONAL TRADE SYSTEM: POLICY AND THEORETICAL PROBLEMS

While the preceding section underlines the developmental advantages that have accrued to the export-promoting countries, a necessary corollary to such a prescription for more than just a handful of LDCs is that the world trading system be reasonably open and accommodating to the trade needs of such a strategy. In fact, the problems that Japan has run into in regard to her international economic policy-making illustrate this point to advantage. It is thus not merely that Japan has often had an 'undervalued' Yen in the sense of generating a net surplus but also that, even if she was not building up exaggerated reserves and was instead spending all her export earnings, she would create waves because her growth rate, and the associated trade expansion, are just too great for the more sluggish rest-of-the-world to accommodate without serious disruptions of sectoral markets that lead to unceasing calls for VERs and other trade restrictions against Japanese exports.

Ragnar Nurkse, as we have seen, was quite aware of this problem for the export-promoting strategy; and the OECD project authors took the precaution also of stressing this when recommending against the import-substitution strategy. In fact, one cannot suppress the thought that the success stories of South Korea, Taiwan, Brazil, Singapore, and Hong Kong would not have been quite so impressive if they had not been built on the failures of the countries sticking overly long to import-substituting strategy and their consequent export (and associated economic) lag.

As it happens, the threats to a liberal international trade order come today from precisely the area of market disruption-related complaints in the DCs in regard to manufactures that must yield to growing imports and from the demands, in turn, from LDCs to extend restrictive arrangements to *primary commodities* as part of the New International Economic Order (NIEO). Both these threats are serious and both raise not merely policy but also theoretical issues of interest to international economists.

Market disruption-related threats

The political economy of tariff-making has received increasing attention recently, with empirical investigation by economists such as Cheh, Riedel, and Baldwin.[52] The result has been to focus on the nature of the adjustment costs that are likely to be imposed by shifts in trade policy or in trade environment, and therefore on the nature of the political opposition to the adoption or maintenance of open trade policies.

At the same time, trade theorists have tried to model the nature of adjustment costs. The model used by Mayer, in his recent work on the distinction between short-run and long-run equilibria, is based on the notion that, in the short run, the adjustment to commodity price change will be not along the usual transformation curve characterized by full mobility of factors but along one resulting from stickiness of capital in each activity and mobility of only labour.[53] On the other hand, we have argued recently that this notion of adjustment costs is too narrow; that the adjustment cost may exist because of, and in fact is more likely to reflect, the stickiness of real wages *à la* Brecher.[54] Equally, it may reflect stickiness of wages combined with initial unwillingness to move, with the former reducing as mobility also improves, so that the short run may well be realistically portrayed as the case where factors will not move and unemployment will ensue because of stickiness of wages.

From a theoretical standpoint, the interesting analytical issues that the threat of market disruption-related imposition of QRs and other trade restrictions poses are the following: (i) what should an exporting country that faces such a threat do by way of optimal policy intervention; and (ii) what should be the GATT rules governing the issue of market disruption-related invoking of trade restrictions? We have shown that the answer to the former question turns out to fall neatly into place in the traditional theory of distortions and welfare. Where the probability of the quota being invoked is endogenous to the level of (first-period) exports, clearly an optimal tariff argument follows: you need to take into account the increased probability of trade restraint, and hence loss of welfare, in the next period as a result of improved export performance in the first period. Moreover, if we also postulate a putty-clay model, such that first-period investments cannot be costlessly reassigned in the

52. Cf. the pioneering paper of John H. Cheh (1974); James Riedel (1977); and the comprehensive and excellent paper by Robert E. Baldwin (1976).

53. Cf. Mayer (1974). Of course, it is not the specificity of capital that causes adjustment problems, as suggested strongly by the work of Cheh (1974) and Riedel (1977), but rather the specificity of labour in the short run.

54. Cf. Bhagwati and Srinivasan (1976), where the analysis of adjustment costs is general enough to embrace the different possibilities discussed in the text above. Among related papers of interest are Tolley and Wilman (1977); Mayer (1977); and Lapan (1976).

second period, clearly, a production tax-cum-subsidy will be required to take this additional complication into account: and this is, of course, nothing but the 'adjustment costs' problem which, as just noted, may be modelled in different ways.[55] Building on this analysis, and the implied notion that the exporting country faces a loss in expected utility from the mere threat of trade restraints, Bhagwati has also suggested how the GATT Article XIX, which regulates (ineffectively, given VERs and bilateral deals) the exercise of market disruption-related invoking of trade restraints, may be revised and compensation rules be devised in regard thereto.[56]

On the other hand, the problem of revision of trade rules in regard to market disruption may be approached analytically by posing the question, not merely from the perspective of the exporting LDCs (just as the existing policies are largely reflecting only the importing DC interests *de facto*), but by considering the problem from the viewpoint of world optimality. If this is done, it is evident that the analytical problem is really one of determining the optimal assignment of adjustment costs between the country of importation and the country of exportation, since one or the other must adjust. As such, the problem becomes analytically similar to the recent analysis of assignment of liability in the 'law-and-economics' literature, with the adjustment costs, however, being spelled out by analytical specification of the nature of stickiness of wages, factor immobility, etc.[57]

Demands for commodity schemes

While the LDCs have been stressing the necessity to keep the DC markets open to increasing imports of manufactures from LDCs, they have simultaneously shifted recently to demanding restrictive and orderly arrangements in the markets for primary products. How is this paradox to be explained?

There are many explanations of the current LDC preference for commodity agreements, in their indexing form as distinct from their stabilization (of prices or perhaps earnings) form, but all would seem to miss the mark. Thus, it is often alleged that the commodity demands stem from the early Latin American preoccupation with the declining terms of trade of primary products, under the aegis of Prebisch and then

55. Both these conclusions, of course, are consistent with the Bhagwati–Ramaswami–Srinivasan–Johnson type of conclusions that the optimal policy intervention should be in the markets where the problems arise. For details, see Bhagwati and Srinivasan (1976).

56. For details, see Bhagwati (1977). The subject has also attracted proposals from other economists, notable among them being Hans Singer.

57. This has been noted in Bhagwati and Srinivasan (1976) and also happens to have been independently suggested by Gerald Meier in an undated paper.

UNCTAD (of which Prebisch was the first secretary-general). But if, indeed, this is so, one has to ask why it is only recently that such demands have come to the centre of the stage: Sherlock Holmes did well to ask why the dog didn't bark! Alternatively, it has been suggested that the UNCTAD believes that economic progress is to be had by monopolistic cartelization and commodity schemes that rig prices at artificially high levels, rather than by the kinds of internal reform that accompany the economic advance in the presently developed countries. This too is a *non sequitur*. There is absolutely no contradiction between believing in the role of internal reforms (on whose dimensions, incidentally, most economists will disagree) and desiring a larger share of the gains from trade. The reasons why commodity schemes with the ultimate objective of indexing, and to be implemented by the LDCs and DCs in concerted action, have come to the forefront of the North–South negotiations have to be surely found elsewhere than in these theories.

There are, on the one hand, economic-philosophical reasons for these demands; on the other hand, there are also accidents-of-history type considerations here. Both must be understood if the demands are to be met by a reasonable response.

The economic-philosophical reasons are essentially the following. First, the LDC economists understand, what we have known with some clarity now since the developments in welfare economics since the 1940s, that the economics of the marketplace is about economic efficiency and not about distributive justice. Thus, it is not intellectually foolish to argue that a price is unjust or unfair when the international income distribution that it reflects is unjust or unfair; rather, these economists know that it is naive to claim any more that opportunity cost is the touchstone of economic justice. Joan Robinson, despite her nascent radicalism, fell into the trap of calling 'exploitation' the payment of a wage below the value of the factor's marginal product; she would probably burn *The Economics of Imperfect Competition* today! Second, many LDC economists find it increasingly baffling that DCs that have not been averse to resorting to indexing for their own constituencies on a massive scale–as with the US agricultural price-support programme–somehow find the idea to be an unacceptable violation of the principles of the marketplace when the idea is sought to be applied internationally: it seems reminiscent of the nineteenth-century English enthusiasm for free trade for the colonies and protection for domestic textiles. Finally, few LDC economists will accept the view that indexing by commodity agreements will disrupt competitive markets that currently assure economic efficiency. Here, there is room for further analysis, since it is not at all evident that the LDC economists' contention that these markets are already characterized by much intervention, willy nilly, and much monopolistic competition to the advantage of the DCs, is altogether bizarre. Thus, while the large number of oft-failing commodity agreements since World War II have been cited as evidence of the difficulty of getting such agreements designed and operated, they can equally well be cited as evidence of the considerable amount of intervention to which most commodity markets have been subjected during this period. Also, Gerry Helleiner has recently compiled the evidence on the degree to which market concentration operates in the world commodity trade and come up with what appeared to us at least to be substantially high figures of trade between related parties and of import concentration (in national markets) in the hands of a very small number of trading firms (see, for example, Helleiner, 1978). Of course, none of these latter facts automatically establish the existence of significant monopsonistic buying by DCs; we have all been sufficiently educated in the theory of entry, working competition, etc., to know that these facts are still consistent with the threat of entry by new firms and, therefore, competitive pricing may still be possible. However, in the face of this factual evidence on the existing structure of international trade in primary products, one needs to await systematic econometric analyses designed to enable us to choose among the two alternative hypotheses.

But if these factors account for why the LDCs are not persuaded that the market efficiency-based criticisms are well taken, the causes of their being wedded to the commodity schemes currently lie instead in political-economic factors that are probably the accidental results of the successes of the OPEC cartel. The OPEC cartel succeeded in unilaterally raising the price of a natural resource sevenfold in two years, against a backdrop of falling (real) aid flows from North to South and increasing sentiment that the path of moral suasion for raising the South's share in world income was unproductive. The OPEC seemed therefore to provide a new model: the LDCs, by acting jointly *qua* producers of commodities, would be able to raise their prices unilaterally. 'Solidarity rather than charity' is the slogan that best captures this transition in the ethos in the South in the early post-OPEC years. Unfortunately, the LDCs were encouraged in this sentiment by DC economists who thought that this commodity power was nothing special to oil but really extended to other commodities: an argument that seems to have held only for bauxite in any significant degree. Thus, the initial shift in the South's strategy from that in the earlier UNCTAD Conferences and Group of 77 deliberations appears to have been toward the formation of producer groups to exercise unilaterally this alleged monopolistic power in individual commodities. Hence, the new-found focus on commodity schemes.

However, it was soon realized that the scope for such unilateral action was strictly limited and certainly self-destroying in the medium run because of induced-substitution possibilities. Since, however, the commodity schemes were 'on' as the focal point of international negotiations, the emphasis soon shifted to making these commodity schemes joint

LDC–DC, or producer-consumer, schemes, with the DC support being induced through political pressures brought from the South *en bloc* at UNCTAD, at CIEC, and so on. Thus, starting as the great new Southern weapon that would bring automatic and increased transfers of the incomes of the affluent countries to the poor ones, the commodity-scheme demands would appear to have become now the mere conduit through which transfers of resources would be made, these transfers to be induced by the exercise of political power, directly exerted by the LDCs *en bloc* at CIEC, and indirectly brought to bear on their behalf (with clearly much greater clout) by the OPEC members.

If this diagnosis is correct, the ultimate and true interest of the LDCs in commodity arrangements lies in their embodying some form of indexing (that would presumably procure higher, average terms of trade for the selected primary commodities than otherwise). This diagnosis would seem to derive additional support from two other observations: (i) the recent Group of 77 and UNCTAD documents, while carefully avoiding exclusive focus on indexing, never fail to include the notion in their proposed objectives for commodity schemes; and (ii) the commodities chosen for inclusion in the UNCTAD Integrated Plan for Commodities are not necessarily those characterized by severe (absolute or relative) instability in prices or earnings and, in fact, include items, such as tea, whose problem has always been that of low trend earnings.

It would thus appear that the alleged UNCTAD/CIEC willingness to negotiate stabilization, as against indexing, versions of commodity schemes is only tactical, designed to get some schemes going and then to make a move to indexing at an appropriate, future stage.

This judgment of LDC intentions is, of course, thoroughly compatible with the view that, by some strange quirk of coincidence, the price stabilization of commodities that are included in the UNCTAD Core Plan would yield a net transfer of resources from the stabilization *per se*: a view advanced recently by Jere Behrman (1977) on the basis of econometric analysis of the markets for these commodities. Thus Behrman estimates that price stabilization for the commodities in the UNCTAD Integrated Plan would have created a modest resource transfer to the LDCs of the order of US $5 billion in present value over the decade 1963–72. His simulations show that any buffer stock scheme intended to raise, rather than merely stabilize, prices is unlikely to succeed, since even a modest price increase of 2 per cent annually in the secular price trends above their historical growth rates would result in accumulation of enormous stocks and would require unrealistically large financing.[58]

58. The analysis in the text focuses on transfer of revenue to LDCs from the price-stabilization schemes. However, if we are interested in the welfare impact of price stabilization along conventional lines–it may be argued that welfare, as distinct from revenue

Turning then to the DCs, we may note that, if the DCs were faced with demands explicitly aimed at indexing, the prospects for commodity agreements would be negligible indeed. On the other hand, the DCs (and the United States specifically) have now indicated willingness to explore stabilization agreements. A cynical motivation behind this might well be to keep the North–South dialogue going for years to come, debating the rules and the specific commodities *ad nauseam*, while giving the appearance of responsiveness to LDC demands at relatively low cost. On the other hand, it appears that several DC policy makers are of the view that price stabilization commodity schemes offer economic advantages to the DCs and that, therefore, here is an opportunity to grant an NIEO demand at a negative cost to the DCs, as long as indexing is firmly ruled out! There are really only two principal arguments underlying this view. First, that purchasers of primary products tend to be risk-averse and would favour price stability; and, second, that the inflationary effects of changes in primary product prices are asymmetrical and lead to a ratchet effect: primary product price increases lead to overall price inflation, whereas their downturn does not reverse the overall price increase.

It is doubtful, however, that these arguments can support the case for an accommodation to the demands for commodity agreements, even if these are confined to stabilization arrangements. The risk-aversion that is admittedly rather strong at the moment surely reflects the phenomenally unusual commodity price boom of 1972–5: its remarkably unusual character having been noted and analysed in the Cooper–Lawrence (1975) study for Brookings. Thus, they write: 'An extraordinary increase in commodity prices occurred in 1973–4. Even leaving aside crude oil as a special case, primary commodity prices on one index more than doubled between mid-1972 and mid-1974, while the prices of some individual commodities, such as sugar and urea (nitrogenous fertilizer), rose more than five times. While the timing differed from commodity to commodity, the sharp upward movement was widespread, affecting virtually all commodities. Most rose dramatically to twenty-year highs, and many went to historical highs.' It is a fairly well-known generalization that when prices are on the upswing, consumers want price stability, whereas, producers want price stability on the downswing. Thus, one should probably treat as transient the present warmth toward price stability in

transfer, impact is of interest only to economists rather than to LDC governments–then there is now an extensive literature on the distribution of welfare gains between producers and consumers from price stabilization, starting from the classic contributions of Waugh, Oi, and Massell. This literature has been surveyed recently by Turnovsky. The empirical issues, such as cost of stabilization, choice of commodities, as well as the econometrics underlying these are discussed among others by Behrman and Brook, *et al.*. Cf. Waugh (1944): Oi (1961); Massell (1969); Turnovsky (1977); Brook *et al.* (1977); and Behrman (1977).

the DCs. Nor is this judgment to be qualified by the argument that users, who fear quantitative shortfalls through withholding of supplies and embargos, would welcome price stability schemes: there is nothing in commodity agreements that would prevent such flow-disruptions and the appropriate method to approach the problem of export controls, so as to restrain their use to agreed rules of the game, may well lie in the general reform of GATT rules, whereby DCs agree to new market-disruption rules that restrain greatly their practice of clamping down on successful LDC exports and thus guarantee freer access by LDCs to DC markets, while LDCs reciprocally agree to a new set of rules that restrain their use of quantitative export controls on primary commodities and thereby maintain freer access by DCs to LDC supplies of primary products.

While, therefore, the risk-aversion argument in favour of price-stabilization commodity schemes is not particularly appealing to us, the macro-economic argument on the ratchet effect is even less so. Admittedly, there is something to it: oil and wage goods obviously qualify for it. There even seems to be some empirical evidence in support of such a ratchet effect.[59] But, surely, it hardly applies to most of the commodities in which LDCs have invested their efforts for the commodity schemes. Again, just as LDCs made the mistake of generalizing from oil to other commodities in arrogating to themselves 'commodity power' for unilateral price-raising, the DCs would appear to be making the mistake of generalizing the ratchet effect from oil, steel, and food to other commodities.

Our conclusions then are the following:

(i) the LDCs have as their major objective an increase in the current transfer of resources from the rich to the poor countries;

(ii) the LDCs stumbled mistakenly into commodity schemes as the new (OPEC-inspired) model for unilaterally achieving this objective;

(iii) the LDCs, having realized that such unilateral power scarcely existed in a significant degree outside oil, switched then to regarding commodity schemes as the conduit through which DCs could be politically pressured into transferring resources via indexing *à la* domestic price-support programmes;

(iv) the 'true' objective of the LDCs is therefore to turn commodity agreements into indexing arrangements and the 'noise' about stabilization etc. in UNCTAD/Group of 77/CIEC documents and demands is, at best, tactical;

(v) the DCs, on the other hand, are opposed to indexing but are inclined, in some cases, to see in price-stabilization arrangements benefits to themselves;

59. For detailed discussion, see the interesting papers of Nicholas Kaldor (1976) and Erik Lundberg (1977).

(vi) these benefits, however, are unlikely to be significant, have been mistakenly exaggerated, and will probably be seen to be so in the near future;

(vii) the North–South willingness, if it crystallizes (as would seem imminent), to negotiate commodity schemes on the basis of price stabilization is then unlikely to lead to more than a transitory accommodation: the LDCs will soon wish to move to indexing, which the DCs will oppose and reject, whereas, the DCs will soon come to see even the stabilization schemes as nuisances, rather than as benefits, to themselves;

(viii) therefore, far from promoting a smooth or amicable North–South relationship, the present focus on commodity schemes as part of the NIEO is a certain recipe for disorder: the LDCs will get next to nothing from the schemes while investing a massive political effort into getting them floated; and the DCs will have accomplished nothing worthwhile if they do mean to improve the flow of resources to the poor countries (though, those who aim at a no-give response should consider this to be a happy outcome, of course);

(ix) therefore, it is of the utmost importance to bury the commodity schemes and to shift attention instead to the more traditional remedies for any of the problems that may be raised for LDCs by commodity revenue instability and to respond to NIEO demands by developing new and efficient resource-transfer proposals;

(x) the traditional remedies for the problems associated with revenue instability include compensatory financing facilities for LDCs to tide over the periods of lean foreign exchange earnings, and domestic buffer stock schemes for those countries that wish to cushion their producers and/or consumers; this being the early, classic prescription of Ragnar Nurkse and also what has transpired satisfactorily with the successive augmentations of the special compensatory financing facilities at the IMF; and, finally, we may note that

(xi) in regard to resource transfers, there are new resource transfer possibilities that amount either to taxing disexternalities (such as overfishing) or rents (such as from mining the seabeds or from skilled migration in the presence of severe immigration quotas) whose adoption could be explored.[60]

APPENDIX

DEFINITION OF PHASES IN THE NBER PROJECT

In order to demarcate in an analytically useful manner the evolution of a country's exchange-control regime, the NBER Project delineated

---

60. For estimates and analysis, see the papers by Richard Cooper and Koichi Hamada in Bhagwati (1977). See also Bhagwati and Partington (1976).

a number of phases which were used in the country studies and are to be found in the two synthesis volumes as well. It should be noted that, while each study identifies the phases through which the country's payments regime passed, there is no presumption, and in fact the evidence shows there to be none as well, that the phases would be gone through necessarily in a predefined sequence.

Phase I: During this period, quantitative restrictions on international transactions are imposed and then intensified. They generally are initiated in response to an unsustainable payments deficit and then, for a period, are intensified. During the period when reliance upon quantitative restrictions as a means of controlling the balance of payments is increasing, the country is said to be in Phase I.

Phase II: During this phase, quantitative restrictions are still intense, but various price measures are taken to offset some of the undesired results of the system. Heightened tariffs, surcharges on imports, rebates for exports, special tourist exchange rates, and other price interventions are used in this phase. However, primary reliance continues to be placed on quantitative restrictions.

Phase III: This phase is characterized by an attempt to systematize the changes which take place during Phase II. It generally starts with a formal exchange-rate change and may be accompanied by removal of some of the surcharges, etc., imposed during Phase II and by reduced reliance upon quantitative restrictions. Phase III may be little more than a tidying-up operation (in which case the likelihood is that the country will re-enter Phase II), or it may signal the beginning of withdrawal from reliance upon quantitative restrictions.

Phase IV: If the changes in Phase III result in adjustments within the country, so that liberalization can continue, the country is said to enter Phase IV. The necessary adjustments generally include increased foreign-exchange earnings and gradual relaxation of quantitative restrictions. The latter relaxation may take the form of changes in the nature of quantitative restrictions or of increased foreign-exchange allocations, and thus reduced premiums, under the same administrative system.

Phase V: This is a period during which an exchange regime is fully liberalized. There is full convertibility on current account, and quantitative restrictions are not employed as a means of regulating the *ex ante* balance of payments.

REFERENCES

Askari, H., and Corbo, V. (1976): 'Export promotion: its rationale and feasibility'. Mimeo.
Balassa, B., and associates (1971): *The Structure of Protection in Developing Countries* (Baltimore: The Johns Hopkins Press for IBRD).

Baldwin, R. (1975): see NBER (3).

—— (1976): 'US tariff policy: formation and effects', *International Trade, Foreign Investment, Employment Discussion Papers*, US Department of Labor, Bureau of International Labor Affairs.

Basevi, G. (1966): 'The United States tariff structure: estimates of effective rates of protection of United States industries and industrial labor', *Review of Economics & Statistics*, pp. 147–60.

Behrman, J. (1976): see NBER (9).

—— (1977): 'International commodity agreements', Overseas Development Council, *NIEO* Series.

Bergsman, J. (1970): see OECD (2).

Bhagwati, J. N. (1968): *The theory and practice of commercial policy: departures from unified exchange rates* Frank Graham Memorial Lecture (1967); Special Papers in International Economics, No. 8 (Princeton: Princeton University Press).

—— (1972): 'Trade policies for development', in *The Gap between Rich and Poor Nations*, Proceedings of an International Economic Association Conference in Bled, Yugoslavia (New York: Macmillan).

—— (1973): 'The theory of immiserizing growth: further applications', in M. B. Connolly and A. K. Swoboda (eds) *International Trade and Money* (Toronto: University of Toronto Press).

—— (1976): 'Protection, industrialization, export performance and economic development', paper prepared for UNCTAD IV conference held in Nairobi.

—— (1977): 'Market disruption, export market disruption, compensation and GATT reform', in J. Bhagwati (ed.) *The New International Economic Order: the North–South Debate* (Cambridge, Mass.: MIT Press).

—— (1978): *Anatomy and Consequences of Exchange Control Regimes*. See NBER (1978).

—— and Desai, P. (1970): see OECD (3).

—— and Krueger, A. (1973): 'Exchange control, liberalization and economic development', *American Economic Review*, 53 (2), pp. 419–27, reprinted in this volume.

—— and Partington, M. (eds) (1976): *Taxing the Brain Drain: A Proposal*, volume I (New York: North-Holland).

—— and Srinivasan, T. N. (1973): 'Contribution to the symposium on the theory of effective protection in general equilibrium', *Journal of International Economics*, 3.

—— (1975): see NBER (6).

—— (1976):'Optimal trade policy and compensation under endogenous uncertainty: the phenomenon of market disruption', *Journal of International Economics*, 6, pp. 317–36.

Brecher, R., and Diaz-Alejandro, C. (1977): 'Tariffs, foreign capital and immiserizing growth', *Journal of International Economics*, 7, pp. 317–22.

Brook, E. M., Grilli, E. R., and Waelbroeck, J. (1977): 'Commodity price stabilization and the developing countries: the problem of choice', World Bank Staff Paper No. 262.

Bruno, M. (1973): 'Contribution to the symposium on the theory of effective protection in general equilibrium', *Journal of International Economics*, 3.

Cheh, J. (1974): 'United States concessions in the Kennedy Round and short-run labor adjustment costs', *Journal of International Economics*, 4, pp. 323–40.

Cooper, R. (1971): *Currency Devaluations in Developing Countries.* International Finance Section, Princeton University Special Papers No. 86.

—— (1977): 'Oceans as a source of revenue', in J. Bhagwati (ed.), *The International Economic Order: The North-South Debate* (Cambridge, Mass.: MIT Press).

—— and Lawrence, R. (1975): 'The 1972-75 commodity boom', *Brookings Papers on Economic Activity*, 3, pp. 671.

Desai, P. (1970): *Tariff Protection and Industrialization: A Study of the Indian Tariff Commission at Work* (Delhi: Hindustan Publishing Corporation).

Diaz-Alejandro, C. (1975): 'Trade policies and economic development', in P. Kenen (ed.), *International Trade and Finance: Frontiers for Research* (Cambridge: Cambridge University Press).

—— (1976): see NBER (8).

Dornbusch, R. (1974): 'Tariffs and nontraded goods', *Journal of International Economics*, 4, pp. 177-85.

Dornbusch, P., Fischer, S. and Samuelson, P. (1977): 'Comparative advantage, trade and payments in Ricardian model with a continuum of goods', *American Economic Review*, 67, pp. 823-39.

Frank, C., Westphal, L., and Kim, K. S. (1975): see NBER (5).

Guisinger, S. (1971): 'The characteristics of protected industries in Pakistan', in H. G. Grubel and H. G. Johnson (eds), *Effective Tariff Protection* (Geneva: General Agreement on Tariffs and Trade).

Haberler, G. (1959): *International Trade and Economic Development* (Cairo: National Bank of Egypt).

Hamada, K. (1974): 'An economic analysis of the duty-free zone', *Journal of International Economics*, pp. 225-41.

—— (1977): 'Taxing the brain drain: a global point of view', in J. Bhagwati (ed.), *The New International Economic Order: The North-South Debate* (Cambridge, Mass.: MIT Press).

Hansen, B., and Nashashibi, K. (1975): see NBER (7).

Helleiner, G. (1977): 'Freedom and management in primary commodity markets: US imports from developing countries'. *World Development*, 6 (January), pp. 23-30.

Hsing, M., Power, J., and Sicat, G. (1970): see OECD (5). 'Journal of International Economics symposium on the theory of effective protection in general equilibrium' (1973): *Journal of International Economics*, 3.

Kaldor, N. (1976): 'Inflation and recession in the world economy', *Economic Journal* (December).

King, T. (1970): See OECD (6).

Kravis, I. (1970): 'Trade as a handmaiden of growth: similarities between the nineteenth and twentieth centuries', *Economic Journal* (December).

Krueger, A. (1975): see NBER (1).

—— (1978): *Liberalization Attempts and Consequences.* See NBER (1978).

Lapan, H. (1976): 'International trade, factor market distortions, and the optimal dynamic subsidy', *American Economic Review*, 66.

Leith, J. (1975): see NBER (11).

Lewis, S. (1970): see OECD (4).

Lewis, W. A. (1969): *Aspects of Tropical Trade: 1883-1965.* Wicksell Lectures (Stockholm: Almquist & Wicksell).

Little, I., Scitovsky T., and Scott, M. (1970): see OECD (1).

Lundberg, Erik. (1977): 'World inflation and national policies'. Stockholm: Institute for International Economic Studies Seminar Paper No. 80.

MacDougall, G. (1958): 'The benefits and costs of private investment from abroad: a theoretical approach', *Economic Record*, 36, pp. 13–35.

Massell, B. (1969): 'Price stabilization and welfare', *Quarterly Journal of Economics*, 83, pp. 284–98.

Mayer, W. (1974): 'Short-run and long-run equilibrium for a small, open economy', *Journal of Political Economy*, 82, pp. 955–67.

—— (1977): 'The national defense tariff reconsidered', *Journal of International Economics*, 7, pp. 363–77.

Meier, G. 'Externality law and market safeguards'. Undated, mimeographed.

Michaely, M. (1975): see NBER (2).

Minabe, N. (1974): 'Capital and technology movements and economic welfare', *American Economic Review*, 64, pp. 1088–1100.

Mundell, R. (1957): 'International trade and factor mobility', *American Economic Review*, 47, pp. 321–35.

National Bureau of Economic Research (NBER) (1975) for (1)–(7); (1976) for (8)–(9):

    (1)   Krueger, A. *Foreign Trade Regimes and Economic Development: Turkey.*

    (2)   Michaely, M. *Foreign Trade Regimes and Economic Development: Israel.*

    (3)   Baldwin, R. *Foreign Trade Regimes and Economic Development: Philippines.*

    (4)   Leith, J. *Foreign Trade Regimes and Economic Development: Ghana.*

    (5)   Frank, C., Westphal, L., and Kim, K. S. *Foreign Trade Regimes and Economic Development: South Korea.*

    (6)   Bhagwati, J., and Srinivasan, T. N. *Foreign Trade Regimes and Economic Development: India.*

    (7)   Hansen, B. and Nashashibi, K. *Foreign Trade Regimes and Economic Development: Egypt.*

    (8)   Diaz-Alejandro, C. *Foreign Trade Regimes and Economic Development: Colombia.*

    (9)   Behrman, J., *Foreign Trade Regimes and Economic Development: Chile.*

    (All New York: Colombia University Press).

—— (1978) (Cambridge, Mass.: Ballinger).

    Krueger, A. *Foreign Trade Regimes and Economic Development: Liberalization Attempts and Consequences* (Cambridge, Mass.: Ballinger).

    Bhagwati, J. *Foreign Trade Regimes and Economic Development: Anatomy and Consequences of Exchange Control Regimes* (Cambridge, Mass.: Ballinger).

Nurkse, R. (1959): *Patterns of Trade and Development*, Wicksell Lectures (Stockholm: Almquist & Wicksell).

Oi, W. (1961): 'The desirability of price stability under perfect competition', *Econometrica*, 29, pp. 58–64.

Organization for Economic Cooperation and Development (OECD) (1970):

    (1)   Little, I., Scitovsky, T., and Scott, M., *Industry and Trade in Some Developing Countries: A Comparative Study.*

    (2)   Bergsman, J., *Brazil: Industrialization and Trade Policies.*

    (3)   Bhagwati, J., and Desai, P., *India: Planning for Industrialization.*

    (4)   Lewis, S., *Pakistan: Industrialization and Trade Policies.*

(5) Hsing, M., Power, J., and Sicat, G., *Taiwan and the Philippines: Industrialization and Trade Policies.*

(6) King, T., *Mexico: Industrialization and Trade Policies since 1940.*

(All Paris: OECD; London: Oxford University Press)

Oyejide, T. A. (1971): 'Tariff protection and industrialization via import substitution: an empirical analysis of the Nigerian experience', *Bangladesh Economic Review*, 1, pp. 331–40.

Ramaswami, V. K., and Srinivasan, T. N. (1971): 'Tariff structure and resource allocation in the presence of substitution', *Trade, Balance of Payments and Growth*, in J. Bhagwati *et al.* (eds) (New York: North-Holland).

Riedel, J. (1977): 'Tariff concessions in the Kennedy round and the structure of protection in West Germany: an econometric assessment', *Journal of International Economics*, 7, pp. 133–44.

Samuelson, P. A. (1964): 'Theoretical notes on trade problems', *Review of Economics & Statistics* (May), pp. 145–54.

Soligo, R. and Stern, J. J. (1965): 'Tariff protection, import substitution, and investment efficiency', *Pakistan Development Review* (Summer), pp. 249–70.

Tolley, G. S. and Wilman, J. D. (1977): 'The foreign dependence question', *Journal of Political Economy*, 85, pp. 232–47.

Turnovsky, S. (1977): 'The distribution of welfare gains from price stabilization: a survey of some theoretical issues'. Paper presented at Ford Foundation Conference on Stabilizing World Commodity Markets.

Uzawa, H. (1969): 'Shihon Jiyuka to Kokumin Keizai [Liberalization of Foreign Investments and the National Economy]', *Economisuto*.

Viner, J. (1953): *International Trade and Economic Development* (Oxford: Clarendon Press).

Waugh, F. (1944): 'Does the consumer benefit from price instability?', *Quarterly Journal of Economics*.

7

Foreign Trade Regimes

What prescriptive conclusions may then be drawn regarding the optimal foreign trade strategy to be followed by developing countries? The issue of the appropriate foreign trade strategy was posed as early as the 1950s by some of the leading international economists of the day, with Ragnar Nurkse arguing for what would be described today as the import-substituting strategy on the grounds of elasticity pessimism and Gottfried Haberler, Jacob Viner, and others arrayed on the other side in favour of what might be described currently as the export-promoting strategy.[1]

Interestingly, Alex Cairncross, in reviewing the relative arguments of Nurkse and Haberler had ended on a somewhat neutral note between these two strategies, appealing for a verdict from empirical evidence in the following terms:

> At the end of it all, the reader may still feel that neither Nurkse nor Haberler has settled the primary issue: how far a shortage of foreign exchange (contrasted with capital, skilled labour, land, etc.) is a limiting factor in economic development. The majority of the under-developed countries are monocultures, dependent for their earnings of foreign exchange on a single commodity (or at most two or three). These earnings are highly inelastic except when exports of the principal commodity form a small fraction of the world's consumption. At the same time, nearly all the plant and machinery that they require has to be imported, so that the scale of industrial investment is limited by the foreign exchange available to pay for it. In those circumstances, what should be the policy of a country seeking to accelerate its development? We know what most countries have done; it would be interesting if we could be told, by an economist of the standing of Nurkse or Haberler, what the results have been and what they should have done. (Cairncross, 1962, p. 208).

1. Cf. Viner (1959), Nurkse (1959) and Haberler (1959). Raul Prebisch has also been identified generally with the import-substituting position. [The following quote from Cairncross appears also in Chapter 6 and has been retained for its appropriateness here.]

From J. N. Bhagwati, *The Anatomy and Consequences of Exchange Control Regimes* (Cambridge, Mass.: Ballinger for the NBER, 1978), pp. 206–18. References to that volume are abbreviated as *Anatomy*.

As it happens, the results of the present Project, as also the earlier analysis in the well-known OECD Project directed by I. M. D. Little, Tibor Scitovsky, and Maurice Scott (1970) do contain an answer to Cairncross's celebrated query. It seems to come down in favour of the export-promoting trade strategy–in the manner and for reasons, and with nuances and reservations, to be discussed in the rest of this chapter.

1 EXPORT-PROMOTING VERSUS IMPORT-SUBSTITUTING STRATEGY AND RELATIONSHIP TO PHASE ANALYSIS

The import-substituting (IS) and export-promoting (EP) trade strategies need to be defined carefully. This is particulary important as the phrase 'import substitution' is often used 'somewhat loosely' as a decline in the ratio of imports in total supply of individual activities. This definition then is a purely statistical artifact without any theoretical meaning or underpinning.[2]

The meanings that we will impart here to the two rival trade strategies are best illustrated by reference to an idealized theoretical model as follows. Thus consider the traditional model of international trade theory where primary factors produce two traded goods X and Y; and with the customary restrictions on production functions, we generate a production possibility curve such as AB in Figure 7.1. If CD is the given international price ratio, a free trade policy that equates domestic to foreign prices of the commodities will bring production to P^* in a perfectly competitive situation. (Note that, under these assumptions, the free trade policy is also socially optimal, an implication to which we will return later).[3] It is evident then that a trade regime that equates EER_x with EER_m in this model happens to be one that also implies the choice of such a free trade policy and will lead to production at P^*. Consider, however, the presence of a foreign trade regime that leads to $EER_x < EER_m$. This will imply a shift in equilibrium production to a ('distorted') point such as $\hat{P}$ where the relative production of the importable commodity Y has moved *up* from what it was at P^*.

We therefore may *define* a policy of import substitution (IS) as one where the effect of the foreign trade regime is to make $EER_x/EER_m < 1$,

2. For a systematic analysis of the measures of import substitution, as used in the statistical literature by economists such as Hollis Chenery, and for a clear statement of the need to define the concept analytically, rather than as a departure from initial import to supply ratio, see Desai (1969).

3. The conditions under which such optimality of free trade may break down have been analysed in depth in the literature on trade and distortions. For a synthesis of these results see Bhagwati (1968, 1971) and Johnson (1965).

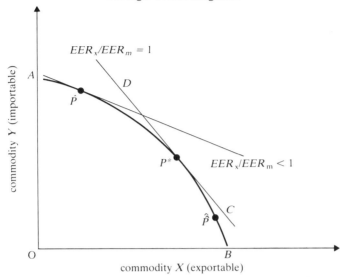

FIGURE 7.1   Definition of import-substituting and export-promoting strategies

implicitly comparing it with the free-trade position that makes $EER_x/EER_m = 1$ and eschewing any welfare connotations from the definition. Asymmetrically, however, we will define the export promoting (EP) policy as one where, by contrast with the IS policy, EER_x/EER_m is restored to unity. This eliminates the bias against the exportables and in favour of the importables that the IS policy (with $EER_x/EER_m < 1$) implies, rather than reversing it in the other direction such that $EER_x/EER_m > 1$, which would lead, for example, to production in Figure 7.1 at a point such as $\widehat{\widehat{P}}$ to the right of P^*.

The reason for this asymmetrical choice of definition of the EP strategy is that the countries that are popularly regarded as 'export-promoting' because of their successful export performance happen to offset, rather than turn on its head, the export bias implied by $EER_x < EER_m$. This is possibly one of the important reasons, as we shall presently see, for their successful *economic* performance.[4]

The link of these definitions with the Phases utilized in the Project studies is relatively straightforward since Phase II, which represents the restrictive foreign trade regime, is essentially one characterized by $EER_x/EER_m < 1$ and therefore by the IS strategy whereas the liberalized trade regimes of Phases IV and V evidently bring this ratio significantly closer to unity and hence are characterized by the EP strategy.

These 'neutral' definitions leave open the question whether the *degree* of import substitution that is implied by the IS strategy is optimal or not.

4. Note that all definitions are essentially arbitrary and must be chosen so as to reflect analytical convenience.

They also do not address the related question as to whether the *pattern* of interindustrial import substitution under the Phase II regimes, as observed in the Project studies, is also suboptimal; and, if so, whether the *pattern* of interindustrial export composition under the Phase IV and V regimes, as actually studied in the Project, is economically more mindful of costs and benefits and hence superior under the EP than under the IS strategy. The answers to both these questions, among others, are pertinent to the explanation of the superior economic performance that, as already noted in the preceding chapter, attends on the EP strategy in Phases IV and V.

2   REASONS FOR SUPERIORITY OF EXPORT-PROMOTING STRATEGY: SOME HYPOTHESES

Drawing in a stylized fashion on the evidence in the Project studies on the many issues already alluded to in *Anatomy*, we may now note that the evidence suggests that, while one source of the economic superiority of the EP strategy is the possible 'neutrality' of the incentives that define the pattern of industrial and export composition under this strategy as against the 'chaotic' non-neutrality of the incentives that arise in the IS strategy, almost certainly the more important source of superiority comes from the mere fact of the improved economic performance that follows from the removal of the bias against exports under the EP strategy.

Pattern of import substitution versus pattern of export composition

We have already noted in depth the chaotic pattern of import substitution that emerges under the IS strategy implied by Phase II. In large part, it should be noted, this is a consequence of the fact that the foreign trade regime leads to indiscriminate import-substituting incentives as a result of overvalued exchange rates. In principle, import-substituting incentives could be far less chaotic and more neutral across different industries if tariffs were utilized instead on an across-the-board basis, for example.

It would appear that, by contrast, the calculations of EER_x for different industries in South Korea during Phase IV suggest a less chaotic pattern of interindustrial incentives (NBER, *South Korea*, p. 84). Whether this contrast is regarded as sufficiently large depends, to a considerable degree, on the significance that is attached to the calculations of EERs, which are the *ad valorem* equivalents of a number of incentives that contain the usual share of 'indirect' incentives such as the link-up of domestic profitability to export sales. It also depends, to some degree, on the significance that is attached to the presence of export *targeting*, which, if it acts as a 'stick' as it definitely did in South Korea in the mid-1960s (NBER, pp. 46–7), would seem to be a counterpart of the physical targeting that attends on import substitution in Phase II economies.

As it happens, there is also some statistical argumentation to suggest that the export promotional policies in a Phase IV country such as South Korea may have led to some wasteful export promotion, rather similar to the wasteful import substitution noted for Phase II countries. Thus, Wontack Hong has produced estimates recently of social losses from certain exports from South Korea.[5]

But when all this is noted, it still seems reasonable to conclude that the EP strategy under Phases IV and V does appear, in practice, to be characterized by a less chaotic and more neutral pattern of interindustrial incentives than does the IS strategy under Phase II. Whether this contrast is truly large and, in turn, makes for a substantial impact on the returns to overall investment is difficult to judge, however.[6] That it should go *some way* toward explaining the superior growth performance of the EP strategy countries, on the other hand, should not be open to serious dispute.

The degree of import substitution and effects of superior export performance

The more important source of superior economic performance of the EP economies would seem to lie, however, not in the efficiency of the export-composition pattern *vis-à-vis* that of the import-substitution pattern, but rather in the indisputable fact of the vastly improved export performance. The interesting and important question is: why? A number of links between superior export and improved economic performance can be suggested and their importance assessed.

First, it should be noted, in conformity with the observation above regarding the relatively greater neutrality of export incentives across

5. Wontack Hong (1976). The Hong study utilizes input-output techniques rather than the technique of valuing inputs and outputs at international prices, which is more appropriate to the problem at hand and which was used to demonstrate the 'extreme' example of wasteful export promotion represented by value subtraction at international prices for exported items in earlier studies of India and Pakistan. For a theoretical examination of the value subtraction phenomenon, see Bhagwati *et al.* (1978).

6. Scepticism about the size of the impact may stem from the somewhat tenuous nature of the effective incentive calculations (as noted); it may also follow from a Harberger-type notional calculation suggesting that the allocative losses tend to be excessively small fractions of national income anyway. The latter argument, however, is conditional on a rather static view of reallocation of given resources: once growing resources are taken into account, as they should be for our present purposes, the estimated losses may be much larger. See the extended discussion of this point in J. Bhagwati (1968) [also reprinted in *EIET*, vol 2, ch. 1].

different exportables under the EP strategy, that the EP trade regime does not equally tend to carry the export subsidization, on the average, to such lengths as actually to make the ratio EER_x/EER_m substantially *greater* than unity, that is, the EP strategy amounts by and large to, and is therefore in fact defined here to be characterized by, having the ratio EER_x/EER_m fairly close to unity.[7]

It would thus appear plausible to conclude that the EP strategy tends generally to be less given to overall excesses than the IS strategy and that, in practice, this may be the source of its asymmetrical economic advantage. If so, we must ask again why this asymmetry exists in practice. The reasons would seem partly to consist in the fact that the successful shift to export-promoting strategy (or Phase IV) generally takes place within the overall context of continuing exchange controls but that the QR-caused bias against exports is offset by giving the import premiums to exporters through schemes such as supply of imported materials at international prices, and so on,[8] and by using exchange rate adjustment more freely and thereby directly reducing import premiums and hence the bias against exports. The result is *generally* (not always) to eliminate or reduce the bias against exports rather than to create excessive bias *for* exports. Because of budgetary considerations, cash subsidies that could conceivably create massive bias for exports are usually not substantial (though not unknown). On the other hand, the import-substituting strategy, especially via the mechanisms of import premiums from QRs, could and did typically cause the EER_m to get way out of line with EER_x (which was then determined almost exclusively by the exchange rate). The costs of such a *substantial* fall in EER_x/EER_m below unity are generally not understood and, in any case, do not fall directly on the budget.

Second, equally important might be the sheer fact that a more comfortable balance of payments position, resulting from improved export incentives and earnings, generally eases up the excesses of the IS strategy. This should be obvious from the well-known demonstration that, under a foreign exchange bottleneck (in the sense of Chenery), additional foreign exchange is more productive than under a savings bottleneck. But it is also apparent from the fact that a comfortable external payments situation

7. For evidence on this, see NBER, *South Korea*, Tables 5–10, which uses *PPPEERs* rather than *EERs* and also see Krueger (1978), Table X-2, where the *EERs* for Israel and South Korea are given for 1955–71 and 1961–70, respectively. Needless to say, there are exceptions on several specific commodities where export subsidization does get carried beyond to EER_x/EER_m being greater than unity in varying degrees: this being part of the chaotic policy incentives commented on earlier; and in the South Korean case the average EER_x/EER_m ratio has also often tended to be higher than unity, while remaining fairly close to it.

8. A great deal of evidence on such schemes is to be found in the Project studies [also see Bhagwati, 1978, ch. 2].

eases up excess capacity (generated largely by the QR regime in the first place), may reduce the need to hold excess inventories, and leads often to elimination of critical bottlenecks, and so on [see Bhagwati, 1978, ch. 5]. It is perhaps remarkable that these kinds of problems, attendant on economies in Phase II, are rarely to be found in Phase IV and V economies that have successfully transited to the EP strategy on a continuing basis.

Third, in regard to the general easing of the balance of payments (and hence of the losses that attend restrictive payments policies) under the EP strategy, it is also worth noting that this effect has been reinforced in the Project countries by the substantial inflow of foreign capital that seems to attend such a strategy.[9] While different political factors help to explain the substantial inflows of foreign funds in South Korea, Brazil, and Israel, these are undoubtedly to be supplemented by economic factors in the case of the former two countries. For South Korea, in particular, the proportion of gross investment coming from foreign saving has run at well over a third on the average and, as a proportion of GNP, foreign saving has run at an average of as much as around 10 per cent during 1960–71 (see NBER, *South Korea*, pp. 106–7).

This inflow is *not* exogenous to the EP strategy, as is sometimes assumed, but can be seriously argued to be a result in large part of the EP strategy itself. Thus, while the bulk of the Korean and Brazilian influx of foreign funds is through public *borrowing* rather than through inflow of direct investment, this borrowing would not have been possible were it not for an export performance that was perceived to be truly remarkable and as a sign of the ability of the country to avoid the 'transfer problem' difficulties that could otherwise be expected to follow from sizeable external borrowing. It is of course well known that private bankers (and the IBRD, Asian Development Bank, etc., which are included under 'private' in at least some statistics) look at debt-service/export ratios, so that loans are rather directly linked, in some fashion, to export performance. Hence, it may even be legitimate to regard Brazil's 'export-led' growth as merging, *via* this link between export performance and foreign borrowings, into what Fishlow calls the 'debt-led' model of economic growth.

Besides, it can be argued that the large-scale inflow of *direct investment*, which has also been more sizeable in South Korea (as a per cent of GNP)

---

9. The general easing of the balance of payments in Brazil was also aided, as Fishlow has reminded the author, by the fact that, from the mid-1960s, the Brazilian terms of trade changed quite favourably. Thus, while exports in nominal terms were increasing at rates of more than 30 per cent, the volume increase was a much more modest (though impressive) 10 per cent approximately.

than in the other countries in the Project, reflects the EP strategy.[10] In fact, it may be argued that, under the EP strategy, both the magnitude of the private (direct) investment inflow *and* its efficacy in promoting economic growth will be greater over the long haul than under the IS strategy. This contrast may be explained as follows. Regarding *magnitude*, an EP strategy, with its lack of discrimination against foreign markets, is likely to attract foreign firms essentially on the nineteenth-century pattern of 'factor endowment' advantages. Whereas in the nineteenth century, this meant natural resources, today it means exploiting Heckscher–Ohlin style low wages. On the other hand, by creating 'artificial' inducement to invest *via* tariffs and/or QRs, so that one gets 'tariff-jumping' investments oriented to the domestic market alone, the IS strategy provides an artificially limited incentive to invest in the country. The lack of complete time-series data on direct investment magnitudes in the countries in the Project and elsewhere prevents a statistical examination of this hypothesis. But it seems reasonable enough, with due adjustments being made for differences among countries on account particularly of their economic size, political attitudes to foreign investment, and political stability more generally.

As regards the *efficiency* of foreign direct investment under the EP strategy, it can again be argued that 'tariff-jumping' investments, induced by the IS strategy, are more likely to imply social losses or (at minimum) reduced gains than investments attracted by Heckscher–Ohlinesque factors. Thus, following a long line of theoretical writings by Uzawa, Hamada, Minabe, and Bhagwati, and independently thereof, Brecher and Diaz-Alejandro have recently argued succinctly that tariff-induced investment in a 2×2 trade-theoretic model of a small open economy that imports capital-intensive goods will, for small changes, *worsen* the welfare loss that the tariff itself implies (Brecher and Diaz-Alejandro, 1977). In this model, it can be shown that successive imports of foreign capital will lead to welfare changes as illustrated in Figure 7.2. Thus the tariff leads to decline in social utility from F to T; successive inflows of capital thereafter reduce welfare until autarky is reached at A; then welfare starts

10. Ian Little has pointed out to the author that, in the case of Taiwan, which is not included in the Project but is a successful example of the EP strategy, foreign direct investment has not been important. In Taiwan, according to his estimates, private foreign investment was negligible in the 1950s, and from 1960 to 1966 it still only averaged about US\$4 mn (including overseas Chinese investment which may be about 30 per cent of the total). This represented 6½ per cent of average fixed capital formation in manufacturing. Judging by approvals, 43 per cent of the cumulative total had gone into electrical machinery and electronics, followed by chemicals, non-electrical machinery and instruments, and the rest nowhere. It is also notable that the multinational company making goods for export to itself or its own sales organization was important only in electronics (and this is also true of South Korea). Another fact which puts foreign investment in perspective is that, in 1976, only 21 out of the 321 largest industrial corporations were foreign.

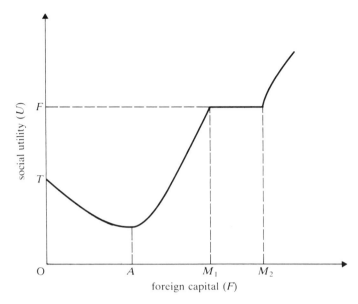

FIGURE 7.2   Welfare effect of successive inflows of capital in presence of tariff distortion.

improving as the domestic price ratio moves toward the international price ratio; with M_1, the two price ratios are equal, as in Mundell (1967), and further inflows will leave welfare at this, free-trade-equivalent, level until complete specialization is reached and then the MacDougall-type (MacDougall, 1960) gains will follow from diminishing returns to inflowing capital. As long, therefore, as the IS strategy leads to inflows within the range OA (short of autarky), which seems reasonable, the inflow of foreign capital will be immiserizing rather than welfare improving.

Finally, there is some statistical argumentation in the Project studies to indicate that the IS strategy may be sometimes growth reducing because the import-substituting industries happen (empirically) to be capital intensive relative to the exportable industries. Systematic evidence on this possibility is found in Chile by Behrman[11] and for Turkey, in particular, by Krueger who presents a detailed statistical exercise of the incremental income that would then have followed from a reallocation of investments within the manufacturing sector so as to reflect a 'moderate import-

11. NBER, *Chile*, pp. 275–80 and p. 286: 'Finally, the foreign-sector regime also might alter the aggregate capital-output ratio through changes in the allocation of investment by destination among production sectors with different capital intensities . . . above, in fact, evidence is reported of more restrictive regimes leading to greater investment in more capital-intensive subsectors.'

substitution' strategy and alternatively a 'balanced export promotion and import substitution' strategy. She concludes that the latter alternative would have resulted in a 'considerably higher rate of growth of manufacturing output'.[12]

It may also be noted here that a more complex programming exercise by Bhagwati and Srinivasan, using the well-known Eckaus-Parikh optimizing planning model for India, also shows that an improved export performance would have resulted in a greater value of the objective function. However, the critical role in this outcome seems to be played, not by the relative capital-output requirements of the exportables and the importables but rather by the fact that the planning model builds into itself the foreign exchange constraint possibility and the 'better-export-performance' alternative enables the planner to get around this with greater benefit as evaluated by the specified objective function.[13]

While the factors just noted are probably the ones that are critical in defining the asymmetrical outcomes under the IS and the EP strategies, some additional factors may be cited that might contribute to the asymmetry but for which no systematic evidence is yet available.

Thus, one could argue that the export-promoting strategy may lead to a *generally* reduced reliance on direct or physical, as distinct from price, measures.[14] Direct controls have been argued with plausibility, in the Project studies as also in the earlier OECD work, to be very costly in practice. It is possible that the general incidence of such direct controls may be significantly less under export promotion because price, distribution, and other controls may make little sense to bureaucrats when firms' outputs are mainly addressed to overseas, rather than domestic, markets. A different, and perhaps more perceptive, formulation of this kind of contrast was well put by an economist familiar with both the Indian (Phase II) and the South Korean (Phase IV) trade regimes. The Indian

12. NBER, *Turkey*, p. 261 and pp. 255–63. Krueger is careful to take into account possible objections regarding the marketability of the resulting increases in exportable production. She also explores the import content and employment implications of the alternative allocational strategies.

13. NBER, *India*, ch. 14. The authors emphasize the illustrative nature of their exercise but conclude that: 'On balance, we still consider the present exercise to be instructive in its illustration of the growth potentiality of additional exports (in the manner precisely set out at the outset of this chapter), simply because any unhappy features of the model will affect both the simulation and the reference runs; and there seems to us to be no clear presumption that the *difference* between the two runs, attributable to the change in the export vector, will be significantly affected. We should also note, to avoid unnecessary confusion, that the Eckaus-Parikh model is a *planning* model and *not* an econometric (behavioural-predictive) model so that the reader should not be surprised by discrepancies between the model's simulation runs and actual developments in the Indian economy' (p. 198).

14. The points in this paragraph and the next two were made, with slight differences in emphasis, in Bhagwati and Krueger (1973).

regime consists mainly of 'don'ts' whereas the Korean regime consists mainly of 'do's'. Whether these contrasts are, in a basic political sense, endemic to the two strategies being contrasted is not clear; but the Project studies do suggest that they exist currently.

In the still more grey area, one may argue that the EP strategy must produce, through international competition, greater efficiency than the IS strategy with its sheltered markets. While this argument is plausible *a priori*, there is as yet no real evidence at all on the subject. The issue besides is complex as the domestic competition may be sufficient to provide the incentive to efficiency under import substitution whereas exports may be to imperfectly competitive foreign markets or may simply be subsidized to the point necessary to offset any possible inefficiency-raised cost disadvantage. There is little convincing evidence on these questions yet.

Then, there is the factor of economies of scale, long recognized in international trade theory and policy discussions relating to customs unions, free trade areas, and similar cases where the size of the market is critical to the analysis of economic efficiency. In relation to the EP strategy, it seems plausible to argue that the creation of incentives (or rather, the elimination of the disincentives) to enter the foreign markets augments the size of the market and hence will lead to greater exploitation of economies of scale. Again, however, the issue is more complex insofar as the growth of firm size may be constrained by other policies and objectives (as in India) so that export promotion may take place from firms with constrained sizes by diversion from domestic production and/or by growth of new licensed firms of small size. Again, therefore, the statistical evidence and analysis of this possible cause of asymmetrical advantage of the EP strategy is not yet available in anything like the degree that would be reasonably compelling; but it does remain a plausible hypothesis.

Finally, it should be noted that there is little evidence that the EP countries are technically more progressive or that they have higher savings ratios because of a larger export sector. The superior economic performance of the EP strategy therefore cannot be additionally explained, at least on current evidence, by these 'dynamic' considerations.

3   CONCLUDING OBSERVATIONS

Thus, on the basis of substantially more detailed and systematic analysis of growth effects than before and on the Phasewise classification of the country experiences, the present Project studies have managed to provide fairly persuasive support to the proponents of the EP strategy, as defined here. The results also point carefully in the direction of a number of unsettled hypotheses that might assist in explaining this superiority of the EP strategy and therefore suggest further areas for systematic investigation.

At the same time, as is evident from the companion synthesis volume of Professor Krueger, the Project throws considerable light on the question as to how the transition to the EP strategy might be successfully made, starting from the restrictive foreign trade regimes associated with the IS strategy. Thus the Project manages to go a substantial way in the direction of filling a lacuna in the previous studies of the trade and payments policies of developing countries.

While however, the Project underlines the developmental advantages that have accrued to the countries utilizing the EP strategy and also illuminates the manner in which restrictive foreign trade regimes may be successfully reshaped toward this end, a corollary to such a prescription for more than just a handful of developing countries is that the world trading system be reasonably open and accommodating to the trade needs of such a strategy. In fact, the problems that Japan has run into in regard to her international economic policymaking illustrate this point to advantage. It is thus not merely that Japan has often had an undervalued yen but also that, even if she was not building up exaggerated reserves and was instead spending all her export earnings, she would create waves because her growth rate, and the associated trade expansion, are just too great for the more sluggish rest of the world to accommodate without serious disruptions of *sectoral* markets that lead to unceasing calls for VERs (voluntary export restrictions) and other trade restrictions against Japanese exports.

Ragnar Nurkse, writing in the 1950s, was quite aware of this problem for the EP strategy. The OECD Project authors took the precaution also of stressing this when recommending against the IS strategy.[15] In fact, one cannot suppress the thought that the success stories of South Korea, Taiwan, Brazil, Singapore, and Hong Kong would not have been quite so impressive if they had not been built partly on the failures of the countries sticking overly long to the IS strategy and their consequent export (and associated economic) lag.

Nonetheless, as the Project results have made clear, even if the growth of protectionism in the international economic system prevents the world markets from accommodating the exports that would ensue if all or many developing countries followed the EP strategy, and therefore they would have to be import substituting in response to this external situation, it does not follow that the Phase II type policies of chaotic import substitution *pattern* have also to be accepted. The latter are, in principle, avoidable by the pursuit of Phase IV and V type liberalized trade regimes,

15. Cf. Nurkse (1959), and Little, Scitovsky and Scott (1970, ch. 8).

while utilizing relatively neutral across-the-board tariffs so as to achieve *both* the required degree of import substitution *and* a rational pattern of it as well. A policy of exchange rate overvaluation, resulting in Phase II, is empirically a typically more expensive way to undertake the import substitution that may be required by an unfavourable external environment.

APPENDIX

DEFINITION OF CONCEPTS USED IN THE PROJECT

Exchange rates

(1) *Nominal exchange rate:* The official parity for a transaction. For countries maintaining a single exchange rate registered with the International Monetary Fund, the nominal exchange rate is the registered rate.

(2) *Effective exchange rate (EER):* The number of units of local currency actually paid or received for a one-dollar international transaction. Surcharges, tariffs, the implicit interest forgone on guarantee deposits, and any other charges against purchases of goods and services abroad are included, as are rebates, the value of import replenishment rights, and other incentives to earn foreign exchange for sales of goods and services abroad.

(3) *Price-level-deflated (PLD) nominal exchange rates:* The nominal exchange rate deflated in relation to some base period by the price level index of the country.

(4) *Price-level-deflated EER (PLD-EER):* The EER deflated by the price level index of the country.

(5) *Purchasing-power-parity adjusted exchange rates:* The relevant (nominal or effective) exchange rate multiplied by the ratio of the foreign price level to the domestic price level.

Devaluation

(1) *Gross devaluation:* The change in the parity registered with the IMF (or, synonymously in most cases, *de jure* devaluation).

(2) *Net devaluation:* The weighted average of changes in EERs by classes of transactions (or, synonymously in most cases *de facto* devaluation).

(3) *Real gross devaluation:* The gross devaluation adjusted for the increase in the domestic price level over the relevant period.

(4) *Real net devaluation:* The net devaluation similarly adjusted.

Protection concepts

(1) *Explicit tariff:* The amount of tariff charged against the import of a good as a percentage of the import price (in local currency at the nominal exchange rate) of the good.

(2) *Implicit tariff:* (or, synonymously, tariff equivalent): The ratio of the domestic price (net of normal distribution costs) minus the c.i.f. import price to the c.i.f. import price in local currency.

(3) *Premium:* The windfall profit accruing to the recipient of an import licence per dollar of imports. It is the difference between the domestic selling price (net of normal distribution costs) and the landed cost of the item (including tariffs and other charges). The premium is thus the difference between the implicit and the explicit tariff (including other charges) multiplied by the nominal exchange rate.

(4) *Nominal tariff:* The tariff–either explicit or implicit as specified– on a commodity.

(5) *Effective tariff:* The explicit or implicit tariff on value added as distinct from the nominal tariff on a commodity. This concept is also expressed as the effective rate of protection (ERP) or as the effective protective rate (EPR).

(6) *Domestic resources costs (DRC):* The value of domestic resources (evaluated at 'shadow' or opportunity cost prices) employed in earning or saving a dollar of foreign exchange (in the value-added sense) when producing domestic goods.

DELINEATION OF PHASES USED IN TRACING THE EVOLUTION OF EXCHANGE CONTROL REGIMES

To achieve comparability of analysis among different countries, each author of a country study was asked to identify the chronological development of his country's payments regime through several phases. There was no presumption that a country would necessarily pass through all the phases in chronological sequence. [The five phases distinguished have been defined at the end of chapter 6 in this volume.]

REFERENCES

Bhagwati, J. (1968): *The Theory and Practice of Commercial Policy: Departures from the Unified Exchange Rates*, Frank Graham Memorial Lecture (1967), Special Papers in International Economics, No. 8 (Princeton: Princeton University Press).
—— (1971): 'The generalized theory of distortions and welfare' in J. Bhagwati *et al.* (eds), *Trade, Balance of Payments and Growth* (Amsterdam: North-Holland).

[—— (1978): *The Anatomy and Consequences of Exchange Control Regimes* (Cambridge, Mass.: Ballinger for NBER).]

—— and Krueger, A. (1973): 'Exchange control, liberalization and economic development', *American Economic Review*, 53 (2), pp. 419–27; reprinted in this volume, ch. 4.

——, Srinivasan, T. N. and Wan, H. Jr (1978): 'Value-subtracted, negative shadow prices of factors in project evaluation, and immiserizing growth: three paradoxes in the presence of trade distortions', *Economic Journal* (March), 88, pp. 121–5; reprinted in *EIET*, vol. 1, ch. 39.

Brecher, R. and Diaz-Alejandro, C. (1977): 'Tariffs, foreign capital and immiserizing growth', *Journal of International Economics*, 7, pp. 317–22.

Cairncross, A. (1962): *Factors in Economic Development* (London: Allen and Unwin).

Corden, W. M. (1974): *Trade Policy and Economic Welfare* (London: Oxford University Press).

Desai, P. (1969): 'Alternative measures of import substitution', *Oxford Economic Papers* (November), pp. 312–24.

Haberler, G. (1959): *International Trade and Economic Development* (Cairo: National Bank of Egypt).

Hong, W. (1976): 'Distortions and static, negative marginal gains from trade', *Journal of International Economics* (May).

Johnson, H. G. (1965): 'Optimal trade intervention in the presence of domestic distortions', in R. E. Caves, H. G. Johnson and P. B. Kenen (eds), *Trade, Growth and the Balance of Payments* (Amsterdam: North-Holland).

Krueger, A. (1978): *Liberalization Attempts and Consequences* (Cambridge, Mass.: Ballinger for NBER).

Little, I., Scitovsky, T. and Scott, M. (1970): *Industry and Trade in some Developing Countries: a Comparative Study* (London: Oxford University Press).

MacDougall, G. D. A. (1960): 'The benefits and costs of private investment from abroad', *Economic Record*, 36, pp. 13–35.

Mundell, R. A. (1967): 'International Trade and Factor Mobility', *American Economic Review*, 49, pp. 321–5.

NBER: see list of references at the end of ch. 6 in this volume.

Nurkse, R. (1959): *Patterns of Trade and Development*, Wicksell Lectures (Stockholm: Almquist & Wicksell).

Viner, J. (1953): *International Trade and Economic Development* (Oxford: Clarendon Press).

8

The Nature of Balance of Payments Difficulties in Developing Countries

In this brief paper I propose to set down a few ideas (1) concerning the kind of balance of payments difficulties that the developing countries face, (2) treating them in relation to traditional analyses of balance of payments problems and then (3) discussing how the balance of payments policies followed by these countries may be sub-optimal as a result of confusion concerning these problems.

1 BALANCE OF PAYMENTS DIFFICULTIES IN THE SENSE OF 'BOTTLENECKS'

Several authors, including Professor Arthur Lewis and others, have recently written about how foreign exchange is the 'bottleneck' to an increase in investment in the developing countries. What I shall do here therefore is to develop and discuss this idea of a 'bottleneck' of foreign exchange, which certainly is not at the heart of traditional balance of payments or trade theory.

It is extremely easy to illustrate how foreign exchange, or rather the opportunity to transform goods one has into goods one wants, can limit the possibility of raising real investment. 'Ceilings' or 'bottlenecks' imposed by foreign exchange or savings (domestically) may be seen readily in relation to a simple model where an economy produces corn with the help of imported tractors purchased with (saved and) exported corn. Suppose that this economy wishes to raise its investment, i.e. at any point of time, increase the stock of tractors. Now, it may be that it is impossible for the Government of the economy to make its inhabitants consume less corn and then transform this additional corn, via trade, into additional tractors. In this case, there is surely a 'savings' ceiling or bottleneck on raising the real investment. On the other hand, assume that it is possible to raise the saving in the economy, in the sense that the inhabitants are persuaded or taxed into consuming less corn. Then if the additional corn cannot be sold abroad, or leads to no additional foreign exchange earnings (implying unit elasticity of foreign demand with respect to price), then no addition to tractors and hence to real investment is possible. In this

From *Measures for Trade Expansion of Developing Countries* (Tokyo: Japan Economic Research Center, 1966).

case, the 'limitation', 'ceiling', 'bottleneck' is provided by 'foreign trade', 'foreign exchange' or, what seems most appropriate, the opportunity to exchange goods in trade.

Once one sees the problem in its most elementary way, as stated above, it is easy to see that what many developing countries are saying is that their ability to raise investment and growth of income is constrained by a foreign exchange bottleneck. This is also the implicit conclusion of many writers on the balance of payment projections and 'gaps' in the future.

Now, what I wish to do here is to see whether these conclusions are not subject to qualification. When one thinks about the question more deeply, certain qualifications do come up.

(1) Practically any factual analysis of underdeveloped countries which one reads shows that export earnings could increase if certain internal policies were followed. For example, this has been shown to be the case for India by Professor Singh in his recent analysis of India's export performance during 1950–62. What appears to have prevented this from happening is that internal objectives, including domestic consumption, have taken more priority than the earning of foreign exchange. Thus, for instance, the export of edible oils, which had an excellent foreign market, was actively controlled in the interest of domestic consumption. Similarly, the modernization of the cotton textile industry has been interfered with in the interest of domestic employment in handlooms. A similar analysis for Egypt by Professor Bent Hansen has also shown that the bottleneck or ceiling (in the strict sense) to investment is not foreign exchange as such; foreign exchange earning could be increased by increasing staple exports but this would be, in his judgment, detrimental to domestic income distribution. A similar problem arises on the import side as well when imported items of consumption are required. If the pattern of consumption could be allowed to shift, via a change in relative prices, then the need for imported goods for consumption could be reduced, making it possible in some cases to increase real investment. Thus, several internal objectives may be the factors really holding up investment; therefore, foreign exchange becomes a bottleneck or ceiling, in the strict sense, only when these internal objectives are taken as constraints on the problem of increasing investment. I do myself think that the latter is the correct interpretation.

(2) A more serious and valid criticism of the foreign exchange bottleneck on increase in investment in the developing countries is that there is not a bottleneck (in the strict sense of not being able to increase export earnings at all) but that these countries think the loss of real income and consumption involved in raising foreign exchange earnings is too high. Let me illustrate this point by a simple diagram (Figure 8.1). The x-axis represents the consumer good and the y-axis the investment good. Let Q represent the bundle initially producible by the country. If the economy

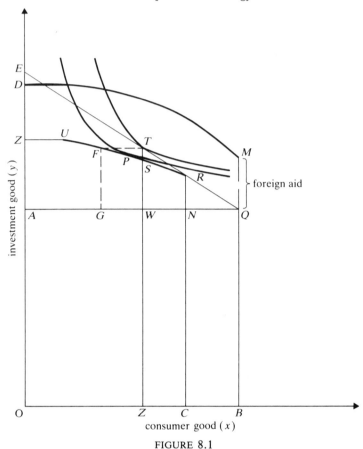

FIGURE 8.1

'saves' QN and transforms this into NR of the investment goods, at the terms of trade represented by the line QR, the real investment goes up by RN. Suppose however that the economy wishes to increase real investment still further. If the terms of trade could be maintained, the economy, for example, could give up another WN of x and now get WT of y. However, if QRSFUZ represents the transformation possibilities instead, yet another WG of x would have to be given up to reach this level (WT = GF) of incremental investment (above BQ). In this case, the economy may prefer to have a lower increment in investment (choosing for example point P on the transformation curve) and thus may not be exhausting all possibilities offered by foreign trade for raising investment. Note that there may be economies whose aim in raising investment may be to reach investment in excess of OZ, in which case there is an exchange bottleneck on raising investment because, at the margin, additional saving of x yields no net y in foreign trade.

In my judgment, however, many economies are still well within QR, many others are on the RSFU range, and few must be on the UZ range of (strict) bottlenecks on investment owing to foreign exchange. Note further that (1) foreign aid would make the task of raising investment considerably easier by raising the whole 'availability' set to BQMD when foreign aid is equal to MQ in units of y; (2) measures which 'increase the access' to foreign markets, would also help by improving the transformation possibilities: for example, measures leading to possible transformation at terms of trade QRT itself, for any level of exchange, would immediately shift the availability frontier for the economy from BQRSFZ to BQRTE.

(3) Finally, I would like to suggest that, if one looks at the problem of raising real investment in the developing countries (at the sacrifice of consumption), and the possibility of an exchange bottleneck thereon, in the context of a model including time, the bottleneck idea becomes even more tenuous. Looking at Figure 8.1 again, it is true that the economy would be constrained, at best, to raising the real investment to OZ (owing to the fact that no aid is available and no improvement in access to markets via reductions, preferential entry etc. is provided). But as soon as one thinks of the next 'period', and the periods thereafter, it is easy to see that increment in the real investment level can be sustained by diverting current investment into producing investment goods other than consumer goods. I have in mind, of course, the Feldman–Mahalanobis type of model which contains this basic idea. When one looks at the problem this way, it is naturally difficult to think of economies which are really constrained, in the strict sense of a bottleneck or ceiling, from raising investment owing to unavailable foreign exchange. India itself, for example, annually imports considerable quantities of capital goods for consumer goods production and also considerable quantities of raw materials for consumer goods industries, plus a very limited quantity of consumer goods. In view of this phenomenon, shared undoubtedly by most developing countries, it seems to me rather odd to argue that the raising of investment in the developing countries in general is subject to a ceiling imposed by unavailable foreign exchange.[1]

2 RELATION TO TRADITIONAL ANALYSIS IN TRADE THEORY

How is such 'bottleneck' or 'ceiling' analysis related to traditional analysis in trade theory? In point of fact, the relationship is extremely simple,

1. Note that I have talked so far only in terms of raising investment. A similar analysis could be carried out for raising income or growth rate of income. Note further that a foreign exchange bottleneck is not necessarily a bottleneck also to income or income growth or any other objective.

as far as I can see. This analysis is nothing more than a 'possibility' analysis, of the kind worked out in traditional theory. After all, there also we define a set of possibilities and then introduce trade to define in turn an availabilities locus. If the economy then wishes to operate outside this locus, it is clearly ruled out unless trade possibilities improve or foreign resources are forthcoming. Traditional theory takes the defined availabilities locus and then works out the methods by which welfare may be maximized, under alternative international and technological assumptions subject to this locus as a constraint. What we have said in relation to bottlenecks is only an extension of the same approach.

(In fact, if the whole question of investment allocation has to be discussed at all meaningfully for any country, developed or developing, the availabilities locus has to be defined carefully. The preceding discussion actually would be a good starting point for the analysis of investment allocation which Ragnar Nurkse began in relation to his notion of stagnant export earning from the developing countries.)

3   NATIONAL POLICIES WITH RESPECT TO BALANCE OF PAYMENTS

Where, indeed, the confusion arises on this score is in the widespread belief that, because bottlenecks may (and are supposed to) exist owing to foreign exchange possibilities, the traditional balance of payments theories of adjustment are therefore somehow irrelevant to the developing countries. This, in my opinion, is an untenable view. To say that the transformation possibilities in trade represent certain constraints which prevent our economic achievement from being still better is surely not to argue that payments analysis is not relevant. Within the constraints imposed by domestic and foreign transformation possibilities, it is still relevant to ask whether any of the adjustment policies will work and which of them will be optimal.

Looking at Indian policy, for example, I cannot help feeling that the notion of an exchange bottleneck has stood for long in the way of a sensible exchange rate policy. What has been equally disastrous is that, now with export promotion measures, and incentives on remittance being increasingly resorted to, a psychology of export maximization has taken hold over the Government. This can be a sensible point of view under certain rare circumstances. But it certainly is not in the Indian case where manufactures represent the marginal exports and use imported components. In view of the non-unified exchange rate implied by the subsidies programme, frequently instances occur of items being exported at f.o.b. value less than value of import content. Further, since exports are of items similar to the import requirements, the exchange-retention export measures frequently lead to the same items being exported at f.o.b.

and rather low prices and imported at c.i.f. and higher prices. The producer of x exports x to earn exchange to import y for his use; the producer of y exports y to import z and so on through the chain. Private advantage and social advantage come to differ considerably.

And the reason for these policies can be traced to exchange 'bottleneck' confusion. Thinking is then conditioned along the lines of export earning maximization as such. Unless the bottleneck idea is seen in relation to the notion of the constraints imposed on transformation possibilities and hence in relation to its implications for investment allocation etc., and balance of payments theories are seen to continue playing a role in economic policy, the national policies with respect to the balance of payments are most likely to be 'sub-optimal'.

9

Indian Balance of Payments Policy
and Exchange Auctions

It is the purpose of this paper to analyse the current Indian balance of payments policy and to examine the case for reform, inclusive of a system of exchange auctions.

The control of foreign trade in India dates back to the Imports and Exports (Control) Act of 1947. It has since been amplified and an effective administrative machinery has been established, especially since the foreign exchange crisis of 1956/7 at the start of the Second Five-year Plan (April 1956–April 1961). Currently all private imports, and part of government imports, are licensed by one of three licensing authorities: (1) The Chief Controller of Imports and Exports (CCI & E); (2) The Iron and Steel Controller (I & SC); and (3) The Development Officer (DO), Tools, Development Wing of the Ministry of Commerce and Industry. Except for iron and steel (cleared by the I & SC) and certain types of machine and certain types of machine tools (licensed by the DO), the CCI & E controls the issuance of all other licences.[1]

The licences issued by the CCI & E are divided into the following categories: (1) *established importers* (EI); (2) *actual users* (AU), which, in turn, are broken down into various categories: for instance, different licences exist for new products, for small-scale industries (which require 'essentiality' certificates from the Development Commissioner for Small Scale Industries), for consumers' cooperative societies, for the 'export promotion scheme' (which gives raw-material licences in relation to past

I wish to thank Padma Desai, Harry Johnson, Ian Little, Donald MacDougall, Manmohan Singh, and V. K. Ramaswami for helpful conversations and comments. V. K. Ramaswami and A. Ghosh (of the Ministry of Commerce and Industry) were most generous with their time and facilities during a visit to India, in late 1960, which was made possible by a grant from the American Philosophical Society. The information presented in this paper is valid up to mid-1960.

1. The import policy is decided semi-annually and announced in what is known as the 'red book', after consultation with Import and Export Promotion Advisory Councils, which include both official and non-official members. The period of validity of different licences is also announced at this time. There are, moreover, ten regional centres for issuing CCI & E licences. As for bilateral trade agreements, of which there were nearly thirty in operation around mid-1960, these amount mostly to an indication of the commodities in respect of which trade is facilitated and licences more freely granted.

From *Oxford Economic Papers*, 14 (1), 1962, pp. 51–68.

TABLE 5.1   Statement showing value of licences issued to various categories of importers during the licensing periods mentioned below (Value in crores of Rs.: 1 crore = 10 million)

(1) Sec. No.	(2) Category	(3) Jan.–June 1951	(4) July–Dec. 1951	(5) Jan.–June 1952	(6) July–Dec. 1952	(7) Jan.–June 1953	(8) July–Dec. 1953	(9) Jan.–June 1954	(10) July–Dec. 1954	(11) Jan.–June 1955	(12) July–Dec. 1955	(13) Jan.–June 1956	(14) July–Dec. 1956
(1)	Established imports	379	293	156	54	81	102	110	110	107	109	108	110
(2)	Newcomers	23	33	3	—	2	2	7	20	12	16	13	9
(3)	Actual users	77	174	23	27	75	57	112	78	92	88	133	82
(4)	Ad hoc	n.a.	n.a.	n.a.	n.a.	n.a.	n.a.	n.a.	20	16	31	30	33
(5)	Raw material	8	1	4	3	3	7	13	18	22	27	32	31
(6)	Capital goods	38	33	25	10	15	10	27	34	40	49	166	161
(7)	Heavy electrical plant	10	14	12	9	7	7	5	6	6	11	13	23
(8)	Iron and steel	n.a.	n.a.	20	73	14	13	20	33	73	150	167	161
(9)	DO tools	n.a.	n.a.	2	4	3	3	2	7	4	4	5	9
(10)	Railway contracts	1	1	negl.	1	negl.	1	9	1	3	9	16	6
(11)	DGS & D	5	9	6	6	3	5	9	6	5	5	7	6
	Total	541	558	251	187	203	207	314	333	380	499	690	631

Category	Jan.–June 1957	July–Sept. 1957	Oct.1957–Mar.1958	Apr.–Sept. 1958	Oct.1958–Mar.1959	Apr.–Sept. 1959	Oct.1959–Mar.1960	Apr.–Sept. 1960
EI	84	4	77	42	33	36	38	60
AU*	100	56	126	127	135	173	223	189
RM	33	15	45	55	66	81	73	116
CG	152	29	45	28	40	52	85	82
HEP	15	3	7	8	5	4	10	5
DO tools	5	3	5	6	5	6	7	13
I & S Controller, Calcutta	36	22	48	40	24	21	32	35
Total	425	132	353	306	308	373	468	500

*Category AU includes licences issued under sub-categories like SSI, Newcomers, Ad hoc, Railway Contracts, DGS & D, Export Proportion Scheme, STC, Tourist Promotion, CCPs, and Foreign Aid.

export performance); (3) *new-comers* (not covered by EI and AU); (4) *ad hoc* (covering items like State Trading Corporation imports and others); (5) *capital goods* (CG); (6) *heavy electrical plant* (HEP); and (7) other miscellaneous types.[2] Of quantitative significance are the EI, AU, CG, and HEP licences (all of which are explained in footnote 2). This is clearly borne out by Table 9.1, which gives the value of different categories of licences issued from January 1951 to March 1959.

Although no statistics of licences issued are yet published for categories like 'consumer goods', 'capital goods', and 'raw materials', it is on the whole true to say that the consumer goods imports by the private sector have come in through the EI licences and represent a falling proportion of this diminishing category.[3] The raw material import licences (inclusive of spare parts) are indicated by the remaining EI, the AU, and other miscellaneous licences, aside from those issued by the I&SC; and CG, HEP, and DO machine tools imports represent capital goods import licences.[4]

Table 9.1 illustrates very clearly the gradual reduction, both absolutely and relatively, of the value of EI licences and consumer goods imports, especially since June 1957. The years since the 1956/7 payments crisis have also witnessed a continuous shortage of exchange to import the raw materials necessary to keep activity at the levels feasible in the light of installed capacity, thereby lending to the AU and EI raw material licences the role of rationing exchange for this purpose. The installation of fresh capacity with the aid of imported capital equipment has been discouraged, in turn, owing to shortage of foreign exchange. Recently, for instance, the applications for import licences for capital goods have been considered only when (1) the applicant himself can make satisfactory arrangements for raising external finance, or (2) credit or payment arrangements have

2. Some definitions are set out here. (1) EI: established importers are precisely defined in terms of a basic period and a specific commodity classification. Quotas are granted to them as percentages of their actual import value in some year in the basic period. (2) AU: actual users are those who require inputs and the licences to them are assessed on several considerations which vary between small-scale industries, consumer co-operative societies, and other categories of users. (3) CG licences are issued for plant and machinery required for fresh installations or extensions, both exceeding the value of Rs. 100,000. Several procedural formalities have to be cleared to secure a CG licence. (4) HEP licences are issued for heavy electrical machinery and plant, provided the value of the project exceeds Rs. 25,000 (f.o.b.). (5) The *miscellaneous categories include licences classified as DGS & D Order (which are licences issued to importers who have orders placed with them by the DGS & D), Railway Contract* (relating to orders placed by the railways), *Replacement Licence* (to replace defective or unsuitable imports), and *Blanket Licence* (mainly for machinery, petroleum oil, and lubricants).

3. A tentative classification of the import licences by way of 'consumer goods', which cannot be reproduced here, supports this statement.

4. The figures for import licences given in Table 9.1 differ, quite naturally, from the figures for imports (c.i.f.), as shown in Table 9.2. The discrepancy is mainly due to time-

been entered into by the government with foreign countries to finance such imports.[5]

On the export side, government intervention is many-sided but not equally extensive. Formerly export control was wide in scope, licences having to be secured prior to export; however, several commodities have now been exempted, including many engineering products, most cotton manufactures, and jute manufactures. In the past the curious procedure of allotting quotas for export of items in 'short supply' has been adopted, without regard to the scarcity of foreign exchange and the consequent possibility of earning high returns (in terms of national advantage) on exports which bring unutilized capacity into operation.[6] This practice, however, has now virtually been abandoned. Instead, government intervention has begun to take the shape of varying inducements to export activities. Drawbacks of duties paid on imported inputs, easier access to raw materials through the 'export promotion' AU licences, cheaper steel

lags between issuance of licences, actual imports, and import payments. After 1956, however, it is substantially due to the bulk of the government imports (PL 480 and capital goods using foreign aid) being unlicensed.

TABLE 9.2   Imports (c.i.f.)

Year	Imports (c.i.f.)	Import licences
	(Rs. billion)	(Rs. billion)
1951/2	9.629	. .
1952/3	6.330	. .
1953/4	5.918	. .
1954/5	6.838	. .
1955/6	7.614	. .
First Plan average	7.266	. .
1956/7	10.995	. .
1957/8	12.336	. .
1958/9	10.296	. .
1959/60	9.237*	. .
1960/1	10.800*	. .
Second Plan average	10.733	

*Estimates only.
Source: MacDougall (1961).

5. At mid-1960 credit facilities were available, in this fashion, from the United States, USSR, and Poland, among other countries. In relation to the applicant himself making arrangements for external finance, the government was willing to consider investment only in the equity capital of the company or long-term loans. Short-term deferred credit payments facilities were not accptable owing to anticipated pressure on the payments position arising from repayment liabilities.

6. Export control was quite extensively exercised: vegetable oils (mainly castor and ground-nut), manganese ore, and several engineering products providing some leading examples.

supplies, and rebate on railway freights have been the chief measures applied, with varying coverage, to exportable products.[7] There is still muddled thinking in some quarters about the level and structure of desirable export subsidies (for instance, the view that subsidies ought to be given only to items not already being exported, on the ground that 'there is no point in subsidizing what is already being exported'). It is fair to say that a large-scale subsidization of exports is still not the policy of the government.

This is, in essence, the Indian payments position that has obtained over the past five years. It is also the situation that is generally conceded as likely to obtain over the next decade: a tight control over imports through import restrictions, a continuous shortage of raw-material imports, careful screening of investments that call for imported equipment, and a generally uneasy feeling that exports need to be pushed up while little is being done to bring this about.[8] This seems to suggest that the Indian policy-makers prefer to balance their payments with an apparently overvalued exchange rate supported by import restrictions (and some degree of price control over major commodities affected by exchange shortage). The rationale of this system must be discussed.

The reason for adjusting the international balance of paments with the use of restrictions is that, until further restriction ceases to be profitable, achieving balance in international accounts with trade restrictions is superior to the use of devaluation.[9] The rate at which exportables can be transformed into importables through trade may happen to fall short of the domestic rate of transformation by virtue of relatively inelastic foreign demand for the country's exportables (as has certainly been true for several *traditional* Indian exports in the immediate past). Moreover,

---

7. Export promotion is now directed at several commodities. At the beginning of the calendar year 1961, concessional prices on raw materials wre being given to engineering goods, cashew kernels, unmanufactured tobacco, silk fabrics, and vanaspati, items whose exports totalled, according to Mr Manmohan Singh's estimate, to over Rs. 350 million in 1959/60. The commodities subject to freight rebate were mostly engineering products, fruits and vegetable preserves, and manganese ore. Export promotion AU licences covered, among other commodities, cotton textiles, engineering commodities, chemicals and allied products, sports goods, and art silk goods. The list of commodities entitled to the drawback of duties had reached beyond 120 items. Priority in movements by rail was also being given to several export products.

8. Sir Donald MacDougall (1961) has estimated, for instance, that a target figure of Rs. 15 billion for exports, per annum, at the beginning of the Fifth Plan (1971) will be necessary if the total import requirements that are likely to be generated, by way of capital goods and raw material inputs, are to be met (*after* making allowance for foreign aid). This calls for an increase by one-half by the end of the Third Plan and another one-half approximately by the end of the Fourth. This figure is in excess of the Planning Commission's own tentative estimates; if anywhere near the mark, it will clearly call for an export subsidy programme which has not yet been formulated.

9. See, for instance Johnson (1958, ch. VI).

the presence of external economies (in the shape of 'infant industry' or some other externalities) could also reinforce the preference for tariffs over devaluation.[10] Once the degree of trade restriction that is considered to be optimal on these grounds has already been adopted, a devaluation becomes preferable to tariffs as a means of correcting deficit in the balance of payments (Johnson, 1958).

In attempting to raise the rate of investment, especially when investment takes the form of machinery and equipment, an economy without an industrial network must necessarily resort to transformation through trade. Structural impossibility of *domestic* transformation of export-type goods (such as jute, textiles, spices, tea, etc.) into the required investment goods implies that trade is the only way in which this transformation can be achieved. If, however, the foreign rate of transformation runs into rapidly diminishing returns, owing to inelastic foreign demand for exports, the extent to which the transformation can be carried out through trade is limited. In the extreme case, where the domestic rate of transformation is zero, the foreign rate of transformation must fall to zero before the possibility of raising the level of investment further is eliminated. When this level is reached, any attempt at further saving, and transformation of it through trade into investment, will be frustrated *ex-post* and the net effect will be merely to give income away to the foreigners, reduce the level of consumption at home, and fail to raise the level of investment.[11] If the rate of investment that is possible is thus limited by the possibility of transformation through trade, political pressures could develop for the grant of foreign aid which, by supplementing the supply of investment goods, would raise the ceiling on feasible investment. The

10. Other arguments could be adduced to support the case for tariffs. One frequently cited argument (Hagen, 1958; Myint, 1963) is that, for economies exporting agricultural items and importing manufactured goods, a wage-differential between the two sectors such that the rural wage is lower than the urban would make a tariff desirable. This argument depends on how exactly the differential is interpreted and there are several difficulties with it (Bhagwati, 1962). A related thesis is that the protection of manufacturing is justified by the presence of a surplus population at a positive wage rate (Myint, 1963). I have shown elsewhere (Bhagwati, 1962) that it is possible to argue the opposite thesis: that a surplus population at a positive wage rate would cause an under-expansion of the labour-intensive activity which may quite well be agriculture; and that, once again, the assumptions underlying one's thesis have to be carefully examined.

11. Taking, for instance, a model where the economy produces corn which is consumed and exported to import tractors which cannot be made at home (Bhagwati, 1960b), we would find that a decision to raise investment would involve a decision to save corn for export and conversion into tractors. Hence, the level of investment could be limited by the possibility of exporting corn. Conceptually, therefore, it is useful to distinguish, in this system, between a limit to the amount of investment imposed by (1) the possibility of saving corn for export; and (2) the possibility of converting the saved corn into the foreign tractors. As long as it is possible to get more tractors through trade, it is meaningful to argue that it is the limitation on the ability to save corn that prevents the State from

exchange rate would then be maintained at the level at which a marginal increase in exports would bring no net increase in imports and any further increase in investment would be supported through the aid programme.

However, as domestic investment takes place by virtue of the imported investment goods, one is faced with the question of allocating the increase in productive capacity among alternative activities. Here the argument about infant industries and optimum tariffs becomes relevant: the imports of investment goods can be utilized to produce a variety of items and the choice of the domestic activities will depend on which activities classify under the infant industry case and whether the trade pattern emerging under non-intervention can be modified by the optimum tariff argument. Thus, for instance, if more machine tools are desired subsequently, it might be advantageous to invest in producing something like rayon for export and to import machine tools therewith rather than to invest in producing machine tools domestically if the domestic rate of transformation of rayon into machine tools is less favourable than the foreign. On the other hand, if the demand for Indian rayon abroad is less than perfectly elastic, the extent to which competitive free enterprise will carry on this trade would be too high and some tariff which improves the domestic profitability of making machine tools would be necessary (on optimum tariff grounds). Moreover, if the machine-tool industry also calls for infant industry protection, there would be a case for a still higher tariff. On the other hand, if rayon happens to be the industry in which the (infant industry) external economies obtain, the result will be to lower the optimum tariff. The net result could even be to make an export subsidy (on rayon) the optimal policy. Once we look at the problem this way, it is relatively easy to see that (1) it may be economical to allow domestic production of even 'luxury' goods like rayon provided these represent merely a more efficient way of getting machinery than by direct domestic production; and (2) as long as *some* domestic consumption of certain goods is permitted, it may be cheaper to import these consumption goods from abroad and to divert the domestic resources employed in producing these consumption goods to the production of some of the capital goods which are imported.[12]

getting more tractors. Where, moreover, it *is* possible to convert corn into tractors domestically, the distinction drawn here between the saving and the transformation constraints on the ability to raise the level of investment would still be valid: as long as any more tractors can be obtained either by domestic transformation or through trade, it would be correct to maintain that it is the limitation imposed by feasible savings that inhibits a rise in the level of investment.

12. This latter point is worth stressing since it is far too often taken for granted that the *import* of consumption goods is an unmitigated evil; and that there is somehow an advantage in importing capital goods, or in importing capital goods to produce capital goods, and so on. Nothing can be said concerning the desirability of any given pattern

The picture would need to be slightly modified, although the general principles are still the same, if there were some structural problems of the following sort. If foreign aid could be utilized only in the specific form of capital goods, then it is quite possible that its acceptance would generate a demand for imports of materials and semi-manufactures exceeding in value the exchange earned by the traditional exports.[13] In this case, if the exchange rate were allowed to depreciate, new exports would arise, earning the exchange to import materials which would then be allocated, at higher domestic prices, among the rival material-using sectors. Where the trade transformation possibility exhibits a divergence between marginal and average terms of trade, once again there would be a case for an optimum tariff until the domestic and the foreign rates of transformation are equalized.[14]

The preceding analysis has been framed with a view to illuminating the Indian situation. Whether the Indian rate of investment has been limited by transformation or by saving feasibility is an interesting question. It is certainly true that, in the Second Plan (and, as Little convincingly argues in his contribution, in the Third Plan as well), several forms of investment which are labour-intensive and do not call for foreign exchange (such as bunding, land drainage, land reclamation by means *other* than the clearing of jungles with heavy tractors that cause a drain on both capital and foreign exchange) could have been attempted. It is also true that not merely have consumer goods been imported, and in considerable sums (Table 9.1, last row), but that capacity has been increased over the last five years in radio sets, refrigerators, cars, food processing, and a variety of consumer goods industries (considerably in excess of any exports directly or indirectly attributable to it). It would be very hard indeed to argue that the limitation on raising the level of investment has been the possibility of transforming savings into investment goods.

What *has* been the case, however, is that, especially since the inception of the Second Plan, subsequent to the early crisis in 1956/7 when a tremendous spurt in the domestic rate of investment spilled over into a

of trade and trade policy without establishing the rates at which different goods, no matter what they are, can be transformed into one another at the margin. The former point is also worth emphasizing since government decisions to set up what appear to be 'inessential' industries are often too readily criticized without bearing in mind their present or foreseeable export value (art silk being an excellent example in India).

13. This is generally believed to be true of the Indian situation and has important policy implications, as argued in the text.

14. For some of the traditional exports, there would probably have to be an increase in the present level of the export duty. It should be noted further that the rising cost of exchange would also lead to a substitution of those projects that are exchange-intensive by those that are not, *both* in terms of import-component of investment and imported inputs, thereby helping to bring into play the drive to economize exchange which can achieve higher real income.

payments crisis, exchange has had to be strictly rationed.[15] Excess capacity has obtained (in the engineering and chemical industries as also in several others) for lack of exchange.[16] Quite recently the rate at which domestic investment can be carried out, using direct imports of capital goods, has been severely restricted. And the policy concerning exports has been only recently changed from control to inadequate promotion (MacDougall, 1961). It is possible to argue that the grant of foreign aid in the specific form of capital goods has generated this imbalance between domestic capacity and available inputs of imported materials. But this argument, while correct as indicating why the structural difficulty arises, does not suffice to justify the means adopted to deal with the problem. As argued earlier, the ideal policy under these circumstances, with the demand for imported materials exceeding the supply made available through export earnings, is to devalue the exchange rate. Since the current practice is to have an overvalued exchange rate supported by import restrictions, the reform called for is devaluation, while retaining (1) the tariffs already levied on grounds of external economies (none being called for an optimum tariff basis, since it is realistic to assume that the foreign supplies of Indian imports are perfectly elastic); and (2) the taxes on exports in less than perfectly elastic demand (and increasing taxes on those traditional exports which are insufficiently taxed). Since countries often prefer not to alter their exchange rate frequently (and, if the structural problem described here disappears in the future, a revaluation may become necessary[17]), it may be considered preferable to have an across-the-board tariff with an equal export subsidy, in lieu of the devaluation.[18] The net result of such a reform would then be to have higher tariff rates, the structure modified on grounds of external economies, and subsidies on

15. There has been an attempt at price control of certain imported items; however, the scope of this control is very limited and covers only relatively few 'essential' items.

16. MacDougall (1961) produces a guess that an annual increment in the value of imports by Rs. 1 billion would have sufficed to put much of the capacity to full use at the end of the Second Plan. This sort of guess is really very difficult to substantiate or refute; like any guess of this sort, however, it reflects a consensus of opinion as to the likely order of magnitude involved. There is the further important problem of getting industries, which do *not* suffer from input or demand difficulties, to resort to multiple-shift working. By economizing on capital requirements, as also on the accompanying foreign exchange cost at this stage of Indian development, an economic policy that succeeds in promoting multiple shifts will step up the rate of growth of the economy, under certain realistic assumptions (Bhagwati, 1960b).

17. MacDougall's careful study (1961) shows how the structural problem is overwhelmingly likely to continue for the next decade.

18. The argument against a devaluation is sometimes supposed to be that it may produce a deterioration in the short-run if imports are in inelastic demand and exports take time to build up. This argument, of course, applies equally to a system of tariffs and subsidies. What *does* appear to me to be an eminently sensible way of dealing with the short-term problem is to devalue and neutralize the export-side by offsetting export taxes, which are

exports (plus taxes on those traditional exports that are in inelastic demand, the taxes varying according to the elasticities). It is in relation to this analysis that we must discuss the case for exchange auctions in India.

Exchange auctions can be considered from two angles: (1) their economic desirability; and (2) their feasibility. The latter is an important consideration indeed. Although the effect of the exchange auctions is similar to that produced by a system of tariff rates,[19] it would be far more difficult to get the former past the IMF, which is bound to associate a system of (discriminatory) exchange auctions with multiple-exchange practices: indeed, this curious preference for tariff rates is just another of the paradoxical anomalies which underlie several attitudes held by international organizations. We shall ignore, for the time being, however, the fact that the IMF is unlikely to sanction the use of exchange auctions, especially now that Brazil has just given up the system in March 1961 after a lengthy period of operation from 1953 (Kafka, 1956), and only later consider the question of feasibility.

We should first settle whether there is any reason to rule out any particular forms of imports altogether. The unusual argument is that certain 'inessential' consumer goods should not be allowed to be imported. This contention needs to be carefully examined. Where the demand is for ruling out such imports while permitting domestic production thereof, there is nothing but a simple confusion involved concerning the question of efficiency in deciding what to produce at home and what to import, as argued earlier. Where, however, the demand calls for the elimination of *both* domestic production *and* imports of 'inessential' items of consumption, the argument is at a more serious level. It is primarily a matter of a social valuation, about which there can be little argument

---

then lifted at a steady rate per annum; the expectation of a steadily increasing incentive to export would bring about the necessary shift of resources and investment in foreign markets in step with the rate at which the incentives are announced to materialize.

19. The two policies, discriminatory tariffs and discriminatory exchange auctions, with fixed exchange rates, would give identical results if two assumptions are made: (1) the rates which emerge from the auctions happen to be those expected by the authorities; hence a system of exchange auctions cannot possibly reproduce exactly a given system of tariff rates *in practice*, except by sheer fluke; (2) unless the level of demand for foreign exchange, overall, has also been guessed at correctly, the adoption of a fixed exchange rate with *given* tariff rates could easily give results diverging from a system of exchange auctions: only a system of *variable* tariff rates could then match a system of exchange auctions. For, a system of exchange auctions would, in any case, give rise to a level of average tariff which would reflect the level of demand for exchange; a system of given tariff rates, unless it happens to coincide with that which is necessary, could mean either too low or too high an average tariff rate to balance the international accounts. Moreover, it should be noted that the use of exchange for 'invisible' imports could be subjected to the auctions system whereas tariffs are normally confined to 'visible' imports. In the auction system I am proposing here, 'invisible' imports would have to be cleared through the auction as well.

on a professional plane among economists.[20] Yet this policy has often been sought to be justified on economic grounds as well. It is claimed, for instance, that when certain goods are not available, the alternative is saving so that, by removing them from the market, one increases the level of saving and investment. The objections to this argument are twofold: (i) although this may be true over relatively short periods, obviously the incentive to save will be reduced if this policy is expected to continue for long and other avenues for expenditure will be found; and (ii) it would be far simpler and surer to use the fiscal machine to increase savings. (The latter objection presumes, of course, that a more stringent fiscal policy is administratively and politically feasible.) An alternative, more plausible line of argument, however, is possible. If tastes are a function of availability, one may be able, by shutting off certain 'inessential' goods from the market, to shift tastes and expenditures towards goods in relatively elastic supply at home: for instance, if washing machines, refrigerators, air-conditioners, and vacuum cleaners are ruled out from the consumers' horizon, they may end up wanting and getting more servants (who are in elastic supply in an over-populated country). There thus seems to me to be a good case, *both* social and economic, in India, for ruling out imports *and* domestic production of certain 'inessential' goods. This can be done quite simply by preventing the imports, and the domestic production, of these goods.[21] There is, however, no case for discriminating against the imports of *other* consumption goods, or capital goods to produce them, or inputs into them.

The effects that a system of exchange auctions would have, in relation to the current system, can be most effectively analysed under the following heads: (1) allocative efficiency; (2) equity; (3) employment; (4) inflationary effects; (5) excess profits and revenue; (6) delays; and (7) export promotion. The current system will be taken to be that previously described: import control administered through EI, AU, CG, and HEP licences, some degree of price control, and inadequate export subsidies. It will further be assumed that an export subsidy programme, corresponding to the desired degree of devaluation, would be adopted

20. Patel (1963) makes out a good case, on *social* grounds, for ruling out the imports and domestic production of certain 'inessential' items.

21. Allowance must be made, of course, as argued earlier, for the establishment of domestic capacity, for potential *exports*, in even 'inessential' goods; however, this would need to be accompanied by excise taxes which rule the commodity out from *domestic* consumption. A conflict, however, could arise if entrepreneurs consider being specialized in foreign markets a serious handicap and cannot be induced to develop an industry like 'rayon' for export if they are not allowed to develop a 'safer' domestic market. This difficulty can be quite serious, if the foreign market is going to be seriously competitive and difficult to keep a firm hold on.

with the proposed exchange auction system: all this would imply is that the exchange would be bought from the exporters at the par value plus the desired subsidy level. The actual method of operating the exchange auction system would clearly have to involve the State buying all exchange from the exporters through the mediation of some authorized banks, for instance, as in Brazil (Kafka, 1956); and the exchange decided to be distributed could then be auctioned. The Brazilians bought exchange from the exporters at an assigned par value and supplemented this with a discriminatory export subsidy programme (the discrimination being mainly between coffee and other exports) which averaged out at one stage to 28 per cent premium on the par value. The exchange earned was auctioned in the shape of certificates, entitling importers to secure 'spot' exchange. The certificates carried a 'remittance' tax, so that the effective import rate turned out to be the par value plus the tax plus the variable auction premium.

Allocative efficiency

In discussing the allocative efficiency of an exchange auction system it is necessary to address oneself, in the Indian context, to two separate questions: (1) Should the exchange auctions be discriminatory between broad categories such as consumer goods, raw materials, and capital goods; if so, in what detail? (2) Should government purchases be exempted from the auctioning system? In the background to this set of questions lies the significant fact that considerable influence on the private sector investment in the Organized Sector (of modern industry) is exercised by the Indian Government as part of its planning programme.

The Brazilian system of exchange auctions specifically exempted the government from the auction process. In the matter of private imports as well, the system was explicitly discriminatory. Certain 'very essential' imports were exempted altogether; so were the imports of equipment against the inflow of capital. Moreover, the auctions were divided into five broad categories, by type of commodities: agricultural supplies and essential raw materials, other raw materials, most industrial equipment, and so on. The auctions were further set apart, frequently for separate currencies: at times, different auctions have been known to have been held for as many as 20 currencies (Kafka, 1956).

In India's case, the government imports consist almost totally of PL 480 US Surplus Food – there is domestic need to maintain a steady price of cereals, primarily due to the existence of a large segment of the population on a fixed and sometimes even falling money wage and/or earnings – and of imports of capital goods under varying aid programmes. The import of capital goods under the aid arrangements is clearly tied up with defined projects, by virtue of international practice, and would be impossible to subject to an auctioning system in any *genuine* sense. Yet, it is necessary that the cost of the exchange should not be understated, as it would clearly be if the different government projects were worked out and implemented on the basis of the current exchange rate. If the government imports of capital goods are to be exempted from the auctioning system, as they will have to be for the reason just given, then it is desirable that the use of a domestic 'surcharge' on the import of equipment under the aid programme, corresponding to the premium which develops in the auction, be levied by the government. This would not merely economize on the use of exchange, where possible, but also reflect more nearly the real cost of importing equipment under the aid programme since the aid must be paid for eventually by resources exported at the transformation rate implied by the rates emerging from the auctions.

Assuming, therefore, that the auctions are to be confined to the allocation of exchange to the private sector, with a surcharge on the import of capital goods by the government, one still has to settle whether the auctions are to be discriminatory between different classes of goods. From the arguments earlier in this paper, it would appear that the auctions should be non-discriminatory between different users, a system of tariffs having already been levied to discriminate in favour of those activities that carry external economies with them. The import of 'inessential' goods would already be excluded; so also the import of capital goods to produce them. Where past mistakes have been made, in setting up capacity to produce 'inessentials' such as refrigerators, the actual users in these industries should be excluded from the actions; and any resale of exchange certificates to such 'inessential' industries could be made a punishable offence. In view of the fact that the government exercises control over the pattern of investment in the Organized Industry sector, it would be necessary, moreover, to admit to the auctions only those CG & HEP applicants who have already been screened by the Capital Issues Committee in relation to the Plan 'priorities' in the matter of investment allocation. Those applicants who are covered by the foreign-aid programme would have to pay the 'surcharge' in common with the public sector. Beyond this set of qualifications, however, the AU raw material licences, CG & HEP, and other applicants should be freely auctioned. Currently, EI licences do result in some of the allocative effects of the auction system, in so far as an EI importer who imports some material, on the strength of his quota, will charge a high price for it, which reflects the high cost of scarce exchange to the actual user (though, the effect would obviously not be *identical* with that when a higher exchange rate would have been allowed to prevail, the quantity of this raw material imported under both systems could easily diverge). The AU licences, on the other hand, by allocating raw material and input imports among different users according to capacity and past imports, define clearly a pattern of imports which has no relation to the efficiency of different units in each sector of use or to the relative efficiencies of different sectors of use. Often the practice of giving licences for imports of identical inputs to *both* EI and AU licencees represents a further discriminatory element with no convincing rationale: the actual users thus get *some* inputs at artificially low prices under AU licences and *others* at high prices through EI licences (though the latter are sometimes ostensibly to supply the users in geographically distant areas). The CG & HEP licences again entitle the successful applicants to secure their exchange at the artificially lower price; the projects chosen being far too exchange-intensive, not merely for this reason, but also because the imported inputs under the current AU system are artificially low in price and hence projects that use more of them get their relative profitability overstated by the current system.[22] The system of exchange auctions would secure greater efficiency in the allocation of exchange than the current system by making the users bid for the exchange.[23]

Equity

Among the arguments against exchange auctions, one should reckon the case for equity. Should not each AU importer, for instance, get his 'fair share' of the exchange? This is, however, no more than a simple feather-bedding argument in support of inefficiency. It would be difficult, on the part of the government, to justify a policy which produces lower income mainly with a view to supporting pressure groups composed of actual users. To use the standard compensation argument, the government should adopt the auctions policy and then proceed to compensate the actual users who are inefficient, if it is keen on supporting the inefficient actual users: this would imply an *open* policy of support which the government would find it very difficult indeed to justify! Another related argument is that small firms are likely to be squeezed out in the 'scramble for exchange'. This is, however, a specious argument because large firms will import to the extent that it is profitable and there is no reason why small firms should not be able to compete if they expect to make equally

22. It is irrelevant to argue, as some officials do, that the licensing authorities tend to make an allowance, when choosing between rival applicants, for the relative exchange-intensities of the different projects submitted. This is insufficient, and almost irrelevant, because the projects submitted for consideration will *already* have been picked from the exchange-intensive range, those that are less intensive in the use of exchange having already been eliminated by virtue of the underpricing of the exchange. Within the government sector again, the use of anything like a shadow price for foreign exchange is far from being the current practice.

23. The question of rigging the bids is unlikely to arise when the auction is not being held in separate sections. If it is supposed, however, that this will happen and if, in practice, it is suspected to happen, minimum bids may have to be introduced (Kafka, 1956).

large profits. If it is thought that small firms are not able to raise finance as easily as the larger firms, despite their equal profitability, then there is a case for general intervention at the level of banking practice, and not for intervention through an inefficient exchange system. If necessary, an actual subsidy could be organized to the smaller firms, though my own view is that the premise that smaller firms suffer from disadvantages not shared by larger firms, for reasons other than relative inefficiency, is untenable.[24] Similar comments apply to the argument that exchange should be allocated so that sectors of use in different parts of the country get a 'fair share'. Once again it is unlikely that geographically distant areas suffer from any special handicaps in exchange auctions; and any failure to bid sufficiently high for exchange is likely to reflect inefficiency rather than geographical distance.

Employment

A related argument would be that, unless the input licences are granted to all firms, it would be difficult for those firms that fail to get import licences in an exchange auction to maintain employment and output in their plants and hence it would be preferable to use an inefficient system which guarantees employment in all plants. This argument, however, assumes that the increase in employment in the efficient firms which get more inputs under the exchange auctions is less than the decrease that accompanies the failure of the inefficient to get exchange (which may be true if the inefficient firms are labour-intensive). It should also be remembered that a policy that creates extra real income will promote greater capital formation and employment in the longer run. Moreover, surely employment is a matter which should be the concern of the overall plan rather than import control.

Inflationary effects

It is sometimes argued that the system of exchange auctions would have inflationary effects. By this, it is meant that the domestic price level would rise. This argument, however, appears to be specious. The current method of import restrictions already raises the price level of the imported goods, except in the few instances of effective price control, and exchange auctions need not have any different overall effect on this price level. Indeed, the auction system, by leading to better allocation of resources and generating

24. The question of the denomination of the certificates was held to be of some significance in Brazil (Kafka, 1956), where it was argued that large denominations would make it difficult for the smaller firms to get hold of exchange. Since reselling by both larger and smaller firms need not be ruled out, the force of this argument seems unclear to me.

higher real income, would lead to a reduction in the price level as compared with the present system. In this connexion, the argument that money expenditure may be sensitive to a rise in the price level of imported commodities seems to be irrelevant as it applies equally to the current system and the auctions method proposed here. Even if it were not so, the rise in the price level of imported goods would be unlikely to raise the level of money expenditure in the economy, as it is believed to in Britain and Australia where many imported items enter directly the cost-of-living index and the wage level is sensitive to this index, since the imported items affect, directly and indirectly, mainly the consumption of the middle class and wage rates are insensitive to price increases except in tiny segments of the economy such as the textile industry.[25] A proponent of the exchange auction system might be further prepared to argue that the system would be, in fact, deflationary in so far as it generates considerable revenue. However, this must be tempered by the fact that export subsidies are assumed in this paper to accompany the institution of exchange auctions. Since export earnings tend to approximate private imports, the net effect on revenue of the auction system proposed here would appear to be insignificant. However, a system of 'surcharge' on the use of foreign aid, equivalent to the premium on auctioned exchange, has been proposed for the government imports (as also the small private sector drawing on foreign aid). Since this will result eventually in the raising of the prices of public sector oututs sold to the private sector, it will have the effect of an indirect tax system. The increased cost of the import-intensive sectors' outputs will be then absorbing any excess expenditure, obviating thereby the need for the government to impose extra taxation for this purpose. Assuming, therefore, that the government, having earned revenue via the higher prices of import-using public sector output, does not raise the revenue it would otherwise have had to, the system of exchange auctions should have no effect on the level of demand (and hence no deflationary or inflationary effect in the Keynesian sense of excess demand) or on the price level, at market prices (if it is assumed that the government taxation, in lieu of these receipts, would have been indirect, as it is sensible to assume in the Indian context) – except, of course, for the reduction in the overall price level following from the higher real income that the auction system brings about.

Excess profits and revenue

In discussing the case for exchange auctions, attention is often confined merely to one aspect of the system of licensing currently used: namely,

---

25. The Second Agricultural Labour Inquiry has shown, for instance, with varying degrees of reservation about its findings, that over the last decade the money earnings of the average landless labourer family have probably fallen, at best not improved. This is a completely plausible result when there is much surplus population.

that the method of import restrictions generates high profits for the established importers and for the actual users who manage to get their exchange at artificially high prices and are not subject to price control (either legally or via evasion). The differences between the imported (c.i.f.) and wholesale market prices of selected items at Bombay, Calcutta, and Madras ports illustrate markedly the large profit margins which accrue to established importers under the present system. There is also believed to be considerable 'trafficking' in AU licences given to small-scale industries. The amount of revenue that could be raised merely by auctioning EI licences would have been Rs. 740 million in 1958/9, assuming 100 per cent auction premium on the value of issued licences (which seems to be a reasonable average in the light of unpublished information on profit margins). The sale of AU, CG, and HEP licences in 1958/9, assuming 20 per cent premium on the value of licences, would have raised the estimate to around Rs. 1.5 billion. Naturally, the revenue so earned must be set against the cost of the export subsidy programme proposed here. A 20 per cent subsidy on the value of exports in 1958/9, making allowance for the fact of its not being extended to jute and tea exports, would have produced a bill of about the same magnitude, if it had raised the total level of exports (net of jute and tea exports) to Rs. 7.5 billion.[26]

Delays

In the matter of delays involved in the current licensing system, one could argue that, although much negotiation has to be gone through to clear a CG licence, for instance, the investor is aware of this lag and hence oves in with his application correspondingly earlier.[27] As for the AU and

26. The effect of the 'surcharge' proposed here on capital goods imports, using foreign aid, and not subjected to auctions, has not been included in the text. This would have come to about Rs. 800 million on government imports in 1958/9 and would have presumably been recovered, through higher public sector (output) prices. It would be sensible to assume, however, that this would have reduced the required taxation by the government, *ceteris paribus*, to reduce private expenditure to the desired level. It may also be noted that, in computing the revenue earned by the government from the auction premia, we have allowed for premia on all private imports, and not merely those presently imported against EI licences. Official estimates of the revenue effect have been confined to the EI figure. Our estimate is higher because the auction system being proposed here embraces all private imports, as it ought to.

27. The Ministry of Commerce and Industry has been in constant touch with the representatives of industry and has occasionally revised its licensing procedure so as to expedite the licensing process. One important aspect of the whole problem, of course, is not merely the delays caused by the whole system, but the amount of money that has to be spent by industry and business, by way of employees' travel to Delhi (where they compete during the tourist season with exchange-spending tourists for expensive hotel accommodation), and so on, to get the licences. Nor must we leave out of reckoning the high-grade civil service talent that is tied up in running the entire system and the expense incurred in the shape of lower-level employees.

EI licences, these are dealt with on a semi-annual basis and it may appear, therefore, that no question of delays can arise. However, this would be a superficial view of the matter. Difficulties arise quite unpredictably; parts which are trivial in value may suddenly require to be imported and negotiations could and do hold up their import, affecting vast areas of production if this bottleneck arises at an early stage of a long productive process. Much of this sort of argument is missed by officials who are inclined to see matters in the light of perfect foresight and/or total bureaucratic efficiency, neither of which assumptions is realistic. Considerable flexibility is needed which just cannot be supplied by the current method of allocating exchange. A system of exchange auctions is bound to increase efficiency by enabling entrepreneurs to invest in capacity, to buy raw materials and parts so as to eliminate quickly shortages whenever necessary and feasible.

Export promotion

It is argued in some official quarters in India that the current system of licensing enables export promotion schemes to be carried out. As noted earlier, there are special AU licences which are handed out to certain export industries. This argument, however, must be dismissed summarily. There is no justification at all for sticking to an inefficient system of import control on grounds of export promotion; since export promotion is made necessary by the over-valuation, it is preferable to collect revenue through exchange auctions and use it for (measurable) subsidies on exports, as proposed here.

A system of exchange auctions thus appears to be a definite improvement over the current system, provided it is characterized, among other things, by: (1) exemption of the public sector imports, which use foreign aid; (2) the subjection of the public sector capital goods imports, using aid, to a 'surcharge' approximating to the premium in the auction; (3) an export subsidy (not extended to some traditional exports) sufficient to generate the supply of exchange necessary to maintain capacity utilization (MacDougall, 1961); and (4) exclusion of applicants, from the auction, for either manufacture or import of 'inessential' goods; and (5) a continuation of the current system of screening applications for licences for investment, so that the entry of applicants for CG and HEP licences to the general exchange auction is to be controlled by the government, in conformity with its planning policy. The only major obstacle to such a system is the real possibility of IMF disapproval, which is of some importance since India is currently drawing upon her quota; and, the fact of maintaining her reserves at a critically low level makes her dependent upon the IMF drawing rights and hence IMF goodwill in a real sense. An ingenious scheme to sidetrack the IMF opposition by formally selling the exchange to the State Trading Corporation which then holds auctions in *commodities*, imported with the exchange, has been suggested unofficially in some circles; whereas this would certainly have the required revenue effects, it will not share any of the other effects with the exchange auction system unless the State Trading Corporation can make accurate guesses. It is, moreover, unlikely that the IMF would be conciliatory to such a scheme which is definitely and obviously a dodge. Indeed, it would be preferable, in this case, to have a system of tariff rates which are maintained sufficiently high to approximate to the (guessed) auction results. The simplest course, of course, would be to devalue so as to bring about the required adjustment, with all the safeguards discussed earlier in the paper. However, it is unlikely that, in view of the irrational fear that attaches to the use of this policy instrument, devaluation will be seriously contemplated.[28]

REFERENCES

Bhagwati, J. (1960a): 'The theory of international trade', *Indian Economic Journal*, 8 (July).
—— (1960b): 'Capacity utilisation in Indian industries', *Indian Statistical Institute* (Planning Unit), New Delhi.
—— (1962): 'Theory of comparative advantage in the context of underdevelopment, growth and planning', Paper read at Seminar on Asian Trade, *Institute of Development Economics*, Karachi, 25 Dec. 1961–2 Jan. 1962.
—— (1963): 'Some recent trends in the pure theory of international trade', R. F. Harrod and D. C. Hague (eds), *International Trade Theory in a Developing World* (London: Macmillan).
Hagen, E. E. (1958): 'An economic justification for protection', *Quarterly Journal of Economics* (November).
Johnson, H. G. (1958): *International Trade and Economic Growth* (London: Allen & Unwin).
Kafka, A. (1956): 'The Brazilian exchange auction system', *Review of Economics and Statistics* (August).
MacDougall, G. D. (1961): 'India's balance of payments', *Bulletin of the Oxford University Institute of Statistics* (May).
Myint, H. (1963): 'Infant industry arguments for assistance to industries in the setting of dynamic trade theory', in R. F. Harrod and D. C. Hague (eds), *International Trade Theory in a Developing World* (London: Macmillan).
Patel, I. G. (1963): 'Trade and payments policy for a developing economy', in R. F. Harrod and D. C. Hague (eds), *International Trade in a Developing World* (London: Macmillan).

28. It may be that this prejudice against devaluation may not prove insurmountable. If Britain devalues in the course of the next year or two, this could provide the right psychological moment for devaluation by India. It seems unlikely that the Government of India would refuse to devalue in step with the sterling; the opportunity could then be taken to devalue *more* than the sterling.

10

The Case for Devaluation

The recent, heavy shortage of foreign exchange, the application to the Fund for standby assistance and the prospects of reduction in the amount of forthcoming aid have brought sharply into focus the balance of payments difficulties besetting the Indian Government. These difficulties are not merely temporary in nature but are certain, by all accounts, to characterize the Indian economy for many years to come.

The years since the payments crisis at the beginning of the Second Plan have witnessed a continuous shortage of foreign exchange to import the inputs and materials necessary to keep activity at the levels feasible in the light of installed capacity. The creation of new capacity which would create a drain on the balance of payments either through the import of capital equipment or through the import of raw materials has been heavily discouraged. In many years recently, applications for imports licences for capital goods have been entertained only when the applicant himself could make arrangements for raising foreign exchange or when payment arrangements had been entered into by the government with foreign countries to finance such imports.

1 CONSOLIDATION OF IMPORT CONTROL

This shortage of foreign exchange has resulted in consolidation of the import control system which dates back to 1947. At the moment, all private imports, and part of Government imports, are licensed by one of three authorities: (1) Chief Controller of Imports and Exports (CCI & E); (2) Iron and Steel Controller; and (3) Development Officer Tools, Development Wing of the Ministry of Commerce and Industry. The bulk of the imports are cleared through the CCI & E.

The licences are divided into the following main categories:
(1) Established importers (EI);
(2) Actual users (AU);
(3) Newcomers (not covered by AU and EI);
(4) *Ad hoc*;
(5) Capital goods (CG);
(6) Heavy electrical plant (HEP); and
(7) Other miscellaneous types.

From *Economic Weekly* (India), 4 August 1962, pp. 457–61.

The EI, AU, CG and HEP provide the bulk of the import licences.

2   SELF-DEFEATING EXPORT MEASURES

On the export side, the Government have now begun to subsidize exports actively. Several varieties of export measures have been devised. These range from drawbacks of duties, rebates, concessional prices for certain inputs and 'export promotion' raw material licences (to replace or more than replace the input content of exports) to continuous exhortation and appeals to the exporters to do their duty by the nation. Most of these measures are cumbersome and sometimes frustrate their own purpose. For instance, unless the 'export promotion' AU licence is issued quickly enough and imports against it are immediately made available, diversion of output from domestic to the foreign markets at a loss could result in a net loss to the exporters and cease to be an incentive scheme. This argument applies also to delays, only much too frequent, in securing rebates and drawbacks.

The present Minister for International Trade sems to think that by merely appointing special officers to look into problems of delays, he can eliminate them. This optimistic belief that one can cure the bureaucracy of its principal hereditary defect is unfortunately bound to be disastrous for our export prospects. In any case, it is clear, and this is important, that the Government in a variety of ways has now admitted that export promotion measures which are tantamount to export subsidies can improve India's export earnings. In other words, the Government admits, in its present inefficient way, that the elasticities of demand facing the export of non-traditional items are large enough to justify an export subsidies programme or a devaluation. I shall be using this particular implicit admission, on the part of the Government, about the efficacy of a devaluation (on the export side), in the course of my argument later in this paper in favour of a devaluation.

3   FOREIGN EXCHANGE NEEDS UNDERESTIMATED

I think a few observations are in order to argue, despite the current crises, that the payments situation over the next few years is likely to be characterized by as great difficulties as in the past five years. It may be naively assumed by some that just because the Third Plan neatly balances the foreign resources against their use, there should be no shortage of foreign exchange. Leaving aside the fact that foreign aid of the magnitude implied in the Plan is unlikely to be forthcoming, one can argue that there are at least three reasons why one would expect a serious shortage of foreign exchange in the future.

(1) It is commonly known that the foreign exchange requirements of projects, both private and public, are deliberately understated in all the calculations because their sponsors wish to work their projects into the plan. This bias towards underestimation is considerable and widely admitted in the governmental circles.

(2) It is also equally well known that the estimated stock requirements of the Third Plan are incredibly low. Of course, there are political reasons why the impossibly low figure of the Third Plan inventory estimate has been written down. Given the fact that nobody wants more than Rs. 10,000 odd crores worth of investment over the five years (erroneously assuming that more cannot be done), it follows that, if you raise the stock figures to what may be regarded a reasonable level, the result would be to eliminate some projects such as, for instance, a steel plant or some fertiliser plants, which few would like to do. Naturally, this understating of stocks means that we are deliberately planning for inflation. The result, of course, would be to add to the inflationary pressure which creates pressures, in turn, on the balance of payments. However, this understating of stocks also adds directly to the balance of payment difficulties because many of these stocks would consist of imported materials.

(3) It is also being admitted by many officials that most of the foreign exchange resources of the Third Plan are already committed to projects and that there is certain to be a great difficulty in financing imports of inputs.

I would argue, therefore, that notwithstanding the serene assurance which the planners have displayed in the Third Plan document, there is little doubt that the problem of a severe foreign exchange shortage, especially to import raw materials, is overwhelmingly likely to continue over the next decade.[1]

4   SUBSIDY: HOW MUCH?

Given these difficulties, the Government's reaction has clearly been to mount what I have described as a cumbersome (and sometimes self-defeating) export promotion programme. This programme, as I have argued, is reducible substantially to an export subsidies programme although it would require a great deal of empirical work to find out the

---

1. This prognostication is corroborated by Sir Donald MacDougall in his paper in *The Economic Weekly* (22 and 29 April 1961) where he argued persuasively concerning the underestimation of foreign exchange needs in India's plans.

extent of effective export subsidies which emerges from all these measures. On the other hand, the Government has continued with heavy import controls, relying upon the licensing system to ration out foreign exchange. It is this system, with an inefficient export subsidies programme combined with import restrictions, that I wish to compare here with a devaluation. I have already compared such a system explicitly with a system of export subsidies plus exchange auctions in the *Oxford Economic Papers*, February 1962. I have shown there how an exchange auctions plus export subsidies scheme would represent an enormous improvement, both from the viewpoint of allocative efficiency and inflation, over the current system. I would only refer the reader to that paper, in case he wishes to examine the case for such a reform. Here I wish instead to discuss the case for devaluation which, while similar to the exchange auction plus export subsidies scheme in several ways, differs from it in two respects:

(1) Whereas the exchange auction scheme would be akin to a fluctuating exchange rate, a devaluation would be a once-for-all change in a fixed exchange rate.

(2) An exchange auction system, continued over a reasonable length of time, would give one a clue to the extent to which the exchange rate is currently overvalued whereas under devaluation there is a genuine difficulty about estimating the extent by which one should devalue.[2]

I shall abstract from all arguments other than that which I regard as constituting the central obstacle to a devaluation. This is the contention that a devaluation would be inflationary. I have come across this argument in several places, both academic and governmental. This argument, however, is very definitely specious.

5   DEVALUATION NOT INFLATIONARY

(1) If, indeed, devaluation will earn one more foreign exchange with which one can bring more capacity into operation with the use of imported inputs, this should represent an improvement in real income (assuming that one has already levied the required taxes to handle the complications introduced by the tariff argument). If the real income rises, with a given money expenditure, clearly the price level ought to fall rather than rise. The standard fear that a devaluation will raise the price level stems from

2. It was pointed out to me by Professor Shenoy that when sterling was devalued in 1949, the Chancellor reportedly looked at the value of sterling in the transferable sterling market and devalued a little in excess of that. Of course, it is possible to argue that this is not a fully satisfactory procedure: the free market is necessarily a restricted market and also unduly subject to speculative fluctuations.

a false comparison between a situation where the payments deficit is met by the use of reserves and a situation where it is eliminated by a devaluation. However, the real comparison ought to be, as is now increasingly realized, between a situation where the payments deficit is eliminated by the use of tariffs and restrictions and a situation where it is eliminated by a devaluation.

(2) The argument that money expenditure may be sensitive to a rise in the price level of imported commodities is irrelevant because this argument applies equally to the (current) system of tariffs and a devaluation. Even if this were not so, it would be a fallacy, in my opinion, to argue that the level of money expenditure in India would rise to match an increased price level of imported goods, since trade union pressures in our country have still not reached the stage where this possibility becomes plausible.

(3) Thirdly, I would argue that the current system of planning is itself inflationary as against a devaluation, on two grounds. The first is that, assuming that trade is balanced, under a devaluation the extra money paid out to exporters because of the devaluation would be picked up (by the Reserve Bank) from the importers. However, under the current system, the Government pays out money to the exporters by way of effective subsidies but does not pick up an equal amount from the importers. Hence, the current system contrasted with a devaluation, at balanced trade, puts more purchasing power into the hands of the public.

(4) Further, if one reckons that, under the Indian system, imports are considerably in excess of exports because of foreign aid, a very substantial opportunity opens up for a 'deflationary' effect following upon devaluation. Assuming that the foreign aid is used substantially by the public sector and that the public sector (having paid more rupees to get its imports after devaluation) will pass on the increased cost to the private sector customers, we find that devaluation will in fact amount to a rise in the price of Government sales and hence *this would be tantamount to an indirect tax*. Thus, if the Government enterprises work on a cost-plus basis, a devaluation will give rise to a substantial indirect tax and abstraction of purchasing power from the private sector. Indeed, this opportunity to collect a lot of purchasing power from the private sector and to put it to use for investment purposes, which a devaluation makes available, is so attractive that it would be foolish to lose such an opportunity. Of course, the market prices would rise and hence devaluation would be 'inflationary' in the popular sense, just like an indirect tax system. However, in the Keynesian sense, the system would, of course, siphon off purchasing power, as argued here.

I do not see any reason why a devaluation would be inflationary as compared with the current system. On the contrary, every argument which I can think of points in the contrary direction. Thus the only argument which can possibly be cited against a devaluation, in the light of the fact that the Government have already admitted that the price elasticities for non-traditional exports are favourable to a devaluation, turns out to be untenable. The onus of proving that a devaluation would prove harmful rather than beneficial would now seem to rest upon the Government.[3]

3. I would recommend a devaluation which would be offset by export taxes on some of the traditional exports. I would also recommend, in view of the fact of short-run inelasticity of supply, that the entire devaluation be neutralised by export taxes and that the export taxes be removed on the non-traditional items, gradually, over a period of, say, five years at 20 per cent per annum. I have discussed this proposal in my paper in the *Oxford Economic Papers* [reprinted in this volume, ch. 9].

PART III
Foreign Assistance

Private, commercial flows have now come to dominate official aid flows to developing countries. However, it would be a mistake to consider aid flows as unimportant. They are still a very substantial amount in nominal magnitudes; private flows are unimportant for a great number of countries outside of Latin America; and even for Latin American countries, the situation ahead seems to suggest dismal prospects for continued borrowing on the scale of the post-OPEC-success 1970s.

These essays on foreign assistance span questions that have evolved over the last three decades. Chapter 11 considers the question as to how aid flows were determined by aid agencies and economists who advocated these flows. In essence it advances a twofold distinction of importance in these proposed methods: those that lead to 'demand-determined' magnitudes, as when the 'needs' of the recipient are established by reference to models that generate investment requirements that must be met by domestic savings supplemented by the foreign assistance that is then elevated to the aid target; and those that lead to 'supply-determined' magnitudes, as when aid is stipulated as, say, 1 per cent of GNP of the donor, in which case it is assumed of course that the resulting sums can be productively used towards the stipulated objectives. This distinction, of course, is analytically clear and conducive to clarity in thinking about the numerous aid-requirements studies that proliferated during the 1950s in particular. In practice, however, one must recognize that the aid agencies, in undertaking such exercises, often must have moved back and forth between the two approaches, in their iterations towards the final magnitudes, as when the 'demand-determined' approach (using any particular model) yielded aid figures that were simply unrealistic from the supply (donor) side and had then to be revised downwards.

Then again, the methods I distinguish and discuss relate to the magnitudes of assistance that were recommended *ex ante*. The *ex post* outcomes are something else: their determination belongs rather to the realm of political economy. While economists have indeed turned their talents now to examining the 'revealed' criteria for aid allocation, for example,[1] it should suffice here to instruct the reader on the subject by recalling an amusing, and I am assured not inaccurate, account of Marshall Plan aid allocations. The recipient delegations were conferring on what requirements to convey to the United States, with the British in the chair.

---

1. Cf. the interesting work of Jere Behrman and Raj Sah (1984) and Bruno Frey (1984).

As successive heads of delegations tabled large figures of projected payments deficits which were to be financed by the Marshall Plan aid, suddenly the leader of the Turkish delegation announced a substantial surplus! The British Chairman diplomatically asked if perhaps the delegate had misread a sign, but to no avail. Evidently, an adjournment had to be announced and a distinguished member of the British delegation was dispatched to confer with the Turkish delegation and explain that, to share in the Marshall Plan funds, one had to come up with payments deficits, not surpluses. The bewildered response was: but we thought that to borrow money you had to show a surplus! Evidently, the ground rules had changed. But the lesson was learnt immediately. When the meeting resumed, an arithmetical error was acknowledged and Turkey indeed had a projected payments deficit!

How 'productive' indeed has foreign assistance been? The truth lies somewhere between Peter Bauer's (1981) distaste and dismissal based on ideological rhetoric and the Brandt Commission's (1980) somewhat axiomatic assumption that aid can only help. Chapters 12–16 can be read as enabling the reader to draw his own inferences on this question by throwing light on some of its central aspects. Different approaches may be distinguished, in turn.

First, chapters 12 and 13 consider the fact that aid flows cannot be treated at their nominal values if their worth to the recipient (or cost to the donor) is to be considered. A dollar worth of aid flow can mean different things depending on the terms and conditions: i.e. whether it is a grant or a loan, what the terms of the loan are and whether it is tied by source and by project or commodity. Chapter 12 considers the question of aid-tying by source in depth; chapter 13 considers the question as to the appropriate way of discounting a loan back to its grant-equivalent present value. That the worth of aid has been substantially less than what the nominal magnitudes indicate, when these and other related constraints and qualifications are quantified and adjusted for, is important to stress when considering the occasional concerns that aid has not yielded adequate returns.

Second, one can extend this general line of analysis yet further and consider situations where the effects of aid on the recipient country as a result of induced deterioration in the terms of trade are so stark that what Professors Richard Brecher, Tatsuo Hatta and I have christened as the phenomenon of 'recipient immiserization' results. This phenomenon has been rigorously demonstrated in the traditional general-equilibrium value-theoretic context, dating back to Professor Wassily Leontief's (1936) classic work. More recently, as the introduction to chapter 14 in volume 1 of these essays makes clear, this possibility of 'transfer paradoxes', such that the recipient is immiserized and/or the donor is enriched, has been demonstrated to arise [consistent with Walras-stability which was shown by Samuelson (1947) to rule out Leontief's paradox in the two-agent, free-trade context] in a wider range of cases, involving bilateral transfers in a multilateral context (see volume 1, chapter 14) and explicit policy interventions such as tariffs, production and consumption taxes and subsidies [Brecher and Bhagwati (1982); Bhagwati et al. (1984)].

Third, however, we can go beyond this neoclassical transfer-theoretic framework and analyse a wider range of concerns that have been expressed regarding foreign assistance. Thus, chapters 14 and 15 in this part address the contention that aid impacts adversely on domestic savings: an outcome that would surely contradict the premises of the 'demand-determined' aid-magnitude exercises I have reviewed in chapter 11 and indeed the presumption that aid was generally made conditional during the 1950s and 1960s on matching domestic savings effort! The thrust of the theoretical, empirical and econometric analysis in chapters 14 and 15 is that both the theory and the evidence on the deleterious effect of aid on domestic savings effort are, at best, inconclusive. Alongside these chapters, however, the reader should also consult two other essays of mine with my former MIT student, Earl Grinols, reprinted in *EIET*. These have developed the question in two other directions: (i) in a dynamic framework, when and how may a short-run adverse impact on domestic savings be offset in the long run (chapter 66 in *EIET*); and (ii) can an economy that has been absorbing foreign aid be destabilized by a politically motivated withdrawal of aid, so that we may then legitimately worry about the 'dependence' caused by foreign aid (chapter 65 in *EIET*)?

Chapter 16 addresses somewhat related concerns, but in regard to the impact of aid embodied in the form of food and other agricultural surpluses. The essay is primarily an exercise in analytical clarification of the numerous issues that arise in evaluating this question and does not extend to an empirical evaluation of the PL 480 programmes of the United States that have resulted in the concerns that are being analysed.

REFERENCES

Bauer, P. (1981): *Equality, the Third World and Economic Delusion* (Cambridge, Mass.: Harvard University Press).
Behrman, J. and Raj Sah (1984): 'What role does equity play in the international distribution of aid?', in M. Syrquin, L. Taylor and L. Westphal (eds), *Economic Structure and Programme: Essays in Honor of Hollis Chenery* (New York: Academic Press).
Bhagwati, J. N. and Grinols, E. (1975): 'Foreign capital, dependence, destabilization and feasibility of transition to socialism', *Journal of Development Economics*, 2: 85–98; reprinted in *EIET*, vol 2, ch. 65.
—— Brecher, N. and Hatta, T. (1982a): 'The generalized theory of transfers and welfare (II): exogenous (policy-imposed) and endogenous (transfer-induced) distortions', New York, 1982, mimeo; forthcoming in the *Quarterly Journal of Economics*.

——— , Brecher, R. and Hatta, T. (1984): 'The paradoxes of immiserizing growth and the donor-enriching "recipient-immiserizing" transfers: a tale of two literatures', *Weltwirtschaftliches Archiv*, 120(2).

Brecher, R. and Bhagwati, J. (1982): 'Immiserizing transfers from abroad', *Journal of International Economics*, 13; reprinted in *EIET*, vol. 2, ch. 68.

Brandt Commission (1980): *North–South: A Program for Survival* (Cambridge, Mass.: MIT Press).

Frey, B. (1984): 'The functions of governments and intergovernmental organizations in the international resource transfer'. Paper presented to the IEA Conference on Economic Incentives in June 1984; forthcoming in volume of proceedings (London: Macmillan).

Gale, D. (1974): 'Exchange equilibrium and coalitions: an example', *Journal of Mathematical Economics*, 1, 63–6.

Grinols, E. and Bhagwati, J. (1976): 'Foreign capital, savings and dependence', *Review of Economics and Statistics*, 58(4) pp. 416–24; reprinted in *EIET* vol. 2, ch. 66.

Leontief, W. (1936): 'Note on the pure theory of capital transfer', in *Explorations in Economics: Notes and Essays Contributed in Honor of F. W. Taussig* (New York: A. M. Kelly).

Samuelson, P. A. (1947): *Foundations of Economic Analysis* (Cambridge, Mass.: Harvard University Press).

11

Aid Flows: Supply-determined *versus* Demand-determined Magnitudes

How much aid should be provided by the rich countries to the poor countries? The determination of the desired aid flows has been a favourite occupation of economists and policy-makers associated with aid programmes. In this chapter we review these exercises in depth, classifying the diverse approaches by their generic types.

Basically, we can distinguish between (i) *supply-determined* and (ii) *demand-determined* aid-requirement magnitudes. The best example of the former is the 1 per cent of GNP target.[1] It represents in essence a frequently agreed upon target of what the DCs *ought* to give to the LDCs under aid programmes, and is at the same time a political assessment of what is *capable* of being achieved in practice. In public debates, it is often claimed that the aid flows at the resulting level can be 'absorbed' productively. But it is clear that the target is politically determined and arrived at quite independently of any detailed assessment of the economic 'returns' to the LDCs from such transfers.

On the other hand, the 'demand-determined' magnitudes of aid requirements are explicitly the result of exercises which start from the recipient countries, assess their aid needs, and then work backwards to the overall aid figures. The exercises in this genre divide broadly into the estimates which are arived at by using macro-models and those which are put together essentially by a qualitative assessment made independently of quantitative model-building. The macroeconomic models, in turn, divide into models which (i) view foreign aid as stepping up domestic availability of savings, (ii) consider aid as expanding the capacity to import goods and services, and (iii) treat both the savings and foreign exchange aspects of foreign aid within the framework of the same quantitative model.

---

1. As we shall argue later, this target has been adopted in the U.N. and UNCTAD resolutions, *not* for official aid flows, but for the sum of official and *private* capital flows to LDCs. This is, as we have already argued, a procedure lacking in any clear rationale and can only obfuscate the issues at stake.

Excerpt from 'Amount and sharing of aid' in J. N. Bhagwati, C. Frank, R. d'A. Shaw and H. B. Malmgren, *Assisting Developing Countries* (New York: Praeger, 1972), pp. 160–96.

1   DEMAND-DETERMINED AID REQUIREMENTS

The distinguishing feature of the models which aim to establish aid requirements on the basis of what can be absorbed by the LDCs is that the precondition of aid flows is taken to be their economically productive use. Thus, any aid flows which result merely in increased consumption in the LDCs, with no impact on the productivity of their economies, would be ruled out by such an approach.[2]

And, yet, this is an ethically unacceptable approach to the international society within which we wish to think of the aid flows. The gap between the *per capita* income levels of the DCs and the LDCs is so enormous, as of now, that simple redistribution of incomes from the DCs to the LDCs, even if no productivity-effect were to follow, would appear to be a moral imperative.[3]

Indeed, if the degree of redistribution that actually occurs *within* the modern welfare states, such as Britain and Sweden, is regarded as indicative of what could be done at the international level (where, in fact, the disparities are much more shocking in view of the abysmal levels of poverty in some heavily populated LDCs),[4] the aid 'requirements' would be far in excess of the magnitudes which the demand-determined models have emerged with (as we shall presently see). And this would be the case even if we were to omit aid flows to countries which are characterized by feudal and conservative oligarchies, where the receipt of aid flows is

2. In practice, additional constraints in defining aid flows are implicitly imposed as well: for, if only productivity of aid were the criterion, we would have to assume that these model-users suppose that the productivity of aid falls sharply to zero just at the level at which they have estimated their magnitudes of aid requirements! We will take up this point later in the text.

3. Indeed, the prospect of reducing this gap in *per capita* income levels by the end of this millenium is also quite dim, if we extrapolate the present trends into the future. If anything, the gap is likely to widen, certainly in absolute terms. Cf. contributions of Bhagwati, Rosenstein-Rodan, Tinbergen, *et al.*, in Bhagwati (1972).

Note also that the transfers of resources on redistributive principles, even more than the productively-oriented aid programmes conceived on the productivity principle, require that aid really accrues to the poorer in the poor countries. The fear that the taxes of the American poor will finance the consumption of the Haitian rich is indeed well-taken. The liberal philosophy requires that the distribution be defined, not among nations as such, but from the rich to the poor. There would then be little enough reason to transfer resources for consumption to the Haitian poor unless the Haitian rich were also contributing *their* share to this enterprise. If anything, these considerations lead to the view that aid should be given, at least in bulk, to the socially progressive nations.

4. Evidence on the standards of living is presented, for a variety of indices such as literacy and health, in Bhagwati (1966, ch. III).

likely to strengthen these regimes, without promoting economic and social progress, and thus frustrate the intended purpose of aid to redistribute world income.[5]

In fact, even if we imposed the requirement that aid should have positive economic returns, the estimates of aid requirements which emerge from such an exercise are, in my judgment, seriously short of anything that we should envisage as 'absorbable' in the LDCs. Purely from a physical point of view, there is *no* reason why we cannot contemplate significantly increased flows of capital and technical assistance, from the DCs, which would build overheads and factories, enable the transformation of agriculture *via* irrigation, new seeds and fertilizers, and permit the implementation of other resource-consuming programmes in the LDCs. It is of course true that the rate at which technical manpower can be mobilized for work in the LDCs, the rate at which technical training can be imparted to residents in LDCs to take over these tasks at future dates, and the ability to turn up useful projects are not unlimited.

It is argued that many potential projects would result in no returns. In this connection, it is necessary to recognize two widely prevalent fallacies: (i) It would be wrong to expect that the returns from these projects in LDCs would be as high as they would be if the projects were alternatively implemented in the DCs. There are several reasons why the LDCs may be inefficient. To begin with, organizational inefficiencies seem to have high correlation with underdevelopment itself. To expect, therefore, that the LDCs should exhibit an extraordinary jump in efficiency in dealing with aid-financed projects, and to deny them aid when they do not, is often irrational. What *is* rational is the insistence that, if aid is to be used for economically productive purposes, the average level of efficiency should be no less than that which characterizes the LDC in general. (ii) The donors must further be prepared to accept the inevitability of some total failures. To expect complete success in aid projects is as utopian as it is to expect that any programme whether of the private or the public sector, in any economy, will be a total success. After all, even the economic efficiency of the capitalist system is supposed to inhere in its ability to weed out the failures (the inefficient firms) rather than in its capacity to prevent such failures from arising. For the laissez-faire critics of the aid programmes, therefore, to argue that the aid programmes should be discontinued because occasionally aid gets used inefficiently is not reasonable.

---

5. Indeed, aid flows which are based on the redistributive, rather than the economic-productivity, principle, are also, from the economic point of view, the more efficient way of granting aid if the productivity of resources in the DCs is greater than in the LDCs. For, in such a case, it would be optimal to invest these resources in the DCs, where they are more productive, and to transfer the incomes for expenditure to the LDCs, than to invest the resources in the LDCs.

Strictly speaking, therefore, even the criterion that aid should produce some positive economic returns in the LDCs cannot rule out the proposition that aid flows can be very much larger than are currently available or which result from the demand-determined requirements models which we presently review. In fact, leaving out aid-transfers for immediate consumption and considering only a strictly *productivity-oriented* point of view, one may wonder whether the following quote from the Soviet academician Sakharov, taken from his celebrated statement which emerged from the Soviet Union several months ago, should be dismissed as altogether utopian:

> In the opinion of the author, it is necessary to have a tax on the developed countries equal to 20 percent of the national income for the next fifteen years . . . Such joint aid would considerably help to stabilize and improve the position of most underdeveloped countries; it would limit the influence of extremists of all types . . . Mankind can develop painlessly only by viewing itself in the demographic sense as a unit, as one family without divisions into nations, except from the point of view of history and traditions.[6]

Twenty per cent of GNP would amount virtually to multiplying the aid flows nearly sixtyfold from their current levels! Clearly, such a visionary programme could not be implemented in any foreseeable future. The time span for approaching such a target would be more like a generation, when we have taken into account the logistic problems of mounting such a major operation. And yet, it would be wrong to deny that equally sharp accelerations in expenditures, and accompanying organizational and technical efforts, have actually been undertaken in wartime (including the recent Vietnam war). Hence, the primary obstacle to a major stepping up of aid remains the lack of political will rather than any lack of suitable opportunities in the LDCs for absorbing aid flows productively.[7]

What are we to make then of the numerous estimates of aid requirements which have been made by a number of economists and agencies, nearly all of which use sophisticated techniques to arrive at

6. The quote is taken from the translation from the original Russian document, in possession of Professor Zacharias of MIT, published in the *Technology Review*, MIT.

7. This lack of political will is *not* confined to the donor countries which must find the additional resources which any expansion of the aid programmes would entail. Opposition to aid flows comes also from elite groups in some LDCs, whose objection to the receipt of aid is based on notions of 'dignity' and fear of foreign domination, values which would appear to have great importance for the elite groups who enjoy higher income levels but which are likely to be unimportant for the groups in these LDCs who are in extreme poverty.

estimates which are well within the range defined by the current aid levels and the extremely modest target for aid at 1 per cent of GNP? Clearly, they use implicit cut-off points for aid inflow, the precise method used varying with the model used for determining the aid flows. Therefore, we will review these different techniques at this stage; only then will we comment on *the utility of these models* from the point of view of determining the aid flow requirements.

Models viewing aid/foreign capital as savings

Although aid serves to add to both domestic savings and foreign exchange, several models have been built, for estimating aid requirements, which focus exclusively on the role of aid in supplementing domestic savings so as to finance the planned investments. Within this broad class of models, we can further distinguish between two basic approaches:

(i) Some models specify a target rate of growth for the LDC recipient(s), work out the investment levels required to sustain this rate of growth, estimate the domestic savings which are feasible, and then argue that the required foreign resources are the difference between the (required) investment and the (feasible) domestic savings.

(ii) The alternative approach estimates the investment requirement of the LDC recipient(s) up to some 'absorptive capacity' limit (not related to a target rate of income growth). Domestic savings are similarly estimated at some feasible level. Then the difference between the (feasible) investment and the (feasible) domestic savings becomes the estimate of the required inflow of foreign resources. In this approach, therefore, the rate of growth of income emerges as a by-product of the exercise, given the productivity of the planned investment (as measured by the marginal capital–output ratio), whereas in models under (i) the rate of growth of income is targeted for and is the starting point of the exercise.[8]

In either case, however, the model leads merely to an estimate of the required foreign *resources*. Its further division into foreign aid, on the one hand, and private capital flows, on the other, has to be determined by extraneous reasoning. Furthermore, in many cases, the foreign aid flow itself is divided into various components such as bilateral grants, surplus commodities, soft and hard loans, and multilateral assistance.

---

8. This distinction between the two approaches is, however, less important than might appear from a purely formal point of view, insofar as models under (i) usually specify their target rate of growth *after* considering the 'absorptive capacity' of the economy for further investments and income growth (as is indeed the case explictly with Rosenstein-Rodan's estimates reviewed presently).

Among the estimates using method (i) are those of: (a) United Nations Experts (1951); (b) Paul Rosenstein-Rodan; (c) Jan Tinbergen; and (d) Paul Hoffman.[9] The estimate using method (ii) explicitly is that of Millikan and Rostow, in their famous *A Proposal*.

United Nations Experts (1951): Among the earliest systematic estimates of the requirements of foreign capital (rather than aid) is that found in the Report of the United Nations Experts on *Measures for the Economic Development of the Under-developed Countries*.

Altogether, the UN Experts produced two estimates, with and without China (mainland) and Mongolia. Their reference base year was 1949, and their period of projection extended to 1950–60. The distinguishing feature of their exercise was the method by which the investment requirements of the LDCs were calculated. These were distinguished into two classes: (i) the investment required in the non-agricultural sector to support an annual transfer, from agricultural employment, of 1 per cent of the total working population; and (ii) the investment required to develop agriculture. The total investment requirements were then calculated on the assumption that the target growth rate of *per capita* income was 2 per cent per annum during 1959–60. The target rate of growth was for the underdeveloped countries en bloc although the investment requirements were broken down by five major areas (Table 11.1). The estimated investment requirements amounted to $19 billion annually, of which roughly $5 billion was assumed to come from domestic savings, the resulting estimate of foreign-capital requirements thus turning out to be $14 billion annually.

This early exercise was extremely impressionistic and was designed to give only broad orders of magnitude. In relation to later exercises of the same genre, it is interesting to note that (i) the relationship between investments and output was left extremely vague (the overall capital-output ratio implicitly used in the exercise may have been as much as 8 to 1 since the rate of growth of income was 2.5 per cent and the savings ratio was 20 per cent;[10] (ii) the required investments were further not

9. The 1964 and 1968 UNCTAD Conferences were also presented with rough estimates based on the savings-investment approach; but, in each case, the measures produced by the trade-gap approach were larger and hence more influential. We may also note here the tentative estimates of savings and foreign exchange gaps contained in the 'Preparation of Guidelines and Proposals for the Second United Nations Development Decade: Developing Countries in the Nineteen Seventies – Preliminary Estimates for Some Key Elements of a Framework for International Development Strategy', *UN Center for Development Planning, Projections and Policies*, Paper submitted to UN Committee for Development Planning, Addis Ababa, 1968. Since these estimates are still unpublished, and the detailed methodology used therein not available for general evaluation, they have not been reproduced and discussed in the present monograph.

10. The Report, in fact, contains an error in arguing that the income would grow at 2.5 per cent, population at 1.25 per cent, and hence *per capita* income at 2 per cent annually! See page 78 of the Report. It would appear, therefore, that the

TABLE 11.1 Estimates by the United Nations Experts (1951) of capital required by under-developed areas annually in industry and agriculture to raise their national income *per capita* by 2 per cent annually

Area (1)	Population mid-1949 (millions) (2)	Expected rate of annual population increase 1950-60 (per cent) (3)	National income 1949 (4)	Net domestic savings 1949 (5)	Capital required (million dollars)			
					Needed for		Total needed (8)	Deficit (col. 8 minus col. 5) (9)
					Industrialization (6)	Agriculture (7)		
Latin American	158	2.25	24,000	1,990	1,580	960	2,540	550
Africa, excluding Egypt	178	1.25	13,200	720	1,780	528	2,308	1,588
Middle East, including Egypt	94	1.50	9,000	540	940	360	1,300	760
South Central Asia[a]	436	1.50	24,000	1,200	4,360	960	5,320	4,120
Far East, excluding Japan[b]	661	0.75	26,400	790	6,610	1,056	7,666	6,876
Total	1,527	1.25	96,600	5,240	15,270	3,864	19,134	13,894

[a]Includes India, Pakistan, Ceylon, the Maldive Islands and the adjacent areas of Nepal and Bhutan.
[b]Includes Burma, China (including Formosa), Korea, Mongolian People's Republic, Philippines, Thailand, British Borneo, Federation of Malaya, Hong Kong, Indonesia, Indochina Macao, Timor, Singapore and New Guinea.

Source: *Measures for the Economic Development of Underdeveloped Countries*, Report to the Secretary-General, United Nations, New York, 1951, p. 76, Table 2.

estimated fully and yet they were treated as such for estimating for foreign capital requirements:

> . . . our estimates include only what is directly required for industry and for agriculture. The total capital requirement, including the capital required for social overheads, greatly exceeds $19 billion;

(iii) there was finally, no attempt at estimating incremental domestic savings, the base-year 1949 savings being taken implicitly as the savings which would be forthcoming through 1950–60 as well.

In relating the estimate of the required foreign capital to foreign aid, the experts produced essentially qualitative arguments and speculation relating to the manner in which private investments and inter-governmental loans and grants could lead to the fulfilment of the proposed target transfer of capital to the LDCs.

Rosenstein-Rodan: The most systematic, early estimate of aid requirements was made by Professor Rosenstein-Rodan. His reference year was 1961 and his period of projection extended to 1976, but was broken down into three periods (of five years each).[11] The aggregate marginal capital-output ratio assumed was 2.8 to 1; however, the estimate was built up from regional estimates of aid requirements, requiring capital–output ratios at country levels.[12] Detailed estimates were further made regarding average and marginal domestic savings rates through the fifteen-year period, for each country. Finally, the target rates of growth for each country were arrived at on the basis of the author's judgment about the country's capacity to increase the rate of investment, based largely on its experience in raising the rate of investment in the preceding five years. Then, the estimated foreign capital requirements were deduced readily by the standard method of taking them to be the difference between the planned investments and the forthcoming domestic savings.

The estimates of foreign-resource requirements were further utilized by Rosenstein-Rodan to arrive at magnitudes of 'developmental capital' which represented a blend of different concepts. Developmental capital embraced both private and official transfers. However, Rosenstein-Rodan, having split the foreign-resource requirements down into official and private flows, proceeded to evaluate them as follows: a third of US surplus agricultural products under PL 480 programmes, were excluded, and

target rate of 2 per cent increase in GNP *per capita* in the LDCs as a group was not treated very seriously by the experts.

11. Two global estimates were presented, differing only in the assumptions made with respect to India. Cf. Rosenstein-Rodan (1969).

12. Rosenstein-Rodan considered altogether seventy-seven countries plus some trust territories separately.

private investment in petroleum and minerals was also evaluated at half its nominal value. The resulting estimates of developmental capital required were an annual inflow of $6.4 billion during 1962–71 and $5.0 billion thereafter.

Tinbergen: The estimate of Professor Jan Tinbergen was made for the European Economic Community (EEC) and published in 1959. Its reference year was 1959 and its period of projection was unspecified. Postulating a target growth rate of *per capita* GNP at 2 per cent per annum for the LDCs (excluding the oil-producers), and a capital–output ratio of 3 to 1, Tinbergen eventually arrived at an estimated foreign-resource requirement of $7.5 billion annually.[13]

Hoffman: Taking as his target the doubling 'in the 1960s, as compared with the 1950s, [of] the annual *per capita* rate of economic growth in one hundred countries and territories containing a billion and a quarter of the world's people . . . increasing the *per capita* economic growth of the less developed countries from an average of one per cent a year in the 1950s to an average of two per cent in the 1960s', Paul Hoffman computed in 1960 the requirements of foreign resources associated with this target (Hoffman, 1960, chapter VI).

Hoffman assumed a capital–output ratio of 3 to 1 and thus deduced that an additional $3 billion would be needed annually to add $1 billion to LDC incomes, amounting to the targeted 1 per cent increment in their growth. With $4 billion *already* accruing to the LDCs by way of private and official flows, the *total* foreign *capital* requirements were estimated at around $7 billion per annum.

Unlike the estimates of the UN Experts and Rosenstein-Rodan, this figure was *globally* arrived at, thus leaving open the question of the distribution of the total flow among different LDC's, countrywise or regionwise. Hoffman argued that:

> The average figures for proposed income increases, covering as they do 1¼ billion people in 100 different country situations, conceal the possibility that, say, ten or fifteen or more key countries will make the most of the opportunities offered, plan and build wisely, make the necessary domestic effort, attract a disproportionate amount of outside investment, and achieve real breakthroughs toward self-propelling, self-generating economices with enormous increases in living standards. Others, with less favorable circumstances or not willing to make the necessary effort, may attain less than the average income increase. And still others may retrogress (Hoffman, 1960, p. 45).

13. Cf. Tinbergen *et al.*(1959), for more details.

A further novelty was Hoffman's nod in the direction of reconciling the results of the savings-investment exercise with the trade aspects of the LDC growth target; a rough estimate of $7 billion worth of foreign exchange requirement was arrived at from this alternative route as well.

Finally, Hoffman speculated about the possible breakdown of the $7 billion target requirements among official and private capital flows without, however, producing firm figures.

Millikan-Rostow: In 1957, Max Millikan and Walt Rostow, in collaboration with Paul Rosenstein-Rodan, produced influential estimates of aid requirements (Millikan and Rostow, 1957). Their reference year was 1953; but no definite period of projection was specified. The estimates were made for five regions: South Central Asia, Rest of Asia, Middle East, Latin America, and Africa.

The estimates of total capital requirements were made on the basis of 'absorptive capacity' notions, derived partly from previous experience in raising investment levels, and partly from notions of the 'stage of development' of the regions. Given a capital–output ratio of 3 to 1, these estimates in turn resulted in an annual income growth rate which varied with the regions, from 4.37 per cent in Latin America to 3.0 per cent in the 'Rest of Asia'; the *per capita* income growth then varied from 2.12 per cent in Latin American and 2.1 per cent in Africa to 1.4 per cent in the 'Rest of Asia'. Further, the difference between domestically feasible savings and the total capital requirements yielded the estimates of *foreign* capital requirements for each region. The aggregate foreign *capital* inflow required annually came to $6.5 billion (as an 'upper limit' estimate, with $5.5 billion as a 'low limit' estimate associated with lower absorptive capacity assumptions).

Models viewing aid/foreign capital as foreign exchange

We now review the principal efforts at estimating foreign capital/aid requirements *via* the difference between the import requirements and the expected export performance of the LDCs.[14] Among these estimates are those of (i) GATT, (ii) United Nations (1962), (iii) Gerda Blau, (iv) Bela Balassa, (v) UNCTAD (1964), and (vi) UNCTAD (1968).[15]

14. Needless to say, in a consistent model, the estimated gaps on savings-investment and on trade account must be identical. The trade-gap approach, however, abstracts from the savings-investment exercise just as the savings-investment exercises (just reviewed) do not examine the trade aspects directly.

15. Among the early trade projections, aimed at providing a quantitative frame of reference for discussing the payments problems of the LDCs, we may also mention: *Economic Survey of Europe in 1960,* UN Economic Commission for Europe, 1961; and Alfred Maizels' well-known study, *Industrial Growth and World Trade* (Cambridge University Press), 1963.

GATT: The interest of the GATT in making projections of the trade of the LDCs, largely to determine their viability in financing their import needs, dates back at least to the annual report on *International Trade: 1956.*[16]

International Trade: 1961 contained, however, the first set of systematic estimates of the foreign exchange gap of the LDCs. Assuming a growth rate of 3 per cent *per capita* income in four LDC regions (which would be consistent with the UN Development Decade target of a minimum 5 per cent growth rate of GNP), and estimating the related production and demands for foodstuffs, agricultural raw materials and industrial products, the study deduced the trade deficit of the LDCs for the year 1975, with 1956–60 as the base period. The overall estimated deficit of $5.8 billion was the result of a deficit of $0.1 billion for Latin America, $2.8 billion for Southeast Asia, and $2.9 billion for all other LDCs (excluding the Middle East petroleum producers).[17]

The GATT study emphasized that 'this gap . . . might well increase by another $15,000 million in the course of the period considered.'[18] But, instead of proceeding to break down the estimated gap into quantitative components which would be met by foreign aid, private capital flows, improved export earnings etc., the study merely offered a qualitative discussion of various courses of action, with emphasis on measures for trade liberalization and promotion (which constitute the GATT's primary responsibility).

United Nations (1962): The 1962 United Nations estimate of the foreign exchange gap, and methods of financing it, was yet more systematic.[19] Its base period was 1959 and its projection was for 1970. The gap was estimated regionally for Latin America, Africa, West Asia, the Far East and other LDCs.[20]

The resulting global gap was $20 billion per annum, the major details of the projections being collected in Table 11.2. Past trends in aid and private capital flows were argued to lead to an estimate of $9 billion for 1970, leading to an unfilled gap of $11 billion. A number of remedial

16. In *International Trade: 1959*, attempts were further made to estimate the import needs of the LDCs during the 1960s on the assumption that their income would grow at 5.2 per cent annually. Further, commoditywise projections have frequently been made by ECAFE, ECLA, and, in particular, FAO.

17. Including the Middle East petroleum producers, the deficit would be reduced to $3.3 billion. Cf. *International Trade: 1961*, GATT, Geneva, 1962, p. 15. For details of the methodology, see the appendix, *ibid.*

18. *Ibid.*, p. 22.

19. Cf. *World Economic Survey*, Part I, United Nations, New York, 1962.

20. In some cases, such as imports, the estimates were made directly at the regional level. In other cases, such as exports, the projections were first made globally and then 'distributed' among the regions. Presumably, the estimators also had some alternative estimates of the gap, which were lower, but which were not published at the time.

TABLE 11.2 UN World Economic Survey, 1962: hypothetical projections of and illustrative requirements for adjustments in the balance of payments of developing countries emerging from an accelerated rate of growth of output (billions of dollars in 1959 prices and exchange rates)[a]

Item	1959 (observed) (1)	1970 (hypothetical) (2)	Remarks on derivation of figures in column 2
(1) Gross domestic product	180	304	Assumed to grow at the historical (1950–59) rate of 4.65 per cent per annum during 1960–65 and to accelerate thereafter by a constant fraction each year so as to reach the United Nations Development Decade target of 5 per cent per annum in 1970.
(2) Gross domestic fixed capital formation	28	52	Assumed to growth in the same relation to gross domestic product as in the period 1950–59.
(3) Commodity imports	21	41	Hypothetical level of imports unadjusted for structural changes and policy measures.
(a) Primary	4	9	
(b) Manufactures	17	32	
(4) Commodity exports	20	29	The gross domestic product of the developed countries was assumed to increase at the same rate as in the period 1950–60 (3.7 per cent per annum).
(a) To developed countries:			
Primary	17	23	
Manufactures	2	4	
(b) To centrally planned economies	1	2	Calculated by using as indicator the target rate of trade turnover of the Soviet Union.
(5) Payments for investment income and other services (net)	4	8	Assumed to be related to total exports and imports.
(6) Gap on current account	5	20	Row (3) and (5) minus row (4).

(7) Inflow of long-term capital and official donations (net)	5[b]	9	Hypothetical level derived by extrapolating past trends.
(8) Initial gap in current and long-term capital account	—	11	Row (6) minus row (7).
(9) Illustrative adjustments through national and international policy measures, assumed and envisaged		7	
(a) Decrease in commodity imports through maintenance of 1959 import ratio		3	Maintenance of the 1959 ratio of imports to gross domestic product, implying decrease in the historical elasticity of import demand for foodstuffs and manufactured goods.
(b) Increase in exports resulting from income acceleration in developed countries		2	Induced by an assumed acceleration of the rate of growth of output in the developed countries so as to reach the target of 4.2 per cent per annum, and corresponding expansion of exportables in the developing countries
(c) Assumed decrease in net payments for investment income and other services		1	Assumed improvements in net income from invisibles.
(d) Assumed increase in inflow of net long-term capital and official donations		1	Additional 10 per cent increase in the level shown in row (7) towards fulfilling the General Assembly target level of capital inflow of 1 per cent of gross domestic product of the developing countries.
(10) Residual gap in the balance of payments remaining to be covered through national and international policy measures additional to those in row (9) [row (8) minus row (9)]		4	

[a]Figures have been rounded to nearest integer.
[b]Including short-term capital.
Source: Adapted from *World Economic Survey*, UN, New York, 1962, p. 6.

measures were suggested, including trade expansion and increased capital flows. There was, in the end, no firm figure produced for foreign capital requirements in 1970, although a 'minimum' of $10 billion, and a 'maximum' of $14 billion may be assumed to be implicit in the calculations of Table 11.2. The breakdown of either of these totals into official *aid* and *private* capital flows was not attempted.

Blau: In 1963, Gerda Blau of the Food and Agricultural Organization (FAO) adapted the 1962 United Nations calculations, to produce two alternative estimates of the LDC foreign exchange requirements for supporting an average 5 per cent growth rate in GNP (Blau, 1964). Essentially, she argued that it was likely that there would be a decline in the terms of trade of the LDCs by 10 per cent, as against the UN assumption of constant terms of trade, thus resulting in an increased foreign exchange requirement of another $4 billion annually by 1970. She also produced a more favourable alternative, under which there would be improved non-primary exports for the adoption of less restrictive trade policies; the gain on this account was estimated at $8 billion by 1970. Thus, altogether she had three estimates of foreign exchange requirements: $20 billion (United Nations), $24 billion, and $12 billion – the last two providing the outer limits to the probable outcome.

In addition, Gerda Blau speculated on the really hard-core gap, which would be left unfilled on current trends of capital flows.

> Thus, whilst it has been possible in 1959 to meet the deficit on current account for the group, as a whole, by inflows of aid and other net capital transfers at a total of $5 billion, the near-doubling of all such net capital inflows to $9 billion in 1970 (a figure based on extrapolating past trends) would not be sufficient . . .

Thus, the three likely estimates of the true, hard-core deficit were: $11 billion, $15 billion, and $3 billion. Presumably, these would have to be filled in by heroic efforts at trade expansion, foreign aid, and/or private investment flows; alternatively, the 5 per cent growth target for the LDCs would not be feasible.

Since Gerda Blau was focusing on the necessity to expand export earnings from primary products, and related institutional changes in the world economy, she did not carry her empirical speculation any further in the direction of suggesting how the total deficit, left *after* all trade measures had been explored, would be divided among official and private capital transfers if the 5 per cent target growth rate in the LDCs was to be met.

Balassa: The most detailed and systematic set of estimates of the foreign exchange trade gap of the LDCs was prepared by Bela Balassa (1964).

TABLE 11.3 Balassa's projections of foreign exchange requirements of LDCs: 1970 and 1975 (billion US dollars)

LDC region			Trade balance					Services balance					Current account balance				
		1960	1970:I	1970:II	1975:I	1975:II	1960	1970:I	1970:II	1975:I	1975:II	1960	1970:I	1970:II	1975:I	1975:II
Latin America	+0.28	(a)	−0.1	−0.1	−0.0	−0.1	−1.76	−2.2	−2.3	−2.4	−2.6	−1.50	−2.6	−2.7	−2.8	−3.2
		(b)	−0.4	−0.4	−0.4	−0.6										
		(c)	−0.6	−0.6	−0.9	−1.1										
Africa	−1.23	(a)	−1.0	−1.2	−0.3	−0.7	+0.21	−0.6	−0.7	−0.9	−1.1	−1.02	−1.7	−2.1	−1.5	−2.2
		(b)	−1.1	−1.4	−0.6	−1.1										
		(c)	−1.3	−1.6	−0.9	−1.6										
Middle East	+1.12	(a)	+1.3	+1.2	+1.4	+1.4	−1.21	−1.6	−1.7	−1.9	−2.2	−0.09	−0.4	−0.6	−0.7	−1.1
		(b)	+1.2	+1.1	+1.2	+1.1										
		(c)	+1.1	+0.9	+1.0	+0.8										
Asia	−1.51	(a)	−3.8	−4.0	−5.0	−5.7	−0.53	−0.7	−0.8	−0.9	−1.0	−2.04	−4.7	−5.1	−6.3	−7.2
		(b)	−4.0	−4.3	−5.4	−6.2										
		(c)	−4.2	−4.6	−5.8	−6.7										
Total: LDCs	−1.34	(a)	−3.6	−4.1	−3.9	−5.1	−3.31	−5.1	−5.5	−6.1	−6.9	−4.65	−9.4	−10.5	−11.3	−13.7
		(b)	−4.3	−5.0	−5.2	−6.8										
		(c)	−5.0	−5.9	−6.6	−8.6										

Notes: Estimates I and II differ in terms of the assumed growth rates in LDCs and DCs. Estimates (a), (b), and (c) differ in the assumed income elasticities of import demand. The current account balance has been obtained by adding the services balance to the (b) estimates for the trade balance.
Source: Balassa (1964), pp. 95–104.

His year of reference was 1960 and his periods of projection extended to 1970 and 1975.

Balassa built up his global estimates from regional estimates, extending to four major geographical units: Latin America, the Middle East, Africa, and Asia. For each of these regions, regarded as a unit for analysis, Balassa projected the export earnings of commodities by seven groups. In making these calculations, Balassa used two alternative assumptions regarding the growth rate of the DCs, and three differing estimates of their income elasticity of demand for imports. Notable among these projections was Balassa's inclusion of exports by the LDCs to the Sino-Soviet bloc. Balassa further calculated the imports of the LDCs on a similar basis, distinguishing again between two alternative growth rates of GNP (and allowing for acceleration in the rate of growth between the two periods: 1960–70 and 1970–5). Given his particular framework of projections, there is no doubt that Balassa's projections were as meticulous and thorough as the data permitted. His results, including the service account projections, have been collected together in Table 11.3. They indicated a foreign exchange gap in the range of $9.5 to $10.5 billion for 1970, and $11.5 to $13.5 billion by 1975.

As with other estimators using the foreign-exchange gap approach, Balassa did not proceed to estimate 'aid requirements', but speculated on a number of alternatives such as expansion of exports via tariff reduction, regional integration and expansion of capital inflows. Nonetheless, his estimates of the gap can be regarded as providing rough orders of magnitude within which capital flows to LDCs would have to fall for the period of projection (although no estimate of foreign *aid* would be possible in the absence of projections on the flow of private capital).

UNCTAD (1964): The UNCTAD Conference in Geneva, in 1964, was presented with estimates of the foreign exchange gap of the LDCs, which were merely an updated version of the 1962 United Nations estimates already discussed.[21]

The year of reference was shifted to 1960, while the year of projection was still 1970; the foreign exchange gap still remained at $20 billion. Of the $11 billion, unfilled gap, $2 billion were 'illustrated' to come from 'increase in exports resulting from acceleration of rate of economic growth in [non-socialist DCs] implicit in OECD target' and $9 billion from 'required contribution of other policy changes: export drive; increased import substitution; measures to improve net balance of service transactions; and achievement of General Assembly target for flow of capital' (UNCTAD, 1964, p. 96).

21. The methodology was thus identical and hence will not be re-discussed (cf. UNCTAD, 1964, pp. 92–101 in particular).

UNCTAD (1968): Similar projections were attempted for the Second UNCTAD Conference in 1968, in New Delhi. The reference year was 1967 and the estimates were for 1975.

Their novelty consisted, however, in being based on detailed studies of 37 LDCs,[22] as distinct from the earlier projections based, at best, on regional trade projections.[23]

Of the alternative 'high' and 'low' estimates produced, the former showed an overall gap of less than $26 billion in 1960 prices and over $28 billion in 1968 prices. The regional-level deficit showed $5.2 billion for Africa, $9 billion for Asia, $8.2 billion for Latin America and $3.3 billion for other LDCs (at 1960 prices).

As with the earlier estimates of different international agencies, however, the 1968 UNCTAD estimate of the gap was not broken down fully into estimates of foreign aid and private capital requirements, etc. Typically, a 'minimum' estimate of $12.9 billion was produced for official assistance (and $5 billion for net private flows). With $7.4 billion left as an unfilled gap, to be taken care of by a possible assortment of measures such as import substitution, more aid, etc., we might put the 'maximum' aid flow, implicit in the UNCTAD exercise, at $21.3 billion and the 'minimum at $7.4 billion.

Models viewing foreign capital/aid as both savings and foreign exchange

Hollis Chenery and Alan Strout have used a highly sophisticated model to build up, from a 1962-base, a wide range of estimates of foreign capital requirements in 1970 and 1975 for as many as fifty LDCs.[24]

Essentially, they use the notion that a country's developmental effort may be constrained by either lack of savings, or lack of foreign exchange, or by lack of skilled labour. These three 'limits' are readily understood by reference to a simple model. Assume that an LDC imports tractors with exported corn, and produces only corn. Suppose that it wishes to raise its rate of investment, to secure more rapid growth: this means that more corn must be saved and exported to secure more tractors. Suppose that the Minister of Finance cannot tax further in order to increase the quantity of corn not consumed: in this case, there is a 'savings' constraint

22. The overall growth rate in GNP, assumed for each region, was at 6 per cent per annum. However, the projections allowed for variations within each region: e.g. in Asia, Taiwan and Thailand were assumed to grow at rates higher than the average while India was assumed to grow below the average.

23. There was also an attempt at computing aid requirements on a savings-investment basis. However, there was no systematic or analytical link between the aggregate estimates produced by these two alternative methods.

24. 'Principal attention has been given to the 25 countries having the largest effect on assistance requirements.' Cf. Chenery and Strout (1966, p. 711).

to the developmental programme. But suppose that the additional corn *is* saved, but that it cannot be transformed through exports into more tractors because the world market cannot absorb more corn.[25] Then, there is a 'foreign exchange' or foreign transformation constraint. Suppose, however, that the additional corn can be saved *and* transformed into more tractors, but that there is no simultaneous expansion of skilled labour to operate these tractors: in this case the developmental programme would be faced with a 'skilled labour' constraint.[26]

Employing a quantitative, economic model approach, built on these threefold constraints, Chenery and Strout computed the foreign aid requirements of the LDCs in the context of exercises which simultaneously classified these LDCs into the relevant 'phase of growth', i.e. the constraint relevant to their programmes.[27]

The resulting estimates of foreign *capital* requirements, available at country-level for the fifty LDCs, totalled up to ranges of $9.3 to $11.9 billion in 1970 and $13 to $17.5 billion in 1975, the associated annual rates of growth in GNP during 1962–75 having a range of 6 to 7.8 per cent. No attempt was made to break these numbers down into foreign aid and private flows.

The 'qualitative' approach

The least formal approach to building up estimates of foreign capital requirements, which purportedly aims at keeping a number of possible constraints to absorption of foreign capital in view, is the one which apparently underlies the World Bank's official declarations on the magnitude of capital requirements of the LDCs.

Thus, in a Ministerial Meeting of DAC in July 1965, President George Woods of the World Bank stated that, on the basis of country studies made by area specialists, it appeared that 'between now and 1970 the less-developed countries might productively use an additional 3 to 4 billion dollars a year.'[28] Since the base-year figure was already over $10 billion for DAC countries, the estimate amounted to $13 to $14 billion annually up to 1970.

25. Technically speaking, we may assume a unitary price elasticity of demand for corn abroad.

26. This presumes, of course, that skilled labour cannot be, or will not be, imported. If this assumption is dropped, there are really only two constraints worth discussing: savings and foreign exchange.

27. The model and the analysis are impossible to summarize adequately; the reader must therefore refer to the Chenery and Strout paper for the full analysis.

28. Quoted in R. Mikesell (1968, p. 91). President Woods was citing the IBRD Annual Report (1964–5), in this connection, which was primarily addressed to saying that while, in the previous years, the IBRD was impressed with the shortage of fundable projects in the LDCs in relation to available external capital, this situation had been reversed and that the available projects totalled up to a sum which exceeded the available funds by some $3 billion to $4 billion.

It is clear that, insofar as the estimate reflects 'judgments' of country specialists at the World Bank, no clear criteria are discernible and hence no critical evaluation would appear possible.[29] In essence, however, the approach would seem to consist in examining the range of productive investments, in different sectors, in greater detail than in the aggregate models reviewed so far, and then deducting the feasible domestic savings to arrive at estimates of the required foreign capital. Since no formal models are employed, any cross-checks attempted in order to examine the trade gap can only be suggestive.

The essential difference in the methods employed, from those implicit in the quantitative-economic models (of savings-investment, trade gaps, etc.), seems therefore to be that formal consistency and model use are not highly valued but, on the other hand, the micro-investment projects and programmes are analysed with greater care (than in the aggregative macro-approaches).[30]

Conclusions on demand-determined aid requirements

What are we to conclude from this detailed review of the prominent exercises aimed at determining aid requirements of the LDCs? Needless to say, none of the exercises is immune to criticism. For example, questions can be raised relating to the relevance of the parameters chosen for model-building or for making 'expert judgments', or relating to the quality of the data which are used by the analysts in question. The most significant problems with these estimates, however, arise at two different levels.

First, the striking thing about nearly all the estimates which we have reviewed is their surprising ability to come up with magnitudes of external-capital capital requirements which uniformly lie within the range between current trends and, at most, an upper limit of 100 per cent addition thereto. They show therefore an overwhelming tendency not to diverge dramatically from the current trends. This uniform 'moderation' is quite surprising, at first sight, when we consider that the estimators reviewed include some prominent supporters of vastly expanded aid programmes, such as Paul Rosenstein-Rodan and Max Millikan.

There appear to be two basic reasons for this phenomenon of 'convergence of values', around a moderate target of external-capital needs of the LDCs. (i) The estimators typically base their futuristic exercises on past trends and experience in the LDCs. Even the complex and

29. An extremely brief description of the World Bank's general methods in preparing the country reports, and the estimates of capital requirements, is contained in Hawkins (1968).
30. Whether the Bank evaluates the projects or the overall developmental programmes adequately is, of course, a different matter, on which there is considerable difference of opinion among economists.

ingenious model of Chenery and Strout is constrained to envisage the target growth rates within the framework defined by past performance and by Plan targets (which, in turn, are formed by such considerations). Since all the estimators have drawn upon identical experience, their parameters tend to converge onto a relatively narrow spectrum, often narrowing in turn the range of external-capital requirements which emerge from the exercises. (ii) But, probably more important, is the constraint which is imposed, often unseen, by the assessment of what is the likely *supply* of external capital. Few estimators are likely to remain uninfluenced by the view that 'irresponsibility' in arriving at 'exaggerated' targets of external-capital requirements will be counter-productive if programmes of increased aid-flows are to be encouraged. Since there can be few, and at best limited, differences of opinion about what the political feasibilities are in this area, the net effect is to produce estimates of external-capital requirements which are both 'moderately immoderate' and also not wildly out of line with one another.[31]

On the other hand, as we have already noted, there is good reason to suppose that the external-capital which can be absorbed with positive marginal productivity in the LDCs is significantly higher than the estimates with which these different exercises emerge. These exercises are better treated, therefore, as differing ways in which economists and aid agencies, faced with the problem of encouraging the expansion of aid flows, have argued for moderate expansion of aid targets before audiences which presumably believe that aid should be given for productive uses rather than for income-distributive purposes (aimed at direct transfer of consumption to relieve poverty immediately).

In fact, it is probable that such estimates may have inadvertently led to the illusion that quite moderate sums of external capital were adequate to make the LDCs grow at the maximum feasible rates or in the optimal fashion. This is likely to have contributed to the public disillusionment with the aid programmes. Continuing difficulties in the LDCs have been difficult to reconcile, in the popular mind, with the 'rapid-results-at-moderate-cost' gloss which seemed to cover some of the early estimates.

A second and related difficulty with these estimates has been that the external-capital requirements approach, which all of them share, does not in itself distinguish between aid and private capital, or between different forms of aid. With given periods of projection (defining the time-horizon for planning), it appears as though it makes no difference whether the foreign-resource deficit is made up by private capital flows,

---

31. Frequently, the Plan targets of growth rates etc. are themselves based on 'realistic' notions of the aid flows that can be expected to come through in the planning period. Hence, the emergence of moderate aid requirements, when based on these Plan targets, or variants thereon, is not particularly surprising, from this point of view as well.

soft aid loans, hard aid loans, or official grants. And yet, it makes all the difference in the world to the welfare of the LDCs and to their growth prospects *beyond* the period of projection. All the approaches which we have reviewed have contributed to this confusion, by focusing on external capital requirements, which in turn have been thrown into lime-light by the 'productivity' approach to estimating aid requirements.[32] The recent concern with the problems of external indebtedness of the LDCs, itself a product of aid-loan programmes in many cases, and with the targets for terms and conditions on the loans and for aid assistance, rather than external capital itself, are all evidence of a growing concern with the very dimensions which nearly all the estimates (which we have reviewed) ignored, or, at best, considered marginally.

In view of these reservations, it would be best to treat such exercises as underlining broadly the fact that the transfer of substantially more capital from the DCs to the LDCs than is currently occurring would be capable of being productively employed.

2   SUPPLY-DETERMINED AID MAGNITUDES

In my judgment, therefore, it follows that the optimal procedure for determining overall aid magnitudes would be to target them at the maximum feasible levels, thus determining them from the supply side. This 'open-ended' approach would appear to be justified in view of *both* the vast difference in the incomes and consumption of the LDCs and the DCs, *and* the extremely low levels of actual resource transfers which are currently occurring.

The '1 per cent of national income' target for assistance, discussed by me elsewhere (cf. Frank *et al.*, 1973), represents essentially such an approach. However, as noted earlier, this target raises a number of difficulties. These relate to the following four issues:

(i)   The target, as adopted, relates to external capital; it thus does not distinguish between aid and private, commercial flows.

(ii) The target referred originally to 'national income', and now refers to GNP, raising the question as to which is an appropriate 'denominator'.

(iii) The target does not extend to a breakdown into subsidiary targets relating to shares of loans, and the terms and conditions on the loans.

(iv) The target necessarily ignores questions such as aid-tying.

---

32. It should be added, in fairness, that estimators such as Rosenstein-Rodan took some pains to draw these distinctions; however, the estimating approach itself tended to minimize the role of such distinctions.

Aid target

It is now widely realized, although full-scale recognition of this point has still not been achieved in the shape of UNCTAD or DAC resolutions, that a target that does not distinguish between commercial (private) and aid (public) flows is inadequate. Apart from the 1 per cent target for external capital, which is extremely valuable, there should be a subsidiary target for official capital flows as well. There seems to be a strong likelihood of the 0.75 per cent target for official flows, mooted at the New Delhi, 1969, UNCTAD Conference, being adopted in the near future. The Pearson Commission Report has also adopted a target of 0.70 per cent for official flows. This is undoubtedly a step in the right direction.

National income or GNP

As adopted in UN, UNCTAD, and DAC targets, in the earlier years, the target relates to 'national income'. However, there were questions relating to the appropriateness of this procedure, with other aggregates such as GNP at market price and NNP at market price being considered. Subsequently, at the Second UNCTAD Conference and subsequently in DAC, the target has been related instead to GNP at market price.[33] We may consider here the principal arguments which have been developed to judge the appropriateness of each concept.

(i) The argument for taking a 'net' estimate is that the burden on the donor country should be related to the goods and services available to it *after* allowance has been made for replacing wornout and obsolete capital equipment. The argument for taking a 'gross' estimate is that, in practice, the estimates of depreciation made by national income accountants are both imprecise and based on different conventions across countries, so that *relative* aid burdens would be biased by taking the available 'net' estimates. (ii) The disagreement among the 'factor cost' and 'market price' proponents is more conceptual, being rooted in the now-defunct proposition that indirect taxes, which divide the two concepts, are passed on to consumers while the direct taxes are not: this proposition, if accepted, would lead to the selection of the 'factor cost' measure. (iii) Whether 'domestic' or 'national' income should be used has also been debated: the reason for preferring the latter is that net income 'from abroad' also adds to the power over resources of the donor country and hence its inclusion measures, more appropriately, the capacity of the country to support the aid burden. From a strictly economic point of view, it would appear that

33. Cf. *The Measurement of the Flow of Resources of Developing Countries* and UNCTAD (1964).

the use of the aggregate, net national product at market prices, would be the most appropriate.

However, this issue is not very important. The distribution of the aid burden among donors that would ensue is affected relatively insignificantly by the choice from among the different alternatives which have been discussed. In Table 11.4, we have computed the nominal aid-burden shares that would result from application of the 1 per cent target to four alternative concepts: net national product at market price, national income, GNP at factor cost and GNP at market price, taking each of the years 1953–66 and fifteen DAC donors (excluding Sweden, for which full data were not available). The differences in the shares, using these alternative definitions of the target, are clearly not significant enough to divert the attention of important international conferences!

On the other hand it is true that the *total* aid flow targeted for could change substantially with the choice of the concept. Thus, a shift from the original UNCTAD and DAC choice of national income to the present alternative of GNP at market prices (which would thus add both indirect taxes and depreciation to the national income total) could, in several cases, raise the aid flow target by up to 20 per cent. However, a shift from national income to national product at market prices would not raise the aid flows by more than 5–10 per cent in most cases. It is not surprising that the LDCs have generally preferred to change the concept to one which produces larger aid flow targets and that the DCs have generally preferred to stick to concepts which produce lower commitments. The issue has thus been primarily political, revolving around the question of how much the DCs and the LDCs can agree upon as a target for the aid flows. The battles over the choice of national income or GNP at market prices were therefore merely proxy for the underlying *political* problem of determining the aid burden of the DCs. In any case, the adoption by UNCTAD and DAC of GNP at market prices as the appropriate base for the 1 per cent target has brought this particular debate to an end.

Aid composition and terms and conditions

However, as we have noted, the official aid target, at 0.75 per cent of the national income of the donor countries, would be meaningless unless there were 'subsidiary' targets concerning the share of grants and the terms and conditions on the loans. The 1965 and 1969 DAC recommendations, aimed at liberalizing and harmonizing the prevalent practices are therefore extremely important. They form an integral part of the problem of defining aid magnitudes.

TABLE 11.4 Percentage shares in aid for fifteen DAC donors on assumption that 1 per cent of (a) GNP at market price, (b) NNP at market price, (c) GNP at factor cost, and (d) national income be given as foreign aid: 1953–66

		1953	1955	1956	1957	1958	1959	1960	1961	1962	1963	1964	1965	1966
Australia	(a)	1.68	1.77	1.79	1.40	1.77	1.82	1.81	1.75	1.74	1.81	1.83	1.79	1.79
	(b)	1.74	1.82	1.84	1.73	1.80	1.85	1.85	1.77	1.78	1.84	1.87	1.82	1.82
	(c)	1.67	1.75	1.77	1.66	1.73	1.79	1.79	1.74	1.75	1.81	1.83	1.78	1.80
	(d)	1.74	1.81	1.82	1.69	1.77	1.82	1.82	1.77	1.77	1.85	1.87	1.81	1.81
Austria	(a)	.54	.63	.64	.67	.68	.66	.70	.72	.71	.71	.71	.72	.71
	(b)	.53	.62	.64	.67	.67	.65	.70	.72	.70	.70	.70	.71	.70
	(c)	.53	.61	.63	.65	.66	.64	.68	.70	.69	.69	.69	.69	.69
	(d)	.51	.61	.62	.65	.66	.63	.67	.69	.67	.68	.68	.68	.67
Belgium	(a)	1.41	1.40	1.39	1.38	1.35	1.29	1.29	1.28	1.26	1.27	1.31	1.31	1.29
	(b)	1.39	1.39	1.38	1.38	1.34	1.28	1.28	1.28	1.27	1.27	1.31	1.32	1.36
	(c)	1.42	1.40	1.40	1.39	1.35	1.29	1.29	1.27	1.26	1.26	1.30	1.31	1.28
	(d)	1.41	1.33	1.39	1.39	1.36	1.28	1.28	1.27	1.25	1.25	1.30	1.31	1.27
Canada	(a)	4.35	4.12	4.40	4.40	4.44	4.19	3.92	3.67	3.67	3.66	3.67	3.73	3.79
	(b)	4.24	3.98	4.26	4.25	4.33	4.07	3.80	3.57	3.57	3.57	3.59	3.66	3.72
	(c)	4.25	4.01	4.28	4.28	4.34	4.10	3.82	3.57	3.55	3.55	3.54	3.59	3.68
	(d)	4.11	3.87	4.08	4.08	4.19	3.94	3.67	3.44	3.46	3.45	3.42	3.47	3.52
Denmark	(a)	.65	.63	.63	.63	.64	.66	.67	.70	.73	.72	.76	.79	.79
	(b)	.66	.64	.64	.64	.65	.67	.68	.71	.74	.73	.77	.80	.81
	(c)	.65	.62	.62	.62	.63	.65	.66	.69	.71	.70	.74	.76	.77
	(d)	.66	.64	.63	.63	.64	.66	.67	.70	.73	.71	.70	.77	.77
France	(a)	5.21	5.30	5.49	5.75	6.38	6.48	6.76	6.85	7.04	7.32	7.38	7.25	7.21
	(b)	5.13	5.29	5.51	5.78	6.03	6.52	6.82	6.90	7.11	7.36	7.44	7.28	7.25
	(c)	4.92	5.04	5.25	5.46	6.05	6.11	6.42	6.50	6.70	6.92	6.96	6.85	6.84
	(d)	4.82	5.03	5.23	5.46	6.11	6.09	6.43	6.51	6.73	6.92	6.96	6.82	6.76

W. Germany	(a)	5.94	6.52	6.71	6.86	7.10	7.15	7.51	8.52	8.64	8.61	8.66	8.40	8.50
	(b)	5.88	6.57	6.76	6.92	7.16	7.19	7.55	8.56	8.66	8.57	8.63	8.64	8.39
	(c)	5.61	6.17	6.39	6.55	6.80	6.84	7.23	8.19	8.33	8.31	8.38	8.43	8.29
	(d)	5.55	6.21	6.39	6.59	6.86	6.85	7.22	8.19	8.29	8.23	8.30	8.30	8.04
Italy	(a)	3.39	3.56	3.61	3.64	3.78	3.72	3.80	3.95	4.11	4.41	4.44	4.40	4.37
	(b)	3.35	3.56	3.62	3.65	3.81	3.75	3.82	3.98	4.15	4.46	4.50	4.46	4.42
	(c)	3.32	3.49	3.52	3.56	3.41	3.66	3.74	3.80	4.06	4.35	4.40	4.37	4.36
	(d)	3.33	3.50	3.52	3.57	3.75	3.68	3.75	3.91	4.09	4.40	4.46	4.42	4.35
Japan	(a)	3.28	3.60	3.75	4.10	4.06	4.25	4.79	5.46	5.65	5.99	6.43	6.56	6.93
	(b)	3.27	3.55	3.68	4.06	4.01	4.19	4.72	5.35	5.52	5.83	6.21	6.31	6.68
	(c)	3.32	3.63	3.79	4.15	4.11	4.31	4.88	5.58	5.81	6.14	6.66	6.78	7.24
	(d)	3.30	3.63	3.72	4.11	4.15	4.26	4.87	5.44	5.71	6.10	6.41	6.62	6.94
Netherlands	(a)	1.08	1.21	1.22	1.24	1.22	1.21	1.27	1.29	1.32	1.33	1.43	1.47	1.48
	(b)	1.06	1.21	1.21	1.24	1.21	1.21	1.27	1.29	1.31	1.34	1.45	1.49	1.49
	(c)	1.06	1.21	1.22	1.26	1.24	1.23	1.29	1.32	1.33	1.35	1.45	1.49	1.50
	(d)	1.05	1.21	1.21	1.26	1.24	1.23	1.29	1.32	1.33	1.36	1.47	1.51	1.50
Norway	(a)	.50	.44	.54	.54	.52	.51	.51	.52	.52	.52	.53	.54	.54
	(b)	.48	.49	.52	.52	.49	.49	.49	.50	.50	.50	.51	.53	.52
	(c)	.49	.51	.54	.54	.51	.51	.51	.52	.52	.52	.53	.54	.54
	(d)	.48	.49	.52	.52	.49	.48	.48	.50	.50	.50	.51	.53	.52
Portugal	(a)	.29	.28	.28	.28	.28	.28	.28	.28	.28	.28	.28	.29	.29
	(b)	.30	.29	.30	.29	.29	.29	.30	.27	.29	.30	.30	.31	.30
	(c)	.30	.29	.29	.29	.29	.28	.29	.29	.29	.29	.29	.30	.30
	(d)	.32	.31	.31	.30	.30	.30	.31	.31	.31	.31	.31	.32	.31
Switzerland	(a)	.93	.95	.95	.94	.93	.93	.95	1.00	1.03	1.05	1.06	1.06	1.05
	(b)	.93	.95	.95	.95	.94	.93	.95	1.00	1.03	1.05	1.06	1.06	1.04
	(c)	.97	.99	.99	.98	.97	.97	1.00	1.05	1.08	1.10	1.11	1.11	1.11
	(d)	.98	1.00	.99	.99	.99	.98	1.00	1.05	1.08	1.10	1.12	1.11	1.09

continued overleaf

TABLE 11.4 Continued

		1953	1955	1956	1957	1958	1959	1960	1961	1962	1963	1964	1965	1966
UK	(a)	8.10	8.20	8.29	8.23	8.30	8.11	8.10	8.11	7.84	7.79	7.74	7.68	7.49
	(b)	8.16	8.31	8.42	8.38	8.50	8.27	8.26	8.32	8.02	7.96	7.94	7.88	7.65
	(c)	7.91	7.99	8.09	8.06	8.17	7.96	8.00	8.05	7.76	7.70	7.61	7.50	7.30
	(d)	8.02	8.12	8.20	8.21	8.32	8.12	8.16	8.23	7.94	7.88	7.81	7.69	7.37
USA	(a)	62.66	61.32	60.30	59.64	58.57	58.76	57.63	55.89	55.48	54.71	53.76	53.70	53.78
	(b)	62.88	61.32	60.26	59.55	58.34	58.64	57.50	55.74	55.35	54.53	53.72	53.74	53.84
	(c)	63.58	62.28	61.22	60.55	59.43	59.66	58.39	56.72	56.37	55.33	54.52	54.49	55.34
	(d)	63.72	62.25	61.37	60.54	59.16	59.68	58.35	56.68	56.15	55.26	54.64	54.65	55.09

Notes: (1) The (a) estimates relate to 1 per cent of GNP at market prices.
The (b) estimates relate to 1 per cent of NNP at market prices.
The (c) estimates relate to 1 per cent of GNP at factor cost.
The (d) estimates relate to 1 per cent of NNP at factor cost.
(i.e. national income).
(2) Exchange rates used:

Australia:	$1.12 US per Australian dollar.
Austria:	26 Schillings per US dollar.
Belgium	50 francs per US dollar.
Canada:	Canadian dollars per US dollar.
1953	0.974
1954	0.966
1955	0.999
1956	0.960
1957	0.985
1958	0.964
1959	0.953
1960	0.9962
1961	1.0431
1962	1.0778
1963–6	1.08108

Table 11.4 (continued)

Denmark:	6.90714 Kroner per US dollar.
France:	4.93706 francs per US dollar.
W. Germany:	1953–60 4.2 DM per US dollar.
	1961 Weighted average of 4.2 DM and 4 DM per US dollar. It came to 4.05 DM per US dollar.
	1962–6 4 DM per US dollar.
Italy:	625 lire per US dollar.
Japan:	360 yen per US dollar.
Netherlands:	1953–60 3.80 guilders per US dollar.
	1961 Weighted average of 3.80 guilders and 3.62 guilders, which was 3.71.
	1962–66 3.62 guilders per US dollar.
Norway:	7.14286 kroner per US dollar.
Portugal:	28.75 esendos per US dollar.
Switzerland:	4.373 francs per US dollar.
UK:	$2.80 US per pound sterling.

(3) Sweden was not considered because complete national income data was not available.
(4) In West Germany the data since 1961 is not comparable with the earlier data because it includes the Saar and West Berlin.

Source: The national income data was taken from the *UN Yearbook of National Income Accounts* and the exchange rates used were taken from the *International Financial Statistics* published by the IMF

It is pertinent, in this connection, to raise the question whether loans need to be made at all.[34] If the purpose of the aid programmes is to transfer resources to LDCs, would not a straightforward transfer *via* grants be the least bothersome method of doing it? It would, among other things, eliminate the problems of watching terms and conditions on loans and worrying about debt-indebtedness (which is a central problem in the aid programmes for a number of LDCs today).

The arguments in favour of loans, as distinct from grants, take different forms.

(i) There is a considerable mythology on this theme, which maintains that grants lead to waste whereas loans, because they have to be repaid, lead to careful and productive expenditures. There is, of course, no logic in this claim. Aid flows occur at inter-governmental level, and the criterion of productivity is already implicit in the bulk of the programmes under which the grants would be made. The mere fact of the loans being repaid does not ensure that the projects or expenditures on which the grants are used will have been carefully chosen. Repayments do not occur from individual projects but are a national responsibility of the recipient country, so that they can always be made from generalized purchasing power over foreign resources, even if individual projects run into economic difficulties. Furthermore, there is nothing to prevent the recipient country, which gets the grants, from dispensing these resources in turn to individual projects etc. on a loan-basis and thereby affecting the efficiency of use of these resources favourably at the project level. Finally, the *overall* efficiency of use of the grants can, and should, be ensured by the imposition of 'economic strings'. At the moment, this task is performed by a number of donor countries, at national level, the prominent example being the guidance and conditions provided by the US Agency for International Development. Such evaluation is also the responsibility of the Consortia and Aid Clubs, which are multilaterally organized, by institutions such as the World Bank and the OECD, for a number of LDCs such as India, Pakistan, Greece and Turkey.[35]

34. This is, of course, a different question from how a given aid flow to an LDC, which consists of hard loans, soft loans, and grants, should be allocated among alternative uses. We are asking a prior, and more important, question as to whether it makes sense to have an official aid programme with a loan-component at all.

35. Recent experience has, however, underlined the delicate nature of such arrangements. Essentially, here is a tough problem which arises directly from the diversity of opinions which can characterize expert evaluation of economic policies. Typically, the donor country or the multilateral agency will think it knows the 'optimal' or the 'correct' answers and that the recipient's policies are ill-informed where they disagree with this view; and similarly, the recipient country will think *it* knows the answers better than the donor or the Consortium. In view of the inherent difficulties of economic evaluation, it seems that the only sensible solution to these problems is to have 'economic arbitration': a suggestion which has recently been mooted also by Paul Rosenstein-Rodan.

(ii) A number of other, rule-of-thumb propositions are in vogue in favour of loans. Schmidt has put together several of these fallacies, some of which are sufficiently widespread to merit discussion here (Schmidt, 1964). For example, it is often argued that grants are suitable for the poorer of the LDCs but loans should be given to the less-badly-off LDCs. However, this makes no sense insofar as the real worth of the loan can be as high or as low as that of a grant, to the recipient. Another fallacy is the claim that grants ought to be given for financing consumption and loans for investment. This is at best a fallacy of misplaced concreteness: consumption may be directly financed by the aid flow (e.g. through PL 480 wheat) but the net effect may still be to increase investment; and the other way around. At worst, the proposition misses the point that the real worth of loans may be identical with that of grants, so that it is absurd to assume that there is any relation at all between either of them and whether the aid flow leads to increased consumption or investment.[36]

(iii) Among the more sophisticated arguments developed in favour of loans is that of Schmidt who argues that, under certain circumstances, it may be possible to maximize the net benefit of aid to the recipient, subject to given cost of aid to the donor, by giving loans rather than grants. This proposition follows when the productivity of the aid flow, at the margin, is greater in the recipient country than in the donor country.[37] This proposition, puzzling as it sounds, is indeed quite obvious. If grants are given, then the ratio of present-value costs to benefits would be 1 to 1. If, on the other hand, a loan is given, since the marginal returns are higher in the recipient than in the donor country, the present-value (discounted) benefit to the recipient will be higher than the cost to the donor, and the ratio of costs to benefits will be less than 1 to 1; hence the superiority of loans over grants. However, this proposition is of little policy relevance, since it rests on a merging together of two separate decisions: the act of a resource transfer to the recipient and the act of investing these resources.

Since the rates of return are different between the recipient and the donor country, it should be possible to invest resources in the country with the higher rate of return (the recipient, in this instance) and thus make one country better off without the other country becoming worse off. What the loan does, in this situation, is to transfer immediately more

36. There is also the difficult problem of distinguishing between consumption and investment, especially in the densely populated Asian LDCs. Increased consumption may well have productivity-effects in some of these countries; and expenditures such as primary education, which were hitherto regarded as social and hence as collective consumption, are increasingly seen as indirectly productive of economic gains through effects on response to agricultural extension, for example.

37. And the reverse proposition, favouring grants, follows when the marginal returns to aid are greater in the donor than in the recipient. Cf. Schmidt (1964).

resources than would a grant costing the donor country (in terms of current discounted value based on the return in the donor country) an identical amount. Thus it amounts to a 'net investment' away from the donor country and a resulting, net gain to the recipient country. We could argue that, for practical purposes, it is sufficient to assume that resources can be invested by the LDCs in the DCs and by the DCs in the LDCs, or that any differences in the rates of returns in the two sets of countries are attributable largely to 'non-economic' objectives (e.g. some countries prefer to invest domestically, at lower rates of return, because they attach value to domestically-originating income as against foreign-earned income). If this were true, as it appears to be, the Schmidt proposition would cease to have any policy significance.

Thus, the arguments in favour of loans for assistance are not persuasive; and it would appear that the ideal form in which aid could be dispensed should be grants. Indeed, Australia has already accepted this policy. The Scandinavian countries are approaching this position rather closely. It would appear, however, that the chances of a universal adoption of such a policy, by all DAC donors, are not at this time particularly bright. However, the adoption of such a long-term target, to be achieved after fulfilment of the recent DAC resolutions on terms and conditions, would be desirable and is worth considering.[38]

Aid-tying

Questions relating to the tying of aid relate to tying by source (e.g. US aid must be spent on supplies), tying by project rather than for general 'balance-of-payments' or 'programmes or 'maintenance' support, and tying by commodity specification. Where the tying is effective, it evidently lowers the value of the aid relative to an untied transfer of resources.

The precise nature of such excess cost, its possible magnitude, and proposals to reduce such costs are discussed in chapter 12 of this volume in relation to the source-tying of aid.[39] Chapter 16, on the other hand, analyses the issues pertaining to the welfare effects of aid-tying by commodity composition, as in the case of food aid under PL 480 programmes of the United States.

38. Such a policy would raise the question of the role of institutions such as the World Bank and the IDA, in developmental assistance. They could essentially serve the role of intermediaries which enable the LDCs to raise loans in the capital markets of the DCs, at better terms than would be possible on their own steam.

39. For this reason the original discussion of aid-tying in this chapter has been abbreviated, as in the text.

REFERENCES

Balassa, B. (1964): *Trade Prospects for Developing Countries* (Homewood, Illinois: Irwin).

Bhagwati, J. (1966): *The Economics of Underdeveloped Countries* (New York: McGraw-Hill), London: Widenfeld and Nicolson).

—— (1972): *Economics and World Order: from the 1970s to the 1990s* (New York: Macmillan).

Blau, G. (1964): 'Commodity export earnings and economic growth', in *New Directions for World Trade*, Proceedings of a Chatham House Conference at Bellagio, 16–24 September 1963 (London: Oxford University Press for Royal Institute of International Affairs).

Chenery, H. and Strout, A. (1966): 'Foreign assistance and foreign development', *American Economic Review* (September).

Frank, C. *et al.* (1972): *Assisting Developing Countries* (New York: Praeger).

Hawkins, E. K. (1968): 'Measuring capital requirements, *Finance and Development* (IMF and World Bank Group).

Hoffman, P. (1960): *One Hundred Countries: One and One Quarter Billion People* (Washington, DC).

Mikesell, R. (1968): *The Economics of Foreign Aid* (Chicago: Aldine Press).

Millikan, M. and Rostow, W. (1957): *A Proposal* (New York: Harper).

Rosenstein-Rodan, J. (1969): 'International aid for underdeveloped countries', *Review of Economics and Statistics* (May) pp. 101–38.

Schmidt, W. (1964): 'The economics of charity: loans versus grants', *Journal of Political Economy* (August), pp. 387–9.

Tinbergen, J. and Centre de Documentation du Comité d'Action pour les Etats-Unis d'Europe (1959): *La Communauté européenne et les Pays sous-développés* (Paris: CAEVE).

UNCTAD (1964): *UNCTAD Conference: Papers and Proceedings*, vol. 1 (New York: UNCTAD).

12

The Tying of Aid

Aid may be tied by source or end-use (via specification of commodities and/or projects). Whereas, however, recent years have witnessed some relaxation in areas such as the project-tying of aid, so that countries like India, Pakistan and Turkey have qualified for increased amounts of aid for non-project, 'maintenance' imports, the trend with respect to tying by source has developed towards comprehensive tying, both in surplus and deficit aid-giving countries. The problems raised by such source-tying of aid have thus become urgent. This urgency is reflected in the resolutions adopted by various UNCTAD organs and subsequent demands for a continuing study of the problems and possible solutions urged on the UNCTAD secretariat and other international organizations such as the OECD.

This paper, therefore, considers the question of source-tying at length.[1] It examines, in particular, the following aspects of the problem:

(1) The methods by which aid is tied by source.
(2) The trend towards increased tying of aid by source.
(3) The reasons for tying aid by source.

The author wishes to thank Mr Andrew Kamarck, Mr J. Saxe and Mr Alan Strout for helpful comments and discussions. Mr T. N. C. Nair and Mr K. B. Nair of the IBM Centre of the Delhi School of Economics kindly made the calculations in Table 12.7.

1. The following symbols have been used in the tables throughout this document: three dots (. . .) indicate that data are not available or are not separately reported; a dash (—) indicates that the amount is nil or negligible; a slash (/) indicates a fiscal year, for example 1965/6. Use of a dash (–) between years, for example 1965–6, signifies the full period involved, including the beginning and end years.

Details and percentages in tables do not necessarily add to totals, because of rounding.

AID	United States Agency for International Development
DAC	Development Assistance Committee for the Organization for Economic Co-operation and Development
EEC	European Economic Community
Exim Bank	Export–Import Bank (United States)
IDA	International Development Association
IDB	Inter-American Development Bank
IBRD	International Bank for Reconstruction and Development
KW	Kreditanstalt für Wiederaufbau (Federal Republic of Germany)
OECD	Organization for Economic Co-operation and Development

From J. N. Bhagwati and R. S. Eckaus (eds), *Foreign Aid: Reading's* (Harmondsworth: Penguin, 1970), pp. 235–93. Originally UNCTAD Secretariat, TD/T/Supp. 4, 1967.

(4) The cost of source-tying to recipient countries.

(5) The gains to aid-giving countries from source-tying.

(6) Methods for reducing the real cost of aid tying by source; and proposals for untying aid.

1 METHODS BY WHICH AID IS TIED BY SOURCE

Tying aid by source must be defined to include all practices by which the recipient country's effective choice to spend the aid on imports from alternative sources, other than the tied source(s), is sought to be proscribed.

Note that our definition would permit aid to be described as source-tied even though, by exploiting switching possibilities (as discussed later), the recipient effectively 'unties' part or all of the aid. At the same time, it would not exclude practices such as simultaneous project-tying, with projects selectively chosen so as to yield the donor country advantages in competitively tendering for them. That some methods of tying could, *ceteris paribus*, cause less real cost to be imposed on the recipient countries, by comparison with other methods, is a separate issue which is examined intensively later.

In general, tying by source can be divided into five major types:

(a) Formal restrictions.

(b) Informal restrictions.

(c) Indirect restrictions.

(d) Export and import credits.

(e) Aid directly in the form of goods and technical services.

Formal restrictions

The most direct form of tying is to require formally and contractually that the recipient country spends the aid funds for importing goods and services only from the designated source(s).

In order to implement such tying, clearly the aid must be disbursed in such a way as to give rise to 'directly identifiable' imports, whose source or origin can be ascertained to ensure that the formal restrictions on procurement by source are not violated.

In these cases, the disbursement procedures vary with countries, depending also on whether the recipient country operates an exchange-control system. In the case of United States aid expenditures, which are formally tied, for example, procurement authorizations are requested from the recipient country and are submitted through the local AID missions for approval in Washington.

Where, however, the aid expenditure does not lead to identifiable, direct imports, it has always been difficult to tie aid by source. This happens typically with the 'local cost' component of project aid, as also with the more common 'budgetary grants' which have been made by donors, such as the United Kingdom, to recipient governments. Even in these cases, however, some donor countries have begun to devise formal restrictions. These usually take the form of 'restricted accounts' arrangements under which the recipient country is required to spend the aid received on specified source(s). The United States has, in particular, resorted to such devices. These arrangements have also been used by the United States to ensure that, although recipient countries are permitted to use aid for procurement in eight designated developing countries,[2] the receipts from such procurement are eventually spent (by these eight countries) on United States goods and services.

It is difficult to quantify the importance of such formal tying of aid in relation to total aid flows, as the relevant data are not generally released. However, it has been estimated that during the years 1961–3 about two-thirds of gross bilateral assistance by DAC member countries was contractually tied or otherwise limited (OECD, 1965, p. 90). The proportion subject to tying has, moreover, increased since the year 1963.

In this connection, it is also relevant to note that some donor countries have sought to impose formal restrictions on shipping to be used for freighting aid-financed imports. However, with the exception of the United States and Japan, all DAC donors have refrained from imposing such restrictions. In the case of the United States, however, legislation under Public Law 83–664 prevents the utilization of aid for financing transportation of aid-financed goods in vessels which do not have United States registry. Further, at least one-half of the aid-financed goods are required by legislation to be shipped in United States bottoms. Similar restrictions have been applicable to goods financed by Export–Import Bank credits, to which we shall refer later.

Informal restrictions

Quite aside from the formal restrictions just described, and the suppliers' credits which are automatically linked to exports from the donor source, as is aid directly embodied in the form of commodities and technical services, it is possible to tie aid by source through 'informal' means. It is frequently pointed out by countries such as the United States which tie aid explicitly and formally, that countries such as France manage, despite overt abstention from formal tying, to arrange that recipient countries spend virtually all of their aid in the donor country. Of course, this is not necessarily proof that informal tying exists. It may be due to the competitive position of the donor countries in international markets; or it may be due to the prevalence of traditional trade ties with such

2. See Lynn (1966).

countries (which secures for the donor an advantage in competing with alternative suppliers); or it may again be due to the influence that the donor country may have in the recipient country through cultural and traditional ties, reinforced by the presence of ex-colonial personnel in the local purchasing agencies and civil service generally (which seems to be partly relevant to the aid expenditures of French-speaking African countries).

On the other hand, there is little doubt that informal tying operates with efficiency in many cases. This can take the form of impressing on the recipient country that any departure from *de facto* tying in purchases would be short-sighted and would cause difficulties in continuing or even granting aid: current United States practices would seem to come fairly close to explicit pursurance of such a policy.

Indirect restrictions

However, much the most subtle form in which source restrictions are applied is neither formal nor informal but what might most aptly be described as 'indirect'. There are essentially two forms in which this is done, at the moment.

One method is to treat the aid flow as part of an over-all trade arrangement, as is done by the socialist countries. An alternative method, practised by the French authorities, is to couple the aid flow with provisions under which the aid is to be spent on French goods and services while France 'reciprocally' purchases from the former French–African territories on a preferential basis. In fact, the entire Franc Zone arrangements, with their monetary and trading implications, are generally recognized as making the question of informal or formal tying somewhat academic. It is interesting to note, in addition, that France has nevertheless resorted to formal tying restrictions in cases where these *de facto* tying arrangements were considered to be inadequate.[3]

Another method, which seems to have gained ground whenever formal and informal restrictions have been considered undiplomatic, is to finance only those commodities and/or projects where the donor country is considered to have a decided advantage in tendering or supplying the specified items. This policy, widely believed to be now practised by the Federal Republic of Germany (and we shall have more to say about this later), can be implemented by letting it be known generally and informally that the chance of securing aid would improve if the project or commodities required were 'suitably chosen' so as to result in directly

3. Thus, for example, the policy of the *Fonds d'Aide et de Coopération* (FAC) has been to tie aid disbursements explicitly via financing conventions signed with local governments: nearly 20 per cent of total French bilateral and multilateral aid was estimated as being informally and formally tied in 1961.

identifiable imports from the donor country despite competitive tendering.[4]

Variations of the preceding policy may also be mentioned. Thus, a donor country wishing to avoid formal and informal tying may reduce the amount of 'local cost' financing or purely budgetary-support grants that will be made. Also, it may deliberately direct projects towards using materials imported from the donor country even though they could have been devised to use cheaper domestic materials that would have necessitated 'local cost' financing.

Export and import credits

Further, there are credits extended to importers or exporters, which are automatically linked therefore to exports from the lending countries. There are essentially two main types to be distinguished here:

(1) On the one hand, there are the so-called suppliers' credits. These are *private* export credits, guaranteed partly or wholly by institutions whose financial support for such activities is directly or indirectly to be traced to official policy. These credits have now reached large proportions (see Table 12.1) and can be obtained from practically all donor countries.[5] These credits can, however, hardly be described as 'international aid', for they are clearly advanced by private exporters whose aim is principally to become established in international markets. The fact that governments, directly and indirectly, help to underwrite, guarantee and promote such credits would seem to make little difference to the fact that they are essentially a means by which the *effective* export prices of capital goods are cut; it is possible to take these credits and discount them back to a current value such that the effective reduction in export price that they make possible can be readily calculated. From this point of view, the efforts at getting the grant of credits co-ordinated by the 'lending' countries, and arriving at rules under which the grant of such credits, and their terms, would be regulated by agreement, would merely represent a form of collusive action by the exporting countries which would artificially inhibit the otherwise *de facto* cutting of their export prices.

4. This need not necessarily imply distortion of choice towards inappropriate or 'low priority' projects in cases where the donor country has taken care to see that the projects were suited to the recipient country and was able to locate a sufficient number of such projects to exhaust the aid commitment planned and requested. However, regardless of how wasteful such an 'indirect' system of ensuring *de facto* tying of aid may be, that it can successfully be used to tie is undoubtedly a fact to be reckoned with.

5. An account of the manner in which these credits are guaranteed in different lending countries, and the role of the governments concerned, is given in a study by the IBRD (1967, see especially pp. 6–7).

TABLE 12.1 Flow to developing countries of guaranteed private export credits net[a] 1960–5 (million US$)

Year	Over 1 up to 5 years	Over 5 years	Total credits
1960	370	93	463
1961	272	221	493
1962	236	399	635
1963	259	293	552
1964	348	533	881
1965	286	455	741

[a]The figures on export credits are annual net increases in outstanding amounts of guaranteed export credits, including the non-guaranteed part of these credits. The IBRD *Report on Suppliers' Credits from Industrialized to Developing Countries*, which is the source of these figures, explicitly points to the unreliability of the information leading to these figures and suggests that they be treated as indicative only.
Source: IBRD (1967).

(2) Of relevance in discussions of tied aid, therefore, are only *public* sector exporter and importer credits such as the sums directly given to purchasers in the importing country on a long-term basis by the Export–Import Bank of the United States, or the credit extended by the Government of Canada, through Canadian exporters, on the basis of specific contracts for the supply of equipment, or the official export credits granted by Italy through the Mediocredito, or the KW (Kreditanstalt für Wiederaufbau) long-term finance that is made available to foreign importers who have placed orders for goods in the Federal Republic of Germany.[6]

Aid directly embodied in goods and technical services

Finally, of relevance to aid-tying by source are the flows which are directly embodied in the form of goods and technical services. The sums involved in such transfers are quite substantial, amounting on the average during 1963–5 to approximately 38 per cent of the total bilateral net aid flow (see Table 12.2). As is indicated further by Table 12.2, the aid in kind is almost wholly from the United States, consisting again primarily of shipments under the PL 480 programme. Aside from the United States, Canada is also an occasional supplier of food aid.

6. It is legitimate to ask whether even these official credits are, after all, not attempts to support export levels and improve export performance, exactly as private export credits (guaranteed or not) are, and whether it is not correct to regard the flows of funds implicit in such credits as ways in which effective supply prices of exports from the 'lending' countries are reduced in order to compete for markets abroad. By the same token, it is not meaningful to expect that untying aid of this kind is feasible for it would undermine the very basis of such credits from the lending countries. This point will be taken up in greater detail later.

TABLE 12.2   Flow of technical assistance and aid in kind to developing countries, 1963–5 (million US$)

Year	Total official bilateral net	Technical assistance	Technical assistance as percentage of total	Aid in kind[a]	Aid in kind as percentage of total	US aid in kind
1963	5712.3	858.4	15.05	1305.2	22.89	1303.0
1964	5440.8	949.6	17.45	1284.6	23.61	1282.0
1965	5773.1	1048.0	18.15	940.3	16.29	940.1

[a]This overstates slightly the amount of shipments in kind because the figures represent the sum of two items: 'Loans repayable in recipients' currencies' and 'Transfer of resources through sales for recipients' currencies'.
Source: OECD (1966, Tables 5–7).

2   THE TREND TOWARDS INCREASED TYING OF AID BY SOURCE

While it is not meaningful to quantify the growth in the prevalence of source-tying, at least partly because data and qualitative information on this subject are closely guarded from scrutiny, there is no doubt that the last few years have witnessed a steady departure from the practice of giving untied aid. This has happened not merely in the countries with deficits in their balance of payments but also in surplus countries such as the Federal Republic of Germany, for reasons which are interesting to discuss.

Deficit countries

United States. The deficit countries have undoubtedly been the pioneers in this trend. The experience of the United States in this respect is both instructive and not without parallel in other countries such as the United Kingdom.

The United States has been steadily tightening its measures in the matter of source-tying. Beginning from 1959, when development loans began to be tied to the United States, all AID loans have now become formally tied and cannot be spent on alternative sources unless inter-agency committees and the AID Administrator grant waivers. In the matter of grant financing, the trend has been parallel: since 1960, procurement under grants has been restricted to the United States and less-developed countries (in the 'free world'), excluding therefore the developed countries of Western Europe and Japan. In March 1966, however, the restrictions were increased and procurement was restricted to the United States and only eight among the developing countries: China (Taiwan), India, Morocco, Pakistan, Philippines, Republic of Korea, Singapore and Thailand where, again, payments for procurement were to be tied to the United States through special letter of credit arrangements. Taking, therefore, this indirect tying into account, it is correct to argue that all United States grants have also now become virtually 100 per cent tied to the United States.

Even in the matter of 'local cost financing', there has been steady tightening in this respect. Wherever the accumulated local currency balances are inadequate for the purpose, and project-financing entails local cost financing, the United States has generally moved in the direction of imposing special letter of credit arrangements which permit payments only for purchases originating in the United States. Up till now, contributions to international organizations have been free of tying. But the latest moves towards tying at least a proportion of the United States contribution to the International Development Association, are indicative of a rapid transition to a full, 100 per cent tying of all United States aid in the near future. Of relevance in this connexion also is the recent report[7] that the Inter-American Development Bank is under pressure, from the United States, to limit the use of IDB ordinary capital outside its member countries.

At the same time, 'informal' tying has increased, in the sense of AID missions seeking to encourage imports from the United States by emphasizing the urgency of the matter to the recipient countries and urging on them the prudence of spending on United States sources even when formal tying is not imposed. Several Latin American countries have thus recently agreed to impose voluntary restraints in their purchases so as to secure them from the United States. Further, commodities of which the United States is a net importer have generally been ruled out from United States aid financing since 1963. Measures to secure full 'additionality', so as to eliminate the possibility of substitution by 'commercial' imports, are being actively studied. In some cases, AID has already successfully imposed limitations on financing projects and/or commodities (via lists) where United States exports would be competitive on commercial terms, thus making it more likely that 'additionality' would follow from aid-tying. Sometimes, loans have been made only in respect of imports 'in excess of normal marketings' of specified commodities.[8]

As a result of these restrictions and actions, the proportion of AID expenditure devoted to offshore purchases has fallen off drastically. The proportion of AID commodity expenditures resulting in off-shore purchases has now been reduced to close to 10 per cent; the proportion of offshore purchases to total AID expenditures (including cash flows and non-commodity expenditures) was reduced to 22.9 per

7. *The Times*, London, 8 May 1967, p. 22.

8. The significant increase in the proportion of PL 480 shipments to the total United States aid flow during the period after 1958/9 should also be taken into account.

cent for the fiscal year 1966 and is expected to be halved within the next two years.

United Kingdom. Until 1962, the United Kingdom had been formally tying only loans provided to countries under section 3 of the Export Guarantees Act: these loans represented only about one-fifth of total disbursements (net of amortization and repayments) by the United Kingdom during this period.[9] A considerable portion of remaining disbursement (not including technical assistance) consisted of financial contributions for budgetary support and 'local financing', which did not in any case give rise to directly identifiable imports in general.

Since then, however, the United Kingdom has generally been tightening terms with respect to tying, under balance of payments pressures. Since 1963 the United Kingdom has tried to ensure, by administrative procedures, that where imports were directly identifiable, these would be procured from the United Kingdom in general. Thus, with respect to 'colonial development and welfare grants', in case of new schemes including grants and/or loans of £25,000 or more, and in case of smaller schemes consisting wholly or largely of imports of capital equipment, direct expenditure on imports from non-United Kingdom sources now requires reference to the Colonial Office which is to sanction such imports only when it is satisfied that the United Kingdom cannot supply the requirements on 'reasonably competitive terms'. The United Kingdom Government has further instituted procedures to examine in respect of all Exchequer loans whether British suppliers could not secure a high share of the imports generated by such loans in the recipient countries, the objective being again to secure orders for the United Kingdom except when the British sources are revealed by consultation to be unreasonably expensive.

Thus, an increasing proportion of the United Kingdom aid expenditures has come to be source-tied as a result of these methods. The matching of aid flows to existing excess capacity in the United Kingdom, thus amounting to tying by selection of projects to be encouraged in the recipient countries, has also been broached in public discussions of aid policy and seems to have played a certain role in United Kingdom aid policy.[10]

Surplus countries

Federal Republic of Germany. The trend in the surplus countries has unfortunately been, even though haltingly, in the same direction as

9. Details of tying in 1963 are given in Krassowski (1965, p. 33).

10. This was specifically discussed, for example, by the Strachey Mission to India some years ago, and seems also to underlie the present indications of British willingness to finance the expansion of Durgapur Steelworks in India when there is excess capacity in the steel-plant-making industry in Britain.

outlined above, and the reasons for this highlight the complexity of the question of getting or keeping aid untied. The experience of the Federal Republic of Germany, which seems to have attempted to play an enlightened role in this respect at the official level, is quite revealing and hence is recorded here at some length.[11]

From the point of view of formal tying, the Federal Republic of Germany had initially been careful not to tie aid significantly beyond that provided through the credits given by the KW out of its own funds, which correspond to the 'Exim-Bank' credits from the United States. The only exceptions had been the indemnification payments to Israel and some loans provided through the budget. In 1962, as a result of this policy, only 9 per cent of the Federal Republic's capital assistance commitments were formally tied.

This was a reflection of the fact that the money and credit section of the Ministry of Economics had held to the argument that the then satisfactory balance of payments situation required that aid from the Federal Republic of Germany be kept untied by source. And yet in 1963 the Federal Government found it advisable to retreat, even though no balance of payments difficulties had occurred or were likely to occur, and formal tying of procurement was applied to 55 per cent of new commitments, whereas (with 3 per cent consisting of offers of consolidation credits) only 42 per cent was left formally untied. Under severe pressure from other donors with payments difficulties the Federal Government retreated marginally, but even in the first half of 1964, over one-third of the Federal Republic's capital assistance remained contractually tied. In 1965, 55 per cent of the total aid flow was left formally untied (with 13 per cent consisting of renewals of former credits and 14 per cent of KW credits from own funds and only 18 per cent being otherwise formally tied).

At the same time, this description understates the effective degree of aid tying by the Federal Republic of Germany. Evidence points to the fact that since 1963, the Government has increasingly sought to finance projects where the Federal Republic of Germany was likely to secure contracts on a competitive basis, thus predisposing the recipients towards acceptance of such projects[12] (even though they may not have been most advantageous to the recipient) and the Federal Government has also been known to boost the import component of projects in preference to 'local cost' financing. The refusal, in many cases, to consider for aid-financing

11. The account here draws on John White (1965, pp. 111–18).
12. 'In 1963 and 1964, several recipient governments began to notice an increasing tendency on the part of German diplomatic representatives to suggest that aid would probably be forthcoming provided that the recipient put up proposals for such and such a project. In several cases, the suggestions were for projects which had a high priority in the recipient's development planning, but the more obvious common factor was the

projects in cases where tenders by the suppliers in the Federal Republic of Germany could be expected to be uncompetitive has led nearly 85 per cent of the loans disbursed by the KW to be spent on suppliers in the Federal Republic. This result has also been accentuated by yet another policy, namely, an occasional refusal to allow contracts to be submitted to international tender. 'Up to the end of 1962, less than half of German capital assistance projects were put up for tender. The others were presumably projects in which a particular firm had had an interest from the start' (White, 1965, p. 113). While the Federal Government has claimed that it has given up this policy, and admits to only a few exceptions to it while even claiming formally that tenders are to be required especially when the project is source-tied to the Federal Republic of Germany, the 'attitudes of German representatives in the field tell a different story from the official one'; and as long as this is so, a prudent recipient government can be expected to treat the capital assistance as effectively tied even though the utilization of an international bidding procedure might have reduced costs.

Why then has a surplus country such as the Federal Republic of Germany, with a powerful economics ministry conscious of the need for keeping aid untied by source, been forced to such methods of aid-tying? The reasons quoted by one source are instructive:

> The principle that German aid should not be currency-tied – that is, tied specifically to the procurement of German goods and services – has been repeatedly criticized by the representatives of German industry. The criticism mounted sharply when the United States took to currency-tying in order to safeguard its balance of payments. Not only did the American decision mean that German exporters lost their share of orders financed from the US Development Loan Fund, which had been considerable, but it also meant, to their far greater chagrin, that they lost a number of established export markets which had previously been independent of aid finance from any country and which were now flooded with American goods purchased with American tied commodity credits. This result was particularly noticeable in Turkey, where German exporters lost the strong position that they had gained in open market competition (White, 1965, p. 113).

likelihood that the contract would be awarded to a German firm. Since there was no evidence that the new tendency was the outcome of intensified study of the recipients' economies, it was taken as evidence of an increased determination to promote German interests, not as the outcome of improved project selection machinery' (White, 1965, p. 114).

Thus, part of the reason for the strong pressure in favour of aid-tying has almost certainly been what might be described as 'competitive aid-tying' prompted by commercial interest. This is quite distinct, of course, from the competitive aid-tying that can occur between deficit countries with one country tying aid to divert expenditure in the contrary direction.[13]

A separate motivation for tying, despite a sound balance of payments position, which the Federal Government has found it difficult to stifle arises from the fact that prestige and political kudos for aid are frequently associated not with the source of finance, but with those who built a project. Cases in which major prestige projects have been financed by the Federal Republic but built by firms from other countries are not common, but they tend to attract much public and press comment when they do occur (White, 1965, p. 114).

Thus, it is clear that even though one would expect a surplus country to take no steps to tie aid, particularly if there were strong opposition to this internationally, there are weighty reasons why it is likely to be forced into such practices. And the experience of the Federal Republic of Germany suggests precisely how the tying will, in such cases, take indirect but effective forms, with little emphasis on the formal tying provisions which would be difficult to defend internationally.[14]

13. Occasional statements and writings of ministers and responsible officials testify to this element of competitive aid-tying very clearly. Thus, take the two following examples: (1) According to *Die Welt*, 17 January 1967, Mr Wischnewski the Federal Republic's Minister for Economic Co-operation, assured his countrymen that the principle of tied aid would be observed even more rigorously in the future, so as to secure orders for materials and machines produced in the Federal Republic, particularly in view of the attitude of other countries. (2) Again, Walter Scheel (1963, p. 23), Minister for Developmental Aid in the former Erhard cabinet, has written that, with regard to the question of source-tying, an international agreement was the ideal solution and that, as long as this was not procured, the Federal Government necessarily had to take into account the attitude of other countries and hence the principle of leaving German aid untied could not be regarded as a 'dogma'.

14. Referring to this conflict between the recognition of an international obligation not to tie aid when there is a surplus in the balance of payments and the need to accommodate domestic pressure for tying, John White has stated cogently that:
'The obvious way of escape from this conflict is simply to avoid making commitments for projects in sectors in which German firms are not competitive, which is the solution that the Federal Government seems consciously to have adopted. The tacit application of this kind of criterion does not necessarily conflict with the recipient's interests, but it clearly limits the range of projects for which German assistance is forthcoming. It therefore puts an onus on the Federal Government to take a far greater initiative in seeking out aid-worthy projects, since the criterion is not one that the recipients can be expected to take into account. So long as the Federal Government maintains a policy of not taking the initiative in seeking project proposals, leaving the recipient to produce projects in conformity with criteria which are in fact not fully stated, there is a continuing danger of an unchecked conflict of interest between German suppliers and the recipients of German aid' (White, 1965, p. 114).

3   REASONS FOR TYING AID BY SOURCE

This leads the discussion directly into the reasons which have been alleged to be, and undoubtedly are, important in the spread of the practices of tying aid by source. The present section merely outlines these reasons; their substance will be examined in later sections that deal with the benefits to donor countries from aid-tying and possible solutions to the question.

The primary cause of tying by the deficit countries, as is evident from the preceding section, remains balance of payments difficulties. This argument has been invoked by both the United States and United Kingdom and undoubtedly is the chief reason for their tying practices. However, it is *also* an argument invoked by countries currently in surplus. For example, Italy has argued in the recent past that the then balance of payments surplus was merely a prelude to increased import spending in support of planned development, so that aid untying would not be adopted as a general policy at the time. Canada and Japan have also continuously produced this reason in support of their tying practices.

In a fundamental sense, the balance of payments ground for tying aid is an argument for avoiding the loss of real income that would follow if the aid transfer did not give rise to a matching demand for imports; for, in such a case, the aid donor would have to adjust its payments accounts by suitable policies which would lead to deterioration in the terms of trade, and hence real income, in general. A similar motivation, of reducing the real cost of making a certain financial transfer of resources, also underlies the desire to tie aid to industries where there is excess capacity in the donor country or where there are already surplus stocks (as in the case of PL 480 shipments). Aid in kind hitherto was primarily to be explained in terms of this motivation, although the unforeseen deficits in food availabilities in countries such as India in the last two years, and the unprecedented sales and depletions of surplus commodities in the United States seem to have reduced this early motivation for expanding PL 480 shipments to complete insignificance.

Further, as we have already seen in the case of the Federal Republic of Germany, an important role is played also by commercial pressure groups who wish to benefit from the orders that they think ought to accrue to donor-country nationals rather than to third countries. This is clearly an important force to reckon with; and it is clear that an element of competitive aid-tying follows from this pressure, for aid-tying by one country on grounds such as deficit in the balance of payments leads to aid-tying by another country whose exporters find their own markets abroad jeopardized by such policies by other donor countries. This competitive element is among the most difficult aspects of the problem of inducing surplus countries to accept (or rather of inducing them to persuade their electorate and pressure groups to accept) aid-tying by other countries on the ground that their own balance of payments is currently in a favourable position. This is irrational, of course, as the deficit country, in so far as it gives up effective tying, is likely to be forced to undertaken other measures which are equally likely to hurt the international industries of the surplus country; but somehow such 'indirect' action is rarely so evocative of a threat as direct action in the form of explicit tying measures.

But, while aid is tied competitively by countries for commercial reasons, the same commercial reasons are undoubtedly responsible in certain cases for leading to the grant of aid (in which case it would not make sense to propose that aid should be untied and expect that aid would remain at initial levels). Thus, for example, the Japanese aid flow, which is exclusively tied formally (except for a negligible amount for multilateral agency contributions and occasionally from consolidation credits), is to be attributed, partly at least, to a desire to support Japanese exports of machinery and manufactures to the developing countries. This is, in fact, the motivating force behind the United States Export-Import Bank's activities. The Exim Bank's direct loans, which are repayable in dollars at near commercial rates of interest, are explicitly directed at financing purchases from the United States, the loans being granted in fact when some explicit imports from the United States are being considered.[15] It is also the motivation behind the activities of the KW in the Federal Republic of Germany on the basis of its own funds, and of similar institutions in Canada, France, United Kingdom and Italy.

Finally, the tendency to tie aid is also to be attributed to a combination of reasons, political and economic, which lead to project-tying of aid in the first instance and to source-tying subsequently. Thus, some countries (the Federal Republic of Germany among them) are keen to tie aid to projects on the ground that this is most likely, in their experience, to lead to an efficient and quick utilization of aid. At the same time, these donor countries feel that the best way to secure credit for their aid in recipient countries is to finance conspicuous projects which are then identified easily in the public mind with the donor country, whereas this political effect is not secured if the aid is not linked to something as conspicuous and dramatic. Further, as pointed out above, it is felt that the credit thus obtained goes in practice to those who actually build the project rather than to those who finance it. Hence the desire to tie aid to both projects and source simultaneously. These political reasons are also accentuated by the fact that, even in the donor countries, few people seem to consider it sensible that orders arising from aid financed at the public expense

---

15. These direct loans of the Export-Import Bank are a fairly sizeable part of the United States assistance programme, running at an average of $564 million during 1960–3, which was about 16 per cent of the total net outflow of aid to the developing countries.

should go to third parties and 'benefit' them instead. These attitudes are particularly important, as we have seen, in the surplus countries and also, because of tying by other countries, extremely difficult to resist.

4   THE COST OF TYING TO RECIPIENT COUNTRIES

In estimating the cost of tying aid by source, it is necessary to note that the actual cost of tying that is incurred by the recipient country may not be the irreducible minimum cost of tying, and that there may exist opportunities for *de facto* untying of aid, or otherwise reducing the cost attached to restricted procurement, which have not been exploited by the recipient country in question.

In estimating empirically the cost of aid-tying by source, therefore, it is important to distinguish between two different questions:

(1) How much cost would be imposed by the tying of aid itself, if the recipient country were maximizing use of available opportunities to substitute, to invite competition and the like.

(2) How much cost is actually to be attributed to the fact that the recipient country does not exploit these opportunities which exist even within the context of source-tied aid.

In practice, of course, these two questions are difficult to disentangle, but they are clearly of considerable relevance to any assessment of the implications of aid-tying as also to an examination of what can be done to reduce, if not minimize, the costs of such tying if it must be accepted to some extent.

In assessing the latter question, it is again necessary to distinguish between what a recipient country could do in principle and what it can reasonably be expected to do in practice when it is aid-dependent and underdeveloped. For example, clever 'programming' aimed at gaining maximum advantages out of substitution possibilities may be somewhat self-defeating if it succeeds in jeopardizing the aid flow itself.

Assuming, for the sake of argument, however, that the recipient country will be doing the maximum necessary in order to minimize the cost of source-tying of aid, what can be expected to be the cost resulting from such source-tying? In dealing with this question analytically, we should distinguish between the case where the aid is also tied by commodity and where it is not.

Case 1: aid tied by source alone

It is readily seen that source-tying will be unsuccessful in its intent in so far as the recipient country would like to spend on purchases from the tied source, from its total pool of foreign exchange from aid and export earnings, an amount that equals or exceeds the amount that is explicitly source-tied. Thus, for example, assume that $300 million of tied aid from the United States is given to India and that, out of its total pool of foreign exchange, India, after considering the relative competitiveness of various alternative sources of supply, would like to spend $350 million on imports from the United States. In this case, it is clear that no effective tying of United States aid has occurred.

The same point may be put a little differently. Suppose that, from the available funds other than the $300 million of United States tied aid, India would have liked to buy $210 million worth of United States goods; and that, from the $300 million of tied aid, India would in any case like to buy $140 million worth of United States goods. In this case, the effective tied aid of $160 million (300 − 140) being less than the $210 million which is being purchased (from other funds) from the United States anyway, India could readily *de facto* untie the United States aid by merely switching existing imports. For the case where there is licensed allocation of foreign exchange, as in India, all that would be necessary is to finance the existing imports, up to $160 million, from the tied fund account, and thus release the same sum for imports from any other sources.[16]

According to this way of looking at the problem, the total pool of funds available to the country is considered as the sum of two parts: the tied aid from a given source and the remainder. And, clearly, it follows that the condition under which tied aid can be regarded as totally untied *de facto* is that the amount that the recipient country would like to spend out of the tied aid funds on sources other than those designated should equal or be less than the amount that the recipient would spend, from the funds not tied to these sources, on the designated sources.[17]

16. If one is dealing with a recipient country not applying exchange controls, then its Government could achieve this objective merely by merging the tied aid funds into the common pool of funds in the foreign exchange market (and would thus be absolved from undertaking intervention in the form of exchange control, for example, to ensure that the purchases from the United States came up to the required tied aid level). In practice, however, one is almost always dealing with recipient countries with exchange control systems, which facilitates the implementation of aid-tying restrictions at the same time that international organizations, and the donor countries through them, eagerly advise the dropping of exchange controls, and the adoption of what are, effectively, flexible exchange rates which they think are not so good for the donor countries themselves. For a theoretical analysis of the effects of aid-tying on multiple exchange rates, see Bhagwati (1968).

17. This condition is, of course, identical with the earlier one when the spending out of the entire pool of funds was considered. Note, however, that whether such possibilities of substitution will be allowed to exist and be exercised is quite a different matter. It is well known that the donor countries increasingly worry about such substitution, when they are in payments difficulties, and have a tendency to impose informal restrictions in this matter as also to indulge in commodity specification which prevents such substitution by earlier, 'commercial' imports. Indeed, since such substitution can occur even among different donors, from their aid funds, it is now increasingly contemplated that the tying

But such a possibility of substitution, with its attendant untying of aid in effect, will not work fully when the funds which would be spent out of the total pool on a source fall short of the tied aid total therefrom. In this case, there will be left a hard core of tied aid, from one or more sources, which is effectively tied even when all substitution possibilities have been exploited.

What is then the cost of this hard core of tied aid which is not merely *de jure* but also *de facto* tied? One is tempted to think that this cost would be measured by the excess cost of the items that would now have to be imported, up to the value of this hard core tied aid, from the tied aid sources; and that this cost would be minimized by following a worldwide tender policy, then ticking off all the competitive tenders from each tied source against the tied aid, leaving a set of unassigned hard core tied-aid flows and unsatisifed import requirements which would then be matched by the authorities in such a way as to minimize the whole cost of this operation. It might also be concluded that such a policy would also eliminate all elements of monopolistic pricing of suppliers under tied aid.

However, there are some important snags to this argument, which imply that the cost of aid-tying in practice will be considerably higher. We will first consider the case where the source-tied aid must be spent on projects (though not on specific projects) and then the case of non-project aid (which again is not tied to specific commodities).

Project aid. To begin with, the worldwide tendering procedure can be gone through for each project; but this is not the same thing as doing it simultaneously and then allocating projects to cheapest sources, as assumed above. For one thing, aid rarely comes in this simultaneous sense, but is a continuing process even for countries with donor-country consortia. For another, few countries have their projects ready for such action and indeed cannot be expected to do so, since total aid prospects are usually unclear and given the limitations also of their technical organizations for this kind of work. Hence, in reality, the costs of tying, even when the donor country does not tie its aid to specific projects, are likely to be considerably greater than indicated above. Moreover, the worldwide tendering on projects, which are then ostensibly assigned to different tied sources according to the successful tenders, will not necessarily yield the maximum number of bids and the widest, most competitive quotations to choose from. If there is a preponderance of tied funds from one source alone, and the free foreign exchange of the recipient country is negligible in comparison, then the suppliers from areas

should be done by specifying commodities in which the donor has the least advantage: this would mean that the donor would be able to secure all orders that it can, on a competitive basis, from all the foreign exchange resources which the recipient country can be put to tender, and ensure thereby the full 'additionality' of tied aid purchases. We shall revert to this later.

other than the tied-aid sources may not deem it worthwhile to tender at all. Further, if the suppliers from the preponderant tied-aid source know about this limited flexibility, then their tenders may well reflect this monopoly position. Even when the tied aid extends to more than one source, the suppliers from all the tied sources may follow similar mark-up policies, for they would have an advantage over other third-source suppliers in so far as third-source entry is limited by the recipient country's lack of manoeuvrability. That such implicit collusion can arise is indisputable; how far it actually arises is difficult to establish. Clearly, such monopolistic charging will be reduced, to the extent that the recipient country's access to free funds is relatively large in relation to tied funds and the tied funds, in turn, are spread over a large number of sources.

Non-project aid. Finally, similar difficulties arise over non-project aid as well. However, they arise from the methods by which the exchange control authorities operate import control. These methods, when combined with tied funds, lead in practice to the possibility of monopoly pricing by suppliers from tied aid sources. In principle, exchange control authorities could issue licences authorizing imports from the tied source(s) only and make these and other licences transferable so that licence-holders could themselves exploit all arbitration possibilities so as to minimize losses, leading to the same result in principle as a worldwide tendering procedure (on the assumption that the importers act with similar energy to seek out the lowest-cost sources of supply).

However, in practice, many governments in fact specify both items and source (where there is tied aid), as the authorities are keen to ensure that only 'priority' uses are permitted. But once both items and source are specified, the donor country specified becomes in effect the only feasible source of supply. The fact that the licensing authorities, in conjunction with the United States AID mission for example, have specified (on the licences) only those items where the United States is regarded as a low-cost supplier will then not necessarily mean that the supplies will come at the competitive rates that would be offered in an open market.

Where the suppliers of the designated items are few in number, explicit collusion cannot be ruled out – even though the aid missions attempt to examine prices and prevent such practices. But even when the suppliers are 'numerous', the fact that the supply is to be undertaken against aid-finance will often lead to a higher price being charged than if it were to be undertaken in a less restricted market. Thus, for example, United States suppliers will treat the aid-financed sales as equivalent to domestic sales and will generally charge f.o.b. prices, for such aid-financed contracts, which are equivalent to domestic prices. But, as is frequently the case, the competitive f.o.b. price charged by many manufacturing concerns is lower than the domestic price – largely because the foreign market is considered to be more 'competitive' owing to the presence of foreign suppliers.[18] Thus, the fact that tying of aid leads United States suppliers, in this example, to price abroad as though they were pricing for a domestic sale, thus treating aid-financed sales as a mere extension of domestic market sales, will also result in the recipient country being overcharged, in relation to the competitive f.o.b. price that it would have secured if the tying of aid had been replaced by free flow of funds, for its imports from the tied source. Note that:

(1) While this need not occur systematically, since some firms may not follow such pricing practices, there is considerable agreement among knowledgeable analysts that there is indeed such a discrepancy between domestic prices and competitive f.o.b. prices in general.

(2) Discussion by the author of this point with procurement officers in one aid mission revealed that the practice under which a domestic price may be charged to foreign purchasers buying under aid-finance was treated as 'legitimate' and, by no means as an exercise of 'monopoly power' which, in fact, it is from a strictly economic point of view.

As these margins, which are lost under tied aid, may be fairly large (if the evidence that obtains with respect to such practices is indicative), the loss imposed on the recipient countries from the tying of aid may be quite considerable despite the recipient country exploiting the substitution possibilities.

The specific problem just discussed arises from a licensing system which specifies imports and source simultaneously in view of, firstly, an aid-tied situation which requires that the imports from the donor source not be allowed to fall below the specified level; as also, secondly, a desire on the part of the recipient country to maintain priority allocation of imports. One way to avoid the problem, however, while maintaining priority uses, would be to permit trade-offs between licensees so that if someone is, for example, in possession of a United States licence for a certain level of imports of item x that he does not want from that source, he can trade it off for a certain level of imports of item x from the United Kingdom with someone who was given a licence for imports of item y from that country. Thus, the exchange would leave the first licensee with the same level of imports of x, but without being limited to United States sources, and the second licensee with the same level of imports of y, but without being limited to United Kingdom sources. Such trade-offs would thus preserve the priority pattern of imports and ensure expenditure of aid on tied sources, while ideally establishing conditions of competition which could help to eliminate the kind of exercise of monopoly power which is otherwise conferred on exporters from tied sources.

18. Evidence on this widely-recognized practice was gathered systematically by Milton Gilbert (1940) for the inter-war period.

The situation may however not be ideal: the trade-offs may be theoretically possible but the market may not be functioning ideally to make use of the opportunities; moreover, if there were a preponderance of funds tied to one or two sources, there may be effective exercise of monpoly power from these sources as the possible trade-offs would be limited and may not be sufficient to ensure effective competition to eliminate the exercise of monopoly power entirely.

Thus, even if optimal policies of procurement were to be followed with respect to both project and non-project imports, so as to exploit substitution possibilities aimed at minimizing the real cost of tied aid, there are sufficient reasons to think that the costs would not be eliminated in practice. Nor can these optimal procurement policies be necessarily followed, for reasons already set out: for example, the sequential character of aid flows which prevents the utilization of simultaneous tendering for different projects. In practice, therefore, the recipient countries would necessarily face the prospect of high cost attached to the hard core of effectively tied aid plus monopolistic prices on a wider range of tied aid flows, even though the aid were assumed to be tied by source and not simultaneously by commodity specification as well.

Case 2: aid tied by specific projects and by commodity

In practice, aid is often tied (at the donor country end) by specific projects, as also by commodity when non-project aid is granted. In either case, therefore, the real costs have to be evaluated in terms of a simultaneous tying by source and commodity specification. As will be readily seen, this practice can be used, with varying degrees of effectiveness, to reduce or even eliminate the possibilities of substitution that were outlined in the preceding discussion.

Aid tied to specific projects

Let us consider first the case of source-tied aid which is also tied to specific projects. The exact costs that are associated with such double-tying will depend critically on the precise method by which the specific projects are chosen for allocation to specific sources.

Method 1. If the projects are allowed to be allocated by source after a worldwide tender for all projects, then the costs which would obtain will be identical with the costs we have already discussed earlier for the case of aid tied by source alone. Clearly, therefore, we are interested here in methods of project selection which do not follow this procedure.

Method 2. An alternative and more realistic procedure is for the recipient country to have a list of projects from which, by mutual consultation, certain projects are assigned to different tied sources on the assumption that these are likely to be the cheaper sources and will impose least excess cost from aid-tying. This may appear to be an approximate, rough and ready way of doing what the system of worldwide tendering and allocation to different tied sources later will accomplish.

However, this is not the case. There is first the simple fact that the relative cheapness of alternative sources may be wrongly estimated by the parties engaged in the exercise: there is no adequate substitute in general for a tendering system. Further, the monopolistic practices discussed in the preceding sub-section will emerge, as soon as a project is allocated in advance to a tied source. In particular, the overpricing resulting from the 'extension of the domestic market' variety of argument will persist in this situation.

Inviting tenders from suppliers within the designated source will be inefficient as an instrument for eliminating monopolistic overpricing if suppliers can enter into collusion (implicitly or explicitly) more easily and readily when they belong to one source rather than several. It is sometimes sought to refute this argument on the grounds that the tenders invited could be on a worldwide basis. However, this could not help if the project was known to be assigned to one specific source already: there would be no incentive for suppliers from alternative sources to tender in such a case.

Needless to say, if the recipient country does not invite tenders even from the suppliers of the designated country, there is every likelihood of the monopolistic pricing being even greater than in the case of explicit monopolistic collusion by suppliers. In fact, there are many cases on record of such overcharging, resulting from the recipient country not having followed a proper tendering procedure even within the feasible limits. It is interesting to note that the reasons for not following even this limited tendering procedure may be several.

(i) Often a foreign firm has been associated with a particular project from the beginning and its getting the order is regarded as practically automatic.

(ii) In some cases the aid actually follows upon a project having been worked out by a specific domestic firm in collaboration with firms or the government in a recipient country, so that tendering is regarded as 'academic' and the firm's prices, provided they are not seen to be outrageously exorbitant, are taken on trust as reasonable.

(iii) In a few cases, further, the lack of tendering has been argued to reflect corruption in the recipient country, with the connivance of influential people in the lending country.

Method 3. Finally, the method of project selection for a tied source may be neither by reference to simultaneous tendering for different projects nor exclusively by choice prior to the invitation of tenders on the selected project.

Several projects, in practice, are 'associated' with certain sources which seem to be the likely source of finance, for a variety of reasons, for them. As Ul Haq indicates in his pioneering analysis of tied aid for Pakistan, the optimal method in such cases is to invite tenders on a worldwide basis and to threaten to shift the project to alternative sources if the 'associated' tied source for the project is unduly expensive (Ul Haq, 1965). Undoubtedly, this method, which is akin to the first method discussed above with the basic difference that projects acquire the likelihood of being assigned to particular sources quite independently of the results of the tenders, is superior to the second method discussed above. However, it would be illusory to think that all monopolistic overpricing, especially the 'extension of the domestic market' variety, will disappear in cases where projects are associated with definite sources and therefore can be expected by suppliers from alternative sources to be assigned to these sources.

In conclusion, it should be mentioned that we have so far discussed the costs of source-tied aid, when also tied to specific projects, on the assumption that the donor country will permit the choice of projects to be made by the recipient country in conformity with the latter's priorities. But this assumption need not be fulfilled. In fact, we have seen already (in an earlier section) how the project choice itself may be dictated by particular supplier interests from a specific donor country – in which case, the cost of such tied-aid may be not merely the costs discussed so far but also that imposed by any possible distortion away from priorities from a developmental point of view (assuming, of course, that the recipient country itself would have exercised such a choice, an assumption which is not as valid as it seems).

Similarly, the costs can be still further increased to the recipient country if the donor country seeks to increase effective tying by reducing the 'local cost' component of the project by artificially raising the import content which is tied to the donor country source.

By such distortion of the choice and design of projects, therefore, the costs of aid-tying may be raised above those which would obtain if the donor country were scrupulous and accommodating about the choice of projects.

Other aid tied by commodity specification

Similar accentuation of difficulties and the cost of source-tying will occur when aid is also tied by end-use other than via projects.

In this case the possibilities of inflated costs of supply of specific items may be reduced by mutual consultation, provided that the donor country is agreeable, so that a process of 'substitution' is mutually allowed for. But, even ruling out costs that may accure from the fact that certain items may not be available from the tied source at all or that the donor country may be interested in supplying specific items of low priority to the recipient (with a view to securing 'additionally' or for other reasons), there will be a 'monopolistic' rise in prices once the commodity specification has taken place. As we have already argued earlier in this section, the aid price is likely to be identical with the domestic price and hence greater than the normal worldwide competitive f.o.b. price. The result might even be yet further monopolistic price exploitation although suitable information and procurement policies could help to reduce this.

Finally, some remarks may be addressed to the assertion sometimes made by donor countries that when import and export credits are granted, as with Exim Bank loans, there is no cost to the *de facto* and automatic tying because, firstly, the recipient countries first choose the items for import themselves and then seek credit; and/or secondly, the credit is given for projects where the national suppliers have already managed to secure contracts on an international tender basis. The first argument is not always factually correct, especially for smaller donor countries, in the experience of countries such as India. But even if it were correct, it is fallacious because, the very fact that the 'aid' is available from a certain source if imports are procured from it, is sufficient to result in real costs of the kind discussed earlier for tied aid. Further, the second argument is also untenable; only if all suppliers everywhere had access to the same credit terms (given as aid by one country for its exports alone), would it be correct to argue that there would be no costs from the tying. Otherwise, the fact, for example, that an Italian firm knows that it has access to Italian aid credits will enable it to tender more cheaply than a firm from the Federal Republic of Germany without such access; whereas if the latter firm also had similar access, it might have tendered yet more cheaply and the recipient country would have been as well off as if the aid were not tied.

To sum up then, source-tying of aid will generally impose costs, inclusive of 'monopolistic' pricing by suppliers, even when ideal procurement policies are followed. Moreover, these costs are likely to be accentuated when the donor countries also specify the end-use, by project or otherwise, of source-tied aid. These costs will vary with:

(1) The flexibility, in substitution, that the recipient country enjoys through access to more than one source of foreign funds.

(2) The extent to which such exploitation of substitution possibilities is permitted by the donor countries.

(3) The willingness and ability of the recipient country, via optimal procurement and related policies, to exploit such substitution and competitive possibilities as exist.

The preceding discussion would be incomplete, however, were reference not made to yet other indirect costs that may arise from the restriction on procurement sources that source-tying will, in general, impose in some degree.

(a) There may be recurring costs from having imported capital equipment which needs expensive repairs, spare parts and even (perhaps) more expensive inputs (such as raw materials and fuel) for processing or operation. Where the buyer follows an 'atomistic' policy, these disadvantages will not be reflected in the price paid; and therefore these costs must be reckoned as additional to those discussed in the preceding paragraphs.

(b) Further, as we remarked earlier, the cost of tying could involve not merely a higher f.o.b. price but also additional shipping expenses. Such additional freight may involve costs for extra distance and also higher freight rates (as with United States shipping) where there are restrictive clauses with respect to the shipping to be used.[19] Moreover, as Ul Haq has pointed out, freight rates which are quoted in tenders not open to suppliers everywhere are typically increased, so that monopolistic raising of freight rates also is not uncommon and needs to be watched when aid is tied (see Table 12.3).

(c) Finally, it is possible that, as with all allocational systems involving direct control, there could be delays associated with finding appropriate items from the donor country to which the aid is tied. Associated with this is the difficulty in establishing trading and commercial relationships with a new area from which tied aid is beginning to come; this itself could cause inefficiency because of delays and may necessitate an expensive 'informational' investment expenditure.

(d) It is also worth mentioning that the effect of restricting procurement to donor countries may be to prevent developing countries from tendering for projects and competing to supply commodities under non-project aid. The effect would thus be to inhibit the growth of export earnings and also, except where supplies are totally elastic, to impose welfare losses on the developing countries who might otherwise have been successful suppliers for aid-financed imports.

Empirical estimates

If we are to examine the cost of source-tying to recipient countries in practice, as revealed by empirical analysis, obviously the estimates can be undertaken only at the recipient country's end, for it is only there that the full scope for substitution (as discussed above), as also the exercise thereof, can be effectively analysed.

---

19. This latter problem is applicable only to the United States. The costs involved can be considerable, for it is well-known that United States shipowners will charge, for aid-financed shipments, freights up to three times the open market rates quoted by other companies. It should be mentioned, however, that the excess freight on PL 480 shipments is covered by the United States authorities rather than by the recipients: though, here too, it qualifies as 'aid disbursed' rather than as an 'export subsidy' in the budgetary accounts.

TABLE 12.3 Instances of higher freight charges under tied credits

Procuring agency	Item	Whether international bids invited	Lowest quotation from tied source	Lowest quotation on international bidding	Percentage difference $((4)-(5))\div(5)$	Remarks
(1)	(2)	(3)	(4)	(5)	(6)	
Pakistan Western Railway	Freight on 18 locomotives (large)	Yes	$14,500 per locomotive	$6800 per locomotive (Norway)	113	Higher freight paid
Pakistan Western Railway	Freight on 20 locomotives (small)	Yes	$9500 per locomotive	$5850 per locomotive (Norway)	62	Higher freight paid
Pakistan Western Railway	Freight on 22 locomotives (large)	Yes	$14,500 per locomotive	$6800 per locomotive (Norway)	113	Higher freight paid
Pakistan Western Railway	Freight on 22 locomotives (small)	Yes	$9500 per locomotive	$5850 per locomotive (Norway)	62	Higher freight paid
Pakistan Western Railway	Freight on 30 locomotives (small)	Yes	$8380 per locomotive	$5850 per locomotive (Norway)	43	Waiver obtained in favour of non-US flag ships. Cost met partly by cash and partly by IBRD loan
Pakistan Eastern Railway	Freight on locomotives (medium)	Yes	$11,500 per locomotive	$7500 per locomotive (Norway)	53	Waiver obtained; costs met from cash.

Source: M. Ul Haq (1965); printed in the Proceedings of the Conference: Adler and Kuznets (1967).

Short of such detailed analysis, it is interesting to note that, firstly, the range of bids, from the highest to the lowest, on international tenders can be very large, thus indicating that the excess cost of procurement from a tied source (even leaving out monopolistic elements) may be significant; and, secondly, the incremental cost, of a monopolistic variety, where tendering is limited or non-existent, can be very high indeed.

A useful source of information on the former point is the spread of bids on IBRD loans and IDA credits. Two sets of samples have become available recently, which cast some light on this question. Before we discuss them, however, it is necessary to point out some of the key limitations, in inferring from them the potential range of excess costs that tying might impose:

(1) Tenders are not easily comparable because of differing clauses, quality differences, different specifications included by different tenderers, etc. Hence, it cannot always be inferred that the observed spread reflects the actual differences in cost of supply that are relevant to our calculations.

(2) Further, while the spread will indicate the *possible* differences in cost of supply from a tied source, it has important limitations in this respect:

(a) The actual source of supply under tied aid may have even higher cost than the highest tender in the IBRD bids, for the simple reason that this high cost may itself have precluded a bid from this source: to this extent, the spread shown will understate the actual cost of tying that can arise.

(b) The tying may be to a source which happens to be a lower-cost source of supply than the highest in the IBRD bids; to that extent, the spread between highest and lowest bids will overstate the actual cost of tying that will arise.

While keeping these qualifications in mind, we note that the sample bids tabulated from IBRD and IDA data in Table 12.4 show that the percentage of potential excess cost, measured as the ratio of the difference between 'high bids' and 'successful bids' to 'successful bids', was on the average 49.3 per cent and that over 31 per cent of the value of contracts awarded (amounting in total to $200.9 million) were characterized by potential excess cost of over 50 per cent, and 62.9 per cent of the value of contracts awarded were characterized by potential excess cost of over 30 per cent.

Turning next to the question of the monopolistic pricing associated with tied aid, Ul Haq has pointed out that tied aid projects in Pakistan were typically subjected to monopolistic pricing:

> ... The quotations offered by the suppliers are often higher
> if the suppliers know that it is a tied credit and come down
> considerably once it is made clear that the supplies will be

TABLE 12.4 Frequency distribution of the ratios of difference between high bids and successful bids to successful bids on competitive tendering for twenty IBRD loans and three IDA credits, 1960–6

	Less than 10%	10–20%	20–30%	30–40%	40–50%	50–100%	100% and over	Total
Number of contracts	12	8	13	12	9	27	11	92
Percentage of contracts	13.0	8.7	14.1	13.0	9.8	29.4	12.0	100.0
Percentage value of contracts to total value	17.6	5.4	14.1	13.0	18.6	28.0	3.3	100.0

Source: UNCTAD secretariat based on IBRD data.

financed against cash or untied credits . . . One of the amusing
examples in the recent experience of Pakistan was that of Atlas
Copco type compressors under French credit.
The French suppliers offered certain quotations which, when
checked against the quotations received from the Pakistani
agents for Atlas Copco, were found to be 33 per cent to 47
per cent higher for various items. (Ul Haq, 1965).

What Ul Haq does not mention, however, is the possibility that, firstly,
there could be 'monopolistic' pricing, in the sense of the f.o.b. price under
tied-aid-financed exports being equal to the domestic price and therefore
higher than the competitive f.o.b. price, for a large range of commodities
under both project and non-project aid; and, secondly, that, where the
substitution possibility is considered limited, even an international tender
may be ineffective in getting the lowest rates.[20]
Among the country studies, which as we have argued are the optimal
way of estimating the actual cost of aid-tying by source, Ul Haq's original
study of Pakistan produced a figure of 14 per cent of excess cost: a loss
of $60 million in a total aid flow of $500 million annually. The somewhat
'low' figure is attributed to two main factors:
(i) The possibility of substitution, and its growing exploitation, as
    Pakistan has access to several alternative aid sources as well as free
    foreign exchange earnings and untied aid.
(ii) A relatively low percentage of tied aid.
However, the estimate is fairly rough and likely to be substantially on
the low side in view of Ul Haq's optimism about avoiding all
'monopolistic' elements in pricing under tied aid.[21]
The UNCTAD country studies promise to throw more quantitative light
on this question. Unfortunately, as of the time of writing the present
report, these studies are incomplete. However, it is relevant in this
connexion to note that, in so far as donor countries tend, for no matter
what reason, to divide up the recipient world into areas of aid-dependence
on particular, rather than diverse, sources, the result would *ceteris paribus*

20. Ul Haq may therefore be over-optimistic in asserting that 'In the case of Pakistan,
the credits advanced by World Bank, IDA, West Germany, UK and Canada, generally
do not suffer from any serious drawbacks, partly because some of these credits are untied
and partly because there are a large number of items that Pakistan can obtain from these
countries at the most competitive prices.' Even when Canada can supply competitively
at $x per unit, under tied aid, its competitive f.o.b. price under untied aid may have been
$(x-y).
21. Moreover, Ul Haq does not, in his quantitative analysis, seem to attach any
significance to factors such as shifts in priority owing to difficulties of procurement from
a tied source etc. Further, the method of measuring the cost of aid-tying used by Ul Haq,
and the subsequent UNCTAD studies, may not fully measure the cost in the strict economic
sense of the term (see Appendix).

be to reduce the substitution and competitive possibilities that were discussed in this section and thereby to enhance the cost of aid tying by source. It is interesting to observe, in relation to this question, that:

(1) While the United States had in the past tended to reduce the degree of aid concentration, with the aid expenditures in thirteen principal countries declining from an average of 92 per cent of the total in 1954–7 to an average of 72 per cent during 1960 and 1961 (Lynn, 1966, p. 21), the recent trend seems to be in the reverse direction, culminating in the policy decision to concentrate United States aid expenditures on fifteen countries.

(2) The examination of aid distribution shows a preponderant dependence by Latin American countries on United States aid, by French-speaking African countries on France, and by Commonwealth countries other than India and Pakistan on the United Kingdom.

Finally, it might be mentioned that a rough-and-ready study of possible excess costs was made when the recipients of United States aid were to be required to shift away from offshore purchases, beginning in 1960. It was estimated at the time that if the recipient countries maintained the same commodity pattern of imports but shifted to United States sources of supply, there would be an average increase of over a third in the cost of imports where the United States was more expensive, but that, computed as the average increase on total commodity expenditure, the excess cost would be about one-half of this proportion.

The impression left by these different estimates is that the tying of aid by source – ruling altogether out of reckoning aid in commodities and technical services, as also suppliers' credits – imposes, in practice (and not in theory alone), costs that are significant enough to justify attempts at promoting measures for the untying of aid. Prior to considering these measures, however, it would be useful to examine some of the arguments produced by the donor countries in support of tying aid.

5   THE GAINS TO DONOR COUNTRIES FROM SOURCE-TYING OF AID

As we have seen earlier, the most powerful and persistent argument produced in support of source-tying of aid deficit countries is that it prevents a deterioration in their balance of payments. In view of its importance, we shall examine this argument carefully, looking closely at the empirical evidence in support of it.

The argument, put in its skeletal form, is that source-tying will divert aid expenditure by recipient countries towards the donor country and thereby reduce the leakage into third-country exports and hence the deterioration in the donor's balance of payments position. There are obvious qualifications to this argument.

(1) More 'return' of the aid by way of demand by recipient countries for export of a donor country will not, in itself, lead to a balance of trade improvement which 'finances' the aid outflow. There has to be a matching release of resources from domestic absorption. It should not be presumed therefore that effective aid-tying by source will necessarily lead to improvement in the balance of payments of the donor country. In fact, it will not if the cause of the donor's balance of payments deficit is excess demand for resources. In such a case, the real problem with the aid process is rather that it involves a transfer of resources for which there is excess demand, so that the important questions then are: (a) Can the aid outflow be undertaken at all? and (b) whether rich countries ought not to seek ways of accommodating this outflow by restraining domestic demand for resources.

(2) Further, even if it were granted that domestic resources were freed to finance the transfer involved as a result of aid-tying by source, the precise impact of such tying is poorly measured by the estimate of the direct spending by the recipient country on the donor's goods and services. Spending on third-country exports will also in turn lead to further, indirect demands for the donor country's exports, so that the net effect of aid-tying on the balance of payments of the donor country will be less than that measured by the primary impact.

(3) Further, the source-tying of aid may (for reasons already examined at length on pp.218–22) be frustrated by 'switching' so that the net impact on the primary spending on donor's exports may be limited. On the other hand, if monopolistic charges accrue to the donor country's suppliers, the net improvement in the payments position would exceed the amount not switched by approximately the transfer implicit in the excess of the monopoly prices over competitive prices.

(4) Finally, the net effect of aid-tying on the balance of payments position must be adjusted for the fact that much of the tying is 'competitive'. The net improvement for the deficit countries therefore will be less than the gross effect, direct and indirect, because their policies will tend to neutralize one another and because the reciprocal tying by the surplus countries will also work to offset any favourable impact effect on the balance of payments.

Empirical estimates of the net effects of aid-tying on the balance of payments of the donor countries are thus notoriously difficult to make. If the estimates are to be meaningful, one would have to have, at the minimum, reasonable guesses concerning:

(a) The extent of aid-tying.
(b) The 'switching' undertaken by the recipient country.
(c) The indirect effects, via third-country respending, on the donor's exports.
(d) The extent of 'competitive, reciprocal aid-tying by donor countries.

Serious analytical attempts at constructing such estimates have been made only in the United States, although purely 'guesswork' estimates are available also for the United Kingdom.

United Kingdom

In the course of an empirical exercise at estimating the balance of payments 'cost' of the United Kingdom foreign aid programme, Andrzej Krassowski (1965) has attempted adjustment for the fact that part of the aid is source-tied.

Taking tied aid to be solely the net Export Credit Guarantee Department loans (under Section 3 of the Export Guarantees Act, 1949), he proceeds to distribute them by destination according to Sterling Area and the rest, subdividing the Sterling Area in turn into 'Africa', 'Caribbean', 'Asia', 'Middle East' and 'Other colonies'. He then assumes that, for the Sterling Area, the 'switching' will be at 30 per cent and elsewhere at 10 per cent, on the sensible presumption that switching is easier when the initial, non-aid-financed trade with the United Kingdom is significant. He further assumes that the switched portion of the tied aid, which is *de facto* untied, will be spent according to the average share of the United Kingdom in imports by the recipient area from industrial countries.

The resulting estimate of the trade diversion in favour of the United Kingdom, attributable to source-tying, comes to £20.54 million for 1963, which amounts to over 50 per cent of the amount that is tied, to over 20 per cent of the net bilateral aid flow, and to under 19 per cent of the entire (multilateral plus bilateral) net aid of the United Kingdom (Table 12.5).

This estimate, however, is subject to serious limitations on the following counts:

(i) The 'switching' estimates are pure guesses.

(ii) The average propensities to spend on United Kingdom goods and services may differ from the marginal propensities, especially when import patterns of the recipient countries are changing significantly owing to developmental programmes.

(iii) No allowance is made for the increment in spending on the exports indirectly by countries in which the aid is spent initially by the recipients; to this extent, the 'gain' from aid-tying is over-estimated.

(iv) The estimate of aid-tying is admittedly confined to the ECGD loans and hence is on the low side.

(v) No adjustment is made for the fact that aid-tying by others may itself be a function of the British aid-tying.[22]

---

22. This last factor, however, is not of great significance in the discussion of United Kingdom aid-tying, in view of the rather limited sums involved. Clearly its significance is paramount for the United States. Moreover, it should be noted that Krassowski has a

TABLE 12.5 Balance of payments effect of source-tying of aid by the United Kingdom, 1963

| | | | Net flow of foreign exchange, 1963 | | | | | | |
| | | | | Tied aid flow returning ultimately to UK | | | | | |
Region	Total aid flow (£ million)	Average percentage share of UK in imports from industrial countries	Tied aid flow (£ million)	Direct (%)	(£ million)	Switched portion (£ million)	Total (£ million)	Amount of tied aid returning to UK if it were untied (£ million)	Balance of payments 'gains' from aid-tying (£ million)
(1)	(2)	(3)	(4)	(5)	(6)	(7)	(8)	(9)	(10)
Sterling area									
Africa	45.4	45	5.5	70	3.85	0.74	4.59	2.48	2.11
Caribbean	6.6	40							
Asia	25.2	25	26.3	70	18.42	1.97	20.39	6.58	13.81
Middle East	12.6	30							
Other colonies	9.0	30							
All other countries	1.2	10	5.7	90	5.13	0.06	5.19	0.57	4.62
Total bilateral	100.0		37.5				30.17	9.63	20.54
Multilateral	13.4								
Total	113.4		37.5						

Sources: Columns (1) – (8) from Krassowski (1965, p. 32).
Columns (9)–(10) calculated.

United States

For the United States, however, there are more systematic estimates of the effect of aid-tying. These consist chiefly of two independent sets of studies, by Lawrence Lynn, Jr and Alan Strout, although earlier the Brookings Institution study by Walter Salant and associates (1963) had produced essentially speculative estimates in the course of predicting the United States balance of payments for 1968.

The Lynn and Strout estimates are characterized by two major elements of sophistication; firstly, the 'switching' possibilities are quantified systematically from the available empirical evidence; and, secondly, the indirect demand for United States exports, via third-country respending of aid is examined intensively so as to see how sensitive the resulting estimates are to various assumptions concerning the reserve-accumulating behaviour of groups of countries, particularly Western Europe. The chief limitations of the estimates consist, firstly, in implicitly treating the tying of aid by other donor countries as autonomous (this assumption makes very little sense for the United States) and, secondly, in not having any reliable estimate of the reserve accumulating behaviour of trading countries.

The 'switching' effect is variously estimated in these studies. Lynn's procedure was essentially to estimate United States exports to a recipient as a linear function of different categories of foreign exchange (distinguishing Exim Bank loans, PL 480 and AID expenditures) and the base-year market share. Using data for forty-three countries for 1958–60 and 1962–3, and taking 1961 as the departure point for the United States aid-tying, Lynn finds that the coefficients of AID expenditure on United States exports change significantly. However, when Lynn drops from the 1962–3 analysis six countries (Bolivia, Ethiopia, India, Pakistan, Sudan and the Republic of Vietnam) where the scope for aid-tying (defined as the excess of estimated expenditure on third countries sought from United States tied-aid funds over normal imports from the United States) is large, the results come out with a slightly larger AID coefficient but the results are closely consistent with the 1958–60 estimates.

Lynn's results thus indicate strongly that the tying of AID funds has resulted in the diversion of trade to the United States for six major aid recipients. For these six countries, the minimum diversion (assuming that all switching possibilities are exploited) has been estimated by Strout using Lynn's data at approximately $74 million and $120 million for 1962 and 1963 respectively. These results, however, are fairly large understatements

detailed statistical analysis of the net impact of aid on the United Kingdom balance of payments, allowing for the effects of the aid flows of other donors: United States, Federal Republic of Germany, France and other DAC countries.

of the total effect of United States aid-tying during this period for the following reasons:

(1) They are minimum estimates.

(2) They relate to six countries, and the possibility of some non-switching by the remaining recipients is not altogether ruled out by Lynn's estimates.

(3) They relate to AID expenditure essentially, and do not include the trade-diversion effects of the Exim Bank loans and PL 480 shipments; Lynn's own analysis underlines the importance of this omission, as his results indicate that during the period 1958–63 the direct expenditure by recipients on United States merchandise exports from United States aid was around 23 per cent for AID expenditures, 80 per cent for PL 480 and 92 per cent for Exim Bank loans. Thus, the amount of trade diversion attributable to these two sources of aid-tying could well be in the range of $500–700 million, bringing the total 'gain' from aid-tying *in toto* to around $600–800 million annually.

Alan Strout has re-computed the estimates of trade diversion from the tying of AID expenditures, by using Lynn's regression estimates of United States market shares for 1958–60 as an alternative set of calculations of United States market shares. He has also made alternative estimates, using similar procedures, for a larger sample of fifty-one countries. These estimates show on the average that tying by AID did have trade-diversionary effects; and that the magnitude of the trade diversion, for 1964, was (for the 51-country sample) anywhere from $490 to $556 million, signifying a proportion of 47 per cent to 54 per cent of 1964 AID-financed exports (to these fifty-one countries). It should be noted that the nominal tying of AID expenditures during fiscal 1964 was only 87 per cent and has increased since. Again, if one adds to this the effect of PL 480 and Exim Bank loan expenditures, the maximum estimate of trade diversion would easily be in the range of $1 billion. The trade diversionary effect of total United States aid-tying may thus be well in the range of 40 per cent of United States aid expenditures.

This conclusion would have to be modified to the extent that the trade diversion reduces in turn the expenditure on United States exports that would otherwise have emerged as a result of respending by third countries (from whom the aid-tying has diverted primary aid expenditure). The extent to which this factor will reduce the 'gain' to the United States balance of payments from aid-tying will be measured by $\Delta \Upsilon A(1 - \lambda)$, where

$$A = \text{total aid flow;}$$

Υ = proportion of the aid flow that the recipient would spend in the donor country in the absence of aid-tying;

$(1 - \Upsilon)A$ = therefore, the amount of aid 'leaking' to third country exports;

$\lambda = $ proportion of 'leaked' aid that returns to the donor country via respending;

$\Upsilon A + \lambda(1 - \Upsilon)A = $ the total amount of aid expenditure that would return to donor country in the absence of aid tying;

$\Delta\Upsilon = $ the additional proportion of aid that the recipient would spend on donor country exports due to aid-tying;

$(\Upsilon + \Delta\Upsilon)A + \lambda(1 - \Upsilon - \Delta\Upsilon)A = $ the total amount of aid expenditure that would return to the donor country under aid-tying; and hence

$\Delta\Upsilon A(1 - \lambda) = $ the amount of additional expenditure on donor country exports, attributable to aid-tying.

It ought to be noted that where $\lambda = 1$, there is no net addition to donor country exports from aid-tying, because in this case the rounds of third-country respending eliminate the effects of the leakage altogether. This will be the case if we assume the third countries accumulate no reserves (i.e. spend all aid expenditure that they earn).[23] Where, however, this is not so, λ will be less than unity and aid-tying will lead to improvement (in donor country exports) which will vary inversely with λ.

Lynn has worked out, for the United States, some ranges of λ which may be used to arrive at very rough orders of magnitude.[24] Taking the matrix of trade relationships for 1958–61, Lynn estimates the average shares of different countries and regions in trade, and assumes these also to be the relevant marginal shares. He next takes alternative assumptions about the reserve-accumulating behaviour of different regions and then arrives at four alternative estimates (Table 12.6) of the percentage of 'leaked' dollars that would accrue back to the United States, namely λ for aid spent in each of four regions: Latin America, Middle East, Africa and Asia.

These are largely illustrative figures. They do, however, underline the sensitivity of λ to the reserve-accumulating assumptions with respect to the West European countries (including EEC). For Assumption 3, which

23. However, in Table 12.6, Assumption 4 (to the effect that third countries do not accumulate reserves) does not yield a value of λ equal to unity because Lynn, on whose work this table is based, did not use a complete world trade matrix but omitted socialist countries and some other unidentifiable categories. This implicitly means assuming 100 per cent reserve accumulation on the part of omitted countries. This qualification applies to all the four estimates of the indirect expenditure on United States exports included in Table 12.6.

24. The technique of analysis used by Lynn was suggested originally by Richard Cooper and had earlier been applied by W. Whitney Hicks (1963), and used also in the Brookings Institution Study of Salant *et al.* (1963).

TABLE 12.6 Alternative estimates of indirect expenditures on United States exports in relation to United States aid[a]

Region of aid expenditure	Direct expenditure on US exports (as percentage of US aid)	Direct leakage into other countries' exports (as percentage of US aid)	Indirect expenditure on US exports on alternative assumptions concerning reserve-accumulating behaviour[b,c]							
			As percentage of aid				As percentage of direct leakage			
			(1)	(2)	(3)	(4)	(1)	(2)	(3)	(4)
Latin America	33.3	66.7	5.6	13.1	16.3	56.3	8.4	19.6	24.8	84.8
Middle East	11.6	88.4	3.8	15.3	20.3	72.6	4.4	17.3	23.1	82.5
Africa	4.4	95.6	2.1	14.0	17.4	85.1	2.2	14.6	18.1	89.1
Asia	10.1	89.9	6.0	23.4	26.6	66.8	6.7	26.0	29.5	74.2

[a]Based on Lynn's regression equations for 1958–61.

[b]Assumption 1: Canada, United Kingdom, EEC, other Western Europe, Australia, New Zealand, South Africa, and Japan add incremental exchange earnings to their reserves.

Assumption 2: EEC and other Western European countries only add increased foreign exchange earnings to their reserves.

Assumption 3: Only EEC countries add increased foreign exchange earnings to their reserves.

Assumption 4: No countries add increased foreign exchange earnings to their reserves.

[c]These calculations are not based on a complete world trade matrix as trade with socialist and some other countries was left out, which implies 100 per cent reserve accumulation by the omitted countries.

Source: Adapted from Lynn (1966, pp. 110–15).

implies that only the EEC countries add incremental foreign exchange earnings to their reserves, λ ranges from 18.1 per cent for Africa to 29.5 per cent for Asia and around 24 per cent for the Middle East and Latin America. However, for Assumption 4 which does away with this possibility, the percentage λ goes up to anywhere from 74.2 to 89.1.

In considering these estimates of λ in arriving at the *net* estimates of the effect of United States aid-tying, using the formula $\Delta \Upsilon A(1-\lambda)$, it is important to remember that they are based on purely illustrative and hypothetical reserve-accumulation behavioural assumptions, as also on average trade shares. However, if we were to assume, as seems plausible at the present time, that Assumption 3 may be closest to reality, the estimate of primary trade diversion of approximately $1 billion would be reduced by about $250 million. The net trade diversionary effect of United States aid-tying (at a nominal level of around 85 per cent) may thus be in the range of 30 per cent of United States aid expenditure.[25]

But if we consider the reciprocal element in aid-tying, the net 'beneficial' effect on the United States balance of payments will be even less. At an approximate estimate that the rest of the aid donors also secure a trade diversionary effect of 30 per cent from their aid-tying, and assuming that measures undertaken by the United States to untie its aid would lead to entire removal of tying by other donor countries, the net effect of United States aid-tying would be further reduced by about $80 million.[26] This

---

25. Alan Strout has pointed out to me, in correspondence, that this estimate may be on the low side because Lynn's estimates of the coefficient for PL 480 and Exim Bank are now believed to be too low. His likely estimate for 1966, at 39 per cent, derived with the use of different higher estimates for PL 480 (at 0.90) and for Exim loans, as also a higher $\Delta\Upsilon$ for AID (thanks to increasing efficacy of aid-tying) and a higher λ than that resulting from Assumption 3 in the text, is derived as follows:

Parameter	PL 480	Exim	AID
Υ (same as untied aid)	0.23	123	0.23
$\Delta\Upsilon$	(0.90–0.23)	(1.00–0.23)	
	= 0.67	= 0.77	0.60
λ	0.40	0.40	0.40
Hence: $\Delta\Upsilon(1-\lambda)$	0.40	0.46	0.36

The US gain in 1966 (for commodities only) thus comes to:

AID (US procurement only): $1190 mn. × 0.36 ≈ $430 million
PL 480 sales   : $1270 mn. × 0.40 ≈ $510 million
Exim direct loans (less 7
  per cent service costs) : $400 mn × (1 − 0.07) × 0.46 ≈ 170 million
      Total   : $1110 million

This is 39 per cent [= 1110 ÷ (1190 + 1270 + 370)] of total US procurement. For 1964, the equivalent figure, assuming a value of $\Delta\Upsilon$ for AID of 0.47, would be slightly less than $1 billion, which exceeds the estimate of $750 million in the text.

26. This estimate is based on the difference between columns (10) and (2), and between columns (11) and (3) in Table 12.7 below.

still leaves fairly large orders of magnitude, at around \$650–700 million, as the net gain from aid-tying by the United States.

General observations

Similar estimates could no doubt be made for the other donor countries notably France and the Federal Republic of Germany; but, unfortunately, they are not available. However, from the preceding analysis, three facts of considerable importance emerge forcefully:

(1) Aid-tying by source is undoubtedly a successful policy instrument for diverting aid expenditure to the donor's exports of commodities and services. In so far as there is, therefore, a matching release of domestic resources undertaken by the donor, it is correct to maintain that aid-tying tends to prevent a deterioration in the donor's balance of payments as a result of the aid flow.

(2) The improvement attributable to the aid-tying varies directly with the reserve-accumulating practices of other trading countries. To put it more specifically, the adverse impact of the untying of aid by the United States on its balance of payments would be significantly reduced if it could be assumed that the western European countries were not likely to put incremental foreign exchange earnings into reserves. The relationship of this conclusion to the more general question of expansion of international liquidity is obvious. Clearly, as long as the countries in current surplus will not agree to an expansion of international liquidity, reserve-accumulating practices will continue to be a serious impediment to the untying of aid. It can also be argued that excessive concern with the balance of payments, and hence resort to practices such as aid-tying by source, originate from a situation where the surplus countries jealously guard their surpluses and the deficit countries are thereby effectively prevented from eliminating their deficits. The only solution (at least in the short-run) to this situation is increased access to international liquidity by the deficit countries.

(3) Finally, it is clear that the competitive element in aid-tying is quite important and has significant quantitative dimensions. For example, the net effect of aid-tying by each donor country, assuming the aid-tying of each country to be autonomous, may be in the range of 20–30 per cent of its aid flow, as we have seen in the preceding empirical discussion. On the other hand, if we were to assume that all aid-tying by DAC member countries were to cease simultaneously, and (by hypothesis) that there were no differentials in the effects of aid-tying between countries all of which may be hypothesized to have a 30 per cent net diversionary effect, and further that the mutual aid-tying would cause no net loss of reserves to the socialist and developing countries but would only cause offsetting gains and losses among the DAC donors, we can work out illustrative but

TABLE 12.7 Estimates of net gain or loss to DAC donor countries if all of them were to untie bilateral aid (excluding technical assistance) simultaneously (millions US$)

Donor country	'Gain' from trade diversion effect, using DAC net bilateral official aid data for years given		Estimates of 'gains' from other donor countries' untying of aid, using the average shares in trade for years given						Alternative estimates of net 'gain' (+) or 'loss' (−) if all donor countries were to untie aid simultaneously					
			1962, using trade diversion estimates of years		1963, using trade diversion estimates of years		1964, using trade diversion estimates of years							
	1963	1964	col. (2)	col. (3)	col. (2)	col. (3)	col. (2)	col. (3)	Columns (4)−(2)	Columns (5)−(3)	Columns (6)−(2)	Columns (7)−(3)	Columns (8)−(2)	Columns (9)−(3)
(1)	(2)	(3)	(4)	(5)	(6)	(7)	(8)	(9)	(10)	(11)	(12)	(13)	(14)	(15)
USA	956.70	843.30	158.13	156.12	157.92	155.88	156.89	154.76	−798.57	−687.18	−798.78	−687.42	−799.81	−688.54
UK	90.63	113.22	237.82	211.37	235.66	209.43	222.80	197.91	+147.19	+98.15	+145.03	+96.21	+132.17	+84.69
France	157.02	140.52	158.11	144.90	160.69	147.25	155.83	142.80	+1.09	+4.38	+3.67	+6.73	−1.19	+2.28
Federal Republic of Germany	100.62	98.34	294.21	267.80	298.74	271.95	289.72	263.67	+193.59	+169.46	+198.12	+173.61	+189.10	+165.53
Other DAC	127.41	119.10	584.09	532.78	591.93	539.94	607.92	554.45	+456.68	+413.68	+464.52	+420.84	+480.51	+435.35
Totals									—	—	—	—	—	—

Methodology: The procedure was to calculate first the net bilateral aid flows, net of technical assistance, for 1963 and 1964. Then the proportion of 30% was applied, by hypothesis partially supported by the empirical work on UK and USA uniformly to these aid figures to arrive at estimates of net (direct and indirect) trade diversion brought about by each country's aid-tying, as recorded in columns (2) and (3). Next, the export data for years 1962, 1963 and 1964 were used, successively, to arrive at the proportions in which the trade-diverted aid expenditure, if untied, would be spent on each country's exports. These proportions were calculated, as follows, the case of UK gains from non-UK countries untying their aid being illustrated here, and where DE = DAC exports, F = French exports, G = Federal Republic of Germany's exports, US = United States exports, UK = United Kingdom exports and ODAC = Belgium + Canada + Netherlands + Portugal + Denmark + Italy + Japan + Norway + Sweden; the table illustrating the ratios measured for United Kingdom. For the UK, for example, the ratio

$$\frac{UK}{DE - US}$$

was taken as the proportion of US trade-diversion, as estimated in columns (2) and (3), which would accrue to UK as additional expenditure on UK exports if US aid were untied. Thus, using column (2) estimate of US trade diversion at $956.70 million and the 1962 ratio, the gain to UK from US untying its aid would amount of $956.70 × 0.18 million. Similarly, for untying on the part of the Federal Republic of Germany, the UK gain would equal $100.62 × 0.159 million. For *all* untying by non-UK countries, the gain then would be the sum of these estimates, equalling $237.82 million in column (4). And so on. This method, of course represents a simple approximation to the 'true' effects. Note that the fact that we have taken DAC exports instead of world exports in the denominator is a simple way of ensuring that all DAC countries taken together do not 'lose' to non-DAC countries; this, in turn, rests on the reasonable assumption that the socialist and developing countries will not accumulate reserves.

Ratios of	1962	1963	1964
$\dfrac{UK}{DE-US}$	0.181	0.179	0.169
$\dfrac{UK}{DE-G}$	0.159	0.158	0.148

Ratios of	1962	1963	1964
$\dfrac{UK}{DE-F}$	0.146	0.145	0.137
$\dfrac{UK}{DE-ODAC}$	0.202	0.202	0.194

Source: Calculated from total net bilateral aid figures for DAC countries in *OECD (1964/5) Reviews*: and United Nations (1964, 1965).

fairly plausible estimates of the amount by which each DAC member country would 'gain' or 'lose' from such a policy.[27] Six such alternative estimates have been presented in Table 12.7, distinguishing among the United States, United Kingdom, Federal Republic of Germany, France and other DAC member countries. It is clear from these estimates that the net gains from tying to all countries are significantly less than the gross gains unadjusted for the reciprocal element. In particular, the deficit country United Kingdom would gain considerably from simultaneous aid-untying. However, while the 'gain' for the United States is also reduced by about one-sixth on all estimates, the fact remains that it would continue to be a major 'loser' from simultaneous aid-untying, chiefly because of the preponderance of its position as an aid-giver among the DAC member countries. Thus, the balance of payments deficit of the United States must continue to serve as an important brake on any move towards a simultaneous untying of all aid flows.

6   METHODS FOR REDUCING THE REAL COST OF AID TYING BY SOURCE
AND PROPOSALS FOR UNTYING AID

The preceding analysis has shown that aid-tying can impose fairly large costs on recipient countries and that the available empirical studies underline the actual existence of such costs. This conclusion is further accentuated by empirical analyses that examine the trade diversionary effects of aid-tying: as trade diversion increases, so will the cost of aid-tying to recipients, other things being equal.

At the same time, it is necessary to recognize that even simultaneous untying of aid by all donor countries is certain to leave the United States in particular with the problem that a large part of procurements from its aid – about 30–35 per cent – is likely to 'leak' into non-United States sources of supply, thus making the task of eliminating its payments deficit correspondingly more difficult (noting again that even trade diversion would not help if domestic absorption is not reduced to permit the elimination of the deficit). Thus, the principal aid-giving country, the United States is unlikely to be enthusiastic about measures for untying aid altogether.

27. The detailed methodology is set out at the bottom of Table 12.7. Estimates were also worked out alternatively on the assumption that the DAC countries could lose reserves, as a group, to non-DAC countries, to see whether this made any difference to the conclusions with respect to effects on individual DAC countries. This was done by simply using world exports instead of DAC exports in the denominator of the formula used in deriving trade shares in Table 12.7 (methodology). The qualitative conclusions, however, with respect to intra-DAC 'gain' and 'losses' were not affected significantly, except for the United Kingdom which naturally turns out as making far more gain from simultaneous aid-tying under the assumption in the text, and even a minor loss on some estimates derived on the alternative assumption now being considered.

Hence, it is necessary to consider two different varieties of proposals, firstly, those that relate to the untying of aid, *while making due adjustments* for the difficulties noted already; and, secondly, those that are based on the assumption (which is more pessimistic) that aid-tying must continue, and which therefore are addressed to the problem of reducing the adverse effects of aid-tying on the recipient countries.

Proposals for untying aid

In the former category, the most optimistic and therefore the least promising, proposal would be that donor countries should forthwith and simultaneously cease to tie all aid by source. As we have already seen, a deficit country with significant aid outflows, such as the United States, is unlikely to agree altogether with such a move.

However, the prospect for such a concerted elimination of aid-tying would improve slightly, though not significantly, if international liquidity could be significantly expanded so that the United States reserve position improves and the reserve accumulation from excess of receipts over payments by other countries is eased. An alternative suggestion, following an analogy with trade liberalization, would be to work out some form of payments arrangement to finance any marginal deficits that may, and in fact must, arise for individual donor countries such as the United States on *aid account alone*. The real problem with such an arrangement for an aid payments union, as recognized by its proponent Vinod Shah (1968), is that it is not possible to identify imports financed by aid as against other imports in so far as recipient countries are in a position to 'switch' between aid and earnings in financing any given imports from a donor country. This 'arbitrariness' makes some kind of convention, in identifying 'truly' aid-financed imports, necessary; and this, in turn, makes the proposal for a payments union directed merely at financing deficits on aid account difficult to implement. Further, it is inevitable in the foreseeable future that the United States with its preponderant aid outflow will run up continuing deficits within such an aid-account payments union, thus making its continued existence precarious.

It is therefore more realistic to consider the possibility of a simultaneous and progressive reduction in aid-tying by small but similar amounts by all donor countries.

Aside from the merit this would have of concerted action and an explicit recognition of competitiveness in aid-tying, it should also be easier for surplus countries such as the Federal Republic of Germany to be able to convince their public that the remaining aid-tying by deficit countries such as the United States was 'justified' because it reflected both the larger aid-flows and the deficit situation.

On the other hand, on this principle of reduction in aid-tying, surplus countries such as France might ultimately be left with some degree of aid-tying while deficit countries such as the United Kingdom might, in view of their lower aid expenditures, be left with none. It may, therefore, be more appropriate if the large-aid, surplus countries were to agree to reduce their aid-tying in larger proportions than other donors.[28] Needless to say, this would leave open a number of questions (such as the identification of the degree of aid-tying by each donor) which may prove delicate.

Proposals on assumption that aid-tying will continue

Short of such proposals for gradual but concerted steps for untying the bulk of current aid flows, there are numerous other measures which are suggested by the analysis in the preceding sections.

These measures can, in turn, be subdivided into those which require initiatory and permissive action by the donor countries and those which can be implemented by the recipients on their own initiative.

Action by donor countries

Among the simpler, but not unimportant, measures that could be adopted are the following:

(1) Greater facility for recipient countries to 'programme' their foreign exchange utilization could be provided. This can be done by adoption of the consortium approach, wherever possible: this enables the recipient country to seek and exploit possibilities of introducing greater competition among aid-financed suppliers, as noted earlier.[29]

(2) At the same time, it would help if the donor countries could avoid joint tying by source and by commodity, which can lead to serious monopolistic exploitation.

(3) Donor countries should further explicitly encourage, even require, competitive tendering on projects – even when the project is left tied by source.

(4) Further, there is need for price vigilance by the donor countries' aid-disbursing agencies.

(5) Moreover, it makes good sense to argue that, since (effective) aid-tying imposes excess cost on recipient countries because the sale of donor

28. This would seem to make more practical sense than the convention suggested by some economists that surplus countries ought to stop all aid-tying. As long as the reduction in aid-tying is mutual and appears therefore to be 'fair', the chance of surplus countries being able to carry their public opinion with them is greater.

29. Such 'programming' would go further, as we have argued earlier, if aid came from diversified sources, and may mean little if aid comes only from one source, is tied and is large in relation to free exchange.

country exports (which are uncompetitive) is being forced, the fair thing to do would be to separate out an estimated sum of this excess cost and to show it directly, in the budget of the donor country, as export subsidy rather than as aid. This would have a two-fold advantage: it would bring aid figures closer to their 'true' value, a matter of some importance when public opinion has become increasingly critical of budgetary appropriations for aid; and it would save the recipient country, *ceteris paribus*, interest payments as a proportion of the excess cost so netted out.[30]

In addition, the donor countries could be persuaded to consider rather more ambitious measures. Since it is advantageous for recipients to have aid from diversified sources, in securing competitive prices, it would be useful if the donor countries would be agreeable to having multilateral aid flows, through IBRD, United Nations agencies, etc., distributed partly with reference to this criterion, and moreover to having these funds available not primarily for social overheads but more freely so as to make realistic the possibility of a shift to multilateral finance in case tied bilateral sources are charging excessive prices.

The donor countries could also explore the possibility of 'swaps' under which, for example, French aid to Gabon could be swapped for United States aid to Guatemala, with source-tying equally offset and thus leaving *de jure* tying levels intact for each donor but increasing the competition possibilities in both Gabon (which is otherwise strictly geared to French aid) and Guatemala (which is otherwise dependent overwhelmingly on United States aid).[31]

In addition, the donor countries could adopt the practice of specifying developing countries as possible sources of supply for aid-expenditure. This practice, if adopted, could also make over time a significant contribution towards the building-up of export earnings via capital goods exports of developing countries with advanced industrial structures such as Argentina, Brazil, India and Mexico.

Finally, as long as the donor countries insist on tying aid outflows, it makes equal sense for the recipient to demand that the repayments be tied as well. This principle is implicit in aid transactions of socialist countries and, as long as outflows are tied, is worth extending to repayments of aid to developed market economy countries (as is indeed effectively the case with the bulk of the United States sales for local currencies).

30. This, for example, is the practice with the excess cost incurred for PL 480 supplies carried by United States flag vessels under PL 480 agreements for sales for foreign currencies (Food for Peace Act of 1966, sec. 108).

31. Such swaps need not pose questions of prestige based on 'who builds something' if they are carried out for non-project aid.

Action by recipient countries

Aside from these actions which could be undertaken by the donors themselves, the recipient countries could try to reduce the cost of aid-tying by self-help measures.

(1) The most obvious thing to do is to adopt sensible procurement practices, including the invitation of tenders and collection of price information from alternative sources. Tendering is, surprisingly enough, followed in relatively few recipient countries.

(2) The other recommendation which emerges from the analysis in this paper, for recipients with extended import controls, is that flexibility in re-transfers of (commodity-specifying) licences between sources is essential and, when removed, increases significantly the possibility of monpolistic pricing by aid-financed suppliers; and hence licences for import, when they specify source and item, should permit flexibility via legalized swapping of licences between sources (as explained on pp. 222–3). It is necessary to recognize that the recipient's import licensing procedures, by specifying both source and items simultaneously, can themselves create monopoly power for foreign suppliers; and that control over the composition of imports, as also aid-tying requirements by source, can be satisfied, while eliminating this monopoly power, by merely permitting swaps (by source) between different licence-holders.

Some of these suggestions are already to be found in the resolutions adopted by international organizations of which both recipients and donors are members. It is also conceded widely that aid-tying needs corrective action. It seems reasonable therefore to expect that some concrete action, along the lines described here, will be feasible in the near future.

APPENDIX

ESTIMATES OF EXCESS COST OF TIED AID AND POSSIBILITIES OF OVERCOMPENSATION AND UNDER-COMPENSATION

This appendix demonstrates, firstly, how the method of estimating the cost of tied aid by finding out the excess cost of commodities purchased under tied aid policy may overestimate or underestimate the compensating flow of funds that would make the recipient country as well off under tied aid policy as it would be if the aid flow were untied instead; and, secondly, how the method of estimating the cost of tied aid by finding out the excess cost that would have to be paid for the bundle of commodities that was purchased under untied aid policy, now that the

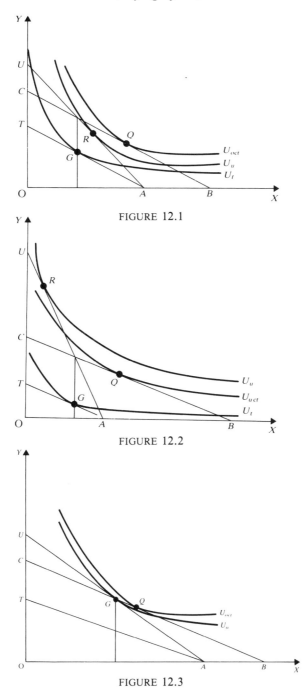

FIGURE 12.1

FIGURE 12.2

FIGURE 12.3

tied aid policy is imposed, would overestimate the compensatory flow of funds that would have to be paid to the recipient country so as to leave it as well off under the tied aid policy as it was prior to the tying of aid.

Estimation from bundle purchased under tied aid policy

The possibility of over-compensation in this case is demonstrated in Figure 12.1. AT represents the availability of combinations of X and Y from a given aid-flow if the aid can be spent only on source-tied basis. However, if the aid were untied, Y could be obtained cheaper from alternative sources and the availability line would then be AU. The bundle G would be demanded under tied aid, R under untied aid, and $U_u > U_t$. Suppose, however, that the recipient economy were to be compensated for the excess cost of the tied aid bundle chosen, namely G, the availability line would shift to BC, the bundle chosen to Q and this would lead to welfare $U_{oct} > U_u$, implying *over-compensation* for the loss resulting from aid-tying. Thus, the excess cost measure overstates the loss imposed by aid-tying.

The possibility of under-compensation is demonstrated in Figure 12.2. Here is illustrated the case where, computing the excess cost of the bundle G purchased under tied aid, given that the tied aid yields Y more expensively than untied aid (with AT and AU the availability lines from given aid flow under tied and untied aid respectively), and giving it to the recipient country such that its availability line now becomes BC, will result in *under-compensation* of the country for losses resulting from aid-tying ($U_{uct} < U_u$). Thus, in this case, the excess cost measure understates the loss imposed by aid-tying.

Estimation from bundle purchased prior to tying

In this case, the excess cost measure will overstate the cost of tying. This is demonstrated in Figure 12.3. AU represents the availability line under untied aid. Let G be the bundle actually purchased. If then aid were to become source-tied, thus resulting in an inferior availability line, AT, with Y more expensive (but not X) to procure from the tied source, then computing the excess cost of this bundle G and compensating the recipient country will lead to the new availability line BC and welfare at $U_{uct} < U_u$, with the new bundle at Q. Thus there will be *over-compensation* for the loss resulting from aid-tying and hence the excess cost measure will overstate the loss imposed by aid-tying.

This result is not surprising; it follows from Samuelson's well-known 'over-compensation' theorem: if prices change and income is changed as to permit the consumption of the original bundle, then over-compensation will necessarily follow unless, of course, Leontief-type fixed consumption patterns are assumed.[32]

REFERENCES

Adler, J. and Kuznets, P. (eds) (1967): *Capital Movements and Economic Development*. (London: Macmillan).

Bhagwati, J. N. (1968): *The Theory and Practice of Commercial Policy*, Frank Graham Memorial Lecture (1967), Special Papers in International Economics, No. 8 (Princeton: Princeton University Press).

Gilbert, M. (1940): 'A sample study of differences between domestic and export pricing policy of United States corporations', *Temporary National Economic Committee Mimeograph*, No. 6, pt I (Washington, DC).

Hicks, W. W. (1963): 'Estimating the foreign exchange costs of untied aid', *Southern Economic Journal*, 30.

International Bank for Reconstruction and Development (1967): *Suppliers' Credits from Industrialized to Developing Countries*, (Washington, DC: IBRD).

Krassowski, A. (1965): 'Aid and the British balance of payments', *Moorgate and Wall Street Review* (Spring).

Lynn, L., Jr (1966): *An Empirical Analysis of US Foreign Economic Aid and the US Balance of Payments, 1954–63*, Ph.D. thesis, submitted to Yale University.

Organization for Economic Co-operation and Development (1964, 1965, 1966): *Developing Assistance Efforts and Policies*, Reviews (Paris: OECD).

Salant, W. *et al.* (1963): *The US Balance of Payments in 1968* (Washington, DC: Brookings Institution).

Scheel, W. (1963): *Konturen Einer Neuen Welt*, (Dusseldorf and Vienna: Econ-Verlag).

Shah, V. (1968): 'Development assistance payments union', *Economica Internazionale*, 21, pp. 244–57.

Ul Haq, M. (1965): 'Tied credits: a quantitative analysis', paper submitted to International Economic Association Round Table Conference on Capital Movements and Economic Development, Washington, DC; reprinted in J. Adler and P. Kuznets (eds) (1967): *Capital Movements and Economic Development* (London: Macmillan).

United Nations (1964, 1965): *Yearbook of International Trade Statistics* (UN).

White, J. (1965): *German Aid* (London: Overseas Development Institute).

32. It is implicitly assumed throughout the analysis in the Appendix that the effect of source-tying is to make the import prices of some (if not all) import items relatively more expensive to those of other commodities. If the prices of all commodities were to go up uniformly, then there would be neither over-compensation nor under-compensation, of course.

13

Alternative Estimates
of the Real Cost of Aid

Economists have been properly concerned recently about the overall net deterioration in the real worth of the foreign aid flow to the developing countries. This has been partly due to the near stagnation in the gross aid flows, the growth in amortization and interest payments on past aid flows, and the rise in the price level of the commodities which aid enables recipients to purchase. Furthermore, it has also resulted from a general net deterioration in the terms and conditions of foreign aid. Defined in the broadest sense, terms and conditions include: (1) the mix of loans and grants in the gross flow, as also the terms of the loans relating to maturity, interest and grace periods on interest and amortization; (2) the tying of aid by source; (3) the tying of aid by projects, 'maintenance' or non-project uses, and by commodity specification (including PL 480 type, direct commodity assistance); and (4) political strings which may involve sacrifice of non-economic objectives or economic policy conditions which *may* result in the imposition of (objectively) sub-optimal economic policies on the recipient countries by messianic but inept experts assisting the donor countries or staffing the multilateral institutions which dispense aid.

In this paper, I wish to concentrate on just one dimension of the terms and conditions of foreign aid: its division between loans and grants and the diverse terms of the loans. Furthermore, I wish to examine this question from the donor country's viewpoint. While it is clear that, from the donor's point of view, grants are more expensive than loans and that 'softer' terms on the loans imply, in general, higher cost than 'harder' terms, the question of the 'real cost' of aid burden to the donor country requires greater precision, especially if we are to discuss important questions relating to (i) the absolute level of the aid-burden borne by individual donors, say, in relation to their GNP levels and (ii) the associated problem of the *distribution* of the overall aid burden among different donors.

It has become customary, since the empirical work of John Pincus, to deflate the figures of the flow of foreign assistance by adjusting them

From Paul Streeten (ed.), *Unfashionable Economics: Essays in Honour of Lord Balogh* (London: Weidenfeld and Nicolson, 1970), pp. 165–209. The original text has been slightly edited. In particular Tables 2–5 have been omitted, with corresponding amendments in the text.

for the present discounted value of the stream of repayments and interest payments involved in loans as distinct from grants.[1]

The procedure involves choosing alternative discount rates by which the stream of amortization and interest is discounted back to current value and then deducted from the nominal value of the aid flow to give the 'real cost' of the aid. The rates chosen vary from the country's own long-term rate (which presumably measures the return that the donor country would have earned if the sum had been invested domestically instead of given abroad via aid) to the profit rate earned by private foreign investors (which presumably measures the cost that the recipient country might have had to pay to borrow foreign capital if the aid had not been forthcoming).[2]

This paper (1) re-examines the Pincus-type approach and outlines an alternative approach to the method of deflation which starts from the basic analytics involved and shows the specific Pincus procedures to be a particular case (section 1); (2) develops alternative estimates of the real cost of foreign aid to the major OECD donor countries for 1962 to 1966 to illustrate the new approach developed here; and (3) compares these estimates (i) with those reached by using the Pincus-approach and (ii) with those resulting from the use of unadjusted, nominal flows of official aid.

1 METHODOLOGY

The correct procedure in estimating the real cost of foreign aid, leaving aside for the time being the thorny questions associated with the tying of aid, is to ask what *would* happen if the aid were not forthcoming. Clearly, there will be a multiplicity of possibilities and effects. But, *at minimum*, one could proceed to consider as a realistic possibility that *some* part of the aid flow would be borrowed, and allowed to be borrowed, on commercial terms whereas the *rest* would have to be absorbed domestically by the donor country. Given the current annual magnitudes of official assistance, it seems highly dubious and unrealistic to argue

1. The estimates by Little and Clifford (1965) follow essentially the procedures as devised by Pincus (1963). These methods were suggested independently by Rosenstein-Rodan (1962). Note that 'non-economic' returns such as political 'influence' are being ignored in the analysis. So also is the possibility that aid may involve zero opportunity cost under conditions of Keynesian unemployment.

2. Note that the benefit the recipient country receives by virtue of foreign aid, and hence the cost to it of withdrawing it, has no relevance in itself to the cost that the donor country suffers from undertaking the aid operation. Hence, taking the private foreign rate of return on capital as the discount rate has *no meaning* insofar as it is used *because* it is considered to indicate the benefit to the borrowing country (which, incidentally, it does not).

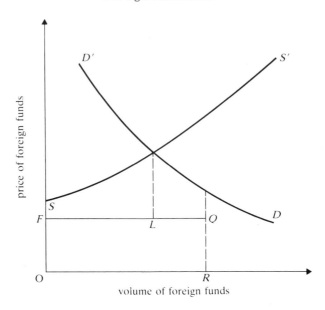

FIGURE 13.1   Alternative estimates of the annual cost of aid

DD' is the demand schedule for foreign funds for the recipient countries and *SS'* the supply schedule of funds to them if aid is not given. Aid is assumed offered at price *OF* and at level *OR = QF*. If it were withdrawn, the amount borrowed would be *FL* which would be below the aid level by *LQ*.

that the same level of funds would be borrowed fully (or not at all) at the commercial terms that would be demanded for *private* lending to the less developed countries (LDCs).

Consider, for example, the idealized Figure 13.1 which illustrates a hypothetical schedule of demand for foreign funds by LDCs, *DD'* , and a supply schedule of such funds from private sources to the LDCs *assuming the withdrawal of aid*. Aid is assumed to be given at 'price' *OF*, in amount *FQ*. If it were withdrawn, the amount 'commercially borrowed' would be *FL* and the volume of funds *QL* would be the rest of the aid flow that would then be ploughed back domestically. It has been argued, so far, that it seems unlikely that *QL* will be zero.

But, for analytical completeness (in the methodological discussion), let us distinguish between (i) *Case I: QL = 0* and (ii) *Case II: QL > 0*. These cases are discussed successively now.

Case I: Borrowing replaces aid totally (QL = 0)

In this case, since aid has been fully replaced by private borrowing on commercial terms, we have a neat case where we can readily identify the difference between the terms on which a *given* amount was granted as foreign aid and the (stiffer) terms on which it would have been *otherwise* borrowed.

Since the 'terms' involve the maturity of a loan, the rate of interest charged and the time profile of repayments (including grace periods), the cost of aid, defined as the benefit forgone by giving foreign aid as against not giving it, will be equivalent in our present case to a time stream of *differences* between (i) the aid stream of amortization and interest payments and (ii) the commercial-borrowing stream of such amortization and interest payments. Thus, for any given value of foreign capital, if *Time Stream I:* $Y_1^f \ldots Y_t^f$ represents the time profile of amortization and interest payments under foreign aid, and *Time Stream II:* $Y_1^b \ldots Y_{t-n}^b$ the time profile thereof under commercial borrowing, then the (opportunity) cost of foreign aid is represented by *Time Stream III:* $(Y_1^b - Y_1^f)$, $(Y_2^b - Y_2^f)$, $\ldots$, $(Y_{t-n}^b - Y_{t-n}^f)$, $(-Y_{t-n+1}^f)$, $\ldots$, $(-Y_t^f)$.

Since time profiles such as this are not easy to deal with, it would be useful if they could be discounted back to their *current* value. *Assuming* that there *is* a discount rate which measures the productivity of capital to the donor country in question, such a discount rate could be used for reducing Time Stream III to a *single*, workable figure of the real cost of foreign aid.

Note, therefore, that we would require, for our calculations, if we are to end up with a single number:

(i) the *actual* Time Stream I of amortization and interest payments;

(ii) the *hypothetical* Time Stream II of amortization and interest payments; and

(iii) a relevant *discount* rate which measures the productivity of resources to the donor country in question.

Case II: Borrowing is less than aid flow (QL > 0)

In this case, clearly two stages of calculation would be involved.

First, for the overlapping part (i.e. *FL* in Figure 13.1), which is equal to the amount borrowed, the same analysis and calculation would apply as in Case I.

However, to this cost, we would have to add the *second* element of cost which relates to the part that is *not* borrowed when the aid is withdrawn (i.e. *QL* in Figure 13.1). To the stream of repayments and interest charge associated with this 'unborrowed' part of the aid flow (*QL*) we would then apply the same, relevant discount rate and reduce it to its discounted current value, deduct it from the aid flow (*QL*) and thus arrive at the real cost of this part (*QL*) of the aid flow.

Thus, in this realistic case we would need to know, in addition to the three items required for Case I:

(iv) the proportion of aid flow that would be (commercially) borrowed.

International comparisons. Are the estimates of real cost of aid to donor countries, thus derived, *directly* comparable from the viewpoint of determining the *distribution of the aid burden*? Two qualifications of significance need to be pointed out, if such comparisons are attempted.

(1) The single numbers of cost of foreign aid, derived by the procedures detailed above, hide an important dimension: namely, the rates of discount (equivalent to the domestic productivity of resources) which are used to arrive at these numbers. Are $X million, calculated as the real cost of aid to the United States at, say, 5 per cent discount rate, equivalent to $X million, similarly, calculated to be the real cost of aid to the United Kingdom at, say, 6 per cent discount rate? Clearly not: for, the same adjusted flow of aid to the United States will be *less* productive than to the United Kingdom (6 per cent > 5 per cent). Hence, unless the discount rate used for all donor countries is identical (which would certainly be an unrealistic assumption in an imperfect world), the mere comparison of the real-cost-of-aid-figures will be misleading *in itself* in judging comparative burdens of aid flow among the donor countries.

(2) Moreover, while different rates of discount may be used, corresponding to the domestic productivity of resources, for computing the aid burden, if the resulting figures are to be compared we would have to assume that the social time rates of discount are identical between the donor countries (unless the capital markets are perfect and the time rate of discount is adequately reflected by the rate of interest).

Do we also have to assume that identical utility weights are to be used in making such international comparisons? This would be necessary, of course, except that we can alternatively compare the distribution of the aid burden, computed without such adjustment, with what we would wish it to be *if* utility weights were assigned on different ethical principles such as, for example, progressive burden-sharing on the basis of *per capita* incomes.[3]

Limitation of Pincus-type procedures. How does the analysis presented above compare with the procedures of computation used by Pincus (1963) and later writers?[4] Their procedure implicitly amounts, in essence, to assuming *either* (1) that all aid, if withdrawn, will be put to domestic use; *or* (2) that if any aid is commercially borrowed, on withdrawal, it

3. This is, in essence, what is done by Kravis and Davenport (1963). The desirability of progressivity in international aid-burden sharing has been stressed by several liberal economists, including Thomas Balogh and Paul Rosenstein-Rodan.

4. In the following discussion, attention is confined to the methods of discounting used in these writings. It should be pointed out here, however, that the qualifications noted in the text, in discussing the question of international comparisons, apply equally to these writings. While these qualifications are noted here for the first time, the new calculations to be presented in section 2 will abstract from the resulting complications.

will be lent at the *same* rate as the discount rate used to reduce the time stream of costs to their current value. Only under either of these assumptions, will it make sense to use a unique rate of discount to deduce the real cost of aid, by the Pincus-type procedure.

But *neither* of these implicit assumptions seems plausible: all aid surely will not be put to domestic use, and the (net-of-recipient-country-tax) commercial lending rates on private foreign loans and investment cannot be expected, in an imperfect market, to equal the (gross-of-own-tax) marginal domestic productivity of resources. Hence, the computational procedure for making calculations of the real cost of foreign aid must be adjusted so as to allow for the possibility of *some* aid being borrowed commercially and the (net) terms of this borrowing being different from the (gross) domestic productivity of resources in the donor country. More realistic calculations will have to proceed, therefore, by making alternative assumptions with respect to (1) how much of foreign aid, if withdrawn, can be expected to be borrowed; and (2) at what (net-of-recipient-country-tax) marginal terms it would be borrowed.

2   ALTERNATIVE CALCULATIONS

We proceed now to present new estimates of the real cost of aid to donors. These estimates, as also those of earlier writers, need to be treated with reasonable scepticism, and are equally more illustrative than definitive, for they rest at several stages on assumptions which are seriously debatable. Since a major purpose of the calculations is to examine the *differences* that emerge in the ranking of donor countries, when the method of discounting is adjusted as argued above, from those resulting from earlier work, we will continue to make identical assumptions except where our method departs from earlier ones.

In what follows, we will work with the following assumptions:

(1) three alternative assumptions concerning the proportion of foreign aid loans that will be borrowed commercially: one-fourth, half and three-fourths;[5]

(2) three alternative *discount* rates: 3, 4 and 5 per cent;[6]

(3) two alternative terms of the commercial borrowing at: 6 per cent interest rate and 5 years maturity; and 15 per cent interest rate and 5 years maturity;[7] and

5. The trade-offs between private investment and official aid could be guessed at by cross-section and time series analysis of recipients, for example.

6. These are again assumptions with respect to the productivity of domestically used resources; they could have been taken to be approximated by the long-term bond rates, as suggested by Pincus (1963) and Little and Clifford (1965), but this seems dubious too.

7. The first terms have been taken simply from the stiffest average terms among donor countries in 1962, of Austria; the second set of terms are much stiffer and hypothesized.

(4) identical application of the preceding three specifications to *all* donor countries, thus ruling out international variations arising from this source.[8]

Note that no allowance is made for the reduction in real cost of aid resulting from aid-tying by source or by commodity or project specification.[9]

The estimates are made for each of the years 1962–6 (though, only the 1962 results are printed here to economize on space), using OECD data produced by the *Development Assistance Committee* (DAC). They cover eleven major donor countries. In common with Little and Clifford (1965), the following assumptions are made in dealing with the different entries in the tables on flow of official assistance, the only differences being those introduced from the changed methods of discounting:

(1) 'grants' are treated at full value;

(2) 'loans repayable in local currencies, net' and 'sales for recipients' currencies, net' are taken as either grant-equivalents (Assumption A) or as involving zero real-cost (Assumption B);

(3) 'multilateral contributions' are treated as grant-equivalents; and

(4) *private* capital transfers are excluded altogether.

Furthermore, since the DAC estimates of aid flows give only the total flows and the *average* interest rates and maturity on loans for each DAC country, we have worked with *two* alternative estimates of *actual* time-paths of loan repayments, based on the alternative assumptions that the *grace-period* on repayment of *principal* is one year or five years (Little and Clifford, 1965).[10]

We have altogether therefore three alternative estimates of the rate of discount, four of the proportion of aid that would be borrowed (including the option of zero lending assumed by Pincus) two of the terms on which commercial borrowing would occur and two of how commodity assistance is evaluated. Further, we have worked with two estimates of the *actual* time profile of amortization and repayments. Hence, for each country, we can have altogether 72 + 12 (on zero-lending terms) = 84 estimates for each year, of its cost of aid.

In practice, however, only United States and Germany have commodity

8. This eliminates one of the two major difficulties noted concerning international comparisons.

9. Aid-tying by source, when effective, amounts to a transfer of real resources from the recipient to the donor country, insofar as the former effectively subsidizes the exports of the latter instead of the latter having to do so. Twenty per cent seems to be around the upper limit of such transfers, according to recent estimates. Cf. Bhagwati (1967).

10. It should be noted, however, that the *ex post* actual time profile will frequently differ from the *ex ante* time profile which is considered in the calculations presented here, thanks to debt-rescheduling adjustments. Note also that, since the completion of the calculations presented in this paper, the DAC has begun to publish data on the *actual* time profiles, so that guesswork in this area is not necessary any longer.

assistance during the years chosen, so that for each of the remaining countries we have only 36 + 6 = 42 alternative estimates. These measures constitute essentially a set of 'sensitivity' exercises, designed to see how far the ranking of countries by calculations of the real cost of their aid can be treated as a reasonably acceptable statistical index for reaching policy conclusions with respect to actual distributions of the aid burden.

The results. The resulting estimates of the real cost of aid, turned into percentages of the GNP of respective donor countries, have been reproduced only for 1962 in Table 13.1 along with the ranks of the different donor countries under each alternative estimate. Furthermore, for comparison, the ranks of the donors by nominal, unadjusted aid flows have also been calculated. Table 13.2 records the weighted average maturity periods and interest rates which have been used in these calculations.

Among the important conclusions which emerge from our calculations (for 1962 and also taking into account the omitted results for 1963–5) are the following:

(1) The real-cost estimates often have a striking impact on the aid-flow estimates as percentage of GNP: the burden reduces dramatically in several cases. Austria, in 1966 for example, shows only one-eighth of its nominal burden if we take the zero-lending assumption at 4 per cent discount rate and a one-year grace period, and as little as one-fourteenth if we take a five-year grace period. In the same year Italy's burden is practically halved for nearly all the estimates. For Portugal, the burden almost disappears at 3 per cent discount rate, zero-lending and a five-year grace period in 1964; and similar calculations in Table 13.2 show the burden even turning negative (at 0.3 per cent of GNP in 1962 for 3 per cent discount rate, zero-lending and five-year grace period), underlining the moral that 'aid' is not always as altruistic as it may appear. Among the nations which seem to emerge rather well, however, are the United States (whose terms and conditions for loans are reputedly soft) and France (whose percentage-of-GNP aid burden continues to be in the range of 0.75 per cent despite the alternative adjustments).

(2) Another important consequence of our deflation is that the ranking of donors by their real cost of aid as a percent of GNP is strikingly different from that for nominal, unadjusted aid figures, generally regardless of the real cost estimates chosen. Among the sensitive countries is Portugal which drops sharply from the first rank in 1964 and 1966 (and second in 1965) by the nominal aid estimates to fairly near the bottom of the scale for some real-cost estimates and does only a little better for estimates based on the assumption either that 50 or 75 per cent would be lent at the highly favourable interest rate of 15 per cent or that the discount rate is at 4 or 5 per cent. On the other hand, Canada rises steeply to a higher rank in 1965 and 1966 by most adjustments.

(3) Finally, the results *are* sometimes sensitive to changes in the assumptions about the proportion of aid that would be lent to LDCs if aid were withdrawn, the terms and conditions on which such lending would accrue, and the discount rate chosen. This is indeed what we would expect from the different combinations of grants and loans, and the different terms and conditions of loans, among the donor countries.[11] The ranks of several countries are admittedly fairly, though not totally, stable: France, for example, remains at the top through all variations whereas the United States varies at maximum from the fourth to the sixth rank (in 1966). On the other hand, a few countries show remarkable volatility in ranking as the assumptions change. Portugal, for example, goes from second to the tenth rank in 1964 at 3 per cent discount rate; and Canada goes from the fifth to the eighth rank in 1965 at 3 per cent discount rate.

It is clearly, therefore, somewhat hazardous to rank donor countries by their aid/GNP shares and deduce conclusions about donor-generosity and aid policy even when the nominal aid flows have been adjusted to real-cost equivalents. The zero-lending Pincus-adjustment itself represents only one of several possible ways of aiming at 'real-cost' estimates from which choice must be made, since the results can, and (as we have shown) in actual practice do, vary with the adjustment-method adopted.

GENERAL NOTES TO TABLE 13.1

(1)   The countries are listed according to their ranks, in descending order, given by the percentage of nominal aid to GNP level.

(2)   The A-estimates, for USA and Germany, represent estimates of 'real cost' of aid, assuming that 'loans repayable in local currencies, net', representing primarily commodity assistance for the USA, are to be treated at full, nominal value. Under the B-assumption, however, they are treated as having zero opportunity cost and thus assigned only zero 'real cost'. The ranks assigned, when there are both A and B estimates, are by A estimates only. The ranks change sometimes, if B estimates are used, but not always.

(3)   The ranks of the countries, for each estimate presented, are given in brackets, directly under the percentage estimates.

11. The precise manner in which changes in ranks are brought about can be inferred by examining the behaviour of the loans in response to alternative methods of adjustment to get their real-cost equivalent.

TABLE 13.1a Total aid as percentage of GNP and country ranking, 1962 (discount rate, 3%)

Interest rate on commercial lending

Proportion of aid loans assumed to be lent to LDCs commercially in case of withdrawal of such aid

Assumed grace period of actual aid loans

Country (1)	Nominal aid (2)	6% Zero 1 yr (3)	6% Zero 5 yr (4)	6% 25% 1 yr (5)	6% 25% 5 yr (6)	6% 50% 1 yr (7)	6% 50% 5 yr (8)	6% 75% 1 yr (9)	6% 75% 5 yr (10)	15% 25% 1 yr (11)	15% 25% 5 yr (12)	15% 50% 1 yr (13)	15% 50% 5 yr (14)	15% 75% 1 yr (15)	15% 75% 5 yr (16)
France	1.40 (1)	1.18 (1)	1.18 (1)	1.19 (1)	1.18 (1)	1.19 (1)	1.19 (1)	1.20 (1)	1.19 (1)	1.20 (1)	1.20 (1)	1.22 (1)	1.21 (1)	1.23 (1)	1.23 (1)
Portugal	1.29 (2)	0.0 (11)	−0.3 (11)	0.03 (11)	−0.01 (11)	0.05 (11)	0.02 (11)	0.08 (11)	0.04 (11)	0.10 (10)	0.07 (11)	0.20 (7)	0.17 (7)	0.30 (5)	0.27 (6)
United States (A)	0.69 (3)	0.53 (4)	0.53 (4)	0.54 (4)	0.54 (4)	0.54 (4)	0.54 (4)	0.54 (4)	0.54 (4)	0.55 (4)	0.55 (4)	0.56 (4)	0.56 (4)	0.57 (4)	0.58 (4)
(B)		0.38	0.38	0.38	0.39	0.39	0.39	0.39	0.39	0.39	0.40	0.41	0.41	0.42	0.42
Netherlands	0.68 (4)	0.64 (2)	0.64 (2)	0.64 (2)	0.64 (2)	0.64 (2)	0.64 (2)	0.64 (2)	0.64 (2)	0.64 (2)	0.64 (2)	0.64 (2)	0.64 (2)	0.64 (2)	0.64 (2)
Belgium	0.62 (5)	0.62 (3)	0.62 (3)	0.62 (3)	0.62 (3)	0.62 (3)	0.62 (3)	0.62 (3)	0.62 (3)	0.62 (3)	0.62 (3)	0.62 (3)	0.62 (3)	0.62 (3)	0.62 (3)
United Kingdom	0.54 (6)	0.24 (5)	0.23 (5)	0.25 (5)	0.23 (5)	0.25 (5)	0.24 (5)	0.26 (5)	0.24 (5)	0.26 (5)	0.25 (5)	0.28 (5)	0.27 (5)	0.30 (6)	0.28 (5)
Germany (A)	0.51 (7)	0.21 (6)	0.20 (6)	0.22 (6)	0.20 (6)	0.22 (6)	0.21 (6)	0.23 (6)	0.22 (6)	0.23 (6)	0.22 (6)	0.26 (6)	0.24 (6)	0.28 (7)	0.27 (6)
(B)	0.51	0.21	0.20	0.21	0.20	0.22	0.21	0.22	0.21	0.23	0.22	0.25	0.24	0.28	0.27

TABLE 13.1a   continued

		Interest rate on commercial lending													
		6%								15%					
		Proportion of aid loans assumed to be lent to LDCs commercially in case of withdrawal of such aid													
		Zero		25%		50%		75%		25%		50%		75%	
		Assumed grace period of actual aid loans													
	Nominal aid	1 yr	5 yr	1 yr	5 yr	1 yr	5 yr	1 yr	5 yr	1 yr	5 yr	1 yr	5 yr	1 yr	5 yr
Country (1)	(2)	(3)	(4)	(5)	(6)	(7)	(8)	(9)	(10)	(11)	(12)	(13)	(14)	(15)	(16)
Japan	0.34 (8)	0.11 (9)	0.09 (9)	0.11 (9)	0.09 (9)	0.12 (8)	0.10 (9)	0.12 (8)	0.10 (9)	0.12 (8)	0.11 (9)	0.14 (9)	0.12 (9)	0.16 (8)	0.14 (9)
Italy	0.19 (9)	0.15 (7)	0.15 (7)	0.15 (7)	0.15 (7)	0.15 (7)	0.15 (7)	0.15 (7)	0.15 (7)	0.16 (7)	0.15 (7)	0.16 (8)	0.15 (8)	0.16 (8)	0.16 (8)
Canada	0.16 (10)	0.09 (10)	0.09 (9)	0.09 (10)	0.09 (9)	0.10 (10)	0.09 (10)	0.10 (10)	0.09 (10)	0.10 (10)	0.09 (10)	0.10 (11)	0.10 (11)	0.11 (11)	0.10 (11)
Austria	0.12 (11)	0.12 (8)	0.12 (8)	0.12 (8)	0.12 (8)	0.12 (8)	0.12 (8)	0.12 (8)	0.12 (8)	0.12 (8)	0.12 (8)	0.12 (10)	0.12 (9)	0.12 (10)	0.12 (10)

TABLE 13.1b Total aid as percentage of GNP and country ranking, 1962 (discount rate, 4%)

		Interest rate on commercial lending													
		6%								15%					
		Proportion of aid loans assumed to be lent to LDCs commercially in case of withdrawal of such aid													
		Zero		25%		50%		75%		25%		50%		75%	
		Assumed grace period of actual aid loans													
Country (1)	Nominal aid (2)	1 yr (3)	5 yr (4)	1 yr (5)	5 yr (6)	1 yr (7)	5 yr (8)	1 yr (9)	5 yr (10)	1 yr (11)	5 yr (12)	1 yr (13)	5 yr (14)	1 yr (15)	5 yr (16)
France	1.40 (1)	1.20 (1)	1.20 (1)	1.20 (1)	1.20 (1)	1.21 (1)	1.21 (1)	1.21 (1)	1.21 (1)	1.22 (1)	1.22 (1)	1.23 (1)	1.23 (1)	1.25 (1)	1.25 (1)
Portugal	1.29 (2)	0.11 (10)	0.11 (10)	0.12 (10)	0.12 (8)	0.14 (8)	0.14 (8)	0.16 (7)	0.16 (7)	0.20 (7)	0.20 (7)	0.29 (6)	0.29 (6)	0.37 (5)	0.37 (6)
United States (A)	0.69 (3)	0.55 (4)	0.55 (4)	0.55 (4)	0.56 (4)	0.55 (4)	0.56 (4)	0.56 (4)	0.56 (4)	0.56 (4)	0.57 (4)	0.57 (4)	0.58 (4)	0.59 (4)	0.59 (3)
(B)		0.40	0.40	0.40	0.40	0.40	0.41	0.40	0.41	0.41	0.42	0.42	0.43	0.44	0.44
Netherlands	0.68 (4)	0.64 (2)	0.64 (2)	0.64 (2)	0.64 (2)	0.64 (2)	0.64 (2)	0.64 (2)	0.64 (2)	0.65 (2)	0.65 (2)	0.65 (2)	0.65 (2)	0.65 (2)	0.65 (2)
Belgium	0.62 (5)	0.62 (3)	0.62 (3)	0.62 (3)	0.62 (3)	0.62 (3)	0.62 (3)	0.62 (3)	0.62 (3)	0.62 (3)	0.62 (3)	0.62 (3)	0.62 (3)	0.62 (3)	0.62 (4)
United Kingdom	0.54 (6)	0.27 (5)	0.26 (5)	0.27 (5)	0.26 (5)	0.28 (5)	0.27 (5)	0.28 (5)	0.27 (5)	0.29 (5)	0.28 (5)	0.31 (5)	0.30 (5)	0.32 (6)	0.31 (5)

TABLE 13.1b continued

		Interest rate on commercial lending													
		6%								15%					
		Proportion of aid loans assumed to be lent to LDCs commercially in case of withdrawal of such aid													
		Zero		25%		50%		75%		25%		50%		75%	
		Assumed grace period of actual aid loans													
Country (1)	Nominal aid (2)	1 yr (3)	5 yr (4)	1 yr (5)	5 yr (6)	1 yr (7)	5 yr (8)	1 yr (9)	5 yr (10)	1 yr (11)	5 yr (12)	1 yr (13)	5 yr (14)	1 yr (15)	5 yr (16)
Germany (A)	0.51 (7)	0.23 (6)	0.23 (6)	0.23 (6)	0.23 (6)	0.24 (6)	0.24 (6)	0.24 (6)	0.24 (6)	0.25 (6)	0.25 (6)	0.27 (7)	0.27 (7)	0.29 (7)	0.29 (7)
(B)	0.51	0.23	0.23	0.23	0.23	0.24	0.23	0.24	0.24	0.25	0.25	0.27	0.27	0.29	0.29
Japan	0.34 (8)	0.12 (8)	0.11 (9)	0.12 (8)	0.11 (10)	0.13 (9)	0.11 (10)	0.13 (9)	0.12 (9)	0.13 (9)	0.12 (9)	0.15 (9)	0.14 (9)	0.16 (8)	0.15 (9)
Italy	0.19 (9)	0.15 (7)	0.15 (7)	0.15 (7)	0.15 (7)	0.16 (7)	0.15 (7)	0.16 (7)	0.15 (8)	0.16 (8)	0.15 (8)	0.16 (8)	0.16 (8)	0.16 (8)	0.16 (8)
Canada	0.16 (10)	0.10 (11)	0.09 (11)	0.10 (11)	0.09 (11)	0.10 (11)	0.10 (11)	0.10 (11)	0.10 (11)	0.10 (11)	0.10 (11)	0.10 (11)	0.10 (11)	0.11 (11)	0.11 (11)
Austria	0.12 (11)	0.12 (8)	0.12 (8)	0.12 (8)	0.12 (8)	0.12 (10)	0.12 (9)	0.12 (10)	0.12 (9)	0.12 (10)	0.12 (9)	0.12 (10)	0.12 (10)	0.12 (10)	0.12 (10)

TABLE 13.1c Total aid as percentage of GNP and country ranking, 1962 (discount rate, 5%)

		Interest rate on commercial lending													
		6%								15%					
		Proportion of aid loans assumed to be lent to LDCs commercially in case of withdrawal of such aid													
		Zero		25%		50%		75%		25%		50%		75%	
		Assumed grace period of actual aid loans													
Country	Nominal aid	1 yr	5 yr	1 yr	5 yr	1 yr	5 yr	1 yr	5 yr	1 yr	5 yr	1 yr	5 yr	1 yr	5 yr
(1)	(2)	(3)	(4)	(5)	(6)	(7)	(8)	(9)	(10)	(11)	(12)	(13)	(14)	(15)	(16)
France	1.40 (1)	1.22 (1)	1.22 (1)	1.22 (1)	1.22 (1)	1.22 (1)	1.22 (1)	1.22 (1)	1.22 (1)	1.23 (1)	1.23 (1)	1.24 (1)	1.25 (1)	1.26 (1)	1.26 (1)
Portugal	1.29 (2)	0.20 (7)	0.23 (7)	0.21 (7)	0.23 (7)	0.22 (7)	0.24 (7)	0.22 (7)	0.25 (7)	0.28 (6)	0.31 (5)	0.36 (5)	0.38 (5)	0.44 (5)	0.46 (5)
United States (A)	0.69 (3)	0.56 (4)	0.57 (4)	0.57 (4)	0.57 (4)	0.57 (4)	0.57 (4)	0.57 (4)	0.57 (4)	0.58 (4)	0.58 (4)	0.59 (4)	0.59 (4)	0.60 (4)	0.61 (4)
(B)		0.41	0.42	0.41	0.42	0.41	0.42	0.42	0.42	0.42	0.43	0.43	0.44	0.45	0.45
Netherlands	0.68 (4)	0.65 (2)	0.65 (2)	0.65 (2)	0.65 (2)	0.65 (2)	0.65 (2)	0.65 (2)	0.65 (2)	0.65 (2)	0.65 (2)	0.65 (2)	0.65 (2)	0.65 (2)	0.65 (2)
Belgium	0.62 (5)	0.62 (3)	0.62 (3)	0.62 (3)	0.62 (3)	0.62 (3)	0.62 (3)	0.62 (3)	0.62 (3)	0.62 (3)	0.62 (3)	0.62 (3)	0.62 (3)	0.62 (3)	0.62 (3)
United Kingdom	0.54 (6)	0.29 (5)	0.29 (5)	0.30 (5)	0.29 (5)	0.30 (5)	0.29 (5)	0.30 (5)	0.30 (5)	0.31 (5)	0.31 (5)	0.33 (6)	0.32 (6)	0.34 (6)	0.34 (6)

TABLE 13.1c   continued

Interest rate on commercial lending

		6%								15%					
		Proportion of aid loans assumed to be lent to LDCs commercially in case of withdrawal of such aid													
		Zero		25%		50%		75%		25%		50%		75%	
		Assumed grace period of actual aid loans													
		1 yr	5 yr	1 yr	5 yr	1 yr	5 yr	1 yr	5 yr	1 yr	5 yr	1 yr	5 yr	1 yr	5 yr
Country	*Nominal aid*														
(1)	*(2)*	*(3)*	*(4)*	*(5)*	*(6)*	*(7)*	*(8)*	*(9)*	*(10)*	*(11)*	*(12)*	*(13)*	*(14)*	*(15)*	*(16)*
Germany (A)	0.51 (7)	0.25 (6)	0.25 (6)	0.25 (6)	0.26 (6)	0.25 (6)	0.26 (6)	0.26 (6)	0.26 (6)	0.27 (7)	0.27 (7)	0.29 (7)	0.29 (7)	0.31 (7)	0.31 (7)
(B)	0.51	0.25 (6)	0.25 (6)	0.25 (6)	0.25 (6)	0.25 (6)	0.26 (6)	0.25 (6)	0.26 (6)	0.27 (7)	0.27 (7)	0.29 (7)	0.29 (7)	0.30 (7)	0.31 (7)
Japan	0.34 (8)	0.13 (9)	0.13 (9)	0.13 (9)	0.13 (9)	0.13 (9)	0.13 (9)	0.14 (9)	0.13 (9)	0.14 (9)	0.14 (9)	0.16 (8)	0.15 (9)	0.17 (8)	0.17 (8)
Italy	0.19 (9)	0.16 (8)	0.15 (8)	0.16 (8)	0.15 (8)	0.16 (8)	0.15 (8)	0.16 (8)	0.16 (8)	0.16 (8)	0.16 (8)	0.16 (8)	0.16 (8)	0.16 (9)	0.16 (9)
Canada	0.16 (10)	0.10 (11)	0.10 (11)	0.10 (11)	0.10 (11)	0.10 (11)	0.10 (11)	0.10 (11)	0.10 (11)	0.10 (11)	0.10 (11)	0.11 (11)	0.11 (11)	0.11 (11)	0.11 (11)
Austria	0.12 (11)	0.12 (10)	0.12 (10)	0.12 (10)	0.12 (10)	0.12 (10)	0.12 (10)	0.12 (10)	0.12 (10)	0.12 (10)	0.12 (10)	0.12 (10)	0.12 (10)	0.12 (10)	0.12 (10)

TABLE 13.2 Average financial terms of official bilateral loan commitments, 1962–6

	Weighted average maturity periods (years)					Weighted average interest rates (per cent)				
	1962	1963	1964	1965	1966	1962	1963	1964	1965	1966
Austria	5.0	19.0	8.8	7.7	6.5	6.0	3.0	5.2	5.5	5.7
Belgium	—	—	20.0	16.2	13.9	—	—	3.0	3.0	2.8
Canada	11.6	12.5	25.1	32.9	34.3	6.0	6.0	4.7	3.4	2.4
France	17.0*	15.0*	15.6*	17.6	15.3	4.0*	4.2*	3.2*	3.8	3.6
Germany	15.2	18.5	18.1	16.9	21.2	4.4	4.3	4.0	4.2	3.3
Italy	5.8	8.7	9.3	6.3	8.0	6.1	6.1	4.3	4.3	3.7
Japan	10.0	15.0	16.0	12.0	14.1	6.0	5.8	5.8	4.4	5.2
Netherlands	26.5	23.8	24.2	23.9	23.6	4.0*	4.8	3.9	3.5	2.0
Portugal	18.9	20.2	16.3	21.5*	25.9*	4.0*	3.3	4.1	3.8*	3.6*
United Kingdom	24.3	21.0	24.0	22.2	23.9	5.8	4.8	4.1	3.3	1.0
United States	28.6	32.5	33.4	27.9	29.3	2.5	2.0	2.5	3.3	3.0
Total DAC countries	24.5	25.1	28.4	22.3	23.5	3.5	3.3	3.1	3.6	3.1

*Gross disbursement data.
Source: *Development Assistance Efforts and Policies: Yearly Review: 1967* (Paris OECD), p. 76.

REFERENCES

Bhagwati, J. (1967): 'The tying of aid', UNCTAD Secretariat, 1 November; prepared for and forthcoming in Proceedings of the second UNCTAD Conference in New Delhi; reprinted in this volume, ch. 12.

Kravis, I. and Davenport, M. W. S. (1963): 'The political arithmetic of international burden-sharing', *Journal of Political Economy* (August), pp. 309–30.

Little, I. M. D. and Clifford, J. (1965): *International Aid* (London: Allen and Unwin).

Pincus, J. (1963): 'The cost of foreign aid', *Review of Economics and Statistics* (November), pp. 360–7.

Rosenstein-Rodan, P. N. (1962): 'Determining the need for and planning the use of external resources', mimeo, Center for International Studies, MIT, Cambridge, Mass.

14

Substitution between Foreign Capital and Domestic Saving

We must now consider a question of some importance, which links the present analysis of foreign capital with the preceding analysis of domestic saving. Can the two be treated as exogenous to each other; or are there any functional links between them?

Although the net result of the latter possibility would be to compound the difficulty of assessing the impact of foreign trade regimes on domestic saving and an overall investment, it must be admitted that there *are* possible links here and that some evidence is also available in support thereof. Note, at the outset, that the links between foreign capital and domestic savings can, in principle, be in both directions.

1 AID INFLOW AS A FUNCTION OF DOMESTIC SAVING

A rising domestic saving ratio may be 'rewarded' by aid donors with greater aid inflows on a 'matching' principle of the kind often discussed by aid agencies. It may equally lead, at higher saving ratios, to lower aid flows as aid agencies may feel that aid is no longer 'necessary' to supplement domestic savings effort. One may therefore hypothesize a reverse U-shaped curve, linking the (independent variable) domestic saving ratio to the (dependent variable) foreign savings (either as ratio to GNP or in absolute magnitude).[1] While there is some evidence in the literature

1. Figure 14.1 illustrates such a relationship between domestic saving and foreign aid flows. The variable F/Y (foreign aid to income) can be replaced by F if the hypothesis is modified to refer to absolute aid flows.

FIGURE 14.1

Excerpts from J. Bhagwati, *The Anatomy and Consequences of Exchange Control Regimes* (Cambridge, Mass.: Ballinger for the NBER, 1978), pp. 165–70, 180–1.

on the pronouncements of donor agencies and aid proponents for the 'matching' principle in aid 'awards', and some supporting evidence in the aid deceleration to South Korea and Taiwan (which were relatively 'successful' in achieving an economic take-off) for the other half of the postulated argument, it should be noted that little support for this type of aid-allocational decision-making process has been found in the cross-sectional analysis of the *ex-post* aid flows among different recipients.[2]

On the other hand, evidence for this bell-shaped relationship may well be detected through a time-series analysis that introduces additional explanatory variables such as shifts in political alliances, growing availability of private foreign capital, and so on. Alternatively, such a relationship may be, not between domestic saving *in toto* and foreign aid, but rather between public savings or tax effort (which are far more reliably measured than total savings and are also a more direct, if incomplete, measure of recipient-governmental effort at raising domestic resources for investment) and foreign aid, at least for the recipient countries with lower saving ratios. Further econometric analysis may thus well rescue some of the hypothesized effect of domestic saving performance on foreign aid inflow.

2   PRIVATE CAPITAL INFLOW AS A FUNCTION OF DOMESTIC SAVING

It is rather more difficult to argue a relationship between domestic saving and private inflow. It may be argued, however, that a higher domestic saving rate, *ceteris paribus*, would imply a higher growth rate (in a Harrod-Domar framework) and that the latter may induce greater private capital inflow. This would yield a monotonic increase in capital inflow with rising saving rates, contrary to the possibly U-shaped relationship that we just discussed for foreign aid.[3] Again, however, as with the latter, there seems

2. Nor, for that matter, has cross-sectional analysis of aid-flow distribution among recipients, using other variables such as *per capita* income, been notably successful. For a review of these analyses and regression estimates, see Bhagwati (1970), app. II).

3. The relationship would be as in Figure 14.2

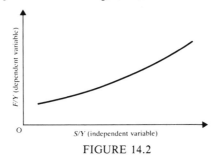

FIGURE 14.2

to be little supporting evidence for any such systematic relationship between private capital inflow and domestic savings.

3 DOMESTIC SAVINGS AS A FUNCTION OF CAPITAL INFLOW

The most influential hypothesis recently has however been that postulating that domestic saving is rather the dependent variable and foreign capital inflow the independent variable, and that foreign capital substitutes for domestic saving. Thus, we may write:

$$S = a + bY + cF \tag{1}$$

where S is saving, Y income, and F the foreign capital inflow, the parameters having the following 'normal' signs: $a < 0$ (the Keynesian assumption), $b > 0$, and $c > 0$.[4] The underlying rationale for this hypothesis is that, as an economy gets more foreign capital, this supplements its available resources, so that it is reasonable to assume that part of this will be expended on increasing current, and part on augmenting future, consumption. With current consumption rising, at given income, the current domestic saving would then fall.[5]

A voluminous amount of cross-country and time-series statistical analysis has been addressed to this issue, essentially regressing domestic saving (as the dependent variable) on income, foreign capital inflow (rarely

---

The net effect of merging the two capital flows, as is done in many of the empirical analyses shortly to be reviewed, would be to moderate (and could even reverse) the decline in F/Y at higher S/Y ratios where the aid curve turns down.

4. Thus, Figure 14.2 modifies to the diagram (where, for simplicity, we assume a negligible 'a') in Figure 14.3.

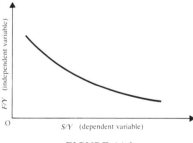

FIGURE 14.3

5. On the other hand, if we assume that the country decides on an optimal time path, given an intertemporal utility function, it is not necessarily true that aid will not be *more than offset* by current consumption. For such 'counterintuitive' results, I am indebted to an unpublished paper of Richard Freeman.

distinguishing between private and official capital),[6] and at times, supplementary independent variables (e.g. exports, as already discussed in the previous section).

The results of several regression studies are summarized here in Table 14.1 and indicate strongly the recurrence of a negative impact, of varying magnitudes, of foreign inflows on saving. The signs are almost always negative. What are we to conclude from this mass of regressions? First, as Papanek has correctly stressed, some caution is necessary in interpreting these results. While it is true that no systematic regression can be fitted that explains low saving ratios as a cause of higher aid flows, this is not the same as ruling this out for some countries (e.g. South Korea after the Korean War's devastation) as a complicating factor that *alternatively* may account for the inverse association between external capital inflows and domestic saving ratios.

Next, the method of computing domestic saving is usually the 'residual' type whereby the payments deficit is subtracted from the estimated investment. If therefore the payments deficit (and hence capital inflow) is overestimated, the saving will be underestimated. Thus the bias in errors of estimation runs systematically in favour of supporting the negative relationship that emerges from the regressions.

But major doubts and difficulties in interpretation also come from other directions. In particular, we could reformulate the saving equation:

$$S = a + b(F) \cdot Y + cF$$

$$b = d + ef \qquad (b,\ e > 0)$$

so that

$$S = a + dY + cF + eFY \qquad (2)$$

and it is being postulated now that, while the recipient government indeed consumes $(1 - c)$ units out of unit inflow of capital, it also increases its domestic saving effort *via* taxation, and so on, so as to yield a higher parameter 'b' – the marginal propensity to save out of income. This formulation would appear to yield estimates that dampen the adverse effect of foreign capital on saving.

Next, we must also note that the adverse impact being discussed is only the primary impact. However, even if foreign capital substitutes for domestic saving, at given income, it will (as long as it adds net to investment) increase (future) income and hence saving on that account. Hence, to evaluate fully the effect of foreign capital on the domestic saving

6. Among the exceptions is Papanek (1973).

TABLE 14.1 Results of major analyses regressing saving on foreign capital flows

Author	Cross-country (C) time series (T) pooled (C, T)	Number of observations	Form of equation	Deflated variables (D) nominal variables (N)	Effect of foreign inflow on saving
Griffin and Enos	C C	32 13	$\dfrac{S_d}{Y} \cdot 100 = a + b\ \dfrac{S_p}{Y} \cdot 100$	N N	−0.73 −0.82
Griffin	T	13	$\dfrac{S_d}{Y} \cdot 100 = a + b\ \dfrac{S_b}{Y} \cdot 100$	N	−0.84
Rahman	C	31	$\dfrac{S}{Y} = a + b\ \dfrac{F}{Y}$	D	−0.2473
Areskoug	T	(22 countries) ≈13–14 observations per country	$I = aB + bY + cF'$	D	−1.53 to +4.30
Weisskopf	T, C	(17 countries) 9–12 observations per country	$S = a\ bY + c\ \dfrac{E}{Y} + dF$	D	−0.227
Chenery	T	(16 countries) 13–14 observations per country	$S = a + bY + c\ \dfrac{E}{Y} + dF$	D	+0.64 to −1.15*
Chenery	C } C	90	$\dfrac{S}{Y} \cdot 100 = a + b\log Y + c(\log Y)^2 + dN + cT + fF$ $\dfrac{Id}{Y} \cdot 100 = a + b\log Y + c(\log Y)^2 + dN + eT + fF$	D D	−0.4894 −0.8892

TABLE 14.1 continued

Author	Cross-country (C) time series (T) pooled (C, T)	Number of observations	Form of equation	Deflated variables (D) nominal variables (N)	Effect of foreign inflow on saving
Papanek	C	85	$S = a + bA + cI_p + dF_0 + eE_p + fE_0$	N	$b \quad c \quad d$ $-1.00, -0.65, -0.38$
			$S = a + b \log \dfrac{Y}{N} + d \log N + eF$ $+ fEp + gE_0$		-0.64
			$S = a + b \log \dfrac{Y}{N} + c \log N + dF$		-0.73
Clark	C, T	(33 countries)	$\dfrac{S}{Y} \cdot 100 = a + b \log \dfrac{Y}{N} - c\dfrac{F}{N} \cdot 100$ $+ dP + eW + fD$	D	-0.58

*12 of 16 negative.

TABLE 14.1 *continued*

List of variables:

Y = GDP.
Sd = Domestic saving.
Sf = Foreign saving.
S = Gross domestic saving.
I = Investment.
B = Net government external borrowing.
F' = Net private capital outflow *plus* change in government foreign reserves *minus* net transfer receipts from abroad.
F = Net foreign inflows
N = Population size.
T = Time.
I_d = Gross domestic investment.
A = Net transfers received by government plus official long-term borrowing.
I_p = Private investment.
E_p = Primary exports.
E_0 = Other exports.
F_0 = Other capital inflows.
P = Decadal rate of population growth.
W = War damage expressed as multiple of 1938 NNP at factor cost.
D = Dummy variable: 0 pre-1955; 1 post-1955.

Sources: Griffin, K. B. and Enos, J. L., 'Foreign Assistance: Objectives and Consequences', *Economic Development and Cultural Change* (April 1970). Griffin, K. B., 'Foreign capital, domestic savings and economic development', *Bulletin of the Oxford University Institute of Economics and Statistics* (May 1970). Rahman, A., 'Foreign capital and domestic savings: a test of Haavelmo's hypothesis with cross-country data', *Review of Economics and Statistics* (February 1968). Areskoug, K., *External Borrowing: Its Role in Economic Development* (New York: Praeger, 1969). Weisskopf, T., 'The impact of foreign capital inflow on domestic savings in underdeveloped countries', *Journal of International Economics*, 2(1) (February 1972). Chenery, H. B., 'Development alternatives for Latin America', (with P. Eckstein) *Journal of Political Economy* (July/August 1970). Chenery, H. B. 'A uniform analysis of development patterns', (with H. Elkington and C. Aims), *Economic Development Reports*, Nos. 148, 158, Harvard University Center for International Affairs. Papanek, G. F. 'Aid, foreign private investment, savings and growth in less developed countries', *Journal of Political Economy*, 81(1) (January/February 1973). Clark, C. *Population Growth and Land Use* (New York: Macmillan, 1967).

K

ratio, the estimated saving functions need to be 'fed' into a growth model. Grinols and Bhagwati have shown that, if we do this in a simple Harrod-Domar model, the impact effect *can* get reversed for a reasonable number of cases in simulation experiments using plausible parametric values[7] (Grinols and Bhagwati, 1976).

Among the studies in the NBER project containing an analysis of the issue of the impact of foreign inflows on domestic saving is that on India. Its conclusions, even on the limited issue of the primary impact effect, are far less conclusive than the results of the studies discussed so far. . . .[8]

On the other hand, Behrman concludes the opposite for Chile and, citing the evidence in support of the substitution hypothesis, he states:

> In one sense, in fact, the support is too strong because the total of the relevant coefficients implies that a permanent increase in real net foreign savings of one unit *ceteris paribus* results in a decrease in real net domestic savings of at least the same order of magnitude. If it were not for the problem of multicollinearity, therefore, one might conclude that in the Chilean case there is support for a rather extreme version of the hypothesis. However, given that the relevant coefficient estimates for the real private domestic savings functions are probably biased upward in absolute value because part of the effects of price and possibly of real monetary balances are incorporated, any deduction about at least the size of the substitution must be qualified. Nevertheless, the conclusion seems warranted that the impact of net real foreign savings on Chilean real domestic savings may be quite significant (Behrman, 1978, p. 285).

REFERENCES

Behrman, J. (1978): *Chile* (NBER Project Country Study) (New York: Columbia University Press).
Bhagwati, J. N. (1970): *Amount and Sharing of Aid* (Washington, DC: Overseas Development Council).
Grinols, E. and Bhagwati, J. (1976): 'Foreign capital, savings and dependence', *Review of Economics and Statistics*, 58(4), pp. 416–24; reprinted in *EIET*, vol. 2, ch. 66.
Papanek, G. F. (1973): 'Aid, foreign private investment savings and growth in less developed countries', *Journal of Political Economy*, 81(1).

7. Cf. Grinols and Bhagwati, (1976). They do not make any adjustment for the assertion sometimes made that foreign inflows *reduce* the efficiency of factor use and thus increase the marginal capital-output ratio. There is no evidence of any value that indicates that aid is utilized any more or less well than average capital use in the developing countries.

[8. This analysis is fully reprinted immediately below as ch. 15 of this volume and hence its brief treatment is omitted here.   GG]

15

Savings and the Foreign Trade Regime

In analysing the impact of India's overall economic policies on the domestic savings effort, we will argue that:

(1) there is little evidence that the marginal propensity to save in the Indian economy was significantly different between the 1950s, when the severity of exchange control (on the average) was less, and the 1960s, when it was more;

(2) detailed analysis does not support the hypothesis that India's absorption of foreign aid has adversely affected her savings effort; this is a conclusion of interest, not merely because of widespread concern with this problem in LDCs today, but because the 1966 economic policy changes toward 'liberalization' were partly motivated by the desire to continue aid flow from the consortium members who had virtually made these policy changes a precondition for continuation of aid;

(3) there is no evidence that the more recent, import-substituting industries which have grown up primarily during the years 1956–70 under the economic regime we have been describing are significantly higher savers than the more traditional industries; and

(4) we do not have adequate data to test the further hypothesis that 'organized' industry *in toto* is a better saver than 'agriculture'. Thus we cannot argue convincingly that the exchange control regime, which buttressed the increasing industrialization, led to greater saving; nor can we establish any other strong links between savings and the Indian foreign trade regime although we consider several possibilities.

1 DOMESTIC SAVINGS AND STRINGENCY OF QRs

It is well known that the data on which Indian national income estimates are based are inadequate and even the methodology of computation is not necessarily the best that could be adopted given the data. The situation regarding savings and investment estimates is even worse: there are no 'direct' estimates for either. In brief, aggregate investment is estimated as the value of goods and services used in investment activity. Savings estimates are obtained as a residual from investment estimates by subtracting therefrom the estimated external capital inflow. This is not

From J. N. Bhagwati and T. N. Srinivasan, *Foreign Trade Regimes and Economic Development: India* (New York: Columbia University Press for NBER, 1975), pp. 228–35 and 241.

to suggest that direct estimates are not available for some components of savings and investment – indeed, relatively accurate direct estimates are available relating to the savings and investment activities of the public sector as well as the large-scale manufacturing sector. But a large proportion has still to be estimated directly.[1]

Given the nature of the data, therefore, it was decided not to attempt to build an elaborate simultaneous-equation model of the Indian economy but rather to work with single-equation regression relationships. The idea is not so much to estimate the marginal propensity to save with great accuracy as rather to obtain some useful insights into overall savings behaviour.

Let us begin, therefore, with the simplest possible relationship:

$$S_t = a_o + a_1 Y_t + u_t \qquad (1)$$

where S_t stands for aggregate savings, Y_t for national income and u_t for a random disturbance term, all variables relating to year t.

In estimating equation (1), we had a choice in defining savings and income (1) in either gross or net terms, (2) at either nominal of real value, and (3) in either *per capita* or aggregate terms. Since the basis on which replacement of capital expenditures is estimated is extremely weak, we decided to define the variables in gross rather than net terms. Again, we decided to concentrate on the relationship between real magnitudes, though in a more elaborate model the impact of monetary factors should be brought in. Finally, to a limited extent we experimented with both alternatives in (3).

The period of our analysis was 1951–2 to 1969–70. There is a belief among some Indian economists that the period since 1965–6 is radically different from the period before, both politically and economically: politically, because the system was exposed to the deaths of Prime Ministers Nehru and Shastri in quick succession in 1964 and 1966; economically, because of (1) the two successive droughts of unprecedented magnitude in 1965 and 1966, (2) aid stoppage during the Indo-Pakistan War of 1965, its resumption in 1966 and subsequent scaling down and (3) the devaluation and liberalization of June 1966. Since we have data only for a four-year period since 1966, we cannot adequately test this belief. However, we do estimate the relationships separately for the entire period and for the period 1951–2 to 1965–6 to see whether there is any sharp break in the income–savings relationship.

From the point of view of the present monograph, perhaps an equally relevant division of the period would be 1951–2 to 1959–60 and 1960–1 to 1969–70 since the exchange control regime was more stringent on the

1. More can be learned about this subject from Rao (1972).

average through the 1960s (the liberalization associated with devaluation being short-lived, as we have seen already). We thus examine the issue whether any significant change in savings behaviour can be observed between the decade of the 1950s and that of the 1960s.

For converting nominal investment to real terms, we had two alternative investment deflators available (denoted by subscripts 1 and 2): one developed by the Perspective Planning Division (PPD) of the Planning Commission and the other put out by the Central Statistical Organization (CSO). Since savings were obtained as a residual from investment by subtracting the external resource flow (i.e., the current account surplus or deficit), we had a number of alternative ways of obtaining real savings, of which the following (denoted by superscripts I and II) were used:

(I) Deflate merchandise imports and exports by their respective unit value indices and take the surplus or deficit on non-merchandise account without deflation.

(II) Deflate the entire current account surplus or deficit by the unit value index of imports, the idea being that, in this way, we capture the real import potential of nominal resource inflow.

Thus, we had four alternative definitions of real savings, $S_1^I(t)$, $S_2^I(t)$, $S_1^{II}(t)$ and $S_2^{II}(t)$ where, for instance, $S_1^{II}(t)$ represents the real savings in year t obtained by subtracting from real investment (defined as the nominal investment deflated by the PPD deflator) the real external resource flow obtained by using procedure II described above. The *per capita* variables are denoted by the same symbols, but in lower case: e.g., s, y, etc.

The results of our regressions are reported in Tables 15.1 and 15.2.[2] The fit as measured by R^2 is quite good in all the regressions. It appears that the estimate of the marginal propensity to save is not very sensitive to the choice of deflators or of the procedure by which the real external resource flow was calculated, though some sensitivity is seen in the period 1960–1 to 1969–70. As is to be expected (given that population, income and savings were rising over time), the marginal propensity to save in each regression involving *per capita* variables is higher than in the corresponding regression with aggregate variables. The goodness of fit of the *per capita* relationship is, however, somewhat poorer.

Let us now examine the results in Table 15.1 and 15.2 for inter-period comparisons of the marginal propensity to save. Clearly, there seems to be little evidence for the view that *either* the post-1966 liberalization years significantly changed the marginal propensity to save from the preceding period (Table 15.1)[3] *or* the 1960s period of relatively tighter exchange

2. The statistical results reported in Tables 15.1 through 15.4 have been taken from Srinivasan *et al.* (1973).

3. Recall, however, our *caveats* in the preceding discussion about the lack of sufficient data for the post-1966 period to test this hypothesis effectively. Table 15.1 is only a weak way of learning about this issue.

TABLE 15.1   Savings regressions, 1951–2 to 1965–6 and 1951–2 to 1969–70

	1951–52 to 1965–66		1951–52 to 1969–70	
(1) (a) S_1^{I} =	$-1453 + 0.24$ Y	$R^2 = 0.94$	$-1053 + 0.21$ Y	$R^2 = 0.93$
	(241) (0.02)		(212) (0.01)	
(b) s_1^{I} =	$-66 + 0.33$ y	$R^2 = 0.87$	$-54 + 0.29$ y	$R^2 = 0.86$
	(12) (0.03)		(10) (0.03)	
(2) (a) S_2^{I} =	$-1476 + 0.24$ Y	$R^2 = 0.93$	$-1323 + 0.23$ Y	$R^2 = 0.95$
	(253) (0.02)		(191) (0.01)	
(b) s_2^{I} =	$-68 + 0.34$ y	$R^2 = 0.86$	$-66 + 0.33$ y	$R^2 = 0.89$
	(12) (0.04)		(10) (0.03)	
(3) (a) S_2^{II} =	$-1509 + 0.24$ Y	$R^2 = 0.93$	$-1216 + 0.21$ Y	$R^2 = 0.94$
	(264) (0.02)		(207) (0.01)	
(b) s_2^{II} =	$-68 + 0.33$ y	$R^2 = 0.85$	$-61 + 0.31$ y	$R^2 = 0.87$
	(13) (0.04)		(10) (0.03)	
(4) (a) S_2^{II} =	$-1532 + 0.24$ Y	$R^2 = 0.93$	$-1486 + 0.24$ Y	$R^2 = 0.96$
	(260) (0.02)		(186) (0.01)	
(b) s_2^{II} =	$-70 + 0.34$ y	$R^2 = 0.86$	$-72 + 0.35$ y	$R^2 = 0.92$
	(13) (0.04)		(10) (0.03)	

Note: Figures in parenthesis are standard errors. Refer to the text for explanation of the regressions.

TABLE 15.2   Savings regressions, 1951–2 to 1959–60 and 1960–1 to 1969–70

		1951–52 to 1959–60		1960–61 to 1969–70	
(1)	S_1^{I} =	$-815 + 0.18$ Y	$R^2 = 0.73$	$-592 + 0.18$ Y	$R^2 = 0.73$
		(520) (0.04)		(698) (0.04)	
(2)	S_2^{I} =	$-1087 + 0.21$ Y	$R^2 = 0.72$	$-1271 + 0.22$ Y	$R^2 = 0.87$
		(607) (0.05)		(560) (0.03)	
(3)	S_1^{I} =	$-532 + 0.16$ Y	$R^2 = 0.63$	$-834 + 0.19$ Y	$R^2 = 0.80$
		(563) (0.05)		(610) (0.03)	
(4)	S_2^{II} =	$-804 + 0.18$ Y	$R^2 = 0.67$	$-1514 + 0.24$ Y	$R^2 = 0.91$
		(600) (0.05)		(741) (0.03)	

Note: Figures in parentheses are standard errors. Refer to the text for explanation of the regressions.

situation was characterized by a higher marginal propensity to save than the somewhat less stringent period of the 1950s (Table 15.2).[4]

2   DOMESTIC SAVINGS AND EXTERNAL RESOURCES

We have postulated so far that savings are a function of income alone. However, it has been argued recently that savings are a function

4. Note again that the early half of the 1950s was very comfortable but the last two years of the decade were already characterized by the strict QR-regime, implying Phase II. Note also that if the marginal propensity to save tends to rise with increasing *per capita* income, its failure to do so in the 1960s may be significant as a possible shortcoming of the QR-regime.

of domestic expenditure, rather than income, so that we should instead write:

$$C_t = \beta_0 + \beta_1(Y_t + F_t) \tag{2}$$

where F_t is the foreign capital inflow, defined as the negative of the balance on current account and C_t is domestic consumption. We therefore estimated the following equation as well:

$$S_t = \alpha_0 + \alpha_1 Y_t + \alpha_2 F_t + u_t \tag{2a}$$

Clearly, when $\alpha_1 = (\alpha_2 + 1)$, this equation will correspond to equation (2). A positive (negative) value for α_2 would be consistent with the hypothesis that external resources complement (substitute for) domestic resources.

The following version of (2a), with F_t lagged by one year, was also estimated:

$$S_t = \alpha_0 + \alpha_1 Y_t + \alpha_2 F_{t-1} + u_t \tag{2b}$$

The idea underlying equation (2b) is that if indeed consumption is related to expected volume of resources available, then it may be reasonable to presume that such expectations for any year are formed on the basis of the actual resources in the previous year. This would suggest that S_t should be related to Y_{t-1} and F_{t-1}. Given that the correlation between Y_t and Y_{t-1} is very high (while that between F_t and F_{t-1} is not), the relation (2b) would, however, do just as well as one with Y_{t-1} instead of Y_t.

The results for both (2a) and (2b) are shown in Table 15.3. Only the results relating to the PPD deflator and the second procedure for calculating the real source flow are reported here. We find that when used in conjunction with income, the explanatory power of contemporaneous external resource flow in explaining savings is virtually nil: the coefficients on F are statistically insignificantly different from zero. The lagged response equations also perform badly: with one exception, the coefficients on F_{-1} are also not significantly different from zero. Thus we infer that domestic savings do not seem to be influenced by external resources.

On the other hand, a mild scepticism toward this conclusion may be in order. For one thing, the introduction of F_{-1} generally seems to lead to higher (*not* lower) coefficients on Y than, for comparable periods, in Tables 15.1 and 15.2. In contrast, a different test suggests an opposite inference: i.e., that domestic savings are a function of $(Y + F)$ rather than (Y). Thus, recall that if we write equation (2) as follows:

$$C = \beta_0 + \beta_1(Y + F) \tag{2}$$

TABLE 15.3 Savings regressions, including foreign capital inflow, various periods, 1951–2 to 1969–70

(1) 1951–2 to 1969–70	(a) $S_1^{II} =$	$-124 + 0.22\ Y - 0.08\ F$	$R^2 = 0.94$
		(0.02) (0.30)	
	(b) $S_1^{II} =$	$-1487 + 0.24\ Y - 0.57\ F_{-1}$	$R^2 = 0.95$
		(0.02) (0.33)	
(2) 1951–2 to 1965–6	(a) $S_1^{II} =$	$-1611 + 0.25\ Y - 0.18\ F$	$R^2 = 0.93$
		(0.03) (0.45)	
	(b)* $S_1^{II} =$	$-1976 + 0.28\ Y - 0.78\ F_{-1}$	$R^2 = 0.95$
		(0.03) (0.38)	
(3) 1951–2 to 1959–60	(a) $S_1^{II} =$	$-553 + 0.16\ Y - 0.02\ F$	$R^2 = 0.63$
		(747) (0.06) (0.49)	
	(b) $S_1^{II} =$	$-1262 + 0.22\ Y - 0.70\ F_{-1}$	$R^2 = 0.75$
		(655) (0.06) (0.42)	
(4) 1960–1 to 1969–70	(a) $S_1^{II} =$	$-641 + 0.19\ Y - 0.29\ F$	$R^2 = 0.81$
		(741) (0.04) (0.57)	
	(b) $S_1^{II} =$	$-862 + 0.21\ Y - 0.49\ F_{-1}$	$R^2 = 0.82$
		(626) (0.04) (0.62)	

Note: Figures in parentheses are standard errors.
*The coefficient on F_{-1} is significantly different from zero at 5 per cent level; other coefficients on F_{-1} are not significantly different from zero, in this table.

and

$$S = Y - C$$

we then have:

$$S = -\beta_0 + (1 - \beta_1)Y - \beta_1 F$$

so that we have the relationship that the coefficient on Y is equal to one plus the coefficient on F (or F_{-1}, if we put in lagged response). We can therefore test whether the coefficients on Y are indeed significantly different from one plus the coefficients on F and F_{-1} in Table 15.3. This test indicates that the hypothesis of equation (2) is *not* rejected by the data in Table 15.3: thus we cannot rule out *altogether* the possibility that external resources substitute for domestic savings.

On balance, therefore, we would conclude that there is not enough evidence, and at best the evidence conflicts, to say whether the absorption of external resources has adversely affected India's domestic savings effort.

Note also that, in regard to our earlier conclusions in this chapter, the introduction of F or F_{-1} into the estimating equation does not significantly affect the conclusions reached (*via* inter-period analysis) regarding the impact of the severity of exchange control on the savings effort.

Sectoral impact

We may next examine the possibility that, even if the overall impact of the external resource inflow on domestic savings is negligible, the impact on certain components thereof may be rather large.

From this viewpoint, it is relevant to distinguish between public and private savings, relating the former to public revenues and the latter to private income alone. Since private income as well as public revenues (to a smaller extent) were in turn correlated with Y, we used Y as the explanatory variable in addition to the external resource flow to reestimate the equations separately for private and government savings. The results are set out in Table 15.4, for the period 1951–2 to 1965–6.

TABLE 15.4   Private and government savings regressions, 1951–2 to 1965–6

$$S_{1p}^{II} = -1135 + 0.19 \ Y - 0.28 \ F \qquad R^2 = 0.91$$
$$\phantom{S_{1p}^{II} = } (304) \quad (0.03) \quad (0.36)$$
$$S_{1p}^{II} = -1433 + 0.22 \ Y - 0.77 \ F_{-1} \qquad R^2 = 0.94$$
$$\phantom{S_{1p}^{II} = } (245) \quad (0.02) \quad (0.28)$$
$$S_{1g}^{II} = -476 + 0.06 \ Y - 0.10 \ F \qquad R^2 = 0.84$$
$$\phantom{S_{1g}^{II} = } (158) \quad (0.01) \quad (0.19)$$
$$S_{1g}^{II} = -543 + 0.06 \ Y - 0.01 \ F_{-1} \qquad R = 0.84$$
$$\phantom{S_{1g}^{II} = } (160) \quad (0.01) \quad (0.18)$$

Notes:. Figures in parentheses are standard errors. The subscripts p and g denote respectively private and public savings. Refer to the text for explanation of the regressions.

As in the case of total savings, the explanatory power of contemporaneous capital inflow is nil in explaining either public or private savings. The lagged capital inflow, however, has a significant negative coefficient in the case of private savings but the marginal propensity to save in the lagged relationship is higher than that in the unlagged one. These results, however, are difficult to interpret, as we would normally have expected the external resource inflow to work primarily through the budget – in view of the larger component of foreign aid – by reducing *public* savings: the significance of the lagged foreign resource inflow in influencing private savings seems to us therefore to be mainly spurious.[5]

5. In fact, we might as well argue that the resource inflow could have improved investment opportunities – in India, the inflow of private foreign investment leads to the same result since joint ventures are actively promoted by government – and could have led to increased private savings *à la* Hirschman to utilize these opportunities! The only 'weak' argument in support of the negative coefficient on F_{-1} is that consumption is a function of available imports which, in turn, reflect foreign aid inflow. This argument would be justified to some extent by PL 480 imports.

Thus we conclude that our analysis contradicts the thesis that incoming foreign resources have seriously interfered with the domestic savings effort. This is probably not surprising since the planning mechanism has, by and large, served to make the domestic tax-and-savings effort keep in step with the aid flow, both because of internal clarity on this objective and external (aid-donor-induced) pressure-cum-ethos in this regard.[6]

REFERENCES

Bhagwati, J. and Desai, P. (1970): *India: Planning for Industrialization* (Paris: OECD; London: Oxford University Press).
Rao, C. R. (ed.) (1972): *Data Base of the Indian Economy* (Calcutta: Statistical Publishing Society).
Srinivasan, T. N., Tendulkar, S. D. and Vaidyanathan, A. (1973): *A Study of the Aggregate Savings Behaviour of the Indian Economy* (New Delhi: Indian Statistical Institute).

6. For relevant details on the tax efforts of the Indian government from 1950 to 1966, see Bhagwati and Desai (1970), pp. 71-3.

16

Food Aid, Agricultural Production and Welfare

The 1950s witnessed a considerable expansion of food aid under the United States PL 480 programme. Since the silos were full, and overflowing, this was regarded at the time as a particularly appropriate way in which to transfer real resources to the less developed countries in need of aid: it would cost very little, if anything. The implicit assumption, of course, was that such aid would be of net benefit to the recipient countries.

This presumption started changing primarily with Theodore Schultz's pointing the finger at the disincentive effects that such food aid would have as far as domestic agricultural production in the developing countries was concerned. His 1960 article in the *Journal of Farm Economics* is the classic statement of this thesis. It would be fair to conclude that the net result has been to turn the orthodoxy around to the opposite viewpoint that food aid, except when addressed to emergency famine situations, is harmful to domestic agricultural production and *hence* harmful to the recipient.

I should like to examine this proposition carefully, drawing in section 1 the essential distinction between the (non-normative) effect on agricultural production and the effect on the welfare of the recipient country. In section 2, I then consider the question why the adverse effect on agricultural production, as argued by Schultz, was not of concern to the recipient countries. In section 3, I develop a series of models and arguments to analyse the possible immiserizing effects of the food transfer on recipient country welfare.

1   ADVERSE EFFECT ON AGRICULTURAL PRODUCTION *VERSUS* IMMISERIZATION OF RECIPIENT

The distinction between effect on agricultural production, and effect on welfare, should be apparent but has been blurred in the discussion of food aid. It is worth making it, therefore, as sharply as possible.

Thanks are due to Alberto Antonini and T. N. Srinivasan for helpful comments.

From S. Guhan and M. R. Shroff (eds), *Essays on Economic Progress and Welfare: Essays in Honour of I. G. Patel* (New Delhi: Oxford University Press, 1985).

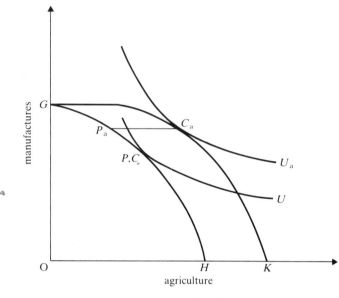

FIGURE 16.1

In Figure 16.1, which treats food and agriculture as equivalent,[1] the recipient country's production possibility curve between Agriculture and Manufactures is *GH*. Production takes place at *P,C*, assuming autarky for simplicity. Now, add Food aid of amount *HK* to the economy. The availability set shifts to *GK*. Consumption will now be at C_a in this aid-inclusive equilibrium; production, at identical price-ratio and hence equal slope as at C_a, will be at P_a.

It is immediately apparent in this case that Agricultural production has declined, as Schultz wisely warns, as a result of the Food aid. However, welfare has increased ($U_a > U$). Inferring welfare loss from adverse impact on Agricultural production, following on Food aid, is therefore a *non sequitur*. The two issues must be kept distinct.

---

1. In practice, they are not. This also raises the possibility that total *agricultural* impact of, say, wheat aid, may be simply to shift production of wheat to production of rice at the margin, if resources are far more mobile between those two products than from either to, say, industry. All the modelling in this paper will continue, however, to treat food and agriculture equivalently, ignoring the further issues raised by the distinction between them.

2   ADVERSE EFFECT ON AGRICULTURAL PRODUCTION

Implied in the Schultz worry about the adverse impact of PL 480 food aid on agricultural production in the recipient countries is the notion, of course, that the addition to domestic supplies by such aid, *ceteris paribus*, drives down the price and hence, given an upward-sloping supply curve of agricultural output, also reduces such output.

All this is immediately evident from Figure 16.2, deployed by Franklin Fisher (1963) in his comment on Schultz, where the *DD* and *SS* curves are the demand and supply curves of the recipient country for Agriculture. Without the aid influx of *WZ*, the domestic price would settle at *OQ* and domestic production at *OV*. The inflow of the food aid lowers the domestic price to *OR* and domestic production by *WV* to *OW*. The case for prosecution rests here.

Why then did the recipient countries such as India, the biggest beneficiary from PL 480 disbursements in the 1950s, not see this? The

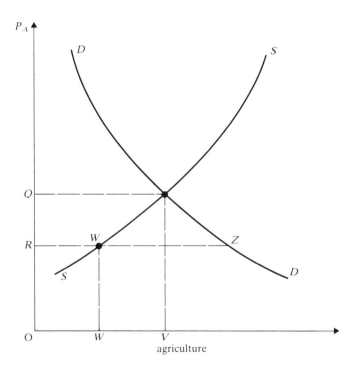

FIGURE 16.2

answer is that they simply did not think that the implicit assumptions underlying the above model were valid. Let me first state the implicit model of the Indian planners during the 1950s when large shipments of PL 480 aid arrived. The assumption underlying Indian thinking was that, corresponding to the projected or planned growth of income and investment during, say, a five-year plan period, there would be a certain demand for agricultural 'wage goods'. To meet this demand, food availability would have to be assured or the relative price of food would rise, resulting in inflation and political instability. Now, add to this argument the further building block of the model: that, with the best efforts in the world, food production could not be increased beyond, say, 4 per cent per annum during the planning period. We then have a wage-goods-constrained model where the 'size' of the plan, i.e. the amount of investment (and hence growth of income) that the planners can achieve, depends critically on available food supplies, since further increments in growth must be achieved on the basis of non-agricultural investments and output which then cause incremental demand for food which would lead to an unacceptable rise in (relative) food prices. Note that this argument does not require that food output be totally inelastic with respect

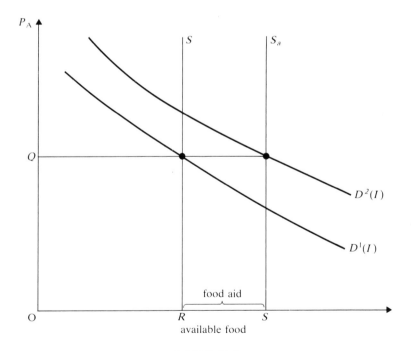

FIGURE 16.3

to its relative price, i.e. a vertical supply curve is not required. For even an upward-sloping supply curve can, in principle, be consistent with the argument that an increased level of investment and income will, *ceteris paribus*, generate an added demand for food which will increase its price beyond an acceptable level. Assuming, or believing that it is proper to assume, that the supply curve is vertical, simply makes the argument even more compelling since the price impact of any excess demand for food translates into a larger price effect that makes the outcome even more intolerable.

Figure 16.3 illustrates these ideas, taking the case of a vertical supply curve for domestic food supply (though, as I just argued, I could have readily allowed for a more elastic upward-sloping supply curve instead). The $D(I)$ curves represent the demand curves for food; for increasing levels of planned investment, they move successively to the right.

Suppose now that the economy cannot allow the price of food, P_A, to exceed OQ. Without food aid, the feasible investment programme will be that yielding $D^1(I)$. Add now food aid of amount RS. The feasible investment then rises to that yielding $D_2(I)$. Food aid therefore permits a larger plan and has not hurt food production.

Note that the critical departure from Schultz's model is in the implied postulate that the relative price of food cannot be allowed to rise beyond the indicated level. It is equally evident that the argument implies that, even if the aid had not been embodied in and effectively tied to food, it would nonetheless have been spent on food imports by the planners: the tying simply makes no difference.

There is room for debate about whether the assumptions underlying the Indian argument were valid. I think the answer has to be judgmental, based on how one assesses two arguments. First, many Indian economists have maintained in regard to the response of agricultural output to price change that, over a planning period of one or even two five-year plans, there was then *de facto* low elasticity of output response to price changes, and that the bulk of the output change had to come from irrigation, extension-service and other infrastructural investments with long gestation lags given the added fact that one was dealing with diverse soil, tenure and other factors impacting on output. Hence, unless the PL 480 programmes were the vehicle for aid transfers for much longer, protracted periods, the wage-goods constraint-model made considerable sense. Second, even if somewhat higher elasticity of response was conceded (at price OQ in Figure 16.3, the supply curve is then less inelastic), the Indians argued that a higher P_A was simply impossible: either if implemented, it would lead to political disruption or it would be infeasible because it would simply generate wage increases and result in overall inflation that would leave P_A, the relative price of food, unchanged. Thus, even if the supply curve was theoretically more elastic at price OQ in Figure 16.3, the economy could not operate above price OQ.

A final remark is in order. The model, as specified in Figure 16.3, assumes that the supply curve for agriculture is independent of the aid provided. This rules out what I have christened the 'goofing-off' effect: i.e. the possibility that the organizational effort going into shifting the agricultural supply curve to the right will be sabotaged if food aid is available 'on tap', as it were. I shall revert to this argument later in section 3 where its welfare implications will be analysed. Here, however, it suffices to note that agricultural production will indeed then fall with food aid, and that investment will be augmented only to the extent that the *net* availability of food expands with food aid.[2]

3   EFFECT ON WELFARE

The effect of PL 480 food aid on welfare is a different type of question altogether. The answer depends naturally on the way in which the inflow of such aid is modelled and the way the objective function is defined. I shall take the question through a succession of 'popular' models. The question of the welfare impact, in turn, can be explored to examine whether such aid can actually immiserize the recipient country.

General-equilibrium static models

The obvious models that come to mind in dealing with the question at hand are the transfer-problem models of general-equilibrium theory. But these have to be adapted to allow for the tying of aid that can result from its embodiment in the form of food.

For the traditional transfer problem, we know in the conventional free-trade, two-agent case, that a transfer from one agent to another involves a primary loss to the donor and a primary gain to the recipient, but that the resulting terms of trade change may offset these primary effects. If so, the donor might be enriched (i.e. made better off) and the recipient be immiserized: a paradoxical outcome first noted by Leontief (1936) that Samuelson (1947) showed to be incompatible with Walrasian market stability.

---

2. In evaluating Schultz's argument, Fisher (1963) notes two complications. First, food aid may be distributed through fixed-price shops at *subsidized* prices. If so, the demand curve for food will generally shift to the right thanks to the income effect. Second, he follows up on a suggestion by Paul Rosenstein-Rodan to argue that food aid will be used to increase investment in food production and hence to shift the supply curve to the right. However, a proper formal treatment of this argument would require an explicit many-period model.

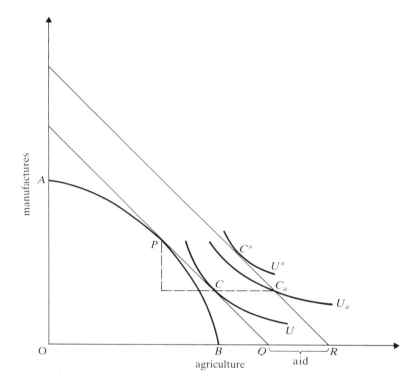

FIGURE 16.4

Recently, thanks to many trade-theoretic and mathematical-economic contributions,[3] we know that these paradoxical outcomes can arise despite Walrasian stability if (1) the number of agents is augmented to three, so that a bilateral transfer takes place in a multilateral context, or (2) the transfer occurs in a two-agent context but in the presence of distortions such as tariffs.[4]

What is of immediate concern in the context of food aid, however, is the fact that food aid is effectively tied; i.e. the donor is likely to impose additionality requirements, such that the recipient cannot simply ship out the food and effectively untie the aid. If so, then the transfer of food aid can be regarded as a case where the transferor induces a distortionary

3. These are reviewed and synthesized in Bhagwati *et al.* (1982).

4. On the former, see especially Johnson (1960), Gale (1974) and Brecher and Bhagwati (1982), each of which independently noted and analysed these paradoxical outcomes, and Bhagwati *et al.* (1983) which provides alternative ways of understanding these paradoxes. On the latter, see Brecher and Bhagwati (1982) and Bhagwati *et al.* (1983).

policy which ensures that gross imports of food increase by the amount of the food aid. This is then the *trade distortion* case. Equally, it may be the case that the donor, concerned by Schultz-like worries, imposes a *production distortion* where the volume of agricultural production in the recipient country is sought to be regulated by the donor of PL 480 aid.

(1) *Trade distortion or import additionality.* Consider then the case where the donor imposes an additionality requirement on imports of food. Using the natural notion that the additional imports must equal the aid inflow, it is possible to show that the recipient need not be immiserized in this case: in fact, it is impossible in the model of Figure 16.4. There, QR worth of aid is given to a small recipient with given external prices and whose production and consumption were at P and C respectively.

The absorption of aid should have shifted consumption to C^* while leaving production efficiently at P. However, the additionality requirement constrains consumption to C_a so that imports of food increase by the full amount of the aid. A consumption tax-cum-subsidy would obviously be necessary to shift consumption from C^* to C_a. But then welfare at C_a must necessarily be higher than at C, so such an additionality requirement cannot immiserize the recipient. In fact, we should note that a consumption tax-cum-subsidy is not even the least-cost method of increasing imports; rather, an import subsidy is.[5] So, an efficient way of meeting the additionality requirement on imports would leave the recipient country still better off than at C_a.[6]

(2) *Production distortion or output additionality.* Similar analysis can be readily extended to the case where the recipient is asked to maintain its agricultural output or to increase it to match the food aid granted.

Where the agricultural output is simply to be not reduced, it is clear that the loss from doing this cannot outweigh the primary gain from the aid inflow. This may be seen readily by contemplating the autarkic case of Figure 16.1 or by taking the other extreme case where the country's external terms of trade are given.

But immiserization can indeed follow if we shift to the requirement that the domestic agricultural production rise to match the aid inflow. This has been demonstrated in Brecher and Bhagwati (1982) and is seen readily by suitably amending Figure 16.4. The reason is simply that the required shift in production, to fulfil the additionality requirement, will impose the conventional 'production cost'. And, if the ease with which

5. This conclusion follows from the theory of optimal intervention to achieve non-economic objectives: see the review in Bhagwati and Srinivasan (1983, ch. 24).

6. If however the transfer element in the food aid is less than its nominal value, the additionality may *exceed* the transfer, increasing the probability of immiserization. I owe this point to my former MIT students, Abbott and McCarthy (1982).

such a production shift can be accomplished is limited, this cost may be large enough to outweigh the primary gain from the aid inflow.[7]

'Goofing-off' or disincentive model

The notion that PL 480 inflow adversely affects welfare has surfaced, on the other hand, for rather different reasons than the additionality arguments deployed above. A main worry has been that the net effect of the inflow will be to reduce domestic agricultural production through making officials goof off, take it easy, fail to mobilize energies and so on. This is a sort of Levi-Strauss effect, somewhat psycho-cultural! It is not too unrealistic, however, to contemplate and casual empiricism seems to support it.

But we need to distinguish between two versions of it. If the bureaucratic and organizational resources that are thus lost to agricultural production are essentially considered worthless outside agriculture (i.e. the opportunity cost of their time and energies is zero because otherwise the bureaucrats simply enjoy the good life and we attach no positive value to that), then the aid is tantamount to causing technical regress in agriculture. Thus, in Figure 16.5, let AB be the pre-aid production possibility curve. BG is the aid inflow that would have normally pushed the availability set out to ADG. However, if agricultural output diminishes due to the goofing-off effect, the production possibility curve shrinks to AE. Adding the aid flow ($EF = BG$), the net availability set is then ADF. The recipient can then be immiserized if the consumption is in the range where AB dominates ADF.[8]

This argument, however, does not apply if the energies lost to agriculture are shifted to other productive use. In that case, we are virtually back to the Schultz-type argument: namely, that added agricultural imports simply shift output composition, *ceteris paribus*, away towards non-agricultural products.

Putty-clay model

A very different argument can be advanced, and may be detected as perhaps the sensible core of truth in some of the debate on the possibly adverse effects of PL 480 aid. This argument basically requires a two-period model with putty-clay features. Assume that when aid has come in, and the economy is closed otherwise as in Figure 16.6, production shifts from P^1 to P^2 and utility goes up in period 1 from U^1 to U^1_a, much

---

7. I might simply note that Walrasian stability exists when the country's terms of trade are given.

8. Needless to say, ADF may wholly dominate AB if the goofing-off effect is small relative to the aid flow.

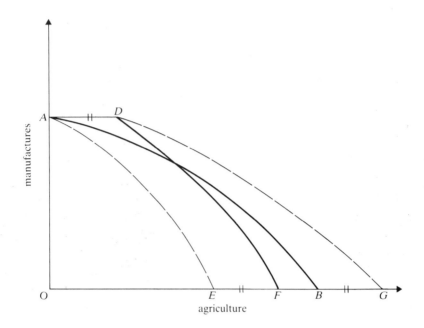

FIGURE 16.5

as I argued in Figure 16.1.[9] However, now let period 2 arrive, with
everything else unchanged for simplicity except that aid has now
disappeared. If production can be reallocated from P^2 back to P^1, utility
will be back at U^1. And, compared to the undiscounted two-period utility
profile $\{U^1, U^1\}$ without aid, we would have a two-period utility profile
$\{U_a^1, U^1\}$. But suppose now that resources simply cannot be transferred
from P^2 back to P^1 when aid has disappeared in period 2. Then, the
second-period utility will fall to U^2, and the two-period utility profile
with aid will instead be $\{U_a^1, U^2\}$. Evidently, with aid, you have more
utility now and less later simply because of the putty-clay nature of the
model. And the economy may well be immiserized in terms of its net
discounted utility today if aid is absorbed under these circumstances.

This model can be readily extended to allow for trade, of course; the
essential result would still be valid provided the putty-clay nature of the
model is retained and myopic behaviour in setting current allocations is

9. I am assuming for simplicity that the first period is characterized wholly by putty
characteristics, so that production can shift from P^1 to P^2 without any difficulty when
aid is received.

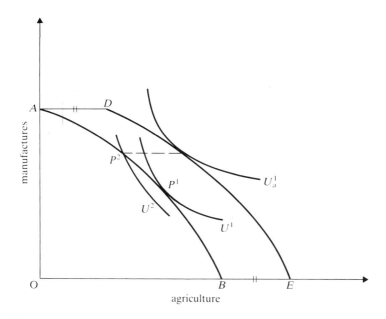

FIGURE 16.6

permitted.[10] In my view, this is the essentially correct case that might be made against PL 480 aid; but the assumptions required to sustain it are not entirely persuasive. Moreover, this case is really different from the usual argument that India would be foolish to let current PL 480 imports adversely affect agricultural production since, when aid dried up, India would have to import the food (no longer available under foreign aid) and then how could it do so? The answer to that alarmist conclusion, of course, is that if India produced more steel than food in period 1, thanks to food aid, it would be able to export more steel in period 2 to buy the needed food. It is only if the external transformation rates (not permitted in Figure 16.6) between steel and food are sufficiently adverse in period 2 and the clay nature of the capacities in steel and food is particularly onerous, and little was done to allow for these facts in making

10. In Bhagwati and Srinivasan (1976), a fairly similar analytical problem is solved where putty-clay considerations are introduced into the analysis of market-disruption-induced QRs in period 2 that are endogenous to export levels achieved in period 1. The optimal policy required for handling the putty-clay problem is shown to be a production tax-cum-subsidy in period 1: a policy that would also emerge as optimal in the problem in the text. If such an optimal policy were indeed followed, aid inflow could never be immiserizing, of course.

current allocations that one would be able to construct the kind of case I built above for PL 480 to be harmful.

Income distribution models

Thus we have a variety of arguments which do yield us some ground for caution in regard to PL 480 aid, even if we do not explicitly allow for income-distributional problems. But suppose that we do. Thus, take Figure 16.1: the shift of production from P to P_a will generally redistribute income. Since food aid is a form of transfer payment, we could then solve the system for the net impact of the transfer, not just on *real wage* in employment at P, but also for the *real income* (which includes *both* the wage and the transfer or what is called in the public finance literature and in sociological discourse, 'entitlement').[11] And it should be easily demonstrable that the real income of any specific group can decline subsequent to the aid inflow. If then we attach a sufficiently large weight to this group and a lower weight to the income of the group that has gained, and the income outcomes from the wage-cum-transfer mechanisms are 'set' and cannot be adjusted, then we do have a decline in overall welfare.

This is a legitimate worry where an adverse effect on agricultural production may be translatable in practice into, say, the immiserization of landless labour and other policy programmes do not provide an offset to this effect. In my judgment, however, the rider at the end of the preceding statement is quite important. Often, the critics have tended to judge policies one by one in terms of their impact on the poor, for instance. The overall welfare weights are more properly applied to the results of the total package of policies instead.

4 CONCLUDING REMARKS

In conclusion, this paper simply attempts to clarify the questions that arise in judging the advisability of food aid, without offering any definitive post mortem on actual experience with the PL 480 programme. Furthermore, I have not attempted to deal with other relevant questions

11. This distinction between 'real wage' and 'real income' therefore fully captures the difference that one can and should make between what one earns from one's endowment of factors, on the one hand, and the income that one commands inclusive of such earnings from sale of factor services plus the transfers from one's entitlements on the *state* (to use the well-known sociological term in discussions of the welfare state) and also from other transfer payments among *private* parties, on the other hand. The wage–income distinction, in this sense, was introduced explicitly in Bhagwati (1959) in connection with the well-known Stolper–Samuelson analysis of the income-distributional implications of alternative trade policies, and has come into wide use.

such as (i) the complications introduced by the fact that PL 480 aid is repayable and hence its grant equivalent is not the same as its nominal value, and also by the fact that the nominal values attached to it are also frequently arbitrary from an economic standpoint since the agricultural markets are not free from intervention, and (ii) the problem of third-country impact, as when PL 480 sales of wheat to India affect Thailand's markets for rice, or the sale of long-staple cotton to India under the PL 480 programme impinges on the world markets for Egyptian cotton.

REFERENCES

Abbott, P. F. and McCarthy, F. D. (1982): 'Welfare effects of tied aid', *Journal of Development Economics*, 11 (1), pp. 63–80.

Bhagwati, J. N. (1959): 'Protection, real wages and real incomes', *Economic Journal* (December), pp. 773–48.

—— and Srinivasan, T. N. (1976): 'Optimal trade policy and compensation under endogenous uncertainty: the phenomenon of market disruption', *Journal of International Economics*, 6, pp. 317–36.

—— and—— (1983): *Lectures on International Trade* (Cambridge, Mass.: MIT Press).

——, R. A. Brecher, and Hatta, T. (1982a): 'The generalized theory of transfers and welfare (II): exogenous (policy-imposed) and endogenous (transfer-induced) distortions', mimeo., July (forthcoming in *Quarterly Journal of Economics*).

——,—— and—— (1982b): 'The paradoxes of immiserizing growth and donor-enriching (recipient-immiserizing) transfers: a tale of two literatures', Paper No. 15, International Economics Research Center, Columbia University, November; appeared in *Weltwirtschaftliches Archiv*, 120(2) (1984), pp. 228–43.

——,—— and—— (1983): 'The generalized theory of transfers and welfare: bilateral transfers in a multilateral world', *American Economic Review*, 73 (September); abbreviated version reprinted as ch.15, vol. 1.

Brecher, R. A. and Bhagwati, J. N. (1981): 'Foreign ownership and the theory of trade and welfare', *Journal of Political Economy*, 89 (June): 497–511.

—— and—— (1982): 'Immiserizing transfers from abroad', *Journal of International Economics*, 13 (November), pp. 353–64.

Fisher, F. (1963): 'A theoretical analysis of the impact of food disposal on agricultural production in recipient countries', *Journal of Farming Economics*, 45, pp.–863–75.

Gale, D. (1974): 'Exchange equilibrium and coalitions: an example', *Journal of mathematical Economics*, 1 (March), pp. 63–6.

Johnson, H. (1960): 'Income distribution, the offer curve and the effects of tariffs', *Manchester School of Economics*, 28 (September), pp. 223–42.

Leontief, W. (1936): 'Note in the pure theory of capital transfer', in *Explorations in Economics: Notes and Essays Contributed in Honor of F. W. Taussig* (New York: McGraw-Hill).

Samuelson, P. A. (1947): *Foundations of Economic Analysis* (Cambridge, Mass.: Harvard University Press).

Schultz, T. (1950): 'Value of US farm surpluses to underdeveloped countries', *Journal of Farm Economics*, 42, pp. 1019–30.

PART IV
International Migration and Investment

The postwar theory of international migration has gone through a number of significant developments, especially as it impinges on questions of skilled migration but also on the more general question of international personal mobility and its consequences. Chapters 17 and 18 examine these developments, both analytical and in policy prescriptions, as they relate to migration from the developing countries. Chapter 19, written jointly with my former MIT student Paul Krugman, on the other hand, reviews and synthesizes the literature on a prior question: Why do people migrate?

The most compelling question to engage theoretical attention at the outset was: does loss of skilled manpower harm the developing countries. As chapter 17 makes clear, the pendulum has swung back and forth on this issue, with each argument generating a counter-argument. The most interesting insight to have emerged from the literature, however, has been that there is no unique way to look at the welfare of the sending (or the receiving) country: the migrants' welfare may be meaningfully considered to be part of the sending or the receiving country's welfare, or part of both or of neither, depending on the specific sociological characteristics of the migration at hand. In turn, this naturally will impact on the answer to the question: how does migration of their skilled people affect the developing countries?

The other question to have engaged major analytical and policy attention has been whether, given the fact of international migration of their people, the developing countries ought not to extend their income tax jurisdiction to their nationals abroad (and thus raise more resources for development, for instance). My proposal that this be done, often characterized as the proposal to 'tax the brain drain' in view of its original formulation, has now been extensively analysed by distinguished lawyers (including Professors Oliver Oldman, Richard Pomp, Frank Newman and Martin Partington), and by eminent economists (such as Professors Koichi Hamada, William Baumol and James Mirrlees) and has also been debated at the UNCTAD.[1] Chapter 18 traces the evolution of this proposal and its intrinsic relationship to the United States and Filippino

1. See in particular the two volumes, Bhagwati and Partington (1976) and Bhagwati (1976), the 1982 Symposium in the *Journal of Public Economics*, and the two interviews with me on the subject in *The Guardian* (1979) and the *Third World Quarterly* (1980).

tax practice which levies income taxation by citizenship nexus rather than by residence.[2] Chapter 17 also has extensive estimates of the revenues that could accrue to developing countries if they would adopt the so-called Bhagwati proposal and follow in the footsteps of the United States and the Philippines.

Yet another policy issue of some interest, but limited in its analytical challenge, has been the issue of capitalizing the human-capital element in skilled migration from the developing to the developed countries so as to put the resulting estimates of (human) capital outflow from the developing countries against the (financial) capital inflow to them. The analytical questions posed by this proposal have been discussed in chapter 17. The difficulties in implementing the proposal, from the data viewpoint, are simply overwhelming and are, I am afraid, the real obstacle to getting such estimates off the ground. However, I must confess that, having been associated with intergovernmental expert-group discussions of the proposal at the UNCTAD, I have had the unhappy experience of seeing the representatives of developed countries raise spurious objections to the proposal on wholly unscientific conceptual grounds that thinly mask political motivations: a spectacle that sits ill at ease with the popular impression in the developed countries that the developing countries indulge in rhetoric and politics at the UN agencies whereas the virtue of scientific argumentation belongs to the developed countries!

International migration raises several other issues which I have considered in my 1978 Ramaswami Memorial Lecture (1979b) and a Plenary Lecture (1979a) to the *Nordisk Migrasjonsforskerseminar* in Norway.[3] In particular, theoretical analysis has been increasingly directed at the interesting question as to whether a capital-abundant developed country would gain by exporting its capital to the labour-abundant developing country or by importing labour from it instead. I posed this question only to discover that V. K. Ramaswami (1968) had already raised it in a much-neglected early contribution in a one-good, two-factor model. The problem, since I raised and discussed it in my Ramaswami Memorial Lecture, has now been extensively analysed: see, in particular, Calvo and Wellisz (1982), Bhagwati and Srinivasan (1983) and several articles in a 1983 Symposium on International Factor Mobility in the *Journal of International Economics*. A distinct, but somewhat kindred problem, proceeds not from the premise of the preceding Ramaswami–Bhagwati type of analysis that the country of immigration has the capacity to enforce

2. See the detailed analysis of the Filipino tax system by Richard Pomp (1985). The historical evolution of the US tax practice is traced briefly in chapter 18 but is dealt with in depth in Bhagwati and Wooton (1982).

3. These are both reprinted as Chs 42 and 44 in vol. 2 of *EIET*. That volume brings together several theoretical papers on international factor mobility, which can be read in conjunction with chs 17–20 in the present volume.

immigration restriction by itself and acceptance of capital inflows by the country of emigration, but rather from the empirical reality that people from the developing country will illegally migrate to the developed country. If so, will foreign capital outflow, in the shape of foreign aid or direct foreign investment, reduce or paradoxically augment this inflow? This question was also raised in my 1979 Norwegian lecture; and it has been the subject of important recent contributions by sociologists such as Saskia Sassen-Koob (1984), which I have considered more extensively in Bhagwati (1984) and am currently engaged in examining further.

Finally, chapter 20 relates to foreign investment. This is a vast topic and I have written extensively on it elsewhere, analysing many complex and richly-textured arguments on the effects of foreign investment and their policy implications, in the Ramaswami Memorial Lecture. Chapter 20 addresses an added argument, of considerable policy interest to the developing countries in view of the recent ideological shift in the United States government and the resulting pressure to extend GATT-type liberalism to foreign investment. This pressure is lent added force by the 'debt crisis' in which some of the developing countries have found themselves. The heat is on to force them into more liberal policies on foreign investment as part of the needed reform to handle the debt situation, lending unfortunate credence to the radical left-wing *caveat* that increased integration into the capitalist world economy would only lead to a mortgaging of one's independence *vis-à-vis* foreign capitalist interests. The main point of chapter 20, jointly authored with Professor Richard Brecher, is simply that the frequent assertion that the neoclassical theoretic case for GATT being extended to embrace free foreign investment flows is identical to the classical case for free trade is simply false.[4] Whether, despite this, one would opt for such extension of GATT to foreign investment is of course a different issue which would require policy judgments concerning the *likely* outcomes of such an extension in practice. For those who would thus vote for such an extension, the contents of chapter 20 may appear unpalatable. I can only remind them that, in economic argumentation, it is absolutely imperative that we keep distinct the question as to 'What can happen' from the question as to 'What is likely to happen'. The former (which is proper theory) is essential for absolute clarity of thought, the latter (which is 'by and large' or 'more or less' economics) is essential for good policy.

REFERENCES

Bhagwati, J. N. (ed.) (1976): *The Brain Drain and Taxation: Theory and Empirical Analysis*, vol. II (Amsterdam: North-Holland).

4. See also the important independent analysis by Professor Gene Grossman (1984) of the theoretical issues pertinent to this argument.

—— (1979a): 'The economic analysis of international migration', Lecture delivered to *Nordisk Migrasjonsforskerseminar*, Nordic Council of Ministers, Oslo, Norway, 1983; reprinted in *EIET*, vol. 2, ch. 44.

—— (1979b): 'International factor movements and national advantage', V. K. Ramaswami Memorial Lecture, *Indian Economic Review*, 14(2), pp. 73–100; reprinted in *EIET*, vol. 2, ch. 42.

—— (1984): 'Incentives and disincentives: international migration', Paper presented to the IEA Conference on Economic Incentives at Kiel in June 1984, *Weltwirtschaftliches Archiv*, December, and forthcoming in volume of proceedings (London: Macmillan).

—— and Partington, M. (1976): *Taxing the Brain Drain: a Proposal*, vol. I (Amsterdam: North-Holland).

—— and Srinivasan, T. N. (1983): 'On the choice between capital and labour mobility', *Journal of International Economics*, 14, pp. 209–21; reprinted in *EIET*, vol. 2, ch. 43.

—— and Wooton, J. (1982): 'The political economy of the global and the schedular income tax systems: a historical analysis of United States and Great Britain', mimeo, July.

Calvo, G. and Wellisz, S. (1983): 'International factor mobility and national advantage', *Journal of International Economics*, 14(1/2), pp. 103–14.

Grossman, G. (1984): 'The gains from international factor movements', *Journal of International Economics*, 17, pp. 73–83.

Guardian (1979): 'Interview with Bhagwati', 19 November, London.

Journal of International Economics (1983): 'International factor mobility: a symposium', 14 May (3/4).

Journal of Public Economics (1982): 'Symposium: income taxation in the presence of international personal mobility', 18 August (3).

Pomp, R. (1985): 'Taxation of citizens abroad: the Philippines case', *Journal of International Law and Politics*, 17 (forthcoming).

Ramaswami, V. K. (1968): 'International factor movements and the national advantage', *Economica*, 35, pp. 309–310.

Sassen-Koob, S. (1984): *The foreign investment connection: rethinking migration*, mimeo, New York.

Third World Quarterly (1980): 'North–South dialogue: an interview [with Bhagwati]', 2(2).

17

The Brain Drain: International Resource Flow Accounting, Compensation, Taxation and Related Policy Proposals

1 INTRODUCTION

This paper is addressed principally to analysing several major issues relating to the phenomenon of international migration of skilled people from the developing countries (LDCs) to the developed countries (DCs), popularly described as the 'brain drain'.

Section 2 places such migration into perspective *vis-à-vis* migrations that occur among LDCs and among DCs, this analysis serving to highlight the special characteristics of the brain drain from LDCs into DCs that must be borne in mind when we turn to the policy-oriented conceptual and measurement analyses of the later sections. Towards that end, the principal dimensions and patterns of the brain drain are also sketched with extreme brevity, for certain policy suggestions in regard to taxing the brain drain, for example, have inter-LDC *distributional* consequences which should reflect the shares of the LDCs in the overall brain drain into DCs.

Section 3 then discusses the possible arguments and modalities for extension of the present international resource accounting framework to include the flows implied by the brain drain.

Section 4 develops the analysis in the direction of examining the reasons why the brain drain 'phenomenon' may also then imply a brain drain 'problem' and, in light thereof, developing the concept of 'loss to the LDCs' from the brain drain – a concept that must be sharply separated from the concept of the 'capital flow' from LDCs to DCs implicit in the brain drain.

Section 5 then discusses the alternative policy proposals that have been advanced in relation to the brain drain, either to mitigate such losses to LDCs or, *more generally*, to tax the brain drain to raise resources for LDCs of origin or LDCs *en bloc*.

Section 6 then focuses directly on alternative proposals to tax the brain drain: distinguishing particularly among the suggestions to tax the DCs for the benefit of the LDCs of emigration to institutionalize an

Prepared for the Division on Transfer of Technology, UNCTAD, in July 1977. Minor editorial changes have been made. *Author's Note*: Since this chapter was written, my views on the feasible and optimal format of an income tax by LDCs on their nationals abroad have evolved, as explicitly spelled out in chapter 18, esp. pp. 352–9.

'international compensation mechanism' and the suggestion to tax the incomes of the migrants themselves. The rationales of such taxes, and the possible objections that may be levelled against them and their possible rebuttal, will be the subject matter of our discussion here.

Section 7 summarizes the major conclusions and recommendations.

2   PATTERNS AND SPECIAL FEATURES OF LDC-TO-DC BRAIN DRAIN

Since the focus of the present paper is exclusively on *analytical* issues arising from policy proposals advanced in regard to the brain drain from LDCs into DCs, this is not the occasion to analyse the available statistical information on such flows. However, a few salient points must be noted, if only because the policy discussions need to take these carefully into account.[1]

First, the impact of the post-Second-World-War shift in the immigration policies of major DCs, away from the earlier racial-origin quotas to more equal access by all nationalities, was to increase significantly the share of the LDCs in the immigration into DCs. Combined with this, of course, was the considerable increase in the share of PTK immigrants – the PTK being the category of professional, technical and kindred workers in the US Immigration and Naturalization Service classification that corresponds generally to the groups of migrants who are considered to constitute the 'brain drain' – in the overall immigration into the United States, in particular, and into Canada and the UK as well.[2]

Second, the pattern of PTK immigration from LDCs to DCs is not necessarily bilateral but will often proceed multilaterally. Indian doctors transit to UK and then to USA; Pakistani PhDs in USA migrate to Canada until they qualify for an entry on immigration visas into USA; Sri Lanka doctors go to the UK while the UK doctors emigrate to the USA, and so on. This imples that, in analysing the statistics, as also the impact of different policy measures, one must take into account a complex pattern of effects. Thus, decline in Canadian PTK immigration followed from the relaxation of the US immigration policies: it was no longer necessary to 'wait' in Canada as much as before. Similarly, tightening entry into

1. The statistical discussions are greatly handicapped by lack of systematic and comprehensive information for most DCs of immigration as also by the lack of comparability of such data across most countries owing to different definitions and coverages. Nonetheless, all is not lost and the interested reader can refer to the recent contributions by Balacs and Gordon (for the UK), Maki and DeVoretz (for Canada) and Lucas, Dellalfar, Pelcovits, etc. (on the USA) in Bhagwati and Partington (1976) and Bhagwati (1976a). Valuable information is also contained in US House of Representatives (1974).

2. For more details, see Bhagwati (1976b).

one country may not reduce the brain drain but merely 'divert' it into another DC.[3]

Third, casual empiricism plus recent statistical exercises lead to the important distinction between 'gross' and 'net' brain drain: many migrants seem to return to LDCs or, at minimum, to shift back and forth. Thus, the policy analysis must take into account the complications from 'to-and-fro' and 'reverse' migrations instead of considering the problem as one of 'permanent' or 'once-and-for-all' migration.[4]

Fourth, a significant portion of the gross immigration consists of 'stay-on' LDC students in DCs. The proportion varies by professions, being clearly negligible in the case of doctors and high for engineers.[5] This fact is critical, for example, to our later discussion of the conventions to be adopted in imputing capital flows to the brain drain since DC-education, insofar as it represents DC-incurred expenditures, may be therefore netted out from the imputation.

Fifth, in anticipating possible LDC interest in several tax and other proposals, the LDC-composition in, and overall size of, the brain drain will be relevant. Here, it is necessary to note that the overall PTK flow into DCs is likely to be a function almost exclusively of the restrictiveness of the DC policies (though these in turn may slightly accommodate to the so-called 'push' factors). On the other hand, the share of the LDCs *en bloc* into this total, as also their *individual* shares therein, will reflect (given randomized access to the immigration queue) the internal labour market situation *vis-à-vis* the external economic prospects and relevant economic magnitudes.[6] This does mean that these levels and patterns are frankly difficult to forecast with accuracy. Thus, for example, recent US legislation has practically shut off immigration of foreign doctors into the US as of early 1977: this could not have been forecast even in 1975! The virtual demise of the huge US space programmes earlier had similarly dealt an unanticipated blow to immigration of scientists, mainly from other DCs, to the point where the European DCs had felt their brain drain problem to be eased sufficiently to have the OECD cease working on a now-obsolete problem.[7] Again, the effect on the LDC-to-DC brain drain of the OPEC countries' enormous demands for PTK manpower imports,

3. Thus, one can distinguish, as in international trade theory on customs unions, between 'brain drain creation' and 'brain drain diversion' as a result of policy changes.

4. Recent statistical exercises suggest that outflow may be as much as 30 per cent of gross immigration of LDC PTKs into DCs. See Balacs and Gordon on the UK, for example, in Bhagwati and Partington (1976).

5. For the statistics, see Table 4 in Bhagwati (1976b), which gives the proportions of different types of immigrants admitted by change of visa status: the conversion of student status being only a subset of the latter, of course.

6. The role of economic factors in explaining migration patterns in numerous econometric studies has been reviewed at length by Krugman and Bhagwati in Bhagwati (1976).

7. On the latter, see Grubel and Scott (1977, ch. 1).

while difficult to analyse, could not have been foreseen as late as 1971.[8]

Sixth, it is useful to place the LDC-to-DC type of 'brain drain' migration into perspective *vis-à-vis* other types of migrations. In particular, two sets of contrasts may be distinguished. On the one hand, the LDC-to-DC migration may be contrasted with the LDC-to-LDC and the DC-to-DC migrations of PTK manpower. On the other hand, the 'brain drain' migration may be contrasted with the 'expulsion', 'exit-from-socialism' and 'flight-from-authoritarianism' type of migrations.

(1) Thus, consider the first contrast. The LDC-to-LDC migration of PTK manpower used to be relatively unimportant in the past, being confined mainly to UN-sponsored technical assistance which deployed LDC experts in other LDCs. However, with the success of OPEC, this type of intra-LDC migration has become extremely important. Its contrast to the LDC-to-DC migration, however, consists in the fact that the OPEC countries have wealth and income but not the developmental attributes that usually go with these: so that while the LDC emigration to the DCs has a great inducement to stay on in the DCs with their 'modern' forms of culture and democratic ways of life, these amenities and advantages of modernization are hardly available in any of the OPEC countries and certainly not in the more traditional societies such as Saudi Arabia and Kuwait. Thus, the Egyptian and other high-level PTK migrants to these countries are far more likely to be 'reverse' migrants: and therefore this migration needs to be regarded, from a policy point of view, as quite a different type of migration than the LDC-to-DC migration of PTK personnel. This argument is only reinforced from the 'demand' side: few of the Middle East oil-rich countries, with their abundant oil and scarce manpower, are likely to want permanent immigration of 'superior' personnel from any one area. Aside from the resentments which are bound to breed from the inherent strains arising from the intellectual superiority of the immigrant and the financial dominance of the native population that hires him, the natives are likely to fear 'reverse assimilation' and loss of identity, thus wanting to have an immigrant PTK workforce that is very definitely *temporary* and variable in terms of its national and cultural composition.[9]

On the other hand, the DC-to-DC PTK migration would seem to contrast with the LDC-to-DC migration in an identical manner – i.e. to be subject to greater reverse migration – but for a totally different reason: namely, that the differences in economic conditions and rewards between

8. For speculation on these effects, see Bhagwati (1976a, p. 8); also see below.

9. This *a priori* observation would seem to be confirmed by the recent success of the South Koreans in landing construction contracts in the Middle East. They are reputed to import Korean labour at all levels, keep it strictly under control and segregated from the local populations, and to remove it as soon as the contract is completed.

LDC and DCs are far more substantial than those among DCs, so that relatively minor relative changes in labour market conditions, for example, may induce reverse migration in the former, but not in the latter, case. This difference also accounts, in large part, for the complacency with which DC-origin economists tend to reject arguments about the disruptive effects of the brain drain on LDC institution-building (which has to be done from a primitive level, frequently), on domestic salary levels (which come under great strain because of the impossibility of matching the tremendously higher DC levels), etc., whereas the LDC-origin economists accept them readily from the immediacy of their LDC experience.

(2) Next, the 'brain drain', which by and large reflects economic and quasi-economic considerations, must be contrasted with three other types of PTK emigration from LDCs: (i) the 'expulsion' type of migration, as with the expulsion of Asian professionals (among others) from Uganda; (ii) the 'exit-from-socialism' type of migration, as with the emigration of PTK 'bourgeoisie' from Tanzania and Chile (under President Allende),[10] where the spread of egalitarianism in the shape of greatly reduced salary and wealth differentials prompts the exit; and (iii) the 'flight-from-authoritarianism' type of migration, where the PTK personnel flee political repression under military or other forms of dictatorships.[11]

These are, of course, 'polar types' and specific PTK migrations may have shades of more than one of these classes of migration. The distinctions are useful, however, in the asymmetries of behaviour that they imply for economic analysis of PTK migration. Thus, for example, remittances may be confidently expected from the 'brain drain' migrants but less so from the 'exit' and 'flight' types and none from the expulsion type where whole families tend to be uprooted. This applies also to flow of externalities in the form of return visits by professionals to LDCs of origin. Again, the brain drain outflow is likely to be smoother and smaller than the 'exit' or 'flight' variety, and therefore less damaging in its immediate impact on the LDCs.

However, from the viewpoint of policy-making, such as the adoption of the brain-drain-related taxes analysed below, these different types of LDC PTK migration into DCs are not likely to be operationally distinguishable and will have to be disregarded, with the exception of possible exemption of those in the 'flight' category who are admitted explicitly as 'political refugees' (an admittedly delimited and small category in any event).

10. Perhaps the emigration of doctors from socialized medicine and high taxes, the twin features of a 'socialist' welfare state in the UK, also falls under this rubric.

11. Examples of this are the flight from Portugal to Brazil under the Salazar regime and from Spain to Latin America generally under the Franco regime. Recent examples would include reverse flights from some countries in Latin America to Portugal and Spain, as the latter have shifted to democratic regimes and the flouting of human rights in the former has increased.

L

3   ON MODIFYING INTERNATIONAL RESOURCE ACCOUNTING
TO INCORPORATE THE BRAIN DRAIN FLOWS

The salient facts about skilled international migration from LDCs to DCs, presented above, have a direct bearing (as we shall presently see) on the questions to which we now turn: (i) should the flow of skilled manpower be incorporated into international accounting on the flows between LDCs and DCs of capital; and (ii) if so, how should this be done?

The international accounting of *capital flows* presently includes only the nominal capital flows that occur at both private and official levels. These also include, of course, flows that are sometimes 'imputed', as in the case of valuation of second-hand machinery imported by multinationals as part of their equity investment in the LDCs. Needless to say, the bulk of these flows run *from the DCs to the LDCs*.

Moreover, it will be recalled that it was customary for many years to regard private and official capital flows as both providing capital 'assistance' to the LDCs, as if the private flows were also some form of aid; and it took much effort to separate out aid from private capital flows and to relate the targets at UNCTAD to aid proper.[12] Nonetheless, the fact remains that an overall balance sheet of international *capital* flows (as distinct from *aid* flows) will include private and official flows alike.

Given this situation, it is well worth investigating whether the migration of skilled manpower from the LDCs to the DCs should not be capitalized and then included in such a balance sheet of 'capital flows', with the concept of capital therefore being broadened but in a thoroughly appropriate manner. The advantage of such a balance sheet of LDC–DC 'capital' flows would be that it would bring into better perspective the overall capital flow situation, and particularly assist in deflating the exaggerated notion still held by many DC observers of the 'assistance' provided by DCs to LDCs through capital flows. In fact, from the viewpoint of capital-flow accounting in LDC–DC economic relations, it would be ideal to separate out three distinct elements: the official flows, the nominal capital flows and the imputed capital flows implicit in (and representing the capitalized equivalent of) the flows of skilled manpower.[13]

How is such capitalization of the brain drain flow to be done?

12. This is not to deny that private capital flows may also be beneficial to LDCs. But then so is trade with LDCs beneficial to DCs, and one does not regard that as aid from LDCs to DCs!

13. It may be noted, with some amusement, that Marxist economists may instead wish to decompose the nominal capital flows into their 'labour-equivalent' and to draw up a balance sheet of overall labour transfers among DCs and LDCs! It is difficult to imagine, however, what use such a balance sheet could be put to, if any.

Fundamentally, there are two approaches that may be taken, with somewhat profoundly different implications. First, one may take the '*historic cost*' approach, under which the educational costs embedded historically in the migrant may be added up to their present worth. Second, one may ask the hypothetical question: if the migrant's services were buyable in a free market, what would be his present worth as an asset? This present worth is clearly given by the '*present discounted value*' of the migrant's marginal product over his expected lifetime.[14]

The two measures will have different implications. Thus, for example, if one takes an unskilled migrant, his educational expenditures are negligible and the imputed capital flow on a historic-cost basis would be negligible. On the other hand, the present discounted value of such a migrant is clearly positive as long as he is employable in the DC of immigration and there would be no decisive reason to exclude his inclusion from a balance sheet of capital flows that would include imputed capital flows.

Next, it is pertinent to note that the educational expenditures embodied in the migrant are not necessarily to be regarded, under either type of imputation procedure, as productive of 'human capital' (in the sense of *socially* productive investment). Thus modern economists are familiar with two other, novel and relevant theories of education which suggest that the higher education embodied in a migrant may instead be a screening device (to enable employers to distinguish the brighter from the duller prospective employees) or an instrument of job competition. In either case, no 'human capital' is involved and education is only *privately* productive of higher incomes to the educated.[15]

Note further that neither measure has affinity to the totally distinct measures of the 'gains to DCs' or the 'losses to LDCs' that are often discussed in regard to the brain drain as well.[16] Indeed, much confusion follows from an inadequate appreciation of this distinction. The distinction should be readily grasped however once an analogy is drawn between the present distinction and the obvious and familiar distinction between a measure of (nominal) capital flows and measures of their welfare effects on the host and the investing countries.

Moreover, it must be noted that the process of imputation is complicated by the presence of two alternative sets of relevant prices: those that pertain to DCs and those that obtain in LDCs. Since these are *segmented* markets, owing to lack of free migration, and since the commodity prices required for the imputation relate in part to non-traded goods and in part to traded

14. For full analysis, see below.
15. For the screening theory of education, see Arrow (1973) and Spence (1973). For job competition theory see Bhagwati (1973), Fields (1974) and Bhagwati and Srinivasan (1977).
16. Nor should any of these measures, in turn, be confused with the measure of the gain in welfare accruing to the migrants themselves.

goods whose prices are not equalized across DCs and LDCs because of artificial and natural obstacles, we are faced with the necessity of developing estimates based alternatively on DC and LDC prices.

Furthermore, the process of imputation is bedevilled by the fact that PTK migration is often 'to-and-fro' rather than of a once-and-for-all variety and by the additional fact that part of the educational expenditure of many migrants is incurred in the DC of immigration. Thus, if we take historic-cost measures, an LDC PTK migrant who has completed some education in the LDC will be evaluated, say, at LDC prices when he migrates; then he acquires additional education in the DC which is, of course, incurred in DC prices; when he returns to the LDC, the reverse flow of capital will then include historic cost measured partly in LDC prices and partly in DC prices, so that one may settle for a convention here as to which prices one should *consistently* use.[17]

Having then noted some of the principal difficulties that the process of imputation will raise, we should also add that such problems are inevitable when imputation of prices is involved: a fact that is fully familiar to national income statisticians that have had to deal with imputing incomes in the non-market sector in LDCs and are now to address themselves to the task of imputing incomes to women's household work. Thus, nothing should be considered insuperable in regard to implementing the suggestion to impute a 'capital' figure to the brain drain flow. Therefore, it is useful to proceed with defining in more depth the two principal types of measures of imputed capital flows that we have distinguished above, focussing first on the simpler once-and-for-all migration case and next on the 'to-and-fro' and 'reverse' migration case.[18]

Once-and-for-all migration

Using the suffixes 'e' and 'i' to refer to the LDC of emigration and DC of immigration, we may now set out the two sets of concepts and their possible variants.

(1) *Historic cost measures.* Here, we can define HC_e as the measure of the direct and indirect educational costs embodied in the migrant at the time of the emigration to the DC.

Simple as this procedure sounds, especially to those familiar with the now-standard techniques for estimating educational costs, note that the estimated costs would be at domestic prices and would have to be converted into 'standard dollar' values or some such *agreed-upon* (now that exchange rates are no longer stable) equivalent, common standard.

---

17. In addition, as we discuss below, the fact that the DC invests in an LDC national's education prior to his formal migration creates obvious problems for estimating the LDC-to-DC flow of imputed capital in this instance.

18. The following discussion is based largely on Bhagwati (1976a, pp. 12–19).

But, more important, there is the difficult problem that arises because the formal act of migration of an LDC national to a DC may follow his acquisition of *some* education in the DC. Should we then estimate his historic-cost imputed flow as the cost of LDC-education alone? Since our focus is on estimating the LDC-to-DC capital flows, this may seem to be more appropriate than leaving the DC-incurred costs in the estimate (though, if we were to count them in, we would still be faced with the problem of choosing between estimating these costs at DC or at LDC prices, the latter being necessary if we wish to make the estimate at *one* set of prices).[19] On the other hand, one can equally soundly argue that what is being measured is the historic cost of education embodied in the LDC national *as and when he migrates to the DC*, so that the question of where that investment came from is not relevant to this particular exercise (though it could well be pertinent to an exercise, for example, aimed at estimating the 'saving in investment costs' to the DCs from having the PTK immigrants from the LDCs). The latter convention is, in fact, the simpler and proper one: and it is the one which ought to be adopted for historic cost measures. It does require, of course, for the *overall* capital-flow accounting between LDCs and DCs, that the DCs be allowed then to include their domestic expenditures on educating LDC students as part of the capital flows from DCs to LDCs. In fact, in so far as foreign aid is utilized for educational expenditures in LDCs, such an accounting is already being made; and extending this practice to DC domestic expenditures on LDC students would both complete this accounting and also be a neater alternative than trying to separate out, in the LDC PTK immigrants, the contributions made by DCs and LDCs to their educational costs.[20]

Identically, then, we may also value the historic cost measure, with the above qualifications and explanations again applicable, at the prices relevant to the DC of immigration: denoting this as the HC_i measure. It is evident that, given the normal excess of DC over LDC educational costs, we should expect HC_i to exceed HC_e.

19. Even if we wish to leave out DC-incurred educational costs, it may still be inappropriate to calculate the historic cost as above since it implies that the act of migration is being notionally shifted to the point in time at which the LDC national arrived in the DC for education. One may still consider migration to have taken place at the actual time of migration and then put a figure on the LDC-education that the migrant might *alternatively* have undertaken prior to actual migration. This 'notional' imputation would then amount to evaluating the migrant's historic cost at his *total* DC + LDC educational expenditures, all these being estimated at LDC prices.

20. It may be noted that if the DC-incurred educational expenses on LDC students in DCs are to be computed as part of DC capital flows to LDCs, they will be recorded at DC prices. Therefore, for consistency, we would want to compute the historic cost measures also such that the DC-incurred educational measures are recorded at these same prices: recording them at LDC prices, for example, would then bias the accounting in favour of DCs!

(2) *Present discounted value measures.* Here, we are faced with a number of alternatives. Basically, the valuation procedure involves pricing the immigrant as an asset that yields a certain income: so that if there were indeed a market for this asset, this would be the valuation that it would command in the market. The alternatives then arise simply from the fact that the market for such an asset may be envisaged in different ways. In particular, we may distinguish among three basic types of concepts: (i) PDV^{PMP} where we assume that the prospective employer takes into account the private marginal product in employment of the immigrant over his lifetime and then bids for the asset; (ii) PDV^{wage} where we assume instead that there may be monopsonistic hiring by employers so that the asset will be valued at capitalized wages which are below the private marginal product; and finally (iii) PDV^{SMP} where we may envisage a situation with the bidding reflecting also the social, rather than the private, marginal product of the immigrant in the DC. These different measures may then be discussed below.

PDV_e^{PMP}. This is the present discounted value in the LDC of emigration, taking the private marginal product of the emigrant. In this measure, we take the present discounted value of the PTK emigrant, as it would emerge in a capital market, from bidding so as to exploit the services of this 'asset'. From the point of view of prospective employers in a decentralized system, the relevant parameters in the calculation are clearly the familiar discount rate, the time-span over which the emigrant would be producing the services, and the estimated private marginal product of the emigrant over this time-span.

PDV_e^{wage}. This is the present discounted value in the LDC of emigration, taking the wage of the emigrant. This measure would diverge from PDV_e^{PMP} if the wage diverged from the private marginal product. This would happen if wage were less than PMP because the employer was monopsonistic (e.g. the State has monopolized the activity, as with medicine). In this case, we can argue that the wage ($< PMP$) would get discounted back to its present value for capitalizing the PTK income: an interpretation that makes sense if we think of this monopsonist as offering a capitalized, current value to the worker for the latter's services over his lifetime.[21] Therefore $PDV_e^{wage} \leq PDV_e^{PMP}$ according as wage $\leq$ PMP.

$PDV_e^{SMP(1)}$. This is the present discounted value in the LDC of emigration, taking the total, social marginal product of the emigrant. This measure would include in the income stream the entire marginal product attributable to the emigrant. This makes sense if we hypothesize a capital market where *countries* are willing to bid for the asset in equation:

---

21. Note however that, in practice, it is extremely unlikely that the estimate of PDV would be undertaken except by reference to the wage earned, so that the distinction between *PMP* and the wage may not be empirically easy to implement.

an LDC would then bid so as to impute the *total*, social marginal product to the emigrant and hence the capitalization would reflect this. Naturally, in the presence of externalities, $PDV_e^{SMP(1)} > PDV_e^{PMP}$.

$PDV_e^{SMP(2)}$. This is also a present discounted value in LDC of emigration, taking the total, social marginal product but *subtracting out* the remuneration (wage) of the immigrant in the LDC. The rationale for this measure would be that, if an LDC were bidding for this migrant-asset, it would probably take into account the 'net' benefit that the LDC derives from the immigrant's presence: and this would then imply subtracting out his domestic remuneration (wage) from his social contribution (SMP) at home. If this is done, as would seem rational for the LDC, then clearly $PDV_e^{SMP(2)} < PDV_e^{SMP(1)}$ but $PDV_e^{SMP(2)}$ may be less *or* greater than PDV_e^{PMP}.[22]

Next, note that these measures again can be computed from the DC data: and here it is not just a question of using different DC 'prices' but also there can be parametric differences such as in the span of working life used in the calculation. Thus, we have:

PDV_i^{PMP}. This is the present discounted value of the immigrant in the DC of immigration. This is the counterpart of PDV_e^{PMP} and discounts back the income stream, defined by the private marginal product, in the country of immigration. The two measures will diverge in so far as the PMPs, at parity conversion, are unlikely to be equal, the discount rates should generally be different and even the working life spans are not identical between DCs and LDCs.

PDV_i^{wage}. This is the present discounted value, using the wage, of the immigrant in the DC of immigration. This is then the counterpart of PDV_e^{wage}.

$PDV_i^{SMP(1)}$. This is the present discounted value of the immigrant in the DC of immigration, taking the social marginal product in the DC. This measure is the counterpart of $PDV_e^{SMP(1)}$ and, for reasons of the kind already spelled out, the two will not generally be identical.

$PDV_i^{SMP(2)}$. This is the present discounted value of the immigrant in the DC of immigration, subtracting out the DC wage from the SMP in the DC, and clearly corresponds to $PDV_e^{SMP(2)}$.

'Reverse', 'net' versus 'gross', 'to-and-fro' migrations

Our discussion of the several possible measures above indicates the difficulties that arise from handling the imputation problems of

---

22. The $PDV_e^{SMP(2)}$ measure is also describable as a 'slavery-equivalent' measure: an employer buying a slave would be taking the 'net' contribution that a slave will make on the plantation and equating that to the notional 'wage' of the slave; and capitalization of the lifetime stream of such 'wages' will then represent the present-discounted-value price of the slave.

permanent, once-and-for-all migrations. As we have already noted, however, the PTK immigrants from LDCs do occasionally happen to return to their countries of origin, or to other LDCs, constituting a 'reverse' flow requiring us to distinguish between 'net' and 'gross' flows. They also, most unfortunately for statisticians and economists, do not seem to make up their minds even then and seem sometimes to swing to and fro between DCs and LDCs. This phenomenon raises problems for our computed imputations of capital flows, to which we address ourselves briefly at this point.

Two critical points need to be noted at the outset. (1) From the viewpoint of measurement, it is clear that relatively unambiguous criteria are necessary at each stage of measurement. Thus, since *ex ante* intentions of migrants are generally *not* reliable, we should stick to *ex post* migrations. Hence, quite regardless of whether a migrant intends to return to his LDC, he should be classified as a migrant as long as he takes an immigrant visa, much the way short-term capital is regarded as such even if the intention may be to hold an asset for ever. A set of simple and feasible conventions could be surely evolved, to classify immigrants as having 'effectively' migrated from one country to another, taking *ex post* movements according to well-defined categories into account. The problems here are no greater than those encountered in allocating financial flows to categories such as short-term and long-term movements. (2) Next, since we have already seen that the presence of two countries involves differential valuations, on any one concept, the question naturally arises about possible consistency in measures at different points of migration of the same person. Thus, if historic cost valuation is adopted, one could evaluate the emigrant from LDC, at initial migration, at LDC valuation. When he returns, one could add to this value the incremental cost of education in the DC at DC valuation *or* evaluate the same at equivalent LDC costs. There seems to be no compelling reason to choose among these alternatives except that one may well put some premium on being consistent and evaluate *all* costs at LDC-equivalent values, whether incurred in LDCs or DCs.[1]

(1) *Historic cost measures.* Take the complex case where the emigrant is educated in the LDC, acquires further education as a non-immigrant student in the DC, works in the DC as an immigrant and then returns to the LDC.

(i) Taking *consistent HC$_e$* valuation, at costs in the LDC, we could measure the imputed flow of capital to the DC as the historic costs incurred up to the point of emigration: hence, the educational costs (direct and

23. Note, however, that if such a convention is followed, the *overall* capital-flows accounting between LDCs and DCs must evaluate an item *identically* everywhere: thus recall our analysis of the historic cost measures in this regard.

indirect) of the DC education would be evaluated at the value of such educational costs if incurred in the LDC, since emigration is not considered to have taken place in the example until *after* the DC education is complete. The reverse flow should then also be measured at the same LDC-equivalent historic cost, HC_e.

(ii) Alternatively, the valuation could be carried through, at each point of cross-over, in terms of DC-equivalent historic costs, HC_i.

(iii) On the other hand, one could take historic values, *as incurred*, evaluating them at the values in the countries where they were incurred, even though this involves adding together values at different 'prices'. Thus, the LDC-educational costs would be recorded at LDC values, HC_e, and the DC-educational costs at DC values, HC_i. Their sum, in our example, would be recorded initially as the flow of imputed capital to the DC and later as the return flow to the LDC.

(2) *Present discounted value measures.* These raise particularly serious computational difficulties, of course, as the valuations must be made (if we stick to the consistency requirement, in the sense of the preceding subsection) entirely with reference to the discount rate, the time-span of remaining working life, and the 'income' (i.e. PMP, wage or SMP) as relevant to either the LDC or the DC. Thus, with LDC valuations, we would need to compute the imputed flow from the LDC to the DC in the foregoing example at the value of the fully trained immigrant; and the return flow to the LDC would measure the same value at 'income' over the working-time-span remaining to the immigrant at the point of the reverse migration. And the same, with DC valuations, would hold for PDV_i measures, taken consistently.

Our analysis therefore indicates the kinds of issues and problems that will arise in developing a set of imputed-capital-flow estimates of the brain drain flow. To emphasize, none of the difficulties attendant on such an exercise is insuperable. In fact, the difficulties are no more substantial than those that statisticians in a number of areas, chiefly national income accounting, have been already successfully addressing themselves to for numerous years and which are, in fact, already subjected to solution by international agreement on conventions for the purpose of standardized national income accounting. And, we might note, professional economists have actually engaged in making statistical estimates of imputed capital, in some form or the other, in relation to the brain drain itself, though not with the precise definitions and objectives we have addressed in this paper.[24]

24. See, for example, Grubel and Scott (1977, chs 10 and 11). Their computations are addressed to the US–Canadian exchange of professional manpower. The arguments produced in this pioneering work against proposals to tax the brain drain are, however, not particularly cogent and do not consider the now-popular version of

4   BRAIN DRAIN PHENOMENON VERSUS BRAIN DRAIN PROBLEM:
     ON DEFINING LDC LOSSES FROM THE BRAIN DRAIN

We may shift now to the alternative, and quite distinct, concept of 'LDC losses' from the brain drain. (There is also, of course, the related concept of the 'DC gains'.) Whereas the imputed-capital-flow concept, discussed in the preceding section, has absolutely no welfare significance in itself, the concept of LDC losses is obviously a welfare-concept and, as such, raises long-familiar issues.

Before we turn to these, note that it is also the concept which is appropriate to the notion of 'compensation': for compensation to LDCs implies some welfare loss which has to be compensated, whereas the use of the imputed-flow-of-capital concept can only be the more limited one, suggested earlier, of preparing a more balanced picture of capital flows between DCs and LDCs.

Note also that, while several LDCs undoubtedly have a brain drain 'phenomenon', one should not jump to the conclusion that they also have a brain drain 'problem': in the sense of a welfare-reducing outflow of PTK personnel. Indeed, much of the debate among economists rests on this precise issue: with DC-based economists often somewhat complacent in this regard and LDC-based economists usually biased in the other direction.

How does one approach the problems of defining the loss of welfare to LDCs from the brain drain? As it happens, the analytical issues involved in an economic evaluation of the consequences of the brain drain for the countries of emigration (and immigration) have been discussed technically elsewhere by the present author (Bhagwati and Rodriguez, 1976). Here, it should suffice to state in non-technical language the main contours that such an analysis should take and what, in fact, can be reasonably presumed to be the consequences of the brain drain for the LDCs.[25]

Conventional economic analysis

Defining the LDCs for this purpose as 'those left behind by the emigrants', and further defining the welfare impact with reference merely to overall

this proposal wherein the LDCs would simply extend their income tax jurisdiction over their nationals working abroad, as do the United States and the Philippines. See, in particular, the Symposium on this question in the *Journal of Public Economics*, August 1982, and especially my introduction to it.

25. The following analysis is borrowed from the author's extended treatment of the issues in 'The Brain Drain', prepared for the 1976 ILO Tripartite World Conference on Employment, Income Distribution and Social Progress and the International Division of Labour.

income (or social utility) – with no weights attached to income-distribution and unemployment rates, for example, for the present – one can cite the basic proposition that an economist would begin his analysis with:[26]

> *As long as the emigration is characterized by: Wage = PMP = SMP, there will be no welfare impact (adverse or beneficial) on those left behind.*

This 'basic' proposition, attributable to Grubel and Scott (1966), merely states that the *claim* that the emigrant makes on the LDC of emigration is his wage that he earns (for that is what enables him, by that amount, to partake of the national income); on the other hand, the *contribution* that he makes to national income is the total (social) marginal product, which is clearly SMP, and which may of course exceed or fall short of his immediate contribution to output in his painful employment, i.e. his PMP (the private, marginal product).

Now, if we assume that the LDC economy is perfectly competitive, so that each person earns a wage which equals his PMP, and that the LDC is further not characterized by any distortions or imperfections in the market system so that the PMP and SMP are also then equal, then it follows that wage = PMP = SMP and that, therefore, the emigrant's claim on the national income will have just been offset by his contribution to it, so that the net result will be to neither harm nor help those who are left behind with his emigration.

But as soon as this basic proposition is formulated, it becomes evident how departures from it can arise in practice and, in fact, will in the realities that characterize the LDCs. Three polar types of such departures from the case for no-impact from the brain drain may be distinguished:

Case I: Wage $\neq$ PMP = SMP
Case II: Wage = PMP $\neq$ SMP
Case III: Wage = SMP $\neq$ PMP

Note that Case III is listed only for completeness' sake; it is not easy to think of a realistic counterpart for it. Besides, the world may be characterized by a combination of two or all of the three cases distinguished. We thus proceed to discuss now, in some depth, Cases I and II which happen to encompass all the principal arguments that can be advanced to illuminate the adverse (and, for that matter, also the beneficial) effects of the brain drain on LDCs of origin.

---

26. PMP stands for private marginal product, i.e. the contribution to output, attributable to the gainful activity of the emigrant, in the activity itself; SMP stands for PMP plus (or minus) gains (or losses) in output, so attributable, but outside of the activity itself.

Case I: wage $\neq$ PMP = SMP. Three classic arguments on how the brain drain can harm the people left behind in the LDCs of emigration relate to Case I by stating conditions under which the emigrant's wage will be *below* the SMP, so that his emigration will deprive the LDC (excluding the emigrant) of the implied net benefit that his presence was contributing.

(1) The first argument relates to a simple point, that the emigration of (a *finite* number of) emigrants will, by altering the proportions in which different factors of production are employed, affect their remuneration. Hence, if emigration implies that the reward of the emigrating labour is increased, it also follows that the emigrants were getting paid *less* than their PMP (over a finite range, considered together).[27] In other words, there was a surplus of the average wage of the emigrants *as a group* over their average addition to output (i.e. w < PMP), which accrued to the LDC of emigration (excluding the emigrants), and which is now lost with the emigration.[28]

The magnitude of this loss depends, of course, on the extent to which the emigrant class of professionals can be substituted for by the country of emigration; and these losses can well be high if the emigrant professionals are not easily replaced or substituted for.

(2) The second argument relates to the emigrant's wage being below his PMP (= SMP) because of monopsonistic pricing of the emigrant professionals. This may be taken to be the case, for example, with the pricing of medical personnel in a nationalized health service of the British variety. Alternatively, it may be the case with any class of professionals where the employer is monolithic (as in some LDCs) and hence the labour market for the profession in question is not competitive but rather is monopsonistic.

(3) The third argument concerns the fact of taxation which can reduce the (net) remuneration of the emigrant class of professionals below their PMP (= SMP). This is very likely to be the case with professionals who, in countries with progressive tax systems, are likely to be net contributors to, rather than net beneficiaries from, the rest of the system.

Case II: wage = PMP $\neq$ SMP. Here again, a number of different examples can be distinguished.

(1) There is first the simple case of 'externality' where the market does not capture for the professional his true worth to society. An important

---

27. To put it another way, the emigrants were driving down their own reward below their marginal product: their increased numbers meant that, while the last member of the labour force did earn *his* PMP in a competitive market, this was not true for the earlier members whose PMP had been higher and whose wage would also have been correspondingly higher if only additional members had not been added to the labour force and had therefore not driven down the wage paid to each.

28. This point was made by Berry and Soligo in a famous article, 'Some welfare aspects of international migration', *Journal of Political Economy*, 77 (1969).

example is probably the case of doctors in many LDCs: their worth cannot really be measured by their earnings, as the mere presence of a doctor in an area, deprived of such services earlier, could be almost priceless.

(2) Then, there is the example of what economists call 'increasing returns to scale': a group of professionals may be worth much more than a subset of them and the wages paid to each member of the group may not reflect this *extra* productivity. This problem is what is referred to in discussions of the 'institution-building' roles of talented emigrants, especially research scientists and professors.

(3) Yet another instance is provided by the fact of educational subsidization of professional training in LDCs, as indeed in most DCs as well. The emigration of the educated, in this situation, could imply no real loss *if* one assumed that the returns to the subsidized-investment-in-education would have accrued to the emigrant anyway (and not to those left behind) *and* that the emigration does not result in an increase in the number of people educated. However, if one postulates an economy in which this emigration leads to other natives being educated by way of replacement, partially or fully, then indeed there is an overall expansion of subsidized education, with increased losses from the subsidization programme, *ceteris paribus*. This is then clearly a case where, thanks to the government subsidy to education, the remuneration enjoyed by the emigrant equals his PMP but his emigration will inflict an *additional* loss such that one must classify this as an instance where wage = PMP < SMP, and therefore the brain drain is harmful.

(4) Yet another, equally important, example that is of interest in the discussion of the brain drain, where a domestic distortion can lead to divergence between the remuneration and the SMP of emigrants, concerns the presence of sticky wages and consequent unemployment. In fact, it is frequently argued, especially in relation to Filippino doctors and Indian engineers (both constituting rather substantial fractions of recent flows of skilled manpower from the LDCs), that there is unemployment in these professions in the LDCs of emigration and that therefore there is not a brain drain problem, but just skilled emigration which is better described as a 'spillover', 'safety valve', 'overflow' phenomenon, with no harm for the LDC of emigration since the SMP of such emigrants is zero.[29]

If this interpretation is assumed to be correct, then clearly we have a situation where wage = PMP = SMP (= 0). However, we have decided to include this phenomenon of emigration from the unemployed into the

---

29. In fact, if the emigrant was receiving a State dole, or subsisting from resources other than his savings while unemployed, it could be argued that the emigration actually improves the welfare of those left behind because his claim on national income (by the amount of his subsistence) exceeded his contribution (which was zero).

class of Case II examples because it can be argued, quite plausibly, that such emigration is *not* one with zero SMP but rather leads to harmful effects and that therefore wage($= 0$) = PMP < SMP. Thus it can be shown (as Hamada and Bhagwati (1975) have formally done) that the outflow abroad of doctors from the overcrowded urban areas with unemployment could inhibit the gradual spillover of such doctors into the rural areas with high social productivity: the (external) brain drain thus slows down the beneficial 'internal diffusion' process which, in a capitalist framework, is an imperfect but real substitute for the Maoist policy of sending doctors to the countryside.

Similarly, it could be argued that the emigration from a pool of currently unemployed professionals could, in the long run, raise the number educated by raising expected returns from such professional training and thus increase educational costs without increasing output, thus *reducing* national income (net of educational costs).[30] Here again we then have wage($= 0$) < SMP (as the emigration reduces SMP and hence the lack of emigration must be construed to increase SMP).

Finally, it should be noted that if the emigration accentuates the sticky-wage distortion by raising the wage level of the emigrant class of professionals through the emulation effect, this will generally accentuate the loss from the emigration noted in the previous paragraph (Bhagwati and Hamada, 1974).

While the preceding examples concern cases where the emigration leads to a loss because the wage is below SMP, one can think of externalities which lead to wage($=$ PMP) > SMP, so that the brain drain is welfare-improving for the LDC of emigration. Two examples may be noted, both relating to the fact that the emigrant's income or output abroad may accrue to the LDC in some fashion.

(5) One example relates to the fact that the output of the emigrant may have the nature of a public good and hence may be available to the LDC as well. This may be the case with professors and research scientists. Besides, their output may be greater because of better facilities and environment in the DCs. On the other hand, the orientation of this output may be towards DC rather than LDC needs. Whether the net effect then is positive for LDCs would then depend on the relative strengths of these offsetting effects.

(6) Another example relates to the notion that distinguished emigrants do not need to be at home but can inspire students and researchers from afar; that, in fact, by working with greater distinction (owing to better facilities leading to superior performance) abroad, they can inspire better. But this argument must be set off against the possibility that the LDC students and researchers may be demoralized into thinking that only work

30. For a formal modelling of this point, see Bhagwati and Hamada (1974).

abroad can lead to distinction and success, thus inhibiting the growth of domestic confidence and capability in scientific achievements: a phenomenon that anyone who has tried to build up institutions in LDCs is likely to be acquainted with.

Additional welfare-impact considerations

The discussion so far has assumed that: (A) the effect of the brain drain on the flow of goods and services, or national income, is an adequate indicator of the consequence of the brain drain on LDC welfare; and (B) the emigration is, in effect, permanent and there are no 'feedback' effects of any kind. Neither of these assumptions, however, is valid and hence they must now be relaxed, each in turn.

(A) *Additional indicators of welfare impact.* Three aspects of the problem of defining welfare consequences more adequately will now be discussed.

(1) *Unemployment.* Note first that our analysis did not attach any significance to unemployment *per se*.[31] However, the increase or reduction in unemployment, consequent upon the brain drain, is of interest in itself.

The precise effect of the brain drain on unemployment, not merely in the class of professionals emigrating but (indirectly) in other occupations as well, will clearly depend on what kinds of labour markets and other related characteristics of the country are postulated. Suffice it here to note, however, that the general argument that, in conditions of unemployment (as at any point of time), emigration will reduce unemployment presupposes that the supply of such professionals does not increase so as to offset this outflow. But this is not at all evident as migration will raise the *expected* wage of such professionals by both *initially* reducing the unemployment pool and because emigration brings into the expected wage the substantially higher foreign salaries. The increased incentive to secure this professional training therefore may well increase the supply of such professionals beyond the level which would offset the outflow, thus *adding* to unemployment, rather than diminishing it.[32] Furthermore, if the emulation effect operates such that the emigration, *via* implied furthering of the integration of the international markets for professionals, leads to an increase in the *actual* salary levels of the class of emigrating professionals (airline pilots presumably being a good example of this 'emulation' effect'), then the probability of

31. Unemployment was considered only in so far as it affected the outcome for national income (or utility), the latter being the only focus of analysis.

32. For a model where the conditions which would generate this possibility are rigorously spelled out, see Bhagwati and Hamada (1974). Another modified model is presented by McCulloch and Yellen (1975).

unemployment level (and rate) increasing (rather than reducing) with the emigration, is increased. And if we visualize a 'leap-frogging' process of secondary wage increases, triggered off by such migration-plus-emulation-induced primary salary increases, unemployment in other labour markets could also increase.[33]

(2) *Income distribution and inequality.* The effect of the brain drain on income distribution and on inequality also needs to be spelled out. But, in doing this, one needs to distinguish among alternative ways of defining these distributional concepts.

Now, if one regards as an egalitarian objective, not merely equality of access but equality of success as well,[34] then a reduction of wage differentials is *prima facie* a virtue. In this event, if the brain drain leads, *via* the emulation effect, to an increase in the professional salary level, this is (in egalitarian terms) an adverse impact. This in fact, is precisely what bothers social and economic planners who worry about the effect that the possibility of emigration has on the domestic ability to maintain desired salary structures: either they can erect emigration restrictions *à la* communist countries so as to eliminate the emulation effect but at the cost of humane values, *or* they must sacrifice their egalitarian objectives.[35] Note that this argument also exposes the shallowness of the assertion, often made by opponents of concern over the brain drain, that the brain drain is a result of 'inadequate' LDC policies such as 'failure' to remunerate their professionals well: it implicitly superimposes on these LDCs their value judgment that they must alter their salary structures in an inegalitarian direction.

An alternative way to look at the inegalitarian impact of the brain drain would be in terms of access: i.e. one could examine whether it permits those at the lower half of the income distribution in an economy to transit to the unequal-and-higher rewards permitted by emigration. In fact, the classic nineteenth-century immigration into the United States from the highly stratified European countries probably fits into this egalitarian version of the consequences of emigration. However, the brain drain from the LDCs hardly fits into this description: enough is known about the inegalitarian access to educational facilities in many LDCs[36] to suggest

33. Again, for formal analysis of such possibilities in a fully-specified model, see Bhagwati and Hamada (1974).

34. This distinction might also be described as one between opportunity and outcome. See Bhagwati (1973).

35. In fact, thanks to the possibility of evasion of emigration barriers, few communist countries can also escape the consequences of the coexistence with countries with greater inequality in rewards for the skilled and talented. Thus, Frederick Pryor's data on East European salary differentials suggest that the East German differentials are larger than others and the explanation seems to lie in the *comparative* ease with which native professionals can slip across to (West Germany in) the outside world (Pryor, 1968).

36. For a discussion of this evidence, primarily in the Indian context, see Bhagwati (1973).

strongly that the access to professional emigration, in consequence, must be regarded as principally available to the better-endowed among the LDC population.

Finally, one could examine the purely income-distributional consequences of the brain drain in terms of either the functional or the personal income distribution. Nothing can be stated categorically one way or the other, however, in regard to either of these: everything depends on the model used to depict the reality in LDCs *and* the precise definition of income distribution chosen; and no 'presumption' would seem to be plausible, at least to the present author. Thus, take a model where emigration leads to a replacement of the educated emigrant by one more educated person, and if it is assumed that sticky wages imply that no more new employment is created, then total output will not change, whereas one unemployed person will have become educated and hence employed. Then, if we take the share of wages in national income, this is unchanged. If one takes the national income *excluding* the increased cost of education (since one more person is being educated), the share of wages has gone up. If one takes the ratio of wages to educated and uneducated workers, this has remained unchanged. If one takes the ratio of *average* wages to the educated to *average* income of the uneducated *plus* unemployed, then this has fallen (since unemployment is reduced). And so on. Indeed, the income distributional consequences have been noted, for the brain drain problem, increasingly of late by general-equilibrium economic theorists (e.g. Bhagwati and Hamada, 1974; McCulloch and Yellen, 1975): and the reader can readily adapt these, and other, analyses to their own preferred indicator of income distribution in the LDC of emigration.

(3) *GNP.* It is not immediately obvious that the welfare of 'those left behind' will not depend, both directly *and* indirectly, on the effect of the brain drain on GNP. Thus, it is possible that a society derives satisfaction from being 'big' in its economic size: an economic counterpart of what is politically the well-known phenomenon of 'big power chauvinism'. But, more respectably, it is clear that a larger economic size could, in turn, produce larger economic gains. Thus, for example, it could lead to better bargaining abilities on economic issues with others in the world economy and hence enhanced share in the gains from trade, investment, etc. Thus, in so far as the brain drain reduces LDC GNP, as it surely must (except in singular circumstances) in the long run, it could *prima facie* have an adverse impact on the LDCs.

(4) *Technical labour force.* Finally, the sheer availability of a technical labour force, with attendant scientific attitudes, may be critical in determining the pace of modernization. As the 1974 US House *Report* on the brain drain put it rather well:

An educated elite plays a primary role in society, and the social loss to the LDCs from this drain can have adverse effects far beyond the impact of specialized disciplines. In general, highly skilled manpower is part of the larger infrastructure of a social elite that is necessary for development. Beyond their specialized areas the scientist, engineer and physician contribute to a nation's political, social and cultural development. They help set the tone of society, and establish national values and goals. . . . In a profound sense, medical and other scientifically trained persons occupy pivotal positions in that they help change values, a necessary condition for changing institutions. . . . Developing countries need not only specific skills but also leadership and organizing ability. A continuing drain of highly trained people can over the long run add to a sense of national frustration, generate a contagious movement, lower the sense of worth of those who remain [that is, the 'left-behind' syndrome], reduce further the small group of potential political and administrative leaders, and reduce the cadre of technically trained people who must be at hand when the process of development gathers momentum.[37]

(B) *To-and-fro migration and 'feedback' effects.* In conclusion, we must note also that the welfare analysis of the brain drain must be modified to take into account the fact that professional migration is no longer a 'permanent' affair but is rather characterized by reverse or even 'to-and-fro' movements by the migrant professionals.

For the present analysis, this phenomenon points to three major qualifications to the contention that the brain drain implies a loss to the LDCs of emigration.

(1) The professionals, returning off and on to their LDCs of origin, can contribute net income to these LDCs in a number of ways. Thus, for example, typically professors and research scientists tend to visit LDC institutions on DC Foundation grants.

(2) Secondly, since the brain can appreciate from better environment, the returning professional might be able to generate *greater* externality to his LDC than when the initial emigration occurred. Thus, for example, recall the fact that the Chinese achievements in atomic capability came from Chinese scientists who had resided and matured in the United States.

(3) And finally, while the inflow of remittances from the emigrants is not conditional on the return or to-and-fro character of the migration, it would seem appropriate to assume that the continued (personal) linkage

37. *Report*, pp. 138–9; quotation marks and footnotes from the original have been omitted.

with the LDC of origin should strengthen, rather than weaken, the impulse to remit (or take savings home on permanent return).

It is not probable that these offsetting factors can be sufficiently large to eliminate the adverse effects of the brain drain on many LDCs of emigration, though it is likely that some LDCs have a brain drain phenomenon but not a brain drain problem.

5   ALTERNATIVE POLICY PROPOSALS IN REGARD TO THE
BRAIN DRAIN: COMPENSATION, TAXATION, ETC.

There are several alternative proposals which have been advanced by economists and policymakers in regard to the brain drain. However, they often have different objectives which are insufficiently distinguished from one another. Nor are their differential requirements in terms of the kinds of actions that need to be taken for implementing them adequately sketched in the documents that contain them. Our first task, therefore, must be to sort out analytically the different proposals and their rationales.

Thus, we may first note that there are basically the following quite different types of proposals in the literature on the brain drain:

(i) proposals aimed at reducing the brain drain: dividing, in turn, into 'restrictive' policies and 'incentive' policies;

(ii) proposals which are aimed at 'compensating' the LDCs for the losses alleged to have been suffered by the LDCs from their PTK emigration: these proposals then being directed, not at reducing the brain drain, but rather at offsetting its ill-effects on the LDCs; these proposals, in turn, dividing into compensation being paid by the DCs *or* by the PTK migrants themselves;

(iii) proposals which are aimed at taxation (of PTK immigrants) to achieve global allocative efficiency, i.e. to maximize 'world welfare';

(iv) proposals which are aimed at *some* form of brain-drain-related taxation in order, frankly, to raise developmental resources for LDCs, *either* by taxing DCs for this purpose on the ground that DCs *benefit* from such PTK immigration and should share these gains with LDCs, *or* by taxing the PTK migrants themselves on the ground that they enjoy DC-quota-restrictions-generated *rents* which can be taxed without ill-effects for developmental spending;

(v) proposals which would tax LDC PTK migrants for LDC developmental spending as an 'inducement', through example of self-help, for the DCs to undertake enhanced aid programs, this constituting therefore an *externality* argument for the proposed tax; and

(vi) proposals which would tax LDC PTK migrants for achievement of efficiency-cum-equity in the LDCs and/or for preventing deleterious effects in the LDCs: this constituting an *LDC-welfare-based* rationale, as against, the *global-efficiency* rationale underlying (iii) above.

Note that (ii)–(vi) above will all raise *some* revenue, in general, for LDCs. However, the *objectives* of the proposals under each are different; and the implied tax-bases (i.e. who pays the tax) are not necessarily identical either. Note additionally that the different proposals differ also according to whether: (i) they require only LDC implementation; (ii) they require only DC action; or (iii) cooperative action by LDCs and DCs is required, this in turn being distinguished by whether bilateral or multilateral action is appropriate or necessary.

Policy proposals to reduce the brain drain

The policy proposals addressed to reducing the brain drain are the more fashionable in most discussions of the brain drain, and divide into 'restrictive' and 'incentive' policy suggestions.

Restrictive policies. The restrictive policy actions are, of course, the LDC counterpart of DC immigration restrictions; the latter already restrict the overall PTK inflow to desired levels while the proposed LDC restrictions can shift the breakdown of their total between LDC and DC sources of emigration. These restrictions can take the form of denial of passports for exiting professionals, requirements of periods of domestic service for newly graduated professionals (as with medical graduates in many countries), or making exit more difficult in other ways (as when the holding of the American Medical Association's ECFMG examination for foreign doctors is forbidden in India). Few of these restrictions can really be applied to those students who 'stay on' abroad after their studies, though even here the government of Sri Lanka (Ceylon) had experimented with making the renewal of passports conditional on transmission of funds, etc., and could well have made the renewal impossible so as to attempt forcing the return of the emigrés.

Typically, however, these kinds of restrictions are both likely to be nuisances and surmountable inequitably by the powerful or the ingenious and to be resented at large by the very professionals who are sought to be held back, with possibly adverse effects on their efficiency and commitment to their societies. Hence, these restrictions are invoked only infrequently and are occasionally cancelled (as recently in Sri Lanka) in response to effective protests by the professionals.

A DC policy action addressed recently to reducing the PTK inflow from LDCs (though not necessarily from LDCs plus DCs), was the now-defunct United States policy ruling that required exchange visitors from LDCs, in PTK categories, to return to their home country or another LDC for a period of two years before they could re-enter the US as immigrants. A later example is the recent US legislative action making the immigration of foreign medical graduates virtually impossible and to rely instead on expanding domestic training facilities.

Incentive policies. As for the incentive policy suggestions, these are generally LDC-focused, and designed to make emigration less attractive. Thus, salary increases, improved research facilities, etc., are typically advocated. But while a number of institutional features of professional life in LDCs could be improved, the basic difficulty lies in the impossibility of significantly narrowing the gap in professional facilities on a wide scale when the DCs and LDCs are so widely apart in their resource situation in the first place. Besides, prescriptions to raise professional salaries yet further towards international levels have inegalitarian and welfare-reducing consequences which LDCs surely cannot ignore. Thus, even if these policies were to be implemented somehow on a significant scale, and were then to reduce the outflow of professional manpower, they would have to be carefully weighed for their other deleterious effects on the LDCs adopting these policies.

Mention also needs to be made here again of the occasional argument that several LDCs have overexpanded their educational facilities and that their PTK emigration is a direct result of such overexpansion and consequent unemployment. Now, in regard to this argument it is certainly likely that if the scale of educational facilities could be reduced in any country experiencing emigration, it would *ceteris paribus* (regardless of unemployment levels) tend to lower emigration to higher-wage DCs by raising, under 'normal' assumptions, the domestic return to education. However, the desirability of such a policy would depend on the precise conditions in the labour market for these professionals and the social objectives of the LDC question. Thus, if the *net* domestic availability (i.e. domestic supply *minus* emigration) of the professionals falls as their total output is restricted, this could well be considered a serious negative effect of the policy. Even if the labour market situation is one characterized by a temporary 'surplus', given the current sticky wage level, it is perfectly conceivable that the reduced domestic availability (including the present surplus) inhibits the diffusion of this kind of professional (e.g. doctors) into the countryside where the social returns to their professional presence is highly valued. However, as already noted in section 4 above, the desirability of restricting educational facilities for the production of the emigrating class of professionals, even when there is current 'unemployment' or 'surplus', is by no means to be taken for granted. Furthermore, it is extremely improbable that a policy of restricting educational facilities for professionals, even if evaluated to be desirable, can be politically implemented, especially when emigration possibilities have made the returns from such educational attainment even more attractive.

Turning next to the incentive policies that the DCs can adopt to reduce the inflow of professionals from LDCs into the DCs, two major types can be distinguished. First, the attraction of permanent emigration can be reduced, *ceteris paribus*, by enabling temporary access to the DC facilities by LDC professionals in a number of ways. Thus, in regard to research-oriented professionals, the major Foundations in the DCs have initiated programmes to finance recurrent and protracted visits by LDC professionals at DC universities and institutes: this permits flirting to be an effective substitute for marriage! Such programmes enable the LDC professionals to retain their domicile in the LDCs where they can proceed with institution-building, etc., at the substantially lower LDC salaries, while enjoying both an increased average income level and intellectual stimulus from the foreign visits. The counterpart of these programmes is the financing of visits by DC scientists to the LDC institutions. In both cases, of course, the results can be deleterious if the programmes are ill-administered: thus, if the LDCs manage them such that the foreign visits are controlled and allocated on a patronage basis, the programme will even generate diversion of professional energy into patronage-cultivation; and the use of funds to bring in low-grade but highly-paid DC scientists may well generate resentment from the indigenous professional community.

Second, a DC policy that could, *ceteris paribus*, reduce the brain drain would be a surtax on the LDC professionals' income in the DCs of immigration: the tax proposal that has been advocated (on several rationales) by the present author in 1973 and later (Bhagwati and Partington, 1976). Econometric analysis of the brain drain into the United States suggests that a reduction in the (net-of-tax) relative wage of the DC and the LDC has a negative, though small, effect on the immigration flows. Essentially, such a tax on the brain drain could be deflecting (in a small way) the DC-restricted immigration, at the margin, away from the LDCs (whose nationals would have to pay the tax) to the DCs (whose emigrating nationals would not have to pay the tax).

Policy proposals to compensate the LDCs for losses caused by the brain drain

Next, we have what are essentially compensatory-financing proposals. These involve *either* compensation schemes to be financed by the *DC of immigration* to compensate for the losses inflicted on the LDCs by the brain drain *or* compensation schemes to be financed by the *emigrants* themselves for these LDC losses.[38]

38. In addition, one could include here the notion that DCs ought to 'replace', through technical assistance, the professionals that they 'take' from the LDCs: in fact, balance sheets of loss and gain of professional manpower through the brain drain and the technical assistance programmes are occasionally drawn up. Quite aside from the fact that the notion

The *moral* rationale for these two alternative methods of compensation may be stated as follows. (1) In the case of compensation paid by the DCs, the moral appeal may rest on the arguments that the coexistence of the prosperous DCs and the poor LDCs leads to this PTK emigration from LDCs and therefore it is fair to expect that the DCs should assist the LDCs in coping with such losses; that, by so doing, the DCs would also be helping to prevent the LDCs from self-protecting, quantitative emigration restrictions that offend against the kind of humane international order that DCs often argue as their ideal; and that if DCs, in turn, are likely to have also *gained* from such PTK immigration (as would seem to be the general presumption in light of immigration policies that are closely geared to national interest), then the moral obligation to assist the poor LDCs to cope with their losses is correspondingly greater. (2) The moral case for making the PTK emigrants pay compensation to the LDCs, on the other hand, is simply that their *considerable* improvement of income, obtained by LDC-permitted emigration that inflicts losses on 'those left behind', imposes a moral obligation on them to share their gains partially with these groups.[39]

Next, it should be noted in regard to the compensatory-financing proposals, whether they relate to the DCs of immigration or the emigrants themselves as assessees, the essential problem with them is that they presuppose a commonly-agreed-upon methodology and procedures for defining the LDC losses which are to be compensated. It is difficult to see, given the wide differences that can sometimes obtain on these issues (as we have noted in section 4), how such an agreement can be readily obtained. But even if it were, it is certain that the losses would fluctuate annually, causing equivalent fluctuations in the compensatory-finance that would be forthcoming (and, if the tax were collected on emigrants, the tax rate would also, in general, fluctuate). Working with LDC-losses as the basis for the transfer of funds (revenue) to LDCs experiencing the brain drain phenomenon is therefore a rather impractical procedure – *unless* it is taken as a general rationale rather than as also providing a firm base for calculating the revenue to be raised for the LDCs.

Note moreover that two main types of taxes on the professional migrants

---

of replacement is tricky, given the quality differences implicit in the professional categories being considered, the two sets of movements have asymmetries of great importance: the emulation effect (considered in section 4) can follow from the emigration and may be only reinforced, rather than offset, by the technical-assistance-sponsored inflow; the LDC may well, and often will, attach significance to having its own stock of professional manpower rather than being dependent on technical assistance that may suddenly vanish; and so on.

39. Note that a moral, as also an efficiency, case for taxing such emigrants, *even if there were no losses imposed on LDCs by the brain drain*, can be developed, as set out below.

might be distinguished when the LDC-losses are the rationale for the tax: (1) the Soviet-style exit tax; and (2) a surtax on post-immigration incomes. The now-defunct Soviet exit tax was rationalized on the assumption that the USSR would be reimbursing itself for the educational costs incurred on the emigrant.[40] The surtax on the post-immigration income of the emigrant could also be calculated and assessed so as to equal the estimated loss to the LDC of emigration; but this would cause practical difficulties in levying the surtax rates so that it is best to regard again the LDC-losses as providing only a general rationale, and *not* a tax-revenue target, if the option of a surtax on post-immigration incomes is chosen as the alternative on the basis of this rationale.

Policy proposal for taxing the brain drain to achieve global (allocative) efficiency

While, however, the proposals for compensation considered above are primarily based on *moral* considerations and therefore cannot be expected to command universal acceptance, it is interesting to note that a case can also be made for taxing LDC PTK immigrants' incomes in DCs (in a manner to be detailed presently) on grounds of *global allocative efficiency*.

This argument is basically a simple and persuasive one. Thus, if the DC and the LDC are characterized by income taxes, the tax rate in the LDC is higher than in the DC, the PTK migration is to the DC, then it will be readily appreciated that the optimal allocation of total DC-plus-LDC PTK labour between the two regions requires that the LDC-origin PTK worker be taxed identically regardless of his residence and work-location. This argument implies that the PTK immigrant into the DC be taxed at the *higher* LDC rate, with double-taxation relief for DC taxes of course. And the difference between the (lower) DC tax rate and the (higher) LDC tax rate constitutes therefore a tax on the brain drain, levied *de facto* in the form of supplementary taxation of the DC incomes of LDC PTK immigrants.[41] While, further, the global efficiency argument does not require that the supplementary-tax revenues accrue to LDCs, granting them in fact to LDCs would constitute a source of revenue as well for the LDCs.

Are LDC tax rates, in fact, generally higher than DC tax rates? Table 17.1 certainly suggests that they are, although we should keep in mind that evasion is probably larger in LDCs and also that the LDC rates could

40. The differences between the exit tax and the tax on incomes in the country of immigration, even if the objectives are identical, are quite profound and favour the latter. See, for argumentation, J. Bhagwati and W. Dellalfar, in Bhagwati and Partington (1976).

41. This version of the proposal by the present author to tax DC incomes of the PTK LDC immigrants was suggested by Professors Oldman and Pomp, in Bhagwati and Partington (1976).

TABLE 17.1 Income tax rates in selected DCs and LDCs

	US Federal tax		Canada Federal tax		UK
	tax	(a)	tax	(b)	
US$5000					(£2000)
S	$491 (9.8%)		$444.84 (8.90%)	$611.02 (12.22%)	$1053.75 (21.08%)
M	322 (6.4)		152.24 (3.04)	229.17 (4.58)	918.75 (18.38)
M+2C	98 (2.0)		32.18 (0.64)	72.49 (1.45)	618.75* (12.38)
US$10,000					(£4000)
S	1530 (15.30%)	$1984 (19.84%)	1559.22 (15.59%)	2065.28 (20.65%)	2553.75 (25.54%)
M	1190 (11.90)	1519 (15.19)	1204.42 (12.04)	1602.27 (16.02)	2418.75 (24.19)
M+2C	905 (9.05)	1148 (11.48)	1057.22 (10.57)	1410.17 (14.10)	2118.75* (21.19)
US$20,000					(£8000)
S	4255 (23.8%)	5456 (27.28%)	4470.45 (22.35%)	5905.70 (29.53%)	6381.25 (31.91%)
M	3400 (17.0)	4455 (22.28)	3974.36 (19.87)	5250.34 (26.25)	6156.25 (30.78)
M+2C	3010 (15.11)	3918 (19.59)	3761.56 (18.81)	4969.22 (24.85)	5677.88* (28.39)
Rate of exchange			US$1 = $1CDN		£1˙ = US$2.5

All data pertain to 1974.

S: single; M: married; M+2C: married with two children.

*Assuming that both children are under 11 years old.

(a) This column includes the federal income tax, the New York State tax and the New York City tax. Deductions for the federal income tax are assumed at 15 per cent of the total remuneration. For the New York State and City taxes standard deductions have been used.

(b) This column includes the federal income tax and the provincial income tax at the minimum rate of 30.5 per cent of the federal income taxes before the special federal 5 per cent tax reduction.

(continued overleaf)

TABLE 17.1 (continued)

	Argentina	Colombia	Mexico
US$5000	($a25,000)	(112,500 pesos)	(62,450 pesos)
S	$325.8 (6.52%)	$1238.44 (24.77%)	$357.82 (7.16%)
M	257.4 (5.15)	1197.33 (23.95)	357.82 (7.16)
M+2C	135 (2.7)	1164.44 (23.29)	357.82 (7.16)
US$10,000	($a50,000)	(225,000 pesos)	(124,900 pesos)
S	1629.8 (16.30%)	3130.67 (31.31%)	1094.26 (10.94%)
M	1514.6 (15.15)	3087.33 (30.87)	1094.26 (10.94)
M+2C	1291.4 (12.91)	3052.67 (30.53)	1094.26 (10.94)
US$20,000	($a100,000)	(450,000 pesos)	(249,800 pesos)
S	5478.6 (27.39%)	7205.11 (36.03%)	4074.04 (20.37%)
M	5325 (26.63)	7158.44 (35.79)	3923.44 (19.62)
M+2C	5037 (25.19)	7121.11 (35.61)	3772.84 (18.86)
Rate of exchange	US$1 = $5.00 (official rate)	US$1 = 22.50 pesos	US$1 = 12.49 pesos

All data pertain to 1974, except for Argentina and Colombia, where data pertain to 1972.
S: single; M: married; M+2C: married with two children.

TABLE 17.1 (continued)

Taiwan	Hong Kong	India†	Korea	Philippines
(NT$190,000)	(HK$28,250)	(Rs.39,550)	(2,400,000 won)	(P34,500)
$397.37 (7.95%)	$248.89 (4.98%)	$1566.53 (31.33%)	$752.5 (15.05%)	$807.6 (16.15%)
345.26 (6.91)	122.79 (2.46)	1566.53 (31.33)	677.5 (13.55)	750.2 (15.0)
275.79 (5.52)	69.69 (1.39)	1566.53 (31.33)	602.5 (12.05)	663.0 (13.26)
(NT$380,000)	(HK$56,500)	(Rs.79,100)	(4,800,000 won)	(P69,000)
1398.42 (13.98%)	1194.69 (11.95%)	5287.67 (52.88%)	2615 (26.15%)	2813.9 (28.14%)
1295.79 (12.96)	896.02 (8.96)	5287.67 (52.88)	2515 (25.15)	2730.4 (27.30)
1145.26 (11.45)	743.36 (7.43)	5287.67 (52.88)	2415 (24.15)	2591.3 (25.91)
(NT$760,000)	(HK$113,000)	(Rs.158,200)	(9,600,000 won)	(P138,000)
4672.63 (23.36%)	3000 (15.0%)	14,329.20 (71.65%)	7290 (36.45%)	8416.2 (42.08%)
4518.68 (22.59)	3000 (15.0)	14,329.20 (71.65)	7165 (35.83)	8310.1 (41.55)
4292.89 (21.46)	3000 (15.0)	14,329.20 (71.65)	7040 (35.2)	8136.2 (40.68)
US$1 = NT$38	US$1 = HK$5.65	US$1 = Rs.7.91	US$1 = 480 won	US$1 = P6.90

†Surcharge included.
Source: Hamada (1977).

not possibly be extended to DC incomes without adjustment for differential cost of living. Nonetheless, the basic argument that LDC tax rates are higher remains valid.

Proposals addressed to raising developmental resources for LDCs

An altogether different objective of some tax proposals related to the brain drain has been frankly the raising of developmental resources for LDCs: this being the direct and principal objective as distinct from being an incidental (and favourably regarded) outcome of policies addressed to other objectives.

In this class of tax proposals we must distinguish again between the proposal for *DCs* to transfer (normal) tax revenues to LDCs on the ground that they enjoy gains from the brain drain and should therefore share these gains for a larger purpose such as developmental spending in the LDCs – note that this argument does *not* require that the LDCs experience any losses from the brain drain, as discussed earlier – and the distinct proposal to tax the *immigrants' incomes* in the DCs instead, the argument in this latter instance being that the immigrants enjoy rents generated by the DC immigration quotas and that these rents should be partially taxed in order to use the proceeds for a larger social purpose such as developmental spending in the LDCs. The simplest analogy to these notions is the scheme, already implemented, whereby the proceeds from the sale of IMF gold at market prices are being used for assisting the LDCs.

Proposals to utilize 'externality' for generating more resources for LDCs

Related to the preceding arguments is the important point made by Professor Jan Tinbergen that a tax on the brain drain, in the form of taxing their DC incomes for developmental spending in the LDCs, could have the 'externality' effect of persuading public opinion in the DCs (through demonstration of self-help by LDC-origin nationals) to vote for more transfers of resources by DCs.[42] Presumably, the DC nationals would not feel, as they often seem to do, that LDCs like to exhort DCs to tax their citizens for aid to LDCs while doing little of it themselves, and that a demonstration of willingness to tax their own successfully emigrated nationals would help to counter this feeling.

In a slightly similar vein, Professor Saul Mendlovitz has argued also that the taxation of PTK LDC immigrants in the DCs could be the first

---

42. Cf. his endorsement of the present author's proposal to tax the brain drain in this form: 'It is my hope that this tax might also help to convince public opinion in the rich countries that more has to be done in the field of development cooperation', in Bhagwati and Partington (1976).

step towards the ultimate adoption of the more broad-based proposals such as a 1 per cent tax on individual incomes in all countries, for raising developmental resources for LDCs.[43]

Note that these arguments also run counter to the assertion sometimes made that all brain-drain-related 'link' proposals to transfer resources to DCs would cut into 'normal' aid flows: that such transfers would substitute for other aid, leaving no increment in the total. Besides, it should be noted that there is absolutely no reason to regard supplementary taxation of LDC PTK immigrants' incomes for transfer to LDCs as a DC contribution of resources (even though the DCs would have to assist in the collection of the revenue, as argued below in section 6). Any legislator who would seek to argue that this was a DC contribution of resources is on exceptionally weak ground and should be readily disabused of such a self-serving notion, so that it should be easy to argue against any attempts to cut down normal aid flows because of revenues from the brain drain tax on LDC PTK immigrants' incomes.

Proposals aimed at providing tax policy instrument to achieve efficiency-cum-equity in LDCs

Finally, we should consider two particular arguments, for taxing LDC PTK immigrants' incomes in DCs, which are designed *not to compensate* the LDCs for losses inflicted by the brain drain, but rather to provide a policy instrument which, if available, would *prevent* the LDCs of emigration from suffering efficiency-cum-equity losses.

The straightforward argument, based on the emulation effect, is that the deleterious effect of the brain drain comes about not merely through the emigration *per se* but rather through the effect it has of underlining vastly higher incomes in the DCs, and then through its effect in raising domestic salary levels through emulation. In this case, the domestic 'distortion' in the salary structure is accentuated by the possibility of emigration for these higher salaries, possibly resulting in income losses through additional unemployment, etc. Furthermore, income inequality would be accentuated also, since the PTK salaries would rise whereas the average wage of the non-emigrant non-PTK workers is unlikely to: so that the salary structure gets skewed. Therefore, both in terms of efficiency and equity, the possibility of emigration to DCs with their significantly higher salary levels creates problems for the LDCs of emigration. In this scenario, the imposition of a brain drain tax on PTK migrants' earnings in DCs would reduce their 'net-of-tax' salaries and thus help to moderate these adverse effects on the LDCs (quite aside, of course, from raising some revenue which could be routed to LDCs).

43. Cf. his Preface in Bhagwati and Partington (1976).

A somewhat more complex argumentation, however, has recently been developed by economic theorists working in the theory of public finance. This argument demonstrates the following: in an economy which is using income taxation to achieve equality of incomes, there is a trade-off between equality and efficiency since the income tax inhibits effort and/or investment in education; the resulting *per capita* income, however, will be lower for LDC nationals if PTK (educated) emigrants can leave and not be taxed on their foreign incomes; the introduction of a tax on foreign earnings of the PTK emigrants will then enable an improvement in *per capita* income of LDC nationals; and that, if an educational subsidy *and* the extension of the income tax to foreign earnings are both introduced into the model (where the income tax distorts the choice of the length of education), these will enable the LDC to achieve the optimal solution in terms of equity-cum-efficiency, equality being achieved with maximum feasible *per capita* incomes.

Having then surveyed the major types of policy proposals, their major features and rationales, we now turn to a more direct focus on the tax proposals, organizing the different arguments now by each type of tax proposal rather than by specific objectives of the different proposals, and also examining some of the practical feasibility aspects of these proposals.

6   MORE ON ALTERNATIVE TAX PROPOSALS

We may distinguish between tax proposals that require DCs to bear the (immediate) tax burden and those that require taxing the incomes of the PTK immigrants' incomes in the DCs of immigration. Of these two major types of tax proposals, the former have received political attention from LDC spokesmen so far, but negligible attention from professional economists and scientists, whereas the latter have received little political attention to date but have instead been the subject of considerable analytical scrutiny from distinguished lawyers and economists while also receiving attention in documentation on the subject of the brain drain in international organizations such as the ILO and the UNCTAD, and in professional legal and economic journals in different countries.

DCs paying the tax

Taking the former kind of proposal first, we can immediately state the possible rationale therefore as *either* that the DCs ought to *compensate* the LDCs for the losses that the brain drain into DCs imposes on the LDCs, *or* that the DCs gain from the brain drain and therefore, regardless of whether there is any loss to the LDCs, they ought to share these gains (based on inflow of LDC nationals) with the LDCs who need developmental resources.

Of these two notions, the former (suggesting compensation for LDCs) would appear to be the main motivating force behind recent pronouncements of LDC spokesmen calling for a brain-drain-related transfer of resources/revenues by DCs. Thus, witness the following two sample statements:

> I would also like to propose the establishment of an International Labour Compensatory Facility (ILCF). It could be elaborated along the lines of the Trust Fund for Compensatory Facilities of the International Monetary Fund. The proposed Facility would draw its resources principally from labour importing countries, but in a spirit of solidarity and goodwill, other ILO members may contribute to it. The accumulated resources will be diverted to developing labour-exporting countries in proportions relative to *the estimated cost incurred due to the loss of labour*.[44]

> The Commission on Development recommends that, in order to *compensate* for the reverse transfer of technology, resulting from such exodus, amounting to several billions of dollars for the last decade, special arrangements including the possibility of establishing special funds, should be made to provide the necessary resources for strengthening the technological capabilities of the developing countries.[45]

However, given the controversy that surrounds the question as to the magnitude, if not the existence, of losses to LDCs in a meaningful and measurable sense, it would appear to be pertinent to rest the case for a brain-drain-related transfer of funds from DCs to LDCs *also* on the former moral rationale: namely, the gains by DCs from the influx of such a brain drain. That such a gain exists is generally conceded, national immigration policies on levels *and* composition having generally been dictated by national interest (except in the case of political refugees: a problem that must be kept distinct from the present problem of the brain drain).[46]

44. Cf. Address by the Crown Prince Hassan bin Talal of Jordan to the 63rd Meeting of the ILO, Geneva, 10 June 1977, page 8, italics inserted. Note the emphasis on 'compensation' and the notion of losses suffered by loss of manpower.
45. Cf. *Report* of the Contact Group on Industrialization and Transfer of Technology, CIEC, Paris, 14 May 1977; italics inserted.
46. The presumption that DCs gain from PTK immigration has recently been challenged by Dan Usher (1977), on the ground that the immigrants receive more from their share in public expenditures than they give up by way of taxes. However, his calculations are not persuasive and do not, in my judgment, undermine the plausible presumption that PTK immigrants, belonging generally to the DC groups that are subject to progressive taxation in DCs, are likely to be making a net contribution to, rather than a net claim

Whether such a DC contribution to LDCs would add to total transfers, or be a mere substitute for other aid flows, is a question that might be posed. It would seem that the substitution of one form of revenue transfer for another has been exaggerated. The presumption of LDC difficulties and DC gains is persuasive, and the moral case for DC revenue transfers based on these two presumptions is one that may find a sympathetic chord in the DCs; in this event, the substitution for other forms of aid may be correspondingly less probable since the moral (or other) case for other forms of resource transfers is surely not identical. It may also be noted that if the proposed tax on DCs is *coupled* with a tax to be borne by the PTK immigrants themselves – as *their* contribution to LDC developmental spending – the acceptability of the former and reduction in the substitutability of both together for other forms of resource transfers to LDCs may be increased.[47]

Taxing LDC PTK immigrants' incomes in DCs

The proposal to tax LDC PTK immigrants' incomes in DCs, as distinct from the proposal to get DCs to transfer resources (from general tax revenues) to LDCs, was originally suggested in 1972 by the present author (Bhagwati, 1972). It has subsequently been explored in depth in several writings by distinguished lawyers and economists, so that its rationales, revenue dimensions, legal and administrative implications, and political-cum-human rights aspects have been laid bare by intensive scrutiny.[48]

The different rationales, and associated implications for the format of the proposed tax, are therefore relatively easy to state. There are basically four different types of arguments that may be produced in justification of such a tax (all mentioned in our earlier analysis but now brought together with additional comments).

Rationale 1. One rationale is that the PTK immigrants ought to be taxed in order to compensate the LDCs for the losses that their migration entails, so that a fraction of their certain economic gains from the migration to DCs is utilized towards this purpose.[49] If the tax rate were to be chosen with reference to the losses, the LDC losses would have to be quantified and then divided up among the emigrants and, strictly speaking, since the losses will generally vary by the kinds of professionals one is

on, the DCs through the tax system; and hence the presumption of DC gain from PTK immigration can only be reinforced on this account.

47. This coupling has been suggested in Bhagwati and Partington (1976), and will be noted again below.

48. Cf. the numerous papers in Bhagwati and Partington (1976), Bhagwati (1976), Hamada (1977) and Balacs (1976), to mention some of the major writings on this proposal.

49. Note again that the 'losses' go well beyond the 'educational costs' that are referred to in the popular writings on the brain drain.

considering, the tax rate would presumably be different by each such class of PTK migrants. However, there is clearly no reason to go in for such 'fine tuning' here any more than with other classes of tax policies already in place in different countries; and it would seem perfectly appropriate to treat the rationale as leading to a general case for such a brain drain tax, with the tax rate actually chosen (at some single figure or schedule) on grounds of practicality and administrative convenience.

Rationale 2. A related, but distinct, rationale on moral principles may be that, even if there is no LDC loss involved, the migration makes these LDC nationals significantly better off and that the LDC tax network should enable the LDCs to tax these incremental incomes, on broadly progressive lines, for LDC social purposes. This moral argument does involve an extension of the progressive tax principle, normally applied to domestically based nationals, to nationals in other countries: and it should be noted that it does not run contrary to 'acceptable' norms of tax behaviour, either.[50]

Rationale 3. Leaving 'moral obligations' aside, there is also the 'purely economic' argument that the extension of the LDC tax schedule to PTK emigrants' earnings in DCs would achieve global efficiency in the sense of permitting optimal allocation of the world supply of PTK manpower. While this argument (already stated earlier) does imply that different LDC emigrants should pay *differential* (own-LDC-related) taxes in DCs, again one could consider for administrative convenience that the actual implementation be undertaken with *identical* supplementary tax rates being applied to all LDC PTK immigrants.

Rationale 4. Then again another rationale runs in terms of the proposed tax providing the LDC with a policy instrument that enables the LDC to achieve greater efficiency and/or equity in the presence of the PTK emigration. These arguments were considered in section 4. Note that they also imply that the tax rates levied could differ by PTKs of different classes and different LDC nationalities. However, on grounds of administrative convenience again, the tax rates could be standardized across all categories of the brain drain.

Rationale 5. Finally, recall the argument that the imposition of such a tax on the PTK immigrants to supplement the LDC developmental spending could have the 'externality' effect of stimulating additional DC transfers of resources to the LDCs, by demonstrating that LDCs were willing to tax the incomes of their own professionals for development in a self-help fashion instead of merely exhorting DC nationals to undertake the tax burden of financing LDC development through increasing aid flows.

---

50. Thus, see the paper of Oldman and Pomp in Bhagwati and Partington (1976). They do note, however, that for a number of reasons the countries that extend their taxation to incomes earned by nationals residing abroad is very small.

M

TABLE 17.2 Estimates for US, Canada and UK, and for all DCs[a,b]

Item	US	Canada	UK
Period over which the stock of professional LDC immigrants is considered. (Tax estimates relates to the terminal year of the period)	1961–71 (11 years)	1963–72 (10 years)	1964–72 (9 years)
Total stock of PTK immigrants in the terminal year of the relevant period[a]	208,309	37,653 (+ 18,315, if certain other professional and technical occupations are not excluded)	60,759 (New Commonwealth and alien LDCs)
Average after-(DC)-tax annual incomes of different categories of immigrants	Physicians, dentists and surgeons $23,807 Scientists (natural) $11,415 Nurses $5987 Engineers $12,550 Technicians $7807	Physicians and dentists $20,734 Nurses, medical and dental technicians $5692 Scientists (natural) $13,438 Teachers $7582 Engineers $13,794	Doctors and dentists £2,280 Nurses £1,025 Scientists (natural and social) £2,050 Teachers £1,823 Engineers £2,054
Estimated total revenue from a 10 per cent tax on disposable incomes of professional LDC immigrants	$231.7 million (1971)	$52.0 million (1972) (of which $13.6 million from certain excluded professions)	£10.8 million (1972) (8.6 million New Commonwealth + 2.2 million alien)

Total revenue (1972):[b] Sum of US, Canada and UK	(≥) $300 million
Total revenue (estimating additional 25 per cent revenue from EEC, Australia and other DCs)	(≥) $375 million
Total UN receipts[c] (total revenue + equal matching contributions by DCs from general revenues)	(≥) $750 million
Total UN receipts (1976) (1976) (additionally allowing for taxation of international civil servants and inflation during the 1970s)	(≥) $1 billion

Notes: The definitions of LDCs in the three studies is broadly comparable, except for negligible differences. However, the definitions of PTK or professional manpower are probably not that close. For Canada, the *detailed* estimates refer only to a subset. However, the *revenue* estimate has been calculated also for the full PTK set, and this is the $52.0 million figure (of which $13.6 million represents the professions omitted by the authors from their detailed calculations, these professions being listed in their Table 1). For definitions of professional immigrants used in the Balacs and Gordon paper for the UK, given the data availability there, see their paper.

[a] Numbers in the original surveys by Bhagwati and Pelcovits on the US, by DeVoretz and Maki on Canada, and by Balacs and Gordon on the UK.

[b] An exchange rate of $2.5 to £1.00 has been used. The Canadian dollar has been simply treated as identical with US dollar.

[c] Estimates of the total receipts that the UN would get if the tax proceeds were matched by an equal contribution by DCs from their general revenues.

Sources: Bhagwati and Pelcovits, appendix to Bhagwati and Dellalfar, for US; Balacs and Gordon, for UK; DeVoretz and Maki, for Canada, all from Bhagwati and Partington (1976).

If any or all of these rationales were indeed to be accepted in order to tax LDC PTK immigrants' incomes in DCs, what order of magnitude would the resulting revenues be, and what legal, administrative and other issues might be raised?

Revenue implications. As it happens, the revenue question has been treated at some length for the USA, UK and Canada and estimates made on the basis of fairly careful calculations. Table 17.2 contains the resulting estimate of US$500 million per annum in 1976 on the following assumptions: (i) the tax would be levied at the rate of 10 per cent on net-of-DC-tax incomes for a period of up to 10 years only after formal migration; (ii) the US categorization of PTK migrants would be (more or less) followed; and (iii) international civil servants would also be included in the coverage.

The figure rises to US$1 billion *if* a *matching* DC contribution of revenue (*à la* first tax proposal, discussed above) is made. Note also that the revenue would be both untied (by source or project or commodity) and fully grant-equivalent, and hence worth about 2 to 3 times as much as an 'average' aid flow of the same nominal magnitude.

Legal and administrative problems. The tax proposal has been extensively explored by lawyers. It would appear that, for it to be constitutionally feasible in the USA, it will have to be a tax imposed by LDCs and collected by DCs, the same being enshrined in a multilateral treaty.[51] There is presumably no constitutional barrier in the UK but the tax, if it is to be acceptable, may have to be imposed by all DCs of immigration so that the constitutional requirements of the US would automatically define the requirements of implementing the tax altogether.

The administrative problems of collection by DCs need not be particularly great. The treaty would make the collection legally enforceable by DC courts whereas the cost of collection need not be large if the existing tax forms can be negligibly amended to identify the immigrants who are eligible and to allow for their supplemental contribution (though the investigative costs to avoid evasion would have to be added separately).

Political problems. Three political problems have been identified. In the UK, a problem with the tax may be that it might be popularly regarded as discriminatory by race since the LDC immigrants would be predominantly from the 'coloured' races.[52] A multilateral treaty, and the fact that the LDCs themselves would be active in seeking such a treaty, ought to counter this notion, however. Identically, it might be feared that such a tax would alienate the professionals from their own LDCs if they resent having to pay the tax. Again, the fact that the payment would not

51. See the Oldman and Pomp analysis in Bhagwati and Partington (1976), and the summary by Partington as well.
52. Cf. Partington's piece on the UK in Bhagwati and Partington (1976).

be identified with the action of any particular LDC, but would be part of a multilateral treaty and conventions, ought to deflect this possible resentment away from 'source-of-origin' LDCs.

Finally, in the DCs generally, the tax may be regarded as being in violation of 'human rights'. In this regard three rebuttals are necessary. First, the tax (unless one is considering exceptionally steep rates that are obviously not going to be acceptable) surely is *not* a quantitative restriction and, in fact, would only cut into some of the very definitely large economic gains made by the migrants. It is, quite definitely, *not* a violation of any fundamental human rights any more than the DC taxation of such migrants, which also reduces their incentive to immigrate, is. Second, the truly *effective* restriction on the free migration of human beings from LDCs to DCs is *not* any LDC policy, present or proposed, but the enormously restrictive *immigration* quotas practised by the DCs themselves. Hence, one might be excused for regarding with some amusement, if not derision, the notion that DCs ought to find such a tax unacceptable on human-rights grounds! And a cynic may well regard such complaints, coming from DC intellectuals and policymakers, as self-serving and better addressed to the immigration authorities of their own governments. Finally, Professor Frank Newman has examined the 'law' at the United Nations on human rights and would appear to argue that a multilateral treaty embodying the proposed brain drain tax could be found consistent with the existing conventions and understandings.[53]

Optimal format of the tax. It would appear that the optimal format of the proposed tax would have to be one where it is levied by LDCs, collected by DCs, and preferably the proceeds are routed through a United Nations agency (such as the UNDP) to the LDCs for developmental spending. The recipients among the LDCs ought to reflect, to a predominant extent, the LDC-nationality composition of the PTK migrants (or else these LDCs would not have interest in supporting the tax, especially as it would cut inward remittances to some extent) while at the same time *not* being tied *completely* into it (or else one would run into opposition from DCs that object strongly to certain LDCs politically and would not wish to be a party to collecting revenues for them). This is, in fact, the format in which the tax has finally been proposed for adoption by the international community in recent writings by its proponents.[54]

These dimensions of the optimal format of the proposed tax can hardly be overemphasized; for the Pakistan government's attempt in January 1976 to tax the foreign earnings of its nationals 'migrating' to the Middle East, *à la* the proposal to tax the brain drain, had to be hurriedly

53. Cf. his contribution in Bhagwati and Partington (1976).
54. Cf. ch. 1 in Bhagwati and Partington (1976); and Bhagwati (1976c,d,e).

withdrawn. It created great resentment against the government, was seen to be unenforceable, and cut into remittances because the potential assessees felt that the remittances might provide a clue to their foreign incomes. Clearly, none of these difficulties would attend a tax where the DCs would collect and enforce the tax which was levied under a collective treaty by DCs and LDCs.

Other alternatives

Finally, two alternative tax and quasi-tax proposals may be listed here, neither of which need to be confined to PTK immigrants.

First, it may be suggested that the United States' practice of tax-exempting contributions to approved charities be extended to contributions made by LDC immigrants to LDCs. Thus, a considerably more lenient ruling for eligibility may apply for contributions by these immigrants to LDC-based developmental and charitable organizations or to international agencies for spending in LDCs.[55] This would seem like a splendid idea and need not be considered to be an alternative to the tax proposals just discussed. This proposal does imply, of course, that there is a small dent being made in the DC revenues by granting such exemptions: therefore, this would appear to be a proposal that mixes private initiative with DC tax-revenue contributions.

Second, following the recent US practice of taxpayers being allowed to earmark part of their taxes to finance Presidential elections, one might suggest that LDC immigrants in DCs be allowed, in the same way, to earmark (up to, say, 30 per cent of their) taxes for routeing to a designated UN agency for developmental spending.

7   MAJOR CONCLUSIONS AND RECOMMENDATIONS

The preceding analytical review of the principal policy-oriented issues related to the brain drain leads to several conclusions of which the few major ones may now be sketched here.

(1) It is possible to measure the imputed capital flows implicit in the flow of PTK manpower from LDCs to DCs. The task of imputation is by no means insuperable and can indeed be undertaken by international agreement on a set of conventions on several procedures and concepts which are no more 'strange' or difficult than those that statisticians and economists continually deal with in arriving at, for example, national income accounts on a standardized basis.

---

55. This suggestion is contained in the paper by Oldman and Pomp in Bhagwati and Partington (1976, p. 182).

(2) Such a measure of imputed capital flows is useful in providing a balanced picture of the capital flows currently taking place between DCs and LDCs, by deflating appropriately the otherwise inflated figure of DC capital flows to LDCs that are often cited as evidence of the benefits derived by LDCs from DCs.

(3) The appropriate measure for any international compensation mechanism, on the other hand, must relate to LDC losses from the brain drain. These can be defined only with complexity and are likely to be only broadly convertible into monetary figures. However, they can form the basis for compensatory tax revenues collected from *either* DCs (from their general tax revenues) *or* the LDC PTK immigrants themselves (as a supplementary tax on their DC incomes).

(4) Rationales can be developed, however, for both these types of taxes (i.e. on DCs *and* on the immigrants) *without* reference to LDC losses.

(5) The rationales for the supplementary tax on LDC PTK immigrants' incomes in DCs, moreover, rest not merely on moral arguments but also on grounds of global allocative efficiency *and* on grounds of LDC equity and efficiency goals. Besides, the revenue implications of such a tax are substantial. Such a tax is therefore worth considering seriously as part of the overall reform of the international economic order under way with the *NIEO* negotiations.

(6) Such taxation can usefully be combined with matching contributions by DCs from their general revenues.

(7) Moreover, it can be supplemented by two DC tax-policy changes: greatly liberalized permission to PTK LDC immigrants to make tax-deductible contributions to LDC-based charitable organizations *and* to international agencies for developmental and social spending in LDCs; *and* permission to PTK LDC immigrants to designate up to a large fraction of their DC tax payments for routeing to LDCs *via* a specially designated internationl agency such as the UNDP.

REFERENCES

Arrow, K. J. (1973): 'Higher education as a filter', *Journal of Public Economics*, 2.
Balacs, P. (1976): *The Brain Drain and Reverse Transfer of Technology* (Geneva: UNCTAD).
Berry, A. and Soligo, R. (1969): 'Some welfare aspects of international migration', *Journal of Political Economy*, September–October.
Bhagwati, J. N. (1972): 'The United States in the Nixon era: the end of innocence', *Daedalus*, 101(4), pp. 25–48.
—— (1973): 'Education, class structure and income equality', *World Development*, 1, pp. 1–36; reprinted in volume 1, ch. 11.
—— (ed.) (1976a): *The Brain Drain and Taxation: Theory and Empirical Analysis*, vol. II (Amsterdam: North-Holland).

—— (1976b): 'The brain drain', *International Social Science Journal*, 28(4), pp. 694–712.

—— (1976c): 'Taxing the brain drain', *Challenge* (July/August).

—— (1976d): 'Brain drain', *Zeitschrift der Österreichen Forschungsstiftung für Entwicklungshilfe*, 2.

—— (1976e): 'L'exode des Cerveaux', *International Social Science Journal* (UNESCO), 18(4).

—— and Hamada, K. (1974): 'The brain drain, international integration of markets for professionals and unemployment: a theoretical analysis', *Journal of Development Economics*, 1(1); reprinted in *EIET*, vol. 2, ch. 47.

—— and Partington, M. (eds) (1976): *Taxing the Brain Drain: a Proposal*, vol. I (Amsterdam: North-Holland).

—— and Rodriguez, C. (1976): 'Welfare-theoretical analyses of the brain drain', in Bhagwati (1976a); reprinted in *EIET*, vol. 2, ch. 46.

—— and Srinivasan, T. N. (1977): 'Education in a "job-ladder" model and the fairness-in-hiring rule', *Journal of Public Economics*, 7; reprinted in *EIET*, vol. 2, ch. 49.

Fields, G. (1974): 'The private demand for education in relation to labour market conditions in less-developed countries', *Economic Journal*.

Grubel, H. and Scott, A. (1966): 'The international flow of human capital', *American Economic Review* (May).

—— and Scott, A. (1977): *The Brain Drain* (Ontario: Wilfrid Laurier University Press).

Hamada, K. (1977): 'Taxing the brain drain: a global point of view', in J. Bhagwati (ed.), *The New International Economic Order: the North-South Debate* (Cambridge, Mass.: MIT Press).

—— and Bhagwati, J. (1975): 'Domestic distortions, imperfect information and the brain drain', *Journal of Development Economics*, 2(3); reprinted in Bhagwati (1976a) and *EIET*, vol. 2, ch. 48.

McCulloch, B. and Yellen, J. (1975): 'Consequences of a tax on the brain drain for unemployment and income inequality in less developed countries', *Journal of Development Economics*, 2(3); reprinted in Bhagwati (1976a).

Pryor, F. (1968): *Public Expenditures in Communist and Capitalist Nations* (London: Allen & Unwin).

Spence, M. (1973): 'Job market signalling', *Quarterly Journal of Economics*, 87.

US House of Representatives (1974): *Brain Drain: a Study of the Persistent Issue of International Scientific Mobility*, Subcommittee on National Security Policy and Scientific Development of the Committee on Foreign Affairs, September (Washington, DC: Government Printing Office).

Usher, D. (1977): 'Public property and the effects of migration upon other residents of the migrants' countries of origin and destination', *Journal of Political Economy*, 85(5), pp. 1001–21.

18

Taxation and International Migration: Recent Policy Issues

Among the recent developments in the theory of international migration and its implications for public policy have been questions relating to the exercise of tax jurisdiction by nation-states over migrants, that is, people who move across national borders. These questions raise not merely narrowly economic but also moral-philosophical and sociological issues since they involve in an essential way the relationship between individuals and nation-states.

More precisely, the questions that have been addressed are the following. First, should nation-states exercise income tax jurisdiction over citizens abroad, quite regardless of status concerning residence and 'migration', as indeed the United States and the Philippines do, or should they follow the 'schedular' system, under which taxation is levied by residence qualification alone? Second, should nations that receive foreign nationals as migrants of one kind or another share the tax revenues raised from such nationals with the countries of origin? Both these questions have immediate policy relevance, and they have been aired recently in international forums dealing with North–South relations, on which they bear.

The first section of this paper is addressed to developing the historical background of these questions. The second section then considers the first issue, tax jurisdiction of nation-states *vis-à-vis* migrants. The third section addresses the second issue, revenue sharing by receiving countries with the sending countries.

1   A BACKWARD GLANCE

The *economic* issues in taxation and migration have their counterparts in the political issues that have surfaced about the voting rights of migrants in receiving countries. As economic analysts have raised the issue whether migrant citizens ought to be allowed total exemption (as with the schedular

From Barry R. Chiswick (ed.), *The Gateway: US Immigration Issues and Policies* (Washington, DC: American Enterprise Institute, 1982), pp. 86–103. The original text has been edited; in particular pp. 92–4 and 101–2 have been substantially abbreviated to avoid repetition of material in Chapter 17 in the present volume.

tax system) from the tax jurisdiction of their countries of nationality – whether there should be 'representation without taxation' – political analysts have raised the reverse question in regard to voting. Should not immigrant aliens who have retained their foreign nationality get the right to vote in their countries of residence – should there be 'taxation without representation'?

Interestingly, there are important and telling contrasts between these two sets of questions that are worth spelling out. The political analysts have come to their question by observing the plight of the unskilled *Gastarbeiters*, guest workers, in western Europe, captured beautifully by Brusati in his poignant portrayal of the Italian immigrant workers in Switzerland in *Bread and Chocolate*. Can one protect the civil rights and liberties of these immigrants if they do not have the vote in a pluralistic democracy?[1] While the United States has seen no public or even academic debate on this issue of granting voting rights to (legal) aliens, the European scene has witnessed rapid progress on the issue, with Sweden granting the vote in local elections to foreign workers in the general election of September 1976.[2]

The neglect of this issue in the United States is an interesting phenomenon that may be explained by the following factors. First, the exploitation of gastarbeiters, who are legal, unskilled aliens, has not been a major factor on the US scene, where the economic-need criterion for setting immigration quotas has played a much more limited role. The adoption of the familial and refugee-oriented immigration system in regard to importation of labour, with a largely uncontrollable border, has spawned a large illegal immigration, where the question of voting rights runs into the immediate and insuperable objection that the presence of the illegal immigrants is not formally sanctioned by the society. The emphasis therefore shifts much more to questions such as the illegals' rights to social security, health, and safety and the implications for census counting and apportionment of seats and federal funds. Second, the legal immigration has largely been familial and refugee oriented, and the economic-need criterion has been applied for the rest mainly to let in the PTK (professional, technical, and kindred) type of brain-drain immigrant, these being categories that (except possibly in the case of large-scale refugee inflows from one source, as with the boat people) plainly do *not* undergo the kind of exploitative experience that the gastarbeiters have experienced. Third, the naturalization process in the United States is probably much easier than in western Europe, so that the anomaly of having resident

1. The grant of the vote is only a necessary, not a sufficient, condition for the guarantee of such rights, of course.
2. See the account of it in Hammar (1977). Professor Hammar, of the department of political science in Stockholm University, is engaged in a detailed study of this election. The question of following Sweden's example is being actively considered in Norway as well.

aliens and foreign workers in one's midst without giving them the right to vote in elections at any level does not appear to be particularly grotesque, if it enters US consciousness at all.

Taxing LDC migrants

By contrast, the tax and international migration questions have come up historically, almost entirely in the context of highly *skilled* migration. They are couched in completely general economic and moral-philosophical terms. Specifically, the present policy formulations derive from my early proposal to tax the brain drain. The specific, and all-too-critical, dimensions of the proposal in regard to who would levy and collect the tax were not spelled out in the original proposal, as briefly stated in a *Daedalus* paper (Bhagwati, 1972). The basic notion that the migrants themselves would pay the tax levied on their incomes in the country of immigration, was, however, spelled out in a later paper in *World Development* (Bhagwati and Dellalfar, 1973). The proposal must be distinguished sharply from the notion of an 'exit tax', which would presumably be levied prior to the migration and, at least in the versions that became current when the Soviet Union was flirting with the notion of its implementation, related to expended educational costs embodied in the migrant. Moreover, the proposal was addressed to highly skilled migrants from the LDCs (less developed countries) to the DCs (developed countries). The underlying moral rationale at the time was twofold. The highly skilled migrants from LDCs ought to make a contribution to LDC development through such an institutionalized tax system. These migrants improved their incomes greatly from the migration across the immigration barriers of the DCs, and it was arguable that, in several cases, their being allowed to migrate resulted in some difficulties – with losses for the countries of emigration. Both these reasons applied with much less force for the DC-to-DC migration; hence the proposal was confined only to the PTK-style immigrants from LDCs to DCs.

A subsequent conference on the proposal, organized at Bellagio, Italy, 15–19 February 1975, with the Rockefeller Foundation's support, led to further variations on the theme, largely as a result of the international-tax-legal, human rights, and constitutional-legal input provided by distinguished lawyers present at the conference. In particular, such a tax on immigrants, which would be levied differentially on them and not on natives of the countries of immigration, could not be levied without considerable difficulty, if at all, by the United States, as it was most likely to be challenged successfully in the US courts. No such constitutional barrier would present itself in the United Kingdom, where the Parliament is effectively sovereign in a world of an unwritten constitution. Since the tax would apply to immigrants predominantly from the non-white part of the commonwealth, the possibility of tax legislation being enacted to support the levy of such a tax on PTK-type immigrants was remote, however, in a context of increasing racial tension.

LDCs' taxes on own migrants: early developments

The feasible format for such a proposal, therefore, seemed to be one whereby the LDCs would themselves levy the tax on their migrants. This, in turn, raised the question, Could such a tax be *collected* by the countries of emigration? If it could not, the responsibility for collection would be entirely that of the levying country. This raises questions, in turn, as to the feasibility of such a tax system. At the time, therefore, I summarized the situation concerning how the tax might be collected by the DCs:

> Thus, if the brain drain tax is to be levied by LDCs, there would be insuperable practical difficulties unless the DC governments were to agree to utilize their revenue agencies to collect it. To do this, clearly a treaty between the DC and the LDC in question would have to be executed making it legally feasible to have the tax enforced in the DC. A major problem that would then be raised by such bilateral treatymaking, which in turn would have to be consistent with domestic constitutional law and with public opinion, is that in this bilateral version the proceeds of the tax would be routed *individually* back to LDCs of origin: for it is easy to imagine several LDCs to which the public opinion in the United States, for example, would condemn the making of such a bilateral 'contribution' and which would therefore be likely to be reflected in the judicial view of the matter if the enforceability of such an LDC-tax were challenged in the courts.
>
> It was thus clear that if for no other reason than purely on the ground of making the tax as judicially acceptable as possible, a *multilateral* version of it would be the best, and this meant that the preferred version of the original *World Development* paper, i.e., the version under which the United Nations would get involved in the brain drain tax in an essential way, became the optimal version of the Bellagio discussions as well.
>
> Given the fact that the LDCs could in principle exercise tax jurisdiction over their nationals abroad, it could then be proposed that the LDCs would delegate their jurisdiction to the United Nations. At the same time, the DCs would make their contribution to the implementation of the tax by offering the UN their collection facilities. The tax revenues would then be

routed to the UN, to be disbursed in the LDCs en bloc, according to the usual criteria for developmental spending as followed by UNDP [United Nations Development Programme] for example. The rationale behind the tax implementation would consist of two arguments, in order of their importance:

(1) Firstly, one would assert the moral principle that, in a world of imperfect mobility, those few who manage to get from LDCs into DCs to practice their professions at substantially-improved incomes ought to be asked to contribute a fraction of their gains for the improved welfare of those left behind in the LDCs; this would effectively be extending the usual principle of progressive taxation across national borders.

(2) Moreover, since there is a widely-held presumption, based on several sound arguments and embodied in numerous international resolutions, that the brain drain creates difficulties for the LDCs, it would also constitute a simple and rough-and-ready way for the emigrating professionals to compensate the LDCs for these losses. In fact, the moral obligation to share one's gains with those who are unable to share in these gains would be reinforced if these others were also hurt by one's emigration.

The tax proposal, in routing the proceeds via UN to LDCs en bloc, would also affirm the growing trend on the part of the LDCs, since the 1964 UNCTAD [United Nations Conference on Trade and Development] Conference, to emphasise their Third World 'bloc', thus enabling them to go beyond their nationalist confines in this act of international policymaking. Furthermore, by bringing together the LDCs and DCs into joint action under UN auspices, it would also affirm the interdependent nature of the present world economy and the need to have coordinated and cooperative action among LDCs and DCs.

It is also clear that, once the tax is made into such a 'global', cooperative policy measure, it could be embodied into a treaty or charter at the United Nations, with the DCs and LDCs signatories to it. This would then increase significantly, and almost certainly guarantee, the possibility of its being politically acceptable, and simultaneously being able to withstand challenges to its constitutionality in the United States.[3]

---

3. Bhagwati (1976, pp. 21–2). Note that as argued in the second section, my views on this question have changed a great deal, and I now favour a different format that does not involve the DCs in any essential way at all.

Fundamentally, therefore, the version of the tax proposal that I emerged with from Bellagio – though not by any means with many converts to the proposal at the conference – was a rather complex one, and one that was unlikely to secure ready following. Nonetheless, the basic idea of taxing the highly skilled migrants in some manner, consistent with the exercise of their accepted income tax jurisdiction by LDCs on their nationals abroad but in a fashion which would make such a policy implementable, found a niche in the concerns at UNCTAD in its work on the brain drain or what it rather describes as the reverse transfer of technology. Thus, at the expert group meeting, 27 February to 7 March 1978, the Group of 77 in the draft recommendations urged the DCs to

> render assistance, either on a bilateral or multilateral basis, to developing countries which exercise or wish to exercise their internationally recognised jurisdiction to tax their citizens abroad under a 'global' tax system; such assistance could take the form either of 'tax collection assistance' and/or of access to information. (Bhagwati, 1976)

Moreover, at the last UNCTAD conference in Manila, the DCs and LDCs adopted, in a rare unanimous affirmative vote, resolution 102(V), which for the first time introduced a reference to tax policies in the context of international migration, providing UNCTAD with a mandate to investigate further the range of questions that have been opened by the proposal to tax the brain drain.[4]

2   OPTIMAL FORMAT OF THE LDC TAX: LATER DEVELOPMENTS

The Bellagio version of the tax derived its specific features from the desire to make the *collection* of the LDC tax by DCs acceptable to the DCs.

---

4. Paragraph 9b of this resolution, adopted on 30 May 1979, states:

Developed countries which admit skilled migrants should:
(i) consider assisting, within national constraints, in the building up of better data on skilled migration and explore ways of systematizing the collection and dissemination of statistical information;
(ii) consider, in the light of the in-depth study by the Secretary-General of the United Nations and his decisions referred to in paragraphs 5 and 6 above, measures related to social security, pension rights, currency control, tax policies and remittances with a view to encouraging contributions to the economic development of developing countries, recognizing that the issues mentioned above involve more than the problems of development and the reverse transfer of technology and recognizing existing national competences in these matters.

Multilateralization of the tax followed, as I have quoted above, from this factor: with the LDCs utilizing the United Nations etc. for this purpose.

However, subsequent analysis has revealed that one may be able to cut through these complexities, as indeed one must if the tax idea is really to be implementable.

The breakthrough came from the realization, and further reflection on the fact, that the income tax system of the United States exactly reflects the original moral rationale of my tax proposal: all citizens are taxed, not just citizens resident within the United States. This 'global' system of income taxation that assesses taxability on the basis of citizenship is also practised by the Philippines and (in theory, though without attempt at enforcement) by Mexico, a point of some interest to those who seek to understand how historical or geographic affinity can diffuse ideas. By contrast, the European countries, and their ex-colonies such as India, have adopted the 'schedular' income tax system that exempts citizens from taxation by several rules of residence, making residence the essential criterion for taxability.[5] Therefore, the collection of such a tax by LDCs themselves, using say the Filipino system of tax collection, may well be possible, especially with DC cooperation at the level simply of bilateral-treaty-covered supply of some tax information. I shall return to this aspect towards the end of this paper. However, I turn initially to the political aspects of the tax from the viewpoint of the LDCs themselves.

The political issue

The question of taxability of citizens abroad raises a basic political issue that must be addressed. If one asserts that the citizens abroad are part of the society that the nation-state represents, it follows that the national tax system ought to embrace them as well. Questions of equity of tax burden, for example, would have to be defined by reference to a population set that cannot properly exclude the citizens abroad. The retention of nationality is often regarded as an index of such membership in the society represented by the nation-state; hence the justification for the adoption of the global tax system based on citizenship.[6] The nature of modern migration is such that the retention of ties to one's nation of origin or emigration is far more common than before. Among the gastarbeiters, this is fostered by the ghettos and the threatening prospect of forced return to one's country. Among the PTKs, the to-and-fro travels promoted by cheap fares and the fact that countries such as the United

5. For a detailed description, see Oldman and Pomp, 'The brain drain; a tax analysis of the Bhagwati proposal', in Bhagwati (1976).

6. In fact, Barry R. Chiswick has reminded me that military conscription is a form of 'tax' that *is* widely levied on nationals living abroad by those countries that do have a draft.

States do not discriminate seriously between natives and resident aliens seem to be among the factors that encourage people to retain their ethnic identities and ties to their own nations. The modern migrants seem to be a part, not merely in a legal-citizenship but also in an emotional and cultural sense, of the societies of their countries of emigration.[7]

Today the economist must construe national welfare as being defined over a population set including the citizens abroad. This precept both runs counter to the concentration in many theoretical studies on the welfare of those left behind and also implies that, in some cases where the immigrants have close affinity to the countries of both immigration and emigration, it would be necessary to (double) count them in the population sets of both countries for analysing the welfare impact of international migration.

Certainly, it is a perfectly appropriate procedure to adopt the global tax system, since the equity issues defined in the context of income taxation should be discussed without excluding the migrants from the population. As Senator Proxmire has reportedly emphasized, there is no reason why the Americans living in Parisian luxury ought not to pay their share of the US tax burden and leave it to be borne only by the proletariat in Detroit. This particular viewpoint has led some public finance theorists such as John Wilson, Koichi Hamada and myself, and James Mirrlees recently to explore the impact of migration on the trade-off between equity and efficiency in the Atkinson model (where the trade-off arises because the income tax is collected to redistribute income for equity but affects efficiency by distorting the choice to educate oneself as more education means more social-and-private income) and in the Mirrlees model (where the efficiency distortion comes from distortion of choice between income and leisure instead). Hamada and I also explored in the Atkinson model the precise implications of the schedular system on distorting the efficiency choices concerning education and migration since it virtually absolves those who work abroad from the domestic tax net (Wilson, 1980; Mirrlees, 1982; Bhagwati and Hamada, 1982).

Taxing firms, not individuals

One interesting complication from the viewpoint of US policy – also confronting the countries wishing to use the global system of income taxation – is that the incidence of the tax on citizens abroad may fall on

7. For some empirical evidence on the fact that many gastarbeiters respond to sociological inquiries by saying that they would not accept naturalization in the receiving countries even if they were to settle permanently in these countries, see the studies cited in Rosemarie Rogers (1978). For the migrants in the highly skilled categories, see Glaser (1978). Glaser's United Nations Institute for Training and Research project underlines similar conclusions. Of course, refugees may be an exception to the point being made. However, it is not unknown for refugees to return to their home countries en masse as the causes that led to their exodus are reversed, as in, for example, Bangladesh and Uganda.

firms rather than on the nationals. This may happen when, say, a US construction firm tenders for a contract in Saudi Arabia. That firm must pay its US citizen-employees salaries that are going to be the net of whatever tax liability follows from the global system, if those employees are to be induced to go abroad. Its rival French firm does not have to pay the French income tax on its French employees; this puts the French firm at a competitive advantage. This is, strictly speaking, a harmonization issue. Since harmonization is not possible as there are two different tax systems involved, the answer is plain. The General Agreement on Tariffs and Trade should allow countries on the global tax system to subsidize their firms' tenders for external contracts, to restore 'true' comparative advantage. In short, given two different objectives, one needs two instruments. The equity issue requires the use of the global tax system; the efficiency-in-comparative-advantage issue requires an appropriate export subsidy (related to the use of national labour).

The two models, however (the equity model that favors the global tax system and the external-comparative-advantage model that favours the schedular system given its existence in rival countries), have played a tug of war in the United States in an endless struggle through most of this century; the construction lobby (occasionally joined by citizens abroad, of course) asks for the adoption of something close to the schedular system, and the equity-minded legislators such as Senator Proxmire ask for the opposite. The exact debate has centred around section 911 of the tax law that states the allowable exclusions from gross taxable incomes of US citizens abroad (not in employ of the US government). Christine Heckman of the Harvard Business School has provided the following capsuled version of the seesaw between restricting and liberalizing this exclusion, that is, between getting closer to or away from the scope of the global system. The period up to the Tax Reform Act of 1976 provides the flavour of the two sets of forces and how, in fact, from a full-fledged global system at the inception, the United States moved to the schedular system in 1926 and then, prompted by equity considerations, gradually wound its way back to the global system, with exemptions whose scope has been changed and debated ever since.

History of 911

(1) *1900–42:* Up to 1925, extreme pressure was placed upon Congress by American industry to develop incentives for industrial expansion overseas. There was concern that many foreign companies doing business in the US had unfair advantages, since foreign nationals generally were exempt from domestic taxes in their home countries. In 1926, as a result of these concerns, the first foreign earned income

exclusion law, Section 213(b)(14), was enacted by Congress. The law permitted US overseas workers to exclude or subtract from their gross taxable income 'amounts derived and received from sources (business conducted) without the United States'; that is, if a person had lived 6 months or more abroad, income earned while residing abroad was exempt from taxation. Up to that time, overseas workers had only been allowed to credit against their US tax bill their income taxes paid to foreign governments.

In 1928, Section 213(b)(14) was designated Section 116(a). Senator Reed of the Senate Finance Committee moved to repeal this section in 1932. He contended that while the intent of the law was to promote American business activity abroad, a foreign income exclusion was not necessary to help foreign trade, and was unfair to citizens resident in the US, who received no similar privilege. Senator Reed further argued that the intent of Section 116(a) had been distorted. He cited cases where American ambassadors, ministers, and officials of the foreign service had used the law to sidestep income taxes. After some debate and compromise, Section 116(a) was amended so that income paid by the US government or its agencies could no longer be excluded or deducted.

> (2) *1942–51:* Continued concern with abuses of the law led Congress to amend Section 116(a) again in 1942. As amended, Section 116(a) applied only to 'an individual citizen of the US, who established to the satisfaction of the Commissioner, that he was a bonafide resident of a foreign country during the entire taxable year', not just 6 months.
> (3) *1951–62:* Residency requirements were again changed in 1951. The amended law established that any income earned overseas by a US citizen could be excluded if (s)he resided abroad for 17 out of 18 months. This part of the law was designated Section 116(a)(2). The purpose of the change was to encourage citizens 'to go abroad on a short term basis to increase technical knowledge in backward areas'.

At the same time another subtle addition to the law, Section 116(a)(1), clarified when certain foreign residents could actually start to claim income exclusion.

In 1953, the amount of excludable income under Section 116(a)(2) was limited to a $20,000 ceiling. In 1954, Section 116(a)(1) became Section 911(a)(1). Section 116(a)(2) was renumbered and subdivided: the residency portion of Section 116(a)(2) became Section 911(a)(2). The provision for a $20,000 ceiling became Section 911(c).

(4) *1962–1975:* In 1963, Congress changed the ceiling to an income exclusion of $20,000 for the first 3 years of residence and $35,000 for each year thereafter. The $35,000 limit was lowered in 1965 to $25,000. By 1975, Section 911 provided for the following:

(i) A $20,000 income exclusion for those who had resided in a foreign country for 17 out of 18 months. A $25,000 exclusion for those with 3 or more years of bonafide residency.

(ii) Permission to subtract the exclusion off the top of earned income; the remainder was the income base for tax calculations. In effect this left the taxpayer in a lower rate bracket than would otherwise have been the case.

(iii) A tax credit on all foreign income taxes paid. However, those claiming the US standard deduction could not claim the foreign tax credit. For example, a worker earning $50,000 paid $230 under the 1975 law. While the 1975 law was more stringent than earlier laws, many felt it still gave unfair tax advantages to a special class of Americans.

(5) *The 1976 Tax Reform Act:* The sweeping Tax Reform Act of 1976, which changed several areas of US tax laws, also altered Section 911 significantly. Among other things, the amended Section 911 provided that:

(i) A maximum of $15,000 could be excluded from earned income by a US citizen who was present in a foreign country for at least 17 out of 18 months. An employee of a charity was allowed a $20,000 exclusion.

(ii) Taxable income remaining after the application of the earned income exclusion was subject to tax at higher-bracket rates. Specifically, the remaining income was to be taxed at the rate applicable before the exclusion.

(iii) Any foreign taxes paid on the $15,000 of excluded income could not be included as part of the foreign tax credit.

(iv) Individuals applying the standard deduction could also apply foreign tax credits.

Thus, as a result of this legislation the exclusion was dropped to $15,000 and income was taxed at higher rates. Under the 1976 law, the family earning $50,000 would now pay $4,214.

As originally enacted, the 1976 Act made the changes effective for the 1976 tax year. However, the sweeping changes in Section 911 brought about by the Tax Reform Act elicited such strong negative reaction that Congress delayed the effect of the 1976 law for one year until January 1, 1977. Further delays were later effected to allow a thorough examination of opposing views of the law. These delays were supported and publicly encouraged by the Treasury. In February 1978, the law was still dormant and scheduled for further debate.[8]

The controversies over what the exemptions ought to be, for schooling, cost-of-living differences, etc., have preoccupied the US legislators and the US Treasury. The adoption of the global tax system is fully consistent with the adoption of treaties to prevent double taxation, so that the net burden of the migrant increases under this formula *only* insofar as the tax liability under the tax system of the country of nationality exceeds the liability in the country of residence/work. For many LDCs, however, this will be the case, even with generous exemptions *à la* present US provisions.[9]

US role in adoption of global tax system by LDCs

Since this conference is focused on US policies concerning immigration, presumably into the United States rather than from it, the question of the appropriateness of the global system, as it applies to US citizens abroad, is not a relevant issue. The issue, however, of whether the United States ought to shift to the schedular system has certainly come to the forefront again, with the controversies over the 1976 act. What concerns me here rather is the *reverse* possibility, namely, the possibility that some LDCs might wish to move to the *global* system. The United States is involved in this issue in so far as the question of tax collection and enforceability may come up in this connection.

At Bellagio, where the lawyers argued that the tax be levied by the LDCs, the question of enforceability and collection was raised and discussed with concern. A possibility considered was to somehow use the DC tax agencies to collect the tax for the LDCs. It may be possible to employ techniques that do not make such demands on the DCs. In particular, the Philippines

8. Heckman (1980, pp. 327–44). The material cited in the text is based on the section entitled *Historical Perspectives*.

9. Compare Hamada (1977, Table 1). Note also that the Filipino system, described later in this paper, adds a small tax of 1 per cent, 2 per cent, or 3 per cent on the taxable earned incomes of Filipinos abroad, *on top of* whatever they pay to foreign governments, thus avoiding raising the double taxation complication by keeping the Filipino tax assessment extremely moderate.

operates a simple version of the global tax system, by utilizing three graduated rates of 1 per cent, 2 per cent, and 3 per cent, which are applied to the earned income of the Filipinos in the United States, for example. The tax is estimated and collected annually by making annual passport renewal conditional on submission of the W-2 form and the tax payment. This system, generally described as the one-two-three system in the Philippines, seems to have worked well. At the rates levied, it does not seem to have led to any significant change in nationality to escape the implied tax burden.[10] It is not beyond the scope of normal bilateral treaties between nations, for the United States to extend assistance by way of information (and systematizing thereof if necessary) on legal, foreign nationals from a particular country in its midst and perhaps even investigating the possibility of sharing tax information between countries to make such collection efforts by LDCs easier and more efficient. That, in fact, is the burden of the recommendation of the UNCTAD expert group meeting.

3   SHARING 'NORMAL' TAX REVENUES

The proposal to tax the incomes of the migrants themselves as with the adoption of the global system, must be distinguished from the idea of getting the developed countries of immigration to share income tax revenues (raised from the migrants simply by the routine taxation apparatus) with the less developed countries of origin. The rationale for such migration-related taxation on developed countries can be provided in two alternative ways. Either the developed countries ought to compensate the less developed countries for the losses that the brain drain imposes on them or, since the developed countries gain from such migration, they ought to share these gains (based on the inflow of less developed country nationals) with the less developed countries that need development resources, regardless of whether there is any loss to the less developed countries.

The latter moral argument reflects a Nozick type of ethical criterion: The human resources 'belong' to the less developed countries and the division of the gains from their working in the developed countries ought rightfully to be shared with the former. This form of argument, evidently not utilitarian in nature, holds if it is contended that these human resources would have been utilized less profitably or not at all in the less developed countries.

10. Professor Richard Pomp has conducted an extended study of the Filipino one-two-three tax system as a consultant to the World Bank and presented his report on it to the Ford Foundation Conference on Taxation of Citizens Working Abroad, in New Delhi, 4–9 January 1981. This paper indicates that the tax collection problems are not insurmountable, even though quite difficult.

Thus, by bilateral or multilateral tax treaties, the United States could agree, for example, to share tax revenues that it earns from the PTK nationals of less developed countries on the basis of some formula.[11] There is legal precedent for such tax sharing, of course. The revenues from taxing the French workers in the canton of Geneva, for example, are shared with the French principalities from which the workers come. Again, the proposal to have the developed countries share their tax revenues with the less developed countries of nationality/origin fits in well with the notion that the less developed countries are self-reliant. These revenues are, after all, paid by their own talented and skilled manpower, which constitutes their 'natural resources'. Their taxes may well be utilized partially to redistribute to the poor in their own countries of nationality rather than fully to redistribute to the poor in the countries of their residence.

I have focused only on two major types of *international* tax issues that have been raised recently in the literature on international migration from LDCs and are still relatively unfamiliar in American literature. The first issue, concerning the exercise of income tax jurisdiction by nations over their nationals abroad, does not directly concern the United States as far as immigrants to the United States are concerned. As already discussed, the LDCs can do this entirely by themselves in principle. The role of the United States, however, in terms of policy accommodation would be to undertake bilateral tax treaties facilitating the flow of information in order to ease the task of tax collection by these countries on their nationals in the United States. The second issue, on the other hand, involves *sharing* tax revenues, pro rata in some agreed fashion to the number of highly skilled migrants. This would involve United States tax policy much more directly, of course.

From the viewpoint of the United States, its *internal* tax policy has ramifications also for issues that have recently come to the forefront and are more familiar on the academic scene, the rights of illegal aliens to federal and local tax-funded benefits being one of them. These are specific to the United States, and of considerable relevance indeed.

REFERENCES

Bhagwati, J. N. (1972): 'United States in the Nixon era: the end of innocence', *Daedalus*, 101(4), pp. 25–48.
—— (1976): *The Brain Drain and Taxation: Theory and Empirical Analysis*, vol. II (Amsterdam: North-Holland).
—— and Dellalfar, W. (1973): 'The brain drain and income taxation', *World Development*, 1(1).

11. The ways in which this can be done have been discussed in Pomp and Oldman (1979).

—— and Hamada, K. (1982): 'Tax policy in the presence of emigration', *Journal of Public Economics* (August).

Glaser, W. (1978): *The Brain Drain: Emigration and Return* (Oxford: Pergamon Press).

Hamada, K. (1977): 'Taxing the brain drain: a global point of view', in J. Bhagwati (ed.), *The New International Economic Order: The North–South Debate* (Cambridge, Mass.: MIT Press).

Hammar, T. (1977): 'The first immigrant election', *International Migration*, 15 (February/March).

Heckman, C. (1980): 'Taxation of Americans working overseas', in R. S. Carlson *et al.* (eds), *International Finance: Cases and Simulation* (Reading, Mass.: Addison-Wesley).

Mirrlees, J. (1982): 'Migration and optimal income taxes', *Journal of Public Economics* (August).

Pomp, R. D. and Oldman, O. (1979): 'Tax measures in response to the brain drain', *Harvard International Law Review*, 60 (Winter), pp. 1–60.

Rogers, R. (1978): 'On the process of international migrants integration into host societies: a hypothesis and comments', Migration and Development Study Group, Discussion Paper no. C/78-16, MIT.

Wilson, J. (1980): 'The effect of potential emigration on the optimal linear income tax', *Journal of Public Economics* (December).

19

The Decision to Migrate: a Survey

1 INTRODUCTION

The decision to migrate has been the subject of analysis by social scientists with diverse backgrounds. Demographers, sociologists and, in recent times, economists have been examining the problems of both internal and international migration, embracing furthermore skilled and unskilled migrations.

From the viewpoint of the focus on this conference, on Brain Drain and Taxation, it is clear that the most interesting aspect of these studies is the sensitivity of the migrant flows to economic rewards; as is, in fact, clearly stated by Lucas and Psacharopoulos in their papers for the conference prior to their econometric exercises directed at precisely this issue. It should therefore be of interest to review here many of the principal results of *earlier* research in this area of inquiry, directing our attention to the findings on economic motivations, and in particular, to the quantitative estimates of the corresponding elasticities of migration flows in regard thereto.[1]

Furthermore, the main focus of our review will be on systematic, econometric analyses, although some nod will be made in the direction of sociological inquiries with potential interest for economists. This narrowing of our review is appropriate since we intend to provide the reader with the perspective required to come to grips with the conference papers of Lucas and Psacharopoulos, DeVoretz and Maki and Bhagwati and Dellalfar on the Bhagwati-type income tax, where the effect of the proposed tax on yields would depend on the elasticity of the migration

---

1. Note however that the economists' studies do not refer exclusively to what might be regarded as 'economic', as distinct from 'non-economic', factors. Thus, for example, in some of the studies on international migration, factors such as 'professional opportunities' are considered; though few of the econometric, as distinct from questionnaire, studies have managed to use anything except what may be regarded as strictly economic factors.

Written with Paul R. Krugman, from J. Bhagwati (ed.), *The Brain Drain and Taxation: Theory and Empirical Analysis*, vol. II (Amsterdam: North-Holland, 1976), pp. 31–51. The conference referred to in the paper was held at Bellagio, 15–19 February 1975, on the subject of taxation in the context of international skilled migration. The papers were eventually published in two volumes: Bhagwati and Partington (1976) and Bhagwati (1976).

flows with respect to the narrowing of the net-of-tax wage differentials between LDCs of origin and DCs of destination.[2]

Our survey will divide the studies reviewed by two major categories, internal and international migration, treating the former in section 2 and the latter in section 3.

2   INTERNAL MIGRATION

We review here 14 econometric studies on internal migration. At the outset, however, it would be useful to state the principal *qualitative* findings on the explanatory variables that seem to emerge from this research.

Principal qualitative findings

Note initially that demographic research appears to have found that migration tends to follow 'economic opportunity'. There is dissension as to the relative importance of wage differences and of job openings; however, both questionnaire-type and statistical evidence lend support to the view that wage rates matter. Furthermore, migration tends to go to areas of high 'urbanization' (though it is not clear, from Bogue (1969) for example, that this effect is considered independent of income as urbanization increases with income). Finally, educated people appear to be more mobile than the uneducated.

These explanatory variables, i.e., wages, education, and urbanization, also turn up in the 14 econometric studies, though there is additional attention paid to variables such as 'distance', and to defining the dependent variable more carefully. By way of summary classification of the findings of the signs of the coefficients, we have put together Table 19.1. The studies use different dependent variables, as clearly indicated in the appropriate headings to each subset of Table 19.1; thus, a distinction is made between studies dealing with gross flows (a), net flows (b), and destination of the migrants (c). Two studies, Sahota (1968) and Gallaway *et al.* (1967), have two models each and hence appear twice in the listing. Finally, note that in each case the question is the effect of a variable on migration from i to j.

---

2. The sociological and demographic studies, which we mainly ignore, appear to rely essentially on a framework analysing migration in terms of 'push' and 'pull' factors, with little recognition of the fact, apparent to any trained economist, that it is generally futile to ask which blade of the scissors cuts the paper. While therefore it is relatively easy for the economist to reinforce his customary sense of superiority *vis-à-vis* these other social sciences by examining the sociological and demographic literature in this area, it is at the same time good to know their findings. The economist reader should find it useful to see for himself the review of these findings in Bogue (1969, ch. 19), as also to consult Parnes (1954), though we briefly report on these in the next section.

TABLE 19.1   Signs of coefficients in 14 econometric studies

(a) Studies of gross flows

Author	Country	Income in j	Income in i	Edu-cation in j	Edu-cation in i	Urban in j	Urban in i	Distance
Sahota	Brazil	+	−	+	−	−	+	−
Beals, Levy and Moses	Ghana	+	−	−	−	+	+	−
Greenwood	Egypt	+	−	+	−	+	+	−
Levy and Wadycki	Venezuela	+	−	?	?	+	−	−
Greenwood	India	+	−	0	0	+	+	−
Gallaway, Gilbert and Smith	US	+	−	0	0	0	0	0
Vanderkamp	Canada	+	+	0	0	0	0	−

(b) Studies of net flows (measured in out direction)

Author	Country	Income	Edu-cation	Urban
Sjaastad	US	− [a]	−	−
Raimon	US	− [a]	0	0
Schultz	Colombia	− [a]	+	0
Bowles	US	− [b]	0	0
Gallaway, Gilbert and Smith	US	− [b]	0	0

(c) Destination of migrant

Author	Country	Income differential	Education differential	Urban differential	Distance
Sahota	Brazil	+	−	+	−
Greenwood	US	+	+	+	−

Notes: For details on the studies, see the discussion in the text. In each case, the question is
what effect a variable has on migration from *i* to *j*. If a variable encourages migration
from *i* to *j*, it receives a + sign; if it discourages, it receives a − sign; if the effect is
indeterminate, a ? is used. A zero indicates that the variable was not considered in the
study.
[a]Income in region considered.
[b]Differential between income in region and in some other region.

Note first that there is complete unanimity on the effect of income on migration to a region.[3] No study here (or anywhere, as far as we can tell) has ever found a perverse effect of destination income on migration. There is also near unanimity on the effect of origin region income, which deters migration; only Vanderkamp (1971) dissents, and we should note that he used only income as an explanatory variable, whereas others used other factors which are surely not independent of income. Hence it is not unlikely that the reason for the discrepancy is that Vanderkamp has found dM/dY while others have found $\partial M/\partial Y$.

Results on education are generally ambiguous. This is not surprising, since the measure of education deployed is educational attainment of the population, which can be argued to have contradictory effects: (1) education is a public service and thus an opportunity which should attract migrants; and at the same time, (2) educated people are more likely to migrate. Furthermore, there are problems of simultaneity. If a region is attractive to migrants, it may (because of differential mobility) tend to have above-average education. This would generate a positive relationship. On the other hand, an abundance of educated people may make a region unattractive for other educated people, etc. Perhaps we should regard it as a vindication of theory that where theory has nothing to say, neither do empirical results.

To say that the effect of education on migration between regions is ambiguous, however, is not to say that the effect of education on the propensity to migrate is unknown. Two studies, those of Bowles (1970), on the US South, and of Levy and Wadycki (1974), on Venezuela, were able to determine the effect of education on the *responsiveness* to other factors, and both found that responsiveness to economic factors increased with education.

The effects of urbanization are a little clearer, but not much. By and large, migrants appear to have a preference for urban areas over and above the income associated with such areas. Urbanization in the origin region, however, is of less certain effect. Again, two arguments can be made, with opposite implications: (1) potential migrants are less likely to leave regions which have been urbanized to their satisfaction; and (2) urbanites are more likely to be well informed about opportunities elsewhere.

The last column of Table 19.1 lists the effect of distance on migration, which is negative – and quite large – wherever tried. Sjaastad (1962) has argued that the effect of distance is too large to be explained solely by cost, and that social and cultural factors should be allowed as an explanation. However, Sahota (1968) carried out a calculation of the cost of moving, which turned out to be substantial. At the same time, Levy

3. In some cases, 'income' is a wage or present discounted value measure. Differences in concepts will be discussed later.

and Wadycki (1974) found educated migrants to be much less affected by distance than others.

These are the principal qualitative conclusions to be drawn from the studies. We will return later to the question of the quantitative significance of income and other factors. But first we give a brief summary of each of the articles. This makes tedious reading, but it is necessary as the studies are in many cases not comparable, but have differences which can be resolved by comparing what they are doing. In particular, researchers investigating the determinants of migration have occasionally been less than careful about both the choice of a dependent variable and the interpretation of results. Some apparently contradictory results have not been about the same thing: some studies have used specifications that are demonstrably incorrect.

Review of individual papers

To systematize our review of the individual papers, we have grouped the papers under three headings. There are 7 studies of gross migration flows, 5 of net flows, and 2 of the destination decision of migrants. Under each heading, we will then discuss what we would expect to find and, in light thereof, review the individual papers.

Gross flows between regions. We have here five studies of LDCs which base their estimates of migration on national censuses in which people were asked where they were born and classified by region. The other two studies in this group are based on somewhat different questions for the US and Canada. The 1960 US census records where people lived in 1955. For Canada, actual annual flows from 1947 to 1966 were calculated from requests for family allowance transfers. Despite the difference in the measures, we will refer to all kinds of gross flow from i to j as M_{ij}, and introduce other symbols: M_i for total migrants out of i, P_i and P_j for the populations of the two regions, and D_{ij} for the distance.

Now, it would seem evident that M_{ij} is likely to be an increasing function of P_i, the population of i, since that is a measure of the number of potential migrants. On the other hand, one *could* argue that the relationship may not be one of strict proportionality because, as with most economic phenomena, at *some* scale of P_i, for say skilled people in any one occupation (e.g., economists), there may be too few people for any one of them to feel that they can interact efficiently, and hence a large proportion would want to migrate, whereas, at a much larger scale, there may be a crowding effect leading to disproportionately more people wanting to migrate; so that we may have the typical U-curve phenomenon here. Nonetheless, a reasonable approximation may well be to treat the phenomenon as one of proportionality, thus implying that M_{ij}/P_i is the appropriate dependent variable in counting gross flows.

Allowing then for the population effect thus, it is clear that we would expect M_{ij} to be larger if: (i) region j is the more desirable; (ii) region i is the less desirable; and (iii) the people of region i are the more prone to migration.

Factor (i), relating to the region of destination, yields variables which can be expected to have relatively unambiguous signs, of course. On the other hand, factors (ii) and (iii) both relate to the region of origin and can clearly yield common variables which pull in contrary directions, as we have already had occasion to note. A way out of this difficulty would be to deflate M_{ij} by M_i. Then one could work with destination variables only to explain the shares of different j's in the emigration from a given i. This deflation was used by Sahota (1968) and Greenwood (1969), but with a serious flaw in specification which we presently note. Yet another cross-sectional approach could be to sum all the flows into j and treat $\Sigma_i M_{ij}$ as the dependent variable and only the destination variables as the independent variables.

We may now turn to the econometric studies of gross migration flows, beginning with five that yield elasticities and ending with two that yield more qualitative results.

(1) *Sahota* (1968) studied data on state of birth and state of residence as reported in the Brazilian census of 1950. He estimated log-linear equations explaining migration by males in two different age groups.

Sahota did not deflate M_{ij} by the population of either state of origin or state of destination. Nor did he include either population as an explanatory variable. This is rather puzzling, and is nowhere justified; its effect on the results is not clear. As explanatory variables, Sahota used a large number of characteristics of the states, and the distance between them. Distance had a substantial negative effect. His income variable was the wage rate in some regressions, and the level of *per capita* income in others. The elasticity of migration with respect to income in the destination state ranged from 1.82 to 2.25; in the origin region it had a negative sign, ranging from -0.77 to -1.69. Other variables are reported in Table 19.1.

(2) *Beals, Levy and Moses* (1967) used the same kind of data from the 1960 Ghana census. The dependent variable was expressed as M_{ij}/P_i, and explained using a log-linear specification. Their explanatory variables included average labour income, population, the fraction who had attended school, and urbanization for both regions. Since population of i appeared on the right-hand side of the equation, the (partial) relationship between M_{ij} and P_i was not restricted to strict proportionality.

The elasticity of migration with respect to home population was significantly greater than one in all regressions; the elasticity with respect to destination population was less than one. No explanation is offered for the latter result; as for the former, they suggest the effect of 'the assured presence of friends of similar background'; presumably they are arguing, then, that Ghanaian regions represent cultural units.

Income in i and j had a negative and positive sign, respectively, and ran from -1.4 to -2.3 for Y_i, from 1.4 to 2.7 for Y_j.

(3) *Greenwood* (1969) carried out a study based on the 1960 Egyptian census which was essentially identical to that of Beals, Levy, and Moses. Using state-of-birth, state-of-residence data from the census, he estimated a log-linear function on M_{ij}, with population of i and j, wage rates, educational level, and urbanization as explanatory variables. Like the previous study, this paper estimated a coefficient on origin region population significantly greater than one, although the coefficient on destination region population was not significantly different from one. Wage rates had the expected signs, with elasticities of 0.651 for destination and -1.406 for origin.

(4) *Levy and Wadycki* (1974) used a similar technique on migration in Venezuela. The principal differences were that M_{ij} was disaggregated by education level, and the econometric techniques were relatively sophisticated. Once again, population of origin region had an elasticity significantly greater than one, except for those with a secondary education or more; for those with less than a secondary education, population of destination had a coefficient significantly less than one. Wage rates, as usual, had the expected signs; for migrants with a secondary education, the elasticity of migration with respect to origin wage ranged from -1.68 to -3.35; the elasticity with respect to destination wage was about 2.

The most important result of this study was that the educated are less deterred by distance and more responsive to differences in wage rates than the less educated.

(5) *Greenwood* (1971), in another paper, estimated the effects of distance, income, and urbanization on rural–urban and urban–urban migration in India (based on the 1961 census). His dependent variable was $M_{ij}/P_i P_j$: i.e., he implicitly accepted the 'gravity hypothesis' for this paper. Income, urbanization, and distance were the explanatory variables. For rural areas the effect of income on migration was positive for both region of origin and destination; for urban areas, the effect of origin income was, as usual, negative. Elasticity of migration with respect to destination income lay in the range 1 to 1.5.

These five studies are all somewhat similar, and show remarkable similarity in some results. In particular, the elasticity of migration with respect to destination income generally lies between 1.0 and 2.5. As further evidence, Sahota cites a similar elasticity, in Sjaastad's (1959) unpublished thesis, of 1.52. These are the only really comparable numbers in the migration literature; as we will discuss later, they are not exactly what we might want to assess the likely response of migration to policy changes, but there really is nothing better available.

There are two more studies of gross migration flows, which are not really comparable to the previous five, except for some qualitative effects.

(6) *Gallaway, Gilbert and Smith* (1967) studied US migration based on the 1960 census. Their dependent variable is M_{ij}/P_i. The explanatory variables were the arithmetic differentials in *per capita* income and unemployment, and distance; the article did not consider P_j's effect on M_{ij}. Although income and unemployment had the right signs, little of the variance in migration was explained. They did not express their results in elasticity terms, so the relative importance of income here is difficult to judge.

(7) *Vanderkamp* (1971) studied migration flows between Canadian provinces, as measured by requests for family allowance transfers. His dependent variable was $M_{ij}/(P_i + P_j)$, which does not have any obvious rationale. The results are again not expressed in elasticity terms. Income and distance were the only explanatory variables; the coefficients on income in both origin and destination areas were positive, but larger for the latter.[4]

Net flows out of (into) a region. There are fewer studies on net flows out of (into) a region and, given our interest in international migration where net flows are just not available in any systematic fashion, this is perhaps not too distressing. Of course, the concept of a net flow is not relevant from the viewpoint of individual decision-making. However, ultimately, policy must try to focus on net flows and hence the following five studies are worth reporting on, if for no other reason than that we are interested in policy issues.[5]

(1) *Sjaastad* (1960) studied the percentage gain (loss) in a state's population from 1940 to 1949 due to in-(out-)migration, for the 'lower 48' US states. Independent variables were *per capita* income, farm population, rate of growth of income, educational level, etc., used in linear regressions. The main result was that income encouraged net in-migration; the results are not easily expressible in elasticity terms, but Sjaastad argues (p. 53) that the effect of income, though significant, is quite small. He also got a uniformly positive coefficient on education, which he argued was the result of an identification problem since educated people are more mobile; states experiencing in-migration tended to have high levels of education.

4. It should be noted that Vanderkamp spends much of his paper discussing return flows, which will not concern us here.

5. A major problem with interpreting net flows is that net figures can be very misleading if care is not taken about what is being added up. For example, the substantial net migration out of the US South since World War II is the difference between a large outmigration of unskilled labour and a smaller immigration of highly skilled labour, so that in some sense migration out of the South is greatly exaggerated by the net figure. Also, the analysis of net migration can sometimes be subject to identification problems, as will be seen later in our discussion.

(2) *Raimon* (1962) used similar data from the 1950s for the US, in a straightforward study. He found that states with above-average income tended to experience net in-migration; and that there was a high rank correlation between net in-migration and either *per capita* income or average earnings per worker.

(3) *Schultz* (1970) studied net migration out of rural areas of Colombia. He found an elasticity of migration with respect to the rural wage rate of about -0.5. The percentage of population aged 10–14 with a primary education was positively related to out-migration; however, the percentage educated in the age group 5–9 had the opposite effect.

(4) *Bowles* (1970) applied a 'human capital' approach to differential migration of age–income–race groups out of the US South. His principal explanatory variable was the estimated present value of the income to be gained by migration. The specification allowed the effect of this variable to change with age and education; separate analyses were run for blacks and whites. He found that: (1) migration was positively affected by the discounted earnings stream; (2) the effect of this stream increased with education and decreased with age; and (3) blacks were more likely to move than whites, but less responsive to economic incentive.[6]

(5) *Gallaway, Gilbert and Smith* (1967), in the second part of their paper, used as a measure of net migration between US states the expression $[M_{ij}/P_i - M_{ji}/P_j]$. They then took as observations only the flows in a direction in which it is positive, regressing them on income and unemployment differentials. This is rather puzzling but they nonetheless got the 'expected' positive coefficient on income.[7]

Migrants' choice of destination. We mentioned above that it might be a good idea to use M_{ij}/M_i as a dependent variable, because it would eliminate those effects on M_{ij} which reflect effects of the propensity to migrate in i. The following two studies did use that variable.

(1)*Sahota* (1968), in the second part of his study of Brazil, regressed (M_{ij}/M_i) in a log-linear equation on differentials in income, wages (i.e., Y_j/Y_i, W_j/W_i), etc. Income had the expected effect, but with a greatly reduced elasticity. He also had a simultaneous model in which migration and wage rates were simultaneously determined, with the resulting elasticity with respect to wages lying between 0.10 and 0.15.

But in the event, these results cannot be accepted because the equation is mis-specified. Let $m_{ij} = (M_{ij}/M_i)$. Then Sahota has $M_{ij} = F(Y_j/Y_i$, etc), with $\partial F/\partial(Y_j/Y_i) > 0$. But this says that if, say, income in i should rise, the proportion of migrants going to any given destination (and thus to all destinations) must fall.

---

6. These results should be compared with those of Levy and Wadycki (1974) in the previous section.

7. A very low R^2 plagues their results and may be due to the omission of any variable representing population of destination.

(2) *Greenwood* (1967), in a study of interstate mobility in the US, uses the same formulation. And he makes the same mistake. Even so, his initial estimate of the elasticity of migration with respect to income in *j* over income in *i* is 0.54. Other explanatory variables are distance, education, urbanization, unemployment, and temperature, but not P_j. He introduces as an explanatory variable the number of persons born in state *i* and living in *j*, which he calls the 'migrant stock'; and, indeed, its influence is plausible. When it is introduced it is significant, and causes the income coefficient to fall to 0.16.

Conclusions to be drawn from the econometric literature

What may we conclude then from the foregoing review of the several econometric studies of internal migration?

Clearly, the one clear reason for migration that emerges is, as Ravenstein wrote long ago, 'the desire inherent in most men to "better" themselves in material respects'.[8]

The evidence that migration is influenced by economic incentives is so uniform and secure that, if anyone should argue for any particular case that economic gain has *no* effect, one should be skeptical; particularly where migrants do in fact gain economically from their move. Furthermore, such evidence as there is suggests that education makes people more responsive to the possibilities of gain from migration.

This is not to deny the importance of non-economic motives, which are clearly important; income variables rarely explain even as much as half of the variance in these studies, and social factors such as race or education (which can be regarded as much as a non-economic as an economic factor) seem to affect responsiveness to economic incentives. For the individual migrant, income considerations may be relatively minor, but the effect of income is nearly always significant and never perverse. So, if, as in some of the brain drain literature which we review presently, an author asserts that there is no relationship between the economic gain from migration and the decision to migrate, one may confidently assume that there is a prima-facie case that the author had only been flirting with his analysis, and not making the scholarly efforts necessary to test the hypothesis adequately.

How large is the effect of income on migration? One should beware of comparing results from widely different sources, but there does not seem to be any alternative. The largest group of more or less comparable studies is the group of studies of gross migration above. These generally imply an elasticity of migration with respect to destination income of, say, between 1.00 and 2.5. Presumably, for highly educated migrants the value should be on the high side of that range, in view of the results in the papers by Bowles (1970) and Levy and Wadycki (1974).

8. Quoted in Lee (1966).

Unfortunately, there is an upward bias in these estimates, since they involve only migration to one region out of several. Presumably an increase in income in *j* would draw migrants from *i*, not only from those who would not otherwise have migrated, but also from those who would have migrated to other regions. We might call these effects 'migration creation' and 'migration diversion'. Migration diversion is clearly of negligible interest for the brain drain problem; poor countries would feel no better if their doctors went to Britain instead of the US. Conceivably, an estimate of the diversion effect could be taken from a study using M_{ij}/M_i as dependent variable. For what it's worth, the studies by Sahota (1968) and Greenwood (1969) using it found relatively low elasticities of migration diversion with respect to income, i.e., around 0.5 or less; but those studies were, as mentioned above, marred by a serious misspecification. If we subtract this figure from the estimates of total effect on migration, we end up with a migration creation elasticity of, say, 0.5 to 2.0 Needless to say, this range has been arrived at by making logical jumps which few would gladly share; but those familiar with the theory and policy of second-best, and those who believe that fiction founded on facts is superior to ignorance, could find these numbers of some use.

But, in using them for analysis of the international brain drain, we need to remember two additional caveats. (1) The differentials in incomes between LDCs and DCs are far more substantial than those built into the studies reviewed above. So the elasticities are estimated from data that fall into a range of observations which do *not* span the values that we are interested in. But the degree of extrapolation involved here is certainly not extraordinary, especially when one recalls that many economists can be found who will argue, for example, that surplus labour (in the sense of zero social marginal product to labour) is impossible at any factor endowment because the production function for agriculture, estimated from the observed range of values, is Cobb–Douglas. (2) Next, in the context of international migration of skilled labour, it is pertinent to remember that one is dealing with restricted access and queues, so that the elasticity of (actual) migration with respect to reduced wage differentials, thanks to a Bhagwati-type income tax, could well be significantly lower than the range indicated above.

We turn our attention now to precisely the issue of the migration of skilled manpower, chiefly from the LDCs to the DCs, and review the contributions in that area.

3 INTERNATIONAL MIGRATION: THE BRAIN DRAIN

Most of the many studies of high-level migration do a once-over-lightly on the motivations of migrants, doing no more than listing a number of plausible reasons before going on to policy questions. One report on a conference stated the reasons quite plainly: 'Statistical analyses and studies of motivation both require surveys and factual information. Policy recommendations, on the other hand, could be made on the basis of assumptions about statistics and motivations, and hence this part of the problem provided greater opportunity for discussion (Oldham, 1968, p. 17).

By and large, adequate data is lacking on migration itself, let alone on likely determinants. So in spite of the immense number of papers that have been written on high-level migration, only a handful provide any useful information about the decision to migrate. Before we turn to these, however, it would be useful to cite Scott's (1970) earlier and most useful review, which groups the reasons for skilled migration under four categories:

(1) *Income differentials.* This is straightforward enough. There are several points that have to be watched carefully, though. (i) It is the whole stream of earnings, discounted to the present in some way, that probably matters. Thus a figure for income at only one point, such as after 5 years of employment, while useful, may be misleading. (ii) If, as is common, there is unemployment among high-level people in the home country, a comparison of earnings if employed may lead to misleading ideas about the income to be gained from migration. (iii) *Per capita* income is not a very useful guide to earnings of professionals and scientists. As Psacharopoulos (1973, p. 132) has shown, the position of graduates of higher education in the wage structure varies considerably among countries.

(2) *Professional opportunities.* It is certainly reasonable to suppose that at least some people move because they cannot do what they would like in an LDC because of a lack of openings or sufficient diversity. Nobody really has any idea how important this is; but our guess is that it affects only a small number of people, but that these people may be exceptionally important.

(3) *Living conditions.* This includes everything from the political environment to the availability of peanut butter. One of the major findings of a UNITAR study (1973) was that members of ethnic minorities are especially liable to emigrate, presumably because of discrimination in the home country.

(4) *Working conditions.* Many scientists who emigrate give the availability of research facilities, libraries, etc., as a reason, and it must surely have some effect.

Scott had very little empirical evidence on which to draw. At this point, a few years later, there is more evidence, though still not very much. We have altogether six studies, of which only the first two were available to Scott: (1) a book by Rudd and Hatch (1968) on British students;

(2) a first rate book by Myers (1972) on foreign students in the US; (3) a book by Psacharopoulos (1973) on returns to education generally; (4) a major sociological UNITAR study by Glaser (1973); (5) a useful article by Kao and Lee (1973) on Taiwan students in the US; and finally, (6) a rather unsatisfactory piece by Sen (1971) on immigration into the US. We will go through these studies, looking for evidence on various motives, then try to sum up what the present state of knowledge is.

(1) *Rudd and Hatch* (1968) devote one chapter of their book on 'graduate education and after' to a study of Britons with graduate education going overseas. Their analysis consisted purely of a questionnaire, which was answered by 678 one-time graduate students who had been overseas at some time between 1957 and 1966. It is a little difficult to be sure what respondents meant, but what is interesting is that many of those who were still overseas in 1966 gave reasons that appear to relate either to income or, less often, to openings and opportunities. (A diehard economic determinist might argue that 'dissatisfaction with Britain' means income, too.)

(2) *Myers'* (1972) work is an extremely helpful piece of research, making the most of inadequate data. What Myers is out to explain is the non-return of students educated in the US, what he calls the 'untrained brain drain'. There are four major parts to his analysis.

(i) The rate of non-return (as measured by statements of intent) for a number of countries was calculated; the rate of non-return was defined as non-returnees as a proportion of students in the US. Myers used the multiple regression technique to analyse variation in this rate, with two interesting results: the rate of non-return was positively associated with *per capita* income in the home country and was negatively related to 'political elitism'. Note that the rate of non-return is not an appropriate measure of the magnitude of brains being drained: if France sent only 2 students to the US, and they both stayed, France would have a 100 per cent non-return rate. So there is not necessarily anything perverse about the finding on income. It may even make sense *a priori*, since poor countries may not be able to provide adequate education at home, whereas if a European comes to the US to study it may be only because he has a particular reason for wanting to be in the US.

In any case, Myers found that the conditions of financial sponsorship were the principal determinant of differences in non-return rates among countries.

(ii) In order to get an index of manpower loss, i.e., brains drained, Myers divided the number of non-returning students by the total number of students at home and abroad who were citizens of the home country. This new index turned out to be essentially unrelated to either *per capita* income or political factors, which is interesting; at least this part of the brain drain seems to afflict rich and poor alike.

(iii) Myers discussed at some length an unpublished study by Herve on non-return. Herve attempted to use an 'effective demand' model of decisions by students. He first calculated a regression equation relating the number of students *per capita* to *per capita* income; then compared actual to predicted values to arrive at a 'surplus' or 'deficit'. The idea was that the number of students a nation can employ depends on income; thus non-return should be related to surplus or deficit. One might argue that what Herve was actually doing was indirectly estimating the return to education in countries, since his surplus countries presumably should have had low earnings for college graduates, either because of competition driving down salaries or because of unemployment. In any case, the analysis did not work for all countries taken as a group, but if Latin America was deleted it did.

(iv) Finally, a questionnaire study was carried out on Peruvian students. They were asked to give, not merely intentions and reasons for their decision, but also estimates of their lifetime earnings streams in the US and Peru, and their subjective estimates of the relative cost of living. There were two surprising results: (a) according to the figures given by the respondents, the present discounted value of income in Peru would *exceed* that in the US; and (b) the comparison between the US and Peru was least favorable to the US for those planning to remain in the US. These results are hard to believe, and Myers was properly sceptical, arguing in particular that his respondents discounted the possibility of unemployment when judging Peruvian incomes.

Myers did not draw any firm conclusions from all this. He failed to find clear evidence that income matters, but argued himself that he was not able to test this properly.

(3) *Psacharopoulos'* (1973) book is concerned with returns to education generally, but in the course of the book, he arrived at two sets of figures which allowed him to carry out an analysis of the brain drain problem. These are: (i) estimates of rates of return to higher education for a number of countries (Psacharapoulos did not compute these himself, rather, he selected them from estimates made by others); and (ii) 'cross' rates of return, which were internal rates of return on the income stream which would be earned if someone were to be educated in a country, then migrate permanently to the US. For his dependent variable, Psacharapoulos worked with the number of professional, technical, and related (PTK) workers admitted to the US in 1969, dividing this by the number of students in higher education in the home country (using the latter, like Myers, as a proxy for the number of potential migrants).

In his first calculations, Psacharapoulos did not use these rates of return. Instead, he regressed migration on home country *per capita* income and distance, and duplicated the result of Myers in finding no significant effect. But he then pointed out, as mentioned above, that this was not surprising, since *per capita* income is a poor predictor of earnings of college graduates.

The estimation was then repeated, with log of migration explained by logs of the two rates of return. The elasticities with respect to cross and home country rates of return were, respectively, 1.563 and −1.072, both significantly different from zero. This is, as far as we can tell, the only estimate available on the effect of economic conditions on the migration of professionals (except for the results reported by Psacharopoulos and Lucas in their papers for this conference itself) and should therefore be treasured as one small candle in a vast darkness, whatever its faults. What is even more remarkable is that the size of the estimated effect is in the same general range as that which characterized the internal migration studies covered above.

Given a set of hard numbers, it would be pleasant just to accept them. But Psacharapoulos' work must be treated with some caution, for a number of reasons. (i) The sample is very small; the need for comparable data reduced the number of usable countries to 13. (ii) The rates of return to higher education are not calculated on a comparable basis; they are taken from a variety of sources, although Psacharopoulos did try to choose studies using similar definitions and techniques. (iii) The correct variables to use in a human capital analysis are not rates of return but present values; these cannot always be used interchangeably. Psacharopoulos presumably had to use rates of return because of data limitations. (iv) Finally, there is something which is not the author's fault, but inherent in the problem, and this is that none of his variables measures quite what we would like it to measure. Immigration of professional and technical workers, as measured by the US Immigration Service, is not really an accurate measure of how many brains the US has drained. The number of college students is not really a measure of potential migrants. And the rates of return are based on average figures for earnings by age and education in each country, whereas those who choose to migrate are probably neither typical of those in the home country with the same education, nor comparable to Americans with the same educational qualifications. (There is some indication that they may be more talented, on the average, than stay-at-homes in either country.)

(4) *Glaser's* (1973) mammoth study for UNITAR is based on a questionnaire, but the questionnaire was designed in such a way as to allow at least rudimentary statistical analysis. Some 20,000 people replied to a long, fairly specific set of questions. (The results reported by Glaser, however, are based only on the first 5500 replies.) Those questioned fell into three groups: LDC students currently studying in developed countries, professionals who had received overseas training and then returned ('returnees') and professionals who had not returned ('stay-ons').

Intentions were gauged by asking whether respondents 'definitely' or 'probably' would either stay or return. With the 'undecided' category, this gave a total of five categories. For many of the analyses, this ordinal variable was transformed into a cardinal variable by letting 'definitely return' = 2.0, 'probably return' = 1.0, etc.

The greater part of the analysis consists simply of cross-tabulations of intentions with various characteristics of migrants. These produced a number of interesting results, of which some are summarized below:

(i)   Members of religious, cultural, or ethnic minorities have a relatively high tendency to emigrate; a conclusion which had been suspected before, but never conclusively shown.

(ii) Contrary to some previous suspicions, there does not appear to be any systematic relationship between emigration and social class.

(iii) It appears that the least able students are the least likely to emigrate.

(iv) Respondents generally cited working conditions and professional needs as reasons to emigrate and personal relations as reasons to remain home.

After examining these cross-tabulations, Glaser carried out a more sophisticated statistical analysis; reasons named by respondents and intentions on migration were formed into trichotomous variables and compared using the statistic 'gamma'. The results of this analysis were that income, quality of jobs, and number of jobs were invariably strong reasons for migration. Opportunity to contribute to one's profession had strong association with migration decisions, but could work in either direction. Friends, family, and patriotism were associated with return. Professional needs turned out to be only weakly associated with the decision on emigration.

Also included was a brief analysis of the effect of income differentials on migration. Respondents were asked to estimate their income after five years of full-time employment at home or in the country of education. These figures were converted into dollars at official exchange rates. The intention to migrate was turned into a cardinal variable, from 1 = definitely return home to 5 = definitely emigrate, and regressed on the proportional gain in expected income from emigration. The estimated coefficient was significantly positive but, Glaser asserts, not very large (there are problems in deciding what is large); only a very small part of variance was explained ($R^2 = 0.033$).

Glaser's mammoth work will probably become a standard reference on motivations of emigrants, so some care should be taken to point out where it appears to be less than satisfactory.

(i) The cross-tabulations and correlations which make up most of the study do not show reasons for emigration; they show associations between the citing of reasons and emigration, which cannot be properly interpreted without some sort of causal model. If X and Y are associated, it may be because Y affects X, but it may also be because Z affects both X and Y.

It is odd that this problem is ignored, since the first chapter contains extensive strictures against confusing association and causation. In all fairness, though, Glaser's technique of grouping reasons into 'clusters' probably reduces the danger from this problem; but more analytical and empirical discussion of these issues (than is available in Glaser's work so far) is called for.

(ii) Because of this problem, Glaser really should have done one of two things: (a) cross-tabulate in more than two dimensions, which is probably the best procedure with ordinal data; but even with 20,000 respondents, any reasonable sized four or five dimensional cross-tabulations will start having empty or nearly empty boxes; or (b) used some sort of multivariate technique; it is not just that, as Glaser says, such techniques give better prediction; if such a technique is really appropriate, simple correlations will give biased results.

(iii) Because of this, we should hesitate to accept at face value the assessments of the relative importance of various factors, although it is not obvious in what ways they may be biased.

(iv) Finally, it is rather peculiar that, on the one hand, income-related questions such as salaries, quality and availability of jobs were among the best predictors of emigration; while on the other hand, the actual income differential explained very little variance. There may be several reasons for this. (a) The question asked of respondents was what they thought they would earn after five years of employment. This ignores both the problem of unemployment, which may vary widely among countries, and the differences in salary patterns by age in different countries (i.e., US salaries tend to start high and grow slowly, while in many countries salaries rise relatively rapidly with age). (b) The business of turning an ordinal into a cardinal variable leaves us uneasy. To illustrate, the quantitative meaning of, say, a shift from 'definitely' to 'probably' return is not clear. (c) The problems of purchasing power are difficult, but one would like a little more information. There is one problem that is particularly worrisome: respondents were asked for estimates of income after five years, in their national currency. How was inflation taken into account? To ask, say, a Brazilian for his income in five years, and convert it to dollars at *current* exchange rates, could overstate what he could earn in Brazil by a factor of two or three.

UNITAR will undoubtedly do some more detailed analysis on their incredible data bank. What Glaser has done so far is more a survey of the data and of the associations found in it than a serious analysis of the decision to migrate.

(5) *Kao* and *Lee* (1973) carried out what amounts to a miniature Glaser-type study of Nationalist Chinese migration to the US. They asked about 'propensity to stay in the US', scaled from 0 to 9, and a number of other variables which were either binary or integer-scaled. These were then

treated as cardinal variables in a number of linear multiple regressions. 'Satisfaction with the American way of life' and 'income satisfaction in the United States' were generally the most important. These are certainly not surprising results; they indicate that both income and non-economic motives matter, which is reassuring.

(6) *Sen*'s (1971) paper takes a cross-section of 47 countries and examines the relationship between various characteristics of a country and emigration of natural scientists, social scientists, engineers, and doctors to the US. He rejects the hypothesis that *per capita* income of sending countries matters, and finds the determinants of emigration to be the number of students in the field, and especially the number of graduate students in the US. This latter relationship is so strong that, in the case of doctors, it could not result even if every graduate students in the US stayed there, which leads Sen to suggest the possible importance of information flows. Unfortunately, little of this can be taken at face value for several reasons, of which we spell out a few here.

(i) Sen's result that income does not matter is based on the use of regressions which use presumably the PTK migrants by different categories deflated by total population in the origin country *or* the total number of PTK migrants, as an absolute number, as the dependent variable, while *per capita* income in origin country is used as the independent variable. For one thing, the use of total migrants is not advisable for reasons which should be apparent from our earlier discussion of the literature on internal migration. Moreover, even the use of the deflated migrants raises the question: why should the deflation with total population (rather than with the population of the PTK class of migrants being analyzed) be correct? Only a systematic examination of the correlation between total and PTK population, if any, and its extent, could indicate the kind of bias that such a deflating procedure would imply. Also, the unsuccessful use of income *per capita* as the independent variable should not be taken as tantamount to explaining away the role of 'economic' factors. Sen should have explored the success of variables such as present discounted values, or relative wage rates, as in the standard literature on migration. The implied rejection of economic motivation in Sen's results must therefore be taken with serious reservations; this is particularly so when we consider the more successful and imaginative use of immigration data in the 1973 work of Psacharopoulos and the work by him and by Lucas in the papers for this conference.

(ii) It is *not* correct econometric practice to take zero-order correlations, discard variables with low R^2, then do a multiple regression on those that remain. The correct way to it is to include all variables in the multiple regression to start with, and use *t*-statistics to test significance.

(iii) Nor is Sen's relationship between graduate students and immigration levels meaningfully assessed. To infer that this implies an information network whereby more graduate students lead to more information and hence to more immigration is to bypass the far more plausible hypothesis that both are non-causally associated for reasons such as the following. (a) Countries which produce a large number of, say, natural scientists would presumably have a large number of students in the field, which would presumably lead to a large number of students overseas as well as at home. And it would also presumably lead to larger emigration, if only because there would be more potential migrants. (b) Moreover, for countries with cultural ties to the US, the US would be a natural destination for both study and migration. If nothing else, the division of the Third World into francophone and anglophone areas would ensure some relationship between overseas graduate study and emigration.[9]

The casual econometrics of this paper merits it, at best, only a minor place in our inventory of useful contributions to the analysis of the brain drain and the associated identification of the variables that matter in the decision to migrate.

4   CONCLUDING REMARKS

The foregoing review of the literature on the decision to migrate is somewhat staggering in its implication that, despite the enormous amount written on the subject of the brain drain, we are forced to rely on the expedient of drawing analogies with a few studies of internal migrations and on literally no more than a mere handful of direct estimates [to be precise, three, of which two (Lucas and Psacharopoulos) have been prepared for this conference and ironically two are by one man]. What have we learned from them?

Starting with the analogy first: in the studies of internal migration, the elasticity of migration with respect to income at the destination was always positive, generally greater than one, never more than three. There was some evidence that highly educated people were more responsive to the possibility of income gains from moving than others. It is tempting to assume that international migration, which is more difficult both physically and psychically, has a lower elasticity with respect to income at the destination. But this does not follow; it is a confusion of the level of a curve – i.e., fewer people migrate abroad – with its slope.

The direct estimates are by Psacharopoulos. His earlier estimate explained migration by internal rates of return; and the elasticity of migration to the US with respect to such a rate was 1.5. This must imply a somewhat higher elasticity with respect to the wage, say 2.0. His later

9. The 'information flow' hypothesis itself is, of course, familiar in the migration literature and has been explicitly postulated, for example, in Greenwood (1967).

estimate, for the conference, uses wages directly, with an estimated elasticity with respect to the US wage of 0.543. Both estimates are based on small samples and imperfect data; taking this into account, they establish a range of reasonable values not too different from that found in the internal migration literature.

Does this allow us to put any bounds on the elasticity (ϵ)? The effect of income is surely positive, but it might be quite small for all we know; so we cannot really give any lower bound other than $\epsilon > 0$. At the same time, the only estimated value for the elasticity of migration with respect to income we have seen that is greater than three was by Quigley (1972) for the exceptional case of nineteenth century Swedish migration to the US, so that one might put the upper bound at 3.0.

Whether one wishes to use any specific estimates, such as those of Psacharopoulos, or a broad range such as 0 to 3.0, must depend on one's taste. Whether these values are considered 'high' or 'low', on the other hand, must of course depend on the uses to which they are put.

REFERENCES

Beals, R. E., Levy, M. B. and Moses, L. N. (1967): 'Rationality and migration in Ghana', *Review of Economics* (November).

[Bhagwati, J. N. (1976): *The Brain Drain and Taxation: Theory and Empirical Analysis*, vol. II (Amsterdam: North-Holland).]

[Bhagwati, J. N. and Partington, M. (1976): *Taxing the Brain: a Proposal*, vol. I (Amsterdam: North Holland).]

Bowles, S. (1970): 'Migration as investment: Empirical tests of the human investment approach to geographical mobility', *Review of Economics and Statistics* (November).

Bogue, D. J. (1969): *Principles of demography* (New York: Wiley).

Gallaway, L. E., Gilbert, R. F. and Smith, P. E. (1967): The economics of labor mobility: an empirical analysis, *Western Economic Journal* (June).

Glaser, W. (1973): *The Migration and Return of Professionals*, Colombia University Bureau of Applied Social Research, a study for the United Nations Institute for Training and Research (UNITAR).

Greenwood, M. J. (1969a): 'An analysis of the determinants of geographic labor mobility in the United States', *Review of Economics and Statistics* (May).

Greenwood, M. J. (1969b): 'The determinants of labor migration in Egypt', *Journal of Regional Science*, 9.

Greenwood, M. J. (1971): 'A regression analysis of migration to urban areas of a less developed country: the case of India', *Journal of Regional Science*, 2.

Kao, C. H. and Lee, J. W. (1973): 'An empirical analysis of China's brain drain into the United States', *Economic Development and Cultural Change* (April).

Lee, E. S. (1966): 'A theory of migration', *Demography*, 3.

Levy, M. B. and Wadycki, W. J. (1974): Education and the decision to migrate: An econometric analysis of migration in Venezuela', *Econometrica* (March).

Myers, R. G. (1972): *Education and Emigration* (New York: McKay).

Oldham, C. H. G. (1968): 'International migration of talent from and to the less developed countries', report of a conference at Ditchley Park.

Parnes, H. J. (1954): *Research on Labor Mobility* (New York: Social Science Research Council).

Psacharopoulos, G. (1973): *Returns to Education* (Amsterdam: Elsevier).

Quigley, J. M. (1972): 'An economic model of Swedish emigration', *Quarterly Journal of Economics* (February).

Raimon, R. L. (1962): 'Interstate migration and wage theory', *Review of Economics and Statistics* (November).

Rudd, E. and Hatch, S. (1968): *Graduate Study and After* (London: Weidenfeld and Nicolson).

Sahota, G. S. (1968): 'An economic analysis of internal migration in Brazil', *Journal of Political Economy* (March/April).

Schultz, T. P. (1971): 'Rural–urban migration in Colombia', *Review of Economics and Statistics* (May).

Scott, A. (1970): 'The brain drain – is a human capital approach justified?', in W. L. Hansen (ed.), *Education, Income, and Human Capital* (New York: NBER).

Sen, A. K. (1971): 'A quantitative study of the flow of trained personnel from the developing countries to the United States of America', *Journal of Development Planning*, 3.

Sjaastad, L. (1959): *The Relationship between Migration and Income in the United States*, Regional Science Association Papers and Proceedings.

Sjaastad, L. (1961): 'Income and migration in the United States', unpublished Ph.D. dissertation, Chicago.

Sjaastad, L. (1962): 'The costs and returns of human migration', *Journal of Political Economy* (October).

Vanderkamp, J. (1971): 'Migration flows, their determinants, and the effects of return migration', *Journal of Political Economy* (September/October).

20

Extending Free Trade to Include International Investment: a Welfare-theoretic Analysis

The classic gains-from-trade theorem of Samuelson (1939) demonstrates that voluntary trade between agents with given endowments must be mutually advantageous: strictly speaking, it cannot be harmful to any of the agents. This fundamental insight underlies institutions such as the GATT which oversee trade among nations. Recently, the United States has proposed that the GATT be extended to include freedom of private investment flows. This proposal presumes that, if free trade exists initially in goods, the subsequent introduction of free capital mobility must also be beneficial to all agents. However, this is simply not true.

Drawing on some of our recent work, section 1 briefly considers why a move to free capital mobility between agents that are already in freetrade may harm an agent, and must indeed do so under certain conditions if the other agent benefits. Section 2 is addressed to explaining this result by reference to the insights obtainable from existing theorems of trade and welfare. In the process, we also show symmetrically that going from no trade to free trade in goods when agents already have free capital mobility among themselves can also create such conflicting-interest, rather than mutually-beneficial, outcomes.

1

Within the standard $(2 \times 2 \times 2)$ model of a two-commodity two-factor world with two countries, Brecher and Choudhri (1982) have shown that a country's welfare can be diminished by the introduction of unrestricted investment from abroad, when there already is free international trade in goods.[1] As they demonstrated, the country would be immiserized (enriched) if the relative price of its importable is raised (lowered) by the advent of untaxed inflows of foreign capital, assuming no 'trade-pattern reversal' in the sense of this price rising above the autarkic level.[2]

1. Also see Grossman (1984) for a welfare analysis of international factor movements in a many-input many-product model.
2. This argument requires, in view of Bhagwati and Brecher's (1980) analysis, that

Written with Richard A. Brecher, from Sanjaya Lall and Frances Stewart (eds), *Theory and Reality in Development: Essays in Honour of Paul Streeten* (London: Macmillan, 1985).

Essentially, the proposition reflects the fact that foreign capital earns what it directly contributes, i.e. the value of its marginal product, and hence any resulting, indirect effect on the terms of trade is then a net social gain or loss depending on whether the terms of trade improve or worsen.

But, as Bhagwati (1982) has noted, this result is symmetric for the capital-exporting country, which thus gains (loses) from capital outflows if its terms of trade improve (worsen). Since a terms-of-trade improvement for one country means a deterioration for the other, we immediately reach the startling conclusion that unrestricted international capital mobility in this instance causes the welfare levels of the two trading partners to move in *opposite* directions.

Although such capital mobility is efficient for the world as a whole – whose utility-possibility frontier is thereby shifted outwards – the movement to the new frontier is never in the northeast direction, given the absence of trade-pattern reversal. Thus, international flows of capital lead to a dramatically unequal 'distribution of gains between investing and borrowing countries', to use a phrase from Singer's (1950) classic article.

This conclusion, that there is *necessarily* a conflicting-interest outcome from introducing capital mobility among the free-trading partners, is dependent of course on the assumed absence of 'trade-pattern reversal'. It assumes also the continued diversification in production before and after the capital flows, so that the same factor price-ratio corresponds to a given price-ratio for goods in both cases. The conclusion would not be generally valid, therefore, in the specific-factors model where the factor price-ratio corresponding to any goods price-ratio will generally change with the inflow or outflow of capital. However, even in such cases, while necessary conflict of interest between the two free-trading agents does not follow, the possibility of harm to one agent cannot be ruled out altogether.

2

How does one explain this result, which has immediate consequences for policy questions of considerable importance? There are three ways in which the result can be intuitively understood.

First, recall the theory of immiserizing growth, as analysed in Bhagwati (1968), which states that growth in the presence of a distortion may be immiserizing. Johnson (1967) showed such immiserization for a small country with a distorting tariff in place; Bhagwati (1973) noted that this

---

production with *and* without the inflow of foreign capital is characterized by diversification (i.e. non-specialization).

implied immediately that capital inflow into such a country would then be more likely to immiserize the country, since there would now be an added loss-causing factor in view of the earnings of foreign capital; and Brecher and Diaz-Alejandro (1977) showed that the immiserization of the host country would *necessarily* follow if, in this $2 \times 2 \times 2$ model, the importable commodity was capital-intensive and capital inflows were not large enough to extinguish the country's imports.[3]

By contrast, the Brecher and Choudhri (1982) case, on which the argument in the present note rests, builds on the *other*, early case of immiserizing growth: namely, Bhagwati (1958), where growth occurs in a large country with free trade, and therefore with a sub-optimal trade policy. The influx of foreign capital as the source of such growth then *necessarily* immiserizes, under the conditions already spelled out.

Second, consider instead the optimal-policy literature, based on the classic work of Kemp (1966) and of Jones (1967), which shows that the optimal policy-mix for national advantage of a large country in the presence of international capital mobility generally involves duty-cum-subsidy on both trade and capital flows. Capital inflow in the presence of free trade is therefore necessarily in the presence of a sub-optimal policy. Hence, reverting to the logic of our first intuitive explanation, one sees immediately the intuition behind the proposition in this note. In fact, as explained by Brecher and Feenstra (1983), the nationally optimal policy towards foreign investment may be prohibitive when taxes on trade in goods are disallowed. Thus, we need not be surprised to find national welfare reduced by the introduction of unrestricted capital mobility when goods trade remains free.

Finally, it is a well-known proposition of international economics that more trade is not necessarily better than less trade from the viewpoint of national welfare. Adding trade in factors, as international capital mobility can be construed; to trade in goods is therefore not necessarily welfare-improving.

All these ways of understanding the results immediately imply the following proposition symmetrically: if we start from a position in which only capital is (perfectly) mobile, the subsequent addition of free trade in goods in the $2 \times 2 \times 2$ model will also lead to necessarily conflicting-outcome situations and hence to a markedly unequal distribution of world gains, again assuming no trade-pattern reversals in the above sense. This will now be demonstrated.

In Figure 20.1, $T_2 T_1$ and $T_2' T_1'$ respectively are the production-possibility frontiers of the home country before and after the inflows of foreign capital have equalized rental rates internationally. By assumption, goods 1 and 2 are produced under constant returns to scale with technology

3. See also Hamada (1974), Minabe (1974) and Uzawa (1969).

that is relatively intensive in capital and labour, respectively. Autarky is at point A, where a community indifference curve touches T_2T_1.

After the capital inflow, the economy cannot be in equilibrium at the autarkic product-price ratio. At this ratio, production would take place at point A', which must lie southeast of A by the Rybczynski Theorem. By the reasoning of Bhagwati and Brecher (1980), however, national income would still be given by the line AB, after payment of foreign profits represented by the length $A'B$ in terms of the second good. (Our analysis would be qualitatively unaffected if foreign profits were given instead by the length EA' in terms of the first good.) Thus, consumption would still lie at point A, implying an excess demand (supply) represented by line segment AB in the domestic market for good 2 (1). This market imbalance would lead to a rise in the relative price of the second good in terms of the first, assuming Walrasian stability.

The market-clearing equilibrium will correspond to production at point

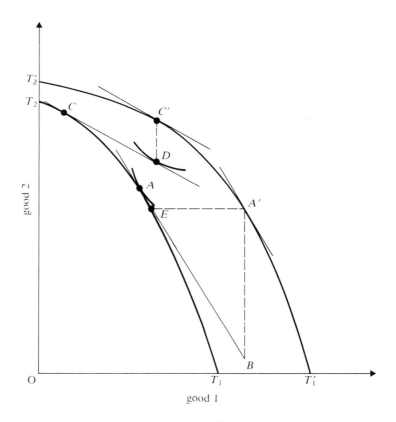

FIGURE 20.1

C' and consumption at point D, with the difference $C'D$ between these two points being absorbed by foreign profits. Thus, after the capital flows but before the trade in goods, the country's relative price of good 2 is above the autarkic level. By similar reasoning, the capital-exporting country will have a relative price of the second commodity below the (foreign) autarkic level, assuming the same factor-intensity ranking as in the home country. (If this ranking were allowed to differ internationally, our principal conclusion below would not be qualitatively changed.) We assume that the product-price ratios now differ between countries, to rule out the uninteresting case where there is no incentive to engage in the commodity trade which is subsequently allowed.

Consequently, when free trade in goods is introduced, the home (foreign) country will lose (gain) if its relative price of commodity 2 decreases, assuming no trade-pattern reversal as defined above. To eliminate the international differences in product prices while preserving equality of world rental rates, the commodity-price ratio of the two countries must move in the same direction, in view of the Stolper–Samuelson Theorem. [We are implicitly assuming the worldwide continuation of incomplete specialization, which is possible under conditions discussed by Brecher and Feenstra (1983), Chipman (1971) and Uekawa (1972).] Thus, once again, one country is immiserized while the other is enriched, given no trade-pattern reversal.

REFERENCES

Bhagwati, J. N. (1958): 'Immizerizing Growth: a geometrical note', *Review of Economic Studies*, 25 (June), pp. 201–5.
—— (1968): 'Distortions and immiserizing growth: a generalization', *Review of Economic Studies*, 35 (October), pp. 481–5.
—— (1973): 'The theory of immiserizing growth: further applications', in Michael B. Connolly and Alexander K. Swoboda (eds), *International Trade and Money* (Toronto: University of Toronto Press).
—— (1982): 'Structural adjustment and international factor mobility: some issues', Paper No. 6, International Economics Research Center, Columbia University, mimeo., August.
—— and Brecher, R. A. (1980): 'National welfare in an open economy in the presence of foreign-owed factors of production', *Journal of International Economics*, (February), pp. 103–15.
Brecher, R. A. and Choudhri, E. U. (1982): 'Immiserizing investment from abroad: the Singer–Prebisch thesis reconsidered', *Quarterly Journal of Economics*, 97 (February), pp. 181–90.
—— and Diaz-Alejandro, C. F. (1977): 'Tariffs, foreign capital and immiserizing growth', *Journal of International Economics*, 7 (November), pp. 317–22.
—— and Feenstra, R. C. (1983): 'International trade and capital mobility between diversified economies,' *Journal of International Economics*, 14 (May), pp. 321–39.

Chipman, J. S. (1971): 'International trade with capital mobility: a substitution theorem', in J. N. Bhagwati *et al.* (eds), *Trade, Balance of Payments and Growth: Papers in International Economics in Honor of Charles P. Kindleberger* (Amsterdam: North-Holland).

Grossman, G. M. (1984): 'The gains from international factor movements', *Journal of International Economics*, 17, pp. 73–83.

Hamada, K. (1974): 'An economic analysis of the duty-free zone', *Journal of International Economics*, 4 (August), pp. 225–41.

Johnson, H. G. (1967): 'The possibility of income losses from increased efficiency or factor accumulation in the presence of tariffs', *Economic Journal*, 77 (March), pp. 151–4.

Jones, R. W. (1967): 'International capital movements and the theory of tariffs and trade', *Quarterly Journal of Economics*, 81 (February), pp. 1–38.

Kemp, M. C. (1966): 'The gain from international trade and investment: a neo-Heckscher-Ohlin approach', *American Economic Review*, 56 (September), pp. 788–809.

Minabe, N. O. (1974): 'Capital and technology movements and economic welfare', *American Economic Review*, 64 (December), pp. 1088–1100.

Samuelson, P. A. (1939): 'The gains from international trade', *Canadian Journal of Economics and Political Science*, 5 (May), pp. 195–205.

Singer, H. W. (1950): 'The distribution of gains between investing and borrowing countries', *American Economic Review, Papers and Proceedings*, 40 (May), pp. 473–85.

Uekawa, Y. (1972): 'On the existence of incomplete specialization in international trade with capital mobility', *Journal of International Economics*, 2 (February), pp. 1–23.

Uzawa, H. (1969): 'Shihon jiyuka to kokumin keizai (Liberalization of foreign investments and the national economy)', *Economisuto*, 23 (December), pp. 106–22 (in Japanese).

Author Index

Subject Index

45.00